Randall Jarrell
and His Age

Photo courtesy of the Randall Jarrell Collection, Special Collections Division
of Jackson Library, The University of North Carolina at Greensboro

Randall Jarrell
and His Age

Stephen Burt

COLUMBIA UNIVERSITY PRESS

NEW YORK

Columbia University Press
Publishers Since 1893
New York   Chichester, West Sussex

My deepest thanks to Mary von Schrader Jarrell for permission to quote from previously
unpublished writings by Randall Jarrell. My thanks as well to Farrar, Straus & Giroux and
to Faber and Faber for permission to quote from *The Complete Poems* by Randall Jarrell
and from *Notebook* by Robert Lowell.

Library of Congress Cataloging-in-Publication Data

Burt, Stephen.
    Randall Jarrell and his age / Stephen Burt.
        p.   cm.
    Includes bibliographical references and index.
    ISBN 0–231–12594–1 (cloth : alk. paper)
    1. Jarrell, Randall, 1914–1965.   2. United States—Intellectual life—20th century.
    3. Poets, American—20th century—Bibliography.   4. Critics—United States—
    Biography.   I. Title.

PS3519.A86 Z596 2002
811'.52—dc21   2002071257

∞

Columbia University Press books are printed
on permanent and durable acid-free paper.
Printed in the United States of America
c 10 9 8 7 6 5 4 3 2 1

to Jessica Bennett

. . . say: "I am yours,
Be mine!"

CONTENTS

ACKNOWLEDGMENTS

No large research project—certainly none I could undertake—could bear fruit without the help and forbearance of many people; those thanked here are only some of them.

First of all I thank Mary Jarrell for the many kinds of help she has made available, in letters, in person and over the phone, and additionally through her published writings. Without her assistance this book could not exist. Having spent month after month in and around the Berg Collection of the New York Public Library, I owe much to it and to its staff, and especially to Stephen Crook. I am also indebted to the staff and resources of other manuscript collections: to the Library of Congress, to the University of North Carolina-Greensboro, to the Beinecke Library and the Yale Review manuscript files at Yale, to the Houghton Library at Harvard, and to Kate Donahue and the University of Minnesota.

Langdon Hammer advised the dissertation from which this book hatched and offered as much help as any student could wish. Jennifer Crewe, my editor at Columbia, provided important support and advice, as did Columbia's two anonymous readers. My student Hannah Brooks-Motl proofread the whole work at a late stage, fixed glitches, and removed a truly startling number of semi-colons. I am also grateful for comments, readings, advice, and assistance from Tim Alborn, Leslie Brisman, John Burt, David Bromwich, Suzanne Ferguson, Richard Flynn, Nick Halpern, John Hollander, James Longenbach, Jenn

Lewin, Stuart McDougal, Thomas Otten, John Plotz, David Quint, Thomas Travisano, and especially Helen Vendler. The stubborn mistakes that remain are of course my own.

Parts of this book have appeared in journals and anthologies, sometimes in earlier versions. About half of chapter 1 appeared in *Metre*, and much of the other half in the anthology *Jarrell, Bishop, Lowell, and Co.* (University of Tennessee). Much smaller portions of chapters 1 and 2 saw print in *Poetry Review* and *Yale Review*. Part of chapter 4 appeared in *PN Review*. Manuscripts uncovered in the course of my work have appeared in the *New York Review of Books*, *Thumbscrew*, and the *Yale Review*. I am grateful to the relevant editors: Justin Quinn and David Wheatley; Suzanne Ferguson; Peter Forbes; J. D. McClatchy; Michael Schmidt; Robert Silvers; and Tim Kendall.

Without my parents, Jeffrey and Sandra Burt, none of this would be possible. Personal, and intellectual, help and happiness came from far too many people to list: some of the most important have been Jordan Ellenberg, Sara Marcus, Mike Scharf, and Monica Youn. Finally, this project—along with everything else in my life—has been improved beyond measure by Jessica Bennett, who sees how things are and knows how they ought to be; her understanding of art, proportion, and intimacy has, I hope, improved my own.

INTRODUCTION

Randall Jarrell showed us how to read his contemporaries; we do not yet know how to read him. Often he seems to have understood the writers around him as posterity would: for some poets (such as Robert Lowell and Robert Frost) he helped to shape that posterity, while for others (such as Elizabeth Bishop) he prefigured it. Many readers know Jarrell as the author of several anthology poems (for example, "The Death of the Ball Turret Gunner"), a charming book or two for children, and a panoply of influential reviews. This book aims to illuminate a Jarrell more ambitious, more complex, and more important than that. He is ambitious partly because his writings refuse certain public ambitions. He is complex in part because his verse style tries so variously to use the artless simplicities of nonliterary speech. And he is important partly because he tells us to forget whether a book seems important, and to care instead for what strikes us as good.

The peers Jarrell admired most—Bishop and Lowell—now belong to a so-called mainstream of American poetry, to which more "radical" or disjunctive writers are said to offer alternatives. Jarrell did not anticipate those developments—if anything, they have made him harder to understand. To see how Jarrell wrote and how to read him is to see how he read his era, and how far his work stands from the course most American poets have followed since his death. It is also to see how Jarrell's literary practice anticipated discoveries in Continental philosophy, in feminist psychology, even in political theory. And it is, finally, to see what he accomplished. To do so, we need to begin with ideas of the self.

Jarrell considered himself first and last a poet; his best-known prose concerns other poets' poetry. Poetry—or lyric poetry, or poetry since the Romantic era—is frequently said to have as its province the inner life, or the psyche, or the self. That general vocation for poetry became Jarrell's special project. His poems and prose describe the distances between the self and the world, the self and history, the self and the social givens within which it is asked to behave. They show how the self seeks fantasy, and how it turns to memory, as refuges from the demands the world makes on it, or from (worse yet) the world's neglect. And they examine how the self seeks confirmation of its continuing existence, a confirmation it can finally have only through other people.

What does it mean to have a self to defend? Irving Howe writes that "by asserting the presence of the self, I counterpose to all imposed definitions of place and function a persuasion that I harbor *something else*, utterly mine—a persuasion that I possess a center of individual consciousness that is active and, to some extent, coherent" (249–50). The philosopher Charles Taylor has shown how ideas of the self have evolved alongside "certain notions of inwardness, which are . . . peculiarly modern" (498). The kinds of selves we find in modern literature, with their never fully revealed interior lives and their ties to autobiography (what Taylor would call "expressive" selves) have often been traced to early Romantic writers (Wordsworth, Goethe) or else to psychoanalysis. More than other American poets, Jarrell made sustained and self-conscious use of those sources.

According to Taylor, we have "come to think that we 'have' selves as we have heads. But the very idea that we have or are 'a self,' that human agency is essentially defined as 'the self,' is a linguistic reflection of our modern understanding" (177). Taylor does not, however, wish to do away with the self: he does not think that we moderns should or can.[1] Other thinkers—especially those indebted to Michel Foucault—have liked to suggest that our notions of the self (or individuality, or interiority) are not only historically contingent but obsolescent, ethically suspect, and politically retrograde. Writing before poststructuralism exerted much influence on American letters, Jarrell took up other challenges to the self, challenges he saw throughout mid-century culture—in supermarkets, in army barracks, in classrooms and lecture halls, on TV, and even within the family. Against all these he insisted that some sense of our presence in our own history, and of our inward difference from the rest of the world, remained prerequisite for our life with other people, for aesthetic experience, and even for ethical action.

Certain concepts of the self have been attacked as implausibly universal, as tending to erase certain sorts of difference. Jarrell's manifestations of selfhood may be seen instead as defenses of difference, among people and among works of art. "That others are now, were, and ever shall be, world without end, *different*," he asks in his only novel, "what else is Romance?" (*Pictures* 176). Far from affirming a complacent, unchanging self (a self that is the possessor of possessions), Jarrell often defends a self he sees as nearly powerless against social forces—against the disempowerment of the young or the losses entailed in growing old.[2] The desire to have and show an inner self is for Jarrell the same thing as the desire to change that self: to be is to change, and so Jarrell's existentially challenged characters respond to systems and situations that seem to erase their inner being with the repeated, insistent plea for change. One well-known poem, "The Woman at the Washington Zoo," ends with the plea "change me, change me!" Elsewhere a new appreciation of a difficult artwork (Berg's *Lyric Suite*) makes Jarrell's narrator "grateful for the best of gifts, a change in one's own self" (*Pictures* 151). Children matter to Jarrell not least because they are guaranteed to change; Jarrell's adults fear that they have become fixed, identical with mere social roles, so that the only change left for them is death. Jarrell's works cohere as defenses of the private self—but for him, in what seems only a paradox, to be oneself is to be able to change; to be always and only the same is not to be at all.

My title plays on Jarrell's first and best-known book of essays, *Poetry and the Age*, and on his preoccupations with youth, age, and aging—the first and last ways in which any self will change. "The taste of the age is, always, a bitter one," one of his essays begins. His work reacted to Auden's *The Age of Anxiety* (a poem Jarrell hated), to the fifties, and to the nuclear age; he liked to remind us, too, that "one judges an age, just as one judges a poet, by its best poems" (*KA* 290; *Age* 13). Jarrell also thought about his own age in years: he grew from a precocious, insecure child into an uneasy, successful young man. As an adult he avoided adult vices, entertaining children and cats while avoiding alcohol and adultery: his literary enemies called him childish, even as he worried about his advancing age. "The Woman at the Washington Zoo" describes animals "Aging, but without knowledge of their age" (*CP* 215); in another poem, an old woman says of "Mother and Father," "They both look so *young*. / I'm so much older than they are" (*CP* 354). Centrally interested in old age and in childhood, his poems consider and challenge the categories into which we sort persons and on which we base our beliefs about them.

Jarrell is hardly the only poet of his era who reconsidered the self. Thomas Travisano has argued that Jarrell, Bishop, Lowell, and John Berryman, whose lives and works so often intersect, collectively address "the problem of selfhood in the postmodern world" (*Mid-Century* 6). Though Jarrell noticed links between his work and Bishop's, he is not often, as Bishop was, a poet of place and nature, nor of foreignness and cultural estrangement.[3] Though he won praise for poems about World War II, he does not usually consider political leadership, heroism, or epic inheritance, leaving those topics instead to his friend Lowell. And though he pays frequent attention to questions of gender, Jarrell finds his special subjects neither in sex nor in the other appetites so important to Berryman. Precisely because he does not take on these issues, Jarrell attends, more than his contemporaries could, to the boundaries and to the fragilities of aesthetic and inner experience, to the self as such and its risky connections to others. No responsible reader would claim that the American mid-century—the age of late Stevens and Williams, Langston Hughes and Auden, early Ashbery and Rich—belongs to Jarrell, or to any poet, alone; my title means instead that Jarrell can help us understand his era and that to know his era well, we need to appreciate him.

My first chapter outlines Jarrell's life. Each subsequent chapter considers a different approach to the self. Chapter 1 addresses the self as it depends on other selves; it shows how Jarrell's poetic style depicts that interdependence. Reacting against his teachers' insistence on poems as self-contained artifacts, Jarrell embraced Wordsworthian views of poetry as troped speech. Such views soon gave Jarrell's verse its distinctive devices: irregular listeners, webs of quotation, multiple speakers, hesitations, self-interruptions, and subtle models of poetic listeners.

Chapter 2 looks at the self within and against society and its institutions, from the army to the academy. Jarrell's working life encompassed the Second World War, the postwar growth of higher education, the concerns about conformity that marked the fifties, and the anxiety about mass cultural forms which continued into the sixties. All of these sharpened Jarrell's sense that literature in general, and his own work in particular, had to distinguish individuals from their social roles. He tried to do so consistently in essays, where his prose style gave him dazzling instruments of appreciation and judgment; it gave him, as well, the means to portray aesthetic experience as something apart from, even opposed to, professional and disciplinary activity. Such portraits, and such contrasts, animate Jarrell's comic novel, *Pictures from an Institution*.

Chapter 3 considers psychoanalytic models of the self—conscious and unconscious, dreaming and waking. Indebted to 1930s Gestalt theory, to Freud and to Freud's heirs, Jarrell reimagined the unconscious, dream work, the death wish, and the persistence of early desires. Where his "confessional" peers cast themselves as patients, Jarrell identified with psychoanalysts: his poems thus explore the intersubjective components of psychoanalysis and of emotion itself.

Chapter 4 examines the self in time, considering how the "I" who speaks a poem or lives a life may understand its past. The chapter begins with philosophical issues concerning personal identity and briefly takes up Jarrell's use of

Proust; it then shows how certain poems about old age, middle age, and child-hood use verbal repetition to depict the persistence of the self.

Chapters 5 and 6 take up kinds of selves, showing how Jarrell investigates assumptions and intuitions about men, women, youth, parents, and children. Every reader has noted Jarrell's interests in childhood; few see the related interests he took in adolescence, as a newly important social phenomenon ("teenagers") and as an inward stage of emotional life. Chapter 5 considers these interests, concluding with a discussion of one of his neglected long poems.

Chapter 6 looks at mothers, fathers and families; it considers several short poems and a children's book before delving into *The Lost World*, a late, long poem based on a year of Jarrell's childhood, and a poem that combines almost all his techniques and interests. My epilogue takes up depictions and valuations of the self in poems and prose about visual art, asking—as Jarrell asked—whether the self can ever be fully depicted. Often I try to advance my general claims through sustained readings of single poems; one of my goals is to demonstrate that Jarrell's poems reward such attention.

Most of the models and theories in this book are ones that Jarrell would have known—those of Freud, for example, or of Jarrell's close friend Hannah Arendt. One exception is my use of object-relations psychoanalysis, a body of thought created in part by the British child analyst D. W. Winnicott. For Winnicott, much human experience has its origins in young children's discovery of distinctions between "I" and "you," self and other, self and mother: children discover a space ("potential space") that may count as self *or* other, or both. Children then find and cathect "transitional objects" (such as a security blanket), which occupy that space. As we grow up, we continue to draw, emotionally and intellectually, on this early "experience in the potential space between the subjective object and the object objectively perceived, between me-extensions and the not-me" (100).[4]

Drawing on Continental philosophers from Hegel to Lévinas, Jessica Benjamin and other feminist thinkers have modified Winnicott's models. Benjamin focuses on "recognition," a kind of intimacy in which I acknowledge my difference from the person with whom I am intimate: "A person comes to feel that 'I . . . am the author of my acts,' by being with another person who recognizes her acts, her feelings, her intentions, her existence, her independence. . . . The subject declares 'I am, I do,' and then waits for the response, 'You are, you have done' " (*Bonds* 21). Such "experiences of 'being with' are predicated on a continually evolving awareness of difference, on a sense of intimacy felt as occurring between 'the *two* of us' " (*Bonds* 47).[5] The poet and critic Allen Grossman has made such encounters a paradigm for poems: "In speaking the poem the speaker of the poem reacquires selfhood by serious reciprocity with another self" (258).[6] For Benjamin all of us seek recognition: people who cannot find it, or failed to find it early enough, tend to imagine life as a choice between loneliness, painful self-consciousness, and separation (from mothers and mother surrogates) on the one hand and unconsciousness, merging (with mother figures) on the other. Alan Williamson has already found just such choices at the core of Jarrell's work.[7]

Some of Jarrell's best interpreters were his contemporaries. Reviews, letters, and the occasional poem by Lowell, Bishop, Karl Shapiro, Delmore Schwartz, and others who knew Jarrell personally have been consistently helpful, as has Mary von Schrader Jarrell, in person and through her memoir, *Remembering Randall*. I am also indebted to previous books about Jarrell's poems, among them Suzanne Ferguson's 1972 survey and monographs by Sister Bernetta Quinn and Charlotte Beck. William Pritchard's *Randall Jarrell: A Literary Life* is invaluable as a biography. Persuasive recent essays by Langdon Hammer and James Longenbach consider Jarrell's relations to gender and power and have provided me with important points of departure.[8] Travisano's volume illuminates Jarrell's interactions with his colleagues and friends. Richard Flynn's monograph, *Randall Jarrell and the Lost World of Childhood*, and especially his subsequent essays, relate the poems well to the cultural criticism and have been important sources for agreement and disagreement. Closest to my approach in some ways has been Williamson, whose psychoanalytically grounded essay (now part of his recent book, *Almost a Girl*) demonstrates how often in Jarrell "separation is cosmic lostness; unity is engulfment, loss of self" ("Märchen" 288).

Other readers approach Jarrell through lenses I have not used. Though I begin with his first important poems and end with his last, I do not proceed book by book; Jarrell arranged his work (in his 1955 *Selected Poems*) in ways that stressed thematic continuities, and I have done likewise here. I have not devoted discrete chapters to war poems or to poems in the voices of women; both groups are examined throughout the book.[9] I have largely left Jarrell's many uses of operatic and orchestral music to critics more qualified to appreciate them. Though Jarrell has been viewed as a Southern writer, he rarely thought of himself that way; his Southern teachers believed him Californian or Jewish.[10] Jarrell translated Chekhov's *The Three Sisters*, Goethe's *Faust, Part 1*, and lyric poems by Rilke and other European authors; his translations have received attention elsewhere, and I do not dwell on them here.[11] Both Edward Brunner's *Cold War Poetry* and Deborah Nelson's *Pursuing Privacy in Cold War America* appeared too late to inform this book; though neither covers Jarrell at length, both bear on my claims, particularly those of Chapters 2 and 6.

A final note concerns Jarrell's vexing and premature death. Continuing arguments about his demise have done more to distract us from his poems than they have to illuminate them. Those arguments have, however, alerted readers to what Mary Kinzie calls his "undercurrent of nihilism" (72). His poems about selves reaching out to other selves often consider how those attempts can fail. I have tried here to show how Jarrell's poems and prose operate, what they can teach us, what his characters need, how some of them find it, and how aesthetic experience can console them when they do not. Those attempts should not occlude the pessimism he manifests sometimes as a bitter detachment, sometimes as a positive wish to leave the world: those overtones can prove hard to build into arguments, but they remain a part of his work that readers should not ignore.

*Randall Jarrell
and His Age*

ANTECHAPTER: RANDALL JARRELL'S LIFE

"Tomorrow," Jarrell complained in 1951, "some poet may, like Byron, wake up
to find himself famous—for having written a novel, for having killed his wife; it
will not be for having written a poem" (*Age* 15). Jarrell's poetic contemporaries
(Robert Lowell makes the best example) indeed became famous for the high
drama of their lives and for their extraliterary deeds: Anthony Hecht even called
Lowell, after his death, "le Byron de nous jours" (32). Jarrell himself displayed a
striking personality, a demanding intellect, and a need for affection: his life, by
his own choice and luck, lacked public drama until its hard last months. This
book addresses Jarrell's literary accomplishment and its contexts; it is not a biog-
raphy. It does, however, hope to revise and deepen our view of the man who
wrote Jarrell's works, and it draws on manuscripts and anecdotes to adumbrate
his career. To that end, I begin with a view of his life.

   Randall Jarrell was born in Tennessee, on May 6, 1914, the oldest child of
Owen and Anna Campbell Jarrell. Asked later in life why he lacked a Southern
accent, he would reply that he learned to talk in California, where his parents
moved in 1915 and where Owen's relatives already lived. Owen worked in Los
Angeles as a photographer's assistant, and it was in Los Angeles that year that
Jarrell's younger brother Charles was born.[1] Soon afterwards the family moved to
Long Beach, where Owen opened his own photography studio. At least from this
time, Anna seems to have been high-strung and sickly: Randall's few comments

later in life portray her as alternately controlling and helpless. Mary von Schrader Jarrell, the poet's widow, recalls that Randall told her, "My mother is a disaster" (*Remembering* 141). Some readers take parts of the late poem "Hope" as portraits of Anna: one passage describes "a recurrent / Scene from my child-hood. / A scene called Mother Has Fainted." Playing out the familiar scene, the children

> did as we were told:
> Put a pillow under her head (or else her feet)
> To make the blood flood to her head (or else away from it).
> Now she was set.
> . . . .
>
> We waited for the world to be the world
> And looked out, shyly, into the little lanes
> That went off from the great dark highway, Mother's Highway,
> And wondered whether we would ever take them—
> And she came back to life, and we never took them.

(CP 308)

Anna left Owen in 1924 to return to her native Nashville, where she taught at a secretarial school; there she could count on help from her relatives, especially from her prosperous brother, Howell Campbell, who owned a candy company. Mary has remembered Randall's descriptions of his mother's kin: "In Nashville, Randall said, he was 'covered with relatives.' The Campbells . . . were an intimate, dominating family of strong wills" (*Remembering* 141). Yet Randall also told his college sweetheart, Amy Breyer, that he had "lived all over, and always been separated from at least half of a very small family, and been as alone as children ever are" (*Letters* 60).[2] The congeries of Nashville relatives lacked, for him, the warmth he found in L.A. Young Randall spent much of his free time at Nashville's Carnegie Library, which became the source of several poems (among them "The Carnegie Library, Juvenile Division") and of some moving prose. He wrote, in an unpublished lecture for librarians,

> A shrew or a hummingbird eats half its weight in twenty-four hours; when I was a boy I read half my weight in a week. I went to school, played, did the things the grown-ups made me do; but no matter how little time I had left, there were never books enough to fill it—I lived on the ragged edge of having nothing to read.

(Berg Collection)

Mary describes the young Randall as "easily bored" and therefore constantly active: besides his constant and voracious reading, Randall was also, by age twelve, a tennis player—in high school he would take up touch football and acting. Young Randall also served as the model for a statue of Ganymede in a Nashville park. The sculptors, Randall learned from his mother years later, had asked to adopt him: "I would," he recalled, "have gone with them like that" (*Remembering* 141).[3]

In the summer of 1926 Randall returned to California to live with his paternal grandparents ("Mama" and "Pop") in a big Los Angeles household along with Randall's great-grandmother ("Dandeen"). The first surviving documents in Randall's hand are a long series of letters from that year, written to his mother in Tennessee. These chatty letters make clear that young Randall enjoyed himself with "Mama" and "Pop" in Los Angeles, and that he wanted to stay. (An early letter concludes, "P.S. Am I writing enough?") Randall was also fascinated by Hollywood:

> I saw a picture show being made last Monday and Sunday night. They made it in a big concrete bowl and they had dogs and Eskimos and igloos and icebergs and snow in it. They had a snowstorm. They threw Christmas tree stuff in front of an airplane propeller and it looked like a blizzard. P.S. I went and saw [radio stations] KNX and KFWB.
>
> (Berg Collection)

Jarrell's mother returned these letters to him in the early 1960s; the happy experiences they describe prompted his late long poem *The Lost World*. (Randall may have been writing poems even then: the same cache of papers includes a long narrative poem, inspired by Kipling, Longfellow, and Rudolph Valentino, called "The Ballad of the Sheik Who Lost His Shine.")

Randall returned to his mother's household in the fall of 1927. His sense of his life there did not improve; he would tell Amy Breyer much later that "just being in Nashville upsets me" (Berg Collection). "In Campbell minds," Mary recalls,

> Randall was expected to Be a Little Man and to aim toward supporting his mother, which, unhappily for Randall, Uncle Howell had done for his mother at an early age.
>
> "They had real gifts for finding me the most *awful* jobs," Randall said. "I wouldn't have minded delivering papers so much—though it was hellish—if I could have hired somebody to do the collecting. The people were so *bad*. They wouldn't pay, and they told lies. And I had to keep going back." They made him sell Christmas seals and ribbons from house

to house, and Randall said, "*Imagine*, pestering people like that in their houses. Wasn't that a wicked thing to make a child do?"

(*Remembering* 141; italics in original)

At Hume-Fogg High School, Jarrell practiced tennis, starred in some school plays, and began his career as a critic with satirical essays in a school magazine and scathing reviews of Nashville Little Theatre shows.[4] His social life sometimes included his mother—they attended movies together ("people thought she was my sister or my date") until she remarried in 1932 (Pritchard 23). During his last year of high school, Jarrell lost many of his books in a fire. The list of lost books he gave the insurers (discovered by Richard Flynn) shows the range and depths of his early interests: it includes two volumes of Proust (in English), D. H. Lawrence's *Fantasia of the Unconscious*, T. S. Eliot, Flaubert, Nietzsche, Tolstoy, and the science fiction novelist Olaf Stapledon (*Last and First Men*) (*Lost* 147–149). After high school, Randall, unsurprisingly, hoped for a literary career. Uncle Howell, however, intended him for the candy company and demanded that he attend a commercial school in Nashville, where he promptly became incapacitated with (perhaps psychosomatic) respiratory illnesses. Howell relented and sent the young man to Vanderbilt; he matriculated in the fall of 1932.

"I had a scientific education and a radical youth," Jarrell recalled in 1950 (*Age* 21). Evidence for both begins at Vanderbilt. So does Jarrell's precocious literary career. In his first term he encountered Robert Penn Warren, then a graduate student, and professor John Crowe Ransom, already a well-known poet. Both men were struck by Randall's precocity and by his tactless self-assurance in class. Over the next few years he found early mentors in them and in the poet and critic Allen Tate. He also took over the college humor magazine, the *Masquerader*, where he opposed attempts to transform it into a serious literary magazine, eventually writing much of its satirical prose himself. By Randall's senior year he had published—with Tate's and Warren's assistance—poems in national magazines. These earliest productions show a prolific, ferociously smart young writer in love with verbal complexity for its own sake and deeply in debt to the early Auden. By the end of 1935 Jarrell had also produced his first notable book review, a characteristically fearless roundup of the year's fiction for the *Southern Review*. "Can you recite a review from memory when you finish it?" Jarrell wrote to Warren that year; "I was astonished to find I could" (*Letters* 5).

Randall combined his literary productivity with prodigious reading in other fields, among them philosophy, economics, and especially psychology, where he found himself fascinated by Gestalt theory. In his senior year he switched his major from English to psychology and then did a year of work (1935–36) at Vanderbilt toward a master's degree in that field. A draft of a capsule biography

Jarrell prepared in 1940 explained that he "studied psychology; but after I had to learn radiophysics I went over into English where I belonged. (I remember . . . thinking it would be better for everybody if I lay down on the table, and let the cat set up the cathode ray oscillograph)" (*Letters* 29).

He made the switch back to English in 1936, completing the coursework for an M.A. in 1937 with courses entitled "Chaucer," "the English Lyric," "American Literature," and "Spenser and His Age." He then began a thesis on A. E. Housman. (Jarrell had at one point wished to write on Auden; the Vanderbilt English professor Donald Davidson prevented him.) Though he may have been hard to take in a classroom, by his last few years in Nashville Randall attracted a following; a clique of students (including the unathletic Peter Taylor) attended his games of touch football for their literary conversation, while a rival literary group congregated at a bar with the poet George Marion O'Donnell.

Vanderbilt had become the de facto headquarters for the Agrarians, the conservative Southern school of social thought represented in *I'll Take My Stand* (1930), to which Davidson, Ransom, Tate, and a very young Warren had contributed. Jarrell—a devotee of Marx and Auden—embraced his teachers' literary stances while rejecting their politics. Taylor remembered that Jarrell "was opposed to Agrarianism from the beginning" (*Conversations* 117–118). One *Masquerader* cover caricatured John Crowe Ransom with a spray can, trying with apparent futility to defend Southern flora from Northern pests. Jarrell's Marxist interests persisted through the forties: he wrote Edmund Wilson (his editor at the *New Republic*) in 1942, "I guess you can tell pretty well what I think about politics, economics and so on—and it's just the opposite of what [Ransom and Tate] think" (*Letters* 59). He made notes for an essay called "The Reactionary Intellectual And What To Do About Him," a critical (and slightly mocking) examination of "Hulme Eliot Pound Wyndham Lewis Winters Tate Criterion writers neo-Thomists other Catholic intellectuals etc" (Berg Collection). His published writings reflect a similar stance: Tate, Jarrell declared in the *Nation* in 1941, was one of the "greatest living poets," and yet "it has been later than [he] think[s] for four hundred years" (*KA* 66).

By 1937 Jarrell had become involved with, and probably engaged to, a sophisticated and literate medical student, Amy Breyer, whose family he had known since high school. Their romance would last until 1938. An unpublished poem about the end of a romance (almost certainly with Breyer) contrasts Jarrell's special dispensation (now ended) with the loneliness he takes to be the normal condition of "Man":

What made me different from the Man I knew,
Engrossed, asleep or asking for his end—

And single in his element, despair—
Was that I had no way to be alone.
You were like weather: good or bad, but there.
That pure, unowned and altering delight
I bought as we buy anything: with ignorance,
The old good of men—the real, fool's gold
That we pay breath by breath for pain
Till we awake in someone else's dream:
Time that one lives through to another time,
Space that the sleeper tenants like a cell—
The winter even waiting will not mend.

(Berg Collection)

Companionship is "fool's gold," the lines suggest—but it is the only gold we can have. Breyer (later de Blasio) made a disastrous first marriage to another doctor. When it ended in the early forties, she wrote to Jarrell again from New Haven, Connecticut, and a moving, introspective exchange ensued; one of its subjects was Amy's psychoanalysis.

In 1937 Kenyon College in Gambier, Ohio, offered Ransom a chair and more money than Vanderbilt gave him; Tate and Jarrell led a campaign to keep him in Nashville through pressure on the Vanderbilt administration. Though three hundred students signed Jarrell's petition, Ransom departed for Kenyon, and Jarrell followed. He would spend two years as an instructor at Kenyon. In 1937–38 Randall lived in Ransom's attic, along with an undergraduate transfer student from Harvard named Robert Lowell. Jarrell spent 1938–39 as the resident faculty member in a small college-owned dorm called Douglass House: among the ten undergraduates there were Lowell, Robie Macauley, and Peter Taylor, who had transferred from Vanderbilt.

Jarrell at Kenyon seems to have combined great tactlessness with great charm. Lowell, writing in 1967, remembered the young man as "upsettingly brilliant, precocious, knowing, naïve, and vexing"; he could be (Lowell continued) "tender and gracious, though he seemed tone-deaf to the amenities and dishonesties that make human relations tolerable" (*RJ* 101–103). Jarrell not only taught English but also coached tennis; Peter Taylor recalled the improbable spectacle of "members of Kenyon's champion tennis team," under their coach's influence, "sitting about the soda shop reading Auden and Chekhov and Proust" (*RJ* 245). Randall also inspired "a good number of . . . ladies and young girls . . . to sewing for him" (*RJ* 244). Taylor would later claim (perhaps self-servingly) "Jarrell treated everybody very badly . . . [Lowell] and I were the only ones who stuck by him through thick and thin" (McAlexander 51).

In 1939 Jarrell submitted his thesis on Housman. (His preface acknowledged debts to William Empson.) That fall Jarrell accepted an instructorship at the University of Texas-Austin. His poems continued to appear in leading journals; in 1940 James Laughlin at New Directions tapped him for the anthology *Five Young American Poets*, along with Mary Barnard, John Berryman, W. R. Moses, and O'Donnell. A first book, *Blood for a Stranger*, appeared from Harcourt, Brace in 1942. Most of the poems from this period share a declamatory style derived from Auden, Empson, and Marxist theory; others, however—including the exemplary "90 North," the crushingly personal "The Bad Music," and the dramatic monologue "The Christmas Roses"—show him finding his characteristic style, attending to the cadences, exchanges, and hesitations of private speech.

During those years Jarrell made his name as a critic. Always witty and self-assured, sometimes enthusiastic, and often caustic or sarcastic, his essays and columns in the *Nation*, the *New Republic*, and elsewhere established him as a reviewer to watch (and to fear). A 1942 attack on Conrad Aiken in the *New Republic* prompted Malcolm Cowley (an editor at the journal) to defend Aiken in print against "Poets as Reviewers." Jarrell responded with a letter to the journal: "I feel as if my decision had been overruled by the Supreme Court" (*Letters* 40–41). When Aiken attacked him again in 1947 over another negative review, Jarrell responded with a valuable list of poets he liked:

> In the last few years I've written favorable or admiring reviews and articles about Robert Frost, Marianne Moore, William Carlos Williams, William Butler Yeats, Dylan Thomas, W. H. Auden, Elizabeth Bishop, John Crowe Ransom, Tristan Corbière, Robert Graves, Walter de la Mare, Robert Lowell, R. P. Blackmur and others; I'd have written similar reviews of T. S. Eliot, Wallace Stevens, William Empson, Louis MacNeice, and Allen Tate if I'd been given their poetry to review.
>
> (*Letters* 193)

Part of the thesis on Housman appeared in *Kenyon Review* in 1939; other critical essays from the 1940s saw print in *Kenyon, Partisan Review, Southern Review*, the *Nation* and the *New Republic*. One important theoretical piece, an invited lecture at Princeton in 1942, saw print only after his death; Thomas Travisano, who found it in the archives, titled it "Levels and Opposites." Jarrell was also reading and rereading Auden. Thorough, and sometimes angry, dissections of Auden's oeuvre appeared in 1941 and 1945, complementing Jarrell's reviews of *The Double Man* (1940) and other individual books. Asked later about Jarrell's essays, the English poet supposedly remarked, "Jarrell is in love with me" (Simpson 110).[5]

At Austin, as at Kenyon, the precocious student was learning to be a teacher. "If I were a rich man," he liked to say later, "I would pay money for the privilege of being able to teach" (*RJ* 105; *Remembering* 31). Several poems from the forties consider Jarrell's place in academia; one of the breezier examples is "Randall Jarrell Office Hours 10–11," in which "Mr. Jarrell" tells his "Lost Students,"

> Come back and you will find me just the same.
> Hunters, hunters—but why should I go on?
> Learn for yourself (if you are made to learn)
> That you must haunt an hourless, nameless door
> Before you find—not me, but anything.

> (CP 463)

Jarrell wrote to Tate that he liked the students at Austin, though he also expressed frustration at his colleagues' indifference to his poems and criticism: "If I had equal amounts of stuff published in the *PMLA*," he complained, "they'd make me a full professor" (*Letters* 51). One colleague, Mackie Langham, inspired warmer feelings: she and Randall wed in 1940.

Like many left-wing Americans, Jarrell was uneasy about the coming of war in Europe; many early poems consider the growing conflict as a vague catastrophe of global capitalism. His letters continue to express a pessimistic Marxism up until February 1943, when he volunteered for the army. Jarrell spent the next several months in the dry heat of Sheppard Field in Texas, where he waited for an assignment. He was then transferred to Chanute Field in Illinois, near Champaign-Urbana, where his tasks included evaluating soldiers' aptitude tests. By the end of the year he had been assigned to Davis-Monthan Field in Tucson, where Mackie and their cat, Kitten, finally joined him. Randall, Mackie, and Kitten would remain in Arizona until 1946.

Numerous letters to Mackie (eighty-five in all) from his army years attest to Jarrell's attachment to her and to Kitten; they also show his feelings about the army. "Everything's so slow, dumb and crude," he wrote in his first days at Sheppard Field; "I've never seen any conversation in a book (well, naturally) that reproduces the way people like these talk; the intelligence, society, vocabulary all *surprisingly* low." On the other hand "People are surprisingly friendly, and I've had not a single unkind word spoken to *me* yet; though I've heard some to others." Astonished by his bunkmates' good-natured ignorance, Jarrell was also appalled at the army's impersonal scale. "I'm just a needle in 75,000 haystacks," one letter decides; another exclaims "It's so *dumb*: the poor soldiers are as dumb as the way they're treated, almost . . . O poor New World!" (Berg

Collection) At Sheppard Field, he told Tate, "we normally spent over four hours a day *just standing in line*" (*Letters* 118).

Jarrell considered becoming a pilot. He underwent training for that job but failed a test for motion sickness (Mary Jarrell, conversation). He may have been of two minds about it all along: a 1943 letter to Mackie promises to "stay safe and on the ground and come back to you. You have to ask for flight duty to get it, I've been told, and I've lost any inclinations that way" (Berg Collection). This and other letters from 1943 contemplate the safer assignment Jarrell eventually obtained at Davis-Monthan. There he operated a celestial navigation tower. Jarrell described his job in a letter to Tate:

> What I do is run a tower that lets people do celestial navigation on the ground. In a tower about forty feet high a fuselage like the front of a bomber is hung. . . . The navigator (sometimes pilots and bombardiers too) sits in it, and navigates by shooting with his sextant the stars that are in a star dome above his head—we move them pretty much as a planetarium operator does . . . besides running and setting up the tower, we record his fixes and other stuff, correct them if he's made mistakes, and so forth.
>
> (*Letters* 121)

"I like the job very much," Jarrell added, explaining that "one trainer in a year certainly saves five or six" bombers and their crews through improved night flight skills. Though Jarrell never saw combat, he trained many flyers who did.

The army gave Jarrell his first distinctive poetic subjects; it also helped him develop his style. His forties poems paint military life in a series of sad, expressive scenes: prisoners loading and unloading garbage, a "drunk sergeant shaving," nocturnal airplanes' "great lights floating in—from Mars, from Mars" (CP 143, 177). Though Jarrell deplored the soldiers' illiterate speech, he also notated their conversation with pleasure and quoted it in some poems; the voices he heard in the army helped him develop the sound of speech in his own work. "One's a very severe critic of literary magazines in the Army," Jarrell decided in another letter; "I think 'The same old game—and done worse than ever,' and the heart sinks" (Berg Collection). In the army, and in his poems about it, Jarrell found himself thinking less about literary conventions and more about the human person as such: writing to Lowell, he described the army as a place where "your knowledge and the other person's ignorance doesn't differentiate you *at all*" (*Letters* 150).

Poems about the army, the army air force, and the war took up most of *Little Friend, Little Friend* (1945) and much of *Losses* (1948). (Other poems on military topics appeared in magazines but were never collected.) These books gained relatively broad attention (*Losses*, for example, received reviews in *Time* and the *New York Times Book Review*). Along with Karl Shapiro (who completed his Pulitzer-Prize-winning *V-Letter* under fire in New Guinea), Jarrell became the prominent highbrow soldier-poet of America's war. By 1945 he was also planning several prose books—one on St. Paul and the origins of theology, another on Hart Crane; none of these projects came to fruition. (He accepted, and later returned, an advance for the volume on Crane.) Jarrell's time in Illinois and Arizona also saw an intense correspondence with Lowell, much of it devoted to the poems in *Lord Weary's Castle*, which Lowell revised with Jarrell's detailed help; Jarrell would later review it with thunderous enthusiasm.

By the end of the war Jarrell had again become a prolific critic, writing a regular column on poetry for the *Nation*, whose book review editor, Margaret Marshall, planned a sabbatical year for 1946–47. Marshall asked Jarrell to describe his qualifications "as a possible Literary Editor of the *Nation*" during her year off. His long enthused answer sheds light on his varied interests; it reads, in part,

> I'm reasonably acquainted with a good many more fields than most potential editors, and this would help me a lot in picking reviewers or judging (and asking for) articles in a particular field. . . . I read very fast, get year-long crazes about particular fields, and read steadily in them, with big shining eyes. Besides the things that I write about. . . . I've been particularly interested in Gestalt psychology, ethnology and "folk" literature, economics (especially Marxist), symbolic logic and modern epistemology, theology and its origins, and a few even queerer things.
>
> (*Letters* 153–154)

Jarrell got the job; he, Mackie and Kitten moved to New York in April 1946.

Jarrell claimed to hate New York's crowds, high cost of living, status-conscious sociability, and lack of greenery, barely alleviated by a midyear move to Queens.[6] He wrote (but never published) a satirical ballad about the five boroughs, "The Man Who Was Born and Died in New York City":

> When he was born the cat was sick with excitement
> And they walked nine blocks to get her a blade of grass;
> And he fell out the window—nobody had a screen—
> And injured in falling a Marching Club and a nun.
>
> . . . .
>
> He met his wife in the subway and proposed to her in a doorway

And they had a little baby and the two of them were three;
And they walked up seven flights of stairs and sat on the fire-escape,
And the same stars shone on them that shine on you and me.

(Berg Collection)

(Jarrell would feel more warmly toward the city when he returned for brief visits later in life, setting his last significant love poem, "A Man Meets a Woman in the Street," in Central Park.) The city Jarrell so disliked as a place to live gave him important friends and influences. He and Peter Taylor became close friends not at Kenyon but in New York: "I doubt I could have ever got started [writing fiction] again after the war," Taylor recalled, "if I had not had Randall to talk to or to listen to" (McAlexander 94). Other important companions included the poets John Berryman and Robert Fitzgerald; Lowell, who liked to visit Manhattan though he lived in Maine; and the classical music critic B. H. Haggin, whose columns in the *Nation* Jarrell had admired. Jarrell orchestrated a dinner party in order to introduce Lowell to Elizabeth Bishop; she remembered "feeling very much at home with Randall Jarrell and his wife, and their big black cat, and Jarrell talked a blue streak while putting Kitten through his tricks" (quoted in Millier 186). It was in this year, too, that Jarrell broadened his style beyond the range of his war poems, writing to (and about) William Carlos Williams and learning from him, Bishop, and others how to expand his repertoire of rhythms and tones.

Another key New York friend was Hannah Arendt, then working at Schocken Books. She later recalled that she "had been impressed by some of his war poems and asked him to translate a few German poems . . . and she edited (translated into English, I should say) some book reviews of mine for the *Nation*" (*RJ* 3). Jarrell's other work for Arendt included a translation of Ferdinand Gregorovius's "Lament of the Children of Israel," included in Schocken's English translation of Gregorovius's book about Roman Jews. Jarrell and Arendt slowly became quite close: by 1951 they were (as she put it) "intoxicated with agreement against a world of enemies," and Jarrell was able to write to her, "Someone said about somebody that 'while that man is alive I am not alone in this world'; I guess I feel that way about you" (*Letters* 250). Jarrell's interest in Rilke—important to his later style—may also be traced to Arendt, who helped him read German poets while he helped her read Americans. In the spring of 1947 Jarrell taught alongside Mary McCarthy at Sarah Lawrence College, soon to become the basis for his satirical novel, *Pictures from an Institution*, which he planned to dedicate to Arendt (*Remembering* 1).

Jarrell worked hard and well finding and editing poetry and book reviews for the *Nation*, though he liked to complain about the job: "I've had so little space,"

Jarrell wrote Berryman, "and most of the reviewable books are so bad, that I haven't been able to do a good many things I meant to do" (University of Minnesota, n.d.). Anyone else might conclude that he did a lot: during his year there the *Nation* printed poems by Bishop ("Faustina"), Robert Graves ("To Juan at the Winter Solstice"), Weldon Kees, Lowell, MacNeice ("Slow Movement"), and W. C. Williams, and book reviews from Arendt, Berryman, Kenneth Burke, Fitzgerald (on Graves's *King Jesus*), Irving Howe (on Palestine), and John Crowe Ransom (on Henry James). Jarrell brought in his onetime hero, William Empson, who reviewed Kafka's *Metamorphosis* and Sartre's *No Exit*.[7] Jarrell offered reviewing work to the young James Baldwin, who forty years later would thank him (along with other editors) for helping Baldwin get his start as a writer (xiii). Jarrell also solicited Robert Penn Warren, Yvor Winters (who had given up reviewing), and George Orwell (who died soon after Jarrell's request arrived) (Beinecke, Margaret Marshall papers).

Jarrell sought academic jobs for the fall of 1947; he chose to join Taylor at the Woman's College of North Carolina in Greensboro (later the University of North Carolina-Greensboro), where Taylor had moved in 1946. Randall and Mackie and Peter and Eleanor Taylor purchased a Greensboro duplex and moved in together. Peter remembered Jarrell's "go[ing] over" his stories from this period "sentence by sentence"—he would also read Eleanor's poetry with careful sympathy. Taylor also remembered Jarrell as hard to live with: Kitten was unavoidable in their duplex, as was classical music played at high volume (McAlexander 100). The Taylors would move in and out of the Greensboro duplex several times over the next few years.

Though he liked to gripe about how little most students knew, Jarrell clearly enjoyed his classes in North Carolina, where he would stay for much of the rest of his life. Writing to Arendt in October 1947, Jarrell mentioned "several good students in modern poetry and writing," one of whom had "turned in a faithful imitation of Robert Lowell. But the only thing to do with the freshmen here is to write a ballet with a Chorus of Peasant Girls" (*Letters* 180). Cleanth Brooks remembered discussing "the advantages of teaching in a coeducational college, a man's college and a woman's college. . . . Randall spoke up for the woman's college, and when asked why, said, in his serious, innocent way, 'I suppose it's because I like girls better than boys' " (Beinecke, Randall Jarrell collection).[8] The next few years were perhaps Jarrell's most productive. In them he wrote many of his best-known essays, including pieces on Bishop, Robert Frost, Marianne Moore, Whitman, and Williams. Jarrell had second thoughts about his reviewing, sending a pan of Archibald Macleish's *Actfive* (1948) to Marshall with instructions not to bother printing it; he would, however, publish other negative reviews throughout the fifties (Beinecke, Margaret Marshall papers).

Jarrell's next book of poems, *The Seven-League Crutches* (1951), reflected his postwar interests in the titles of its three sections: "Europe," "Children," and "Once Upon a Time." The "Europe" poems grew, in turn, from Jarrell's 1948 summer job at the Salzburg (Austria) Seminar in American Civilization. This U.S.-government-sponsored event, housed in a castle called Leopoldskron, brought American teachers to European students; there Jarrell fell in love with German Romanticism and with the vistas of Mitteleuropa. He also fell in love with Elisabeth Eisler, a Viennese ceramics artist in her late twenties, who had signed up for Jarrell's class in American poetry. The two spent much of the summer together and then exchanged intimate, passionate letters. Jarrell decided at the end of the year to stay with Mackie, telling Elisabeth that their correspondence would have to lose its romantic character.

These years also saw more stateside honors. One well-known essay, "The Obscurity of the Poet," began in 1950 as an address given at Harvard. Jarrell also accepted other teaching engagements at summer writers' conferences. At one such conference in Boulder, Colorado, in 1951, Randall encountered an adult student named Mary von Schrader (they were introduced, she recalled, by W. D. Snodgrass) (*Remembering* 131). Randall and Mary spent the evening together, ending up at the library; they quickly became inseparable. By the end of the summer Randall had asked Mackie for a divorce.

He and Mary were already planning their new life. Yet Randall had already agreed to spend the academic year 1951–52 teaching at Princeton, where he and Mackie, before their divorce, had arranged to rent a house.[9] Living alone for the first time since the war, Jarrell spent much of his year writing letters to Mary (far more survive than could be included in his published *Letters*). Mary recalled his obsession with mail delivery: "What Princeton needs," he quipped to her, "is an Institute of Advanced Postmen" (*Remembering* 13). At Princeton Jarrell wrote a few poems (some, such as "The Lonely Man," clearly set there) and finished a number of essays. He also gave a series of lectures on Auden, some reworked from his earlier writings. The ambitious and witty talks remain in manuscript, with some fragments apparently never delivered. One lecture proposes to "start an Early Auden Society, to be called the Friends of *Paid on Both Sides*, and give a performance of it every five years, in Iceland." Another argues that though many of Auden's changes have been for the worse, he "*has* begun to get better again . . . and is *not* locked away in that real graveyard of poets, My Own Style, going on like a repeating decimal until the day someone drives a stake through his heart" (Berg Collection).

Mary and Randall were married in California in November 1952. They moved first to the University of Illinois at Champaign-Urbana, where Jarrell taught for one term, and then back to Greensboro, where they made their home with Alleyne and Beatrice, Mary's preteen daughters from her previous marriage. "To be married to Randall," Mary would write, "was to be encapsulated with him. He wanted, and we had a round-the-clock inseparability" (*Remembering* 135). A Greensboro graduate, Emily Wilson (later Herring), recalled that when students invited Jarrell to read in a dorm, "Mrs. Jarrell came with him, and they held hands or he stood by her, entwining his arm in the curve of her shawl" (quoted in Quinn, *Randall Jarrell* 133). In Greensboro, Randall finished his first books of prose—*Poetry and the Age* (1953) and *Pictures from an Institution* (1954). The former, collecting his essays and reviews, established itself as a touchstone of mid-century practical criticism; the latter sold well enough to pay for a sports car. (Automobiles had joined tennis among Jarrell's serious hobbies; he subscribed to *Road and Track* and recorded his fascination in two sparkling essays for *Mademoiselle* and *Vogue*.)

Despite a few long new poems (chief among them "The End of the Rainbow," set in California) and a 1955 *Selected Poems*, Jarrell had come to feel blocked as a writer of verse. He complained to Mary that "a wicked fairy has turned me into a prose writer" (*Remembering* 51). Some of his energy surely went into teaching, as the awed memoirs of his students attest.[10] A complex fight over the Woman's College curriculum also ate into his time. Jarrell kept on writing reviews and essays about poetry, among them "The Collected Poems of Wallace Stevens." He had, though, begun to turn his critical energies elsewhere: new essays and lectures (many given repeatedly on various college campuses) reflected his dismay at American education and mass culture. Jarrell also began a translation of Chekhov's *Three Sisters* (staged on Broadway in 1964); an anthology of short fiction (*The Anchor Book of Stories*, 1958); and a translation of Goethe's *Faust, Part 1* (published posthumously in 1976). A ballet scenario and a psychoanalytic explication of T. S. Eliot stand among other projects he never completed.

In 1956 Jarrell was asked to serve as consultant in poetry at the Library of Congress (the position now called Poet Laureate). Someone (likely the family of a disgruntled student) told the Library that Jarrell had been a Communist, which almost derailed the nomination; nevertheless, he, Mary, Alleyne, and Beatrice moved to Washington, D.C. that fall. Jarrell by all accounts performed splendidly, soliciting poets to record their works, requesting that they will their manuscripts to the library, arranging public programming in Washington and elsewhere, involving himself in the city's intellectual life, and answering random letters from literary-minded citizens. He largely extricated himself from reviewing, ending his regular stint at the *Yale Review*, because the negative comments he would have made conflicted with his consultant duties (*Yale Review* files). Living at 3916 Jenifer Street NW, near the Maryland line, Randall and

Mary loved Washington almost inordinately: it offered museums and orchestras along with civility, greenery, and tennis. "I'm not a native Washingtonian," he wrote, "but I wish I were—it's my favorite American city" (to Johanna Curran, 3 January 1957; Library of Congress). Their frequent trips to the National Zoo (on Connecticut Avenue, a long walk from their house) generated two important poems, "Jerome" and "The Woman at the Washington Zoo."

The new job also brought a higher profile: one public lecture, "The Taste of the Age," gathered local and national attention (in the *Washington Post*, the *New York Times*, even *House Beautiful!*) and brought him a wave of requests for reprints (Library of Congress). Jarrell had been anxious for years about the academic-formalist turn fifties poetry seemed to have taken, objecting in 1955 to the "many young poets" for whom "poetry is a game . . . they play with propriety, as part of their social and academic existence" (*KA* 231). At the library he tried to help nurture alternatives, offering advice to Jonathan Williams of *Jargon* and to the new editor of the *Colorado Review* about running a magazine, and to Princeton University Press about starting a poetry list. Invitations to lecture or teach brought the Jarrells on trips from Washington to Dallas, Cincinnatti, Columbus, Ohio, and San Francisco, where he discovered the Beats: Jarrell quarreled in public with Allen Ginsberg but took a liking to Gregory Corso, whom Mary remembered as "pleasingly promising," "a streetwise waif" (*Remembering* 41).

That winter Corso came to visit the Jarrells at Jenifer Street; he stayed for six weeks, inviting Jack Kerouac over, writing "a poem a day," and never revising. "Disenchanted with Corso," Mary recalled, "Randall was relieved" when Corso moved out (*Remembering* 41–42). Another visitor was Robert Lowell, then on the cusp of a manic episode. "I wish all the San Francisco poets would eat all the University poets and burst," Jarrell wrote to Karl Shapiro the following year; "it's pretty awful to look at Mass Culture, and at its side High Culture, and hardly know which you like less" (*Letters* 436). Randall did like Italy, where the Jarrells, the Taylors, and their children traveled for the summer of 1958: they stayed at Levanto and Buonassola, near Robert and Sally Fitzgerald. Mary and Eleanor have both left glowing records of that occasionally fractious summer, during which Peter finished stories, Randall played with the children, and Eleanor (with Randall's help) revised what would become her first book of poems.

The Jarrells returned to Greensboro, where they moved into "a rustic house on a red clay road in a small forest" (*Remembering* 143). Randall worked on *Faust* and on *The Woman at the Washington Zoo*, which garnered the National Book Award in 1960. *A Sad Heart at the Supermarket* (1962) collected more essays, most of them on education and American culture. In early 1962 Michael di

Capua, an editor at Macmillan, invited Jarrell to translate a few Grimms' tales. Jarrell soon offered him not only translations (of *Snow White*, among other stories) but also an original children's book, *The Gingerbread Rabbit*, which Garth Williams would illustrate. The charming but unsteady narrative follows its titular animal as he runs away from a kitchen to live as a real animal in the forest. Jarrell's next and far superior children's book, *The Bat-Poet*, paired him with the illustrator Maurice Sendak, who was years away from his own fame: Sendak would later call "working with Randall . . . the most charmed experience of my career" ("Unlimited"). Two more children's books followed, both with Sendak's pictures: the much longer *The Animal Family* (1965) and *Fly by Night*, published posthumously in 1976.

Jarrell welcomed the Kennedy era, remarking in a televised discussion "What a pleasure to think that for the next few years our art and our government won't be complete strangers" (quoted in *Remembering* 156). The White House Conference on the Arts in November 1962 became the stage for his final verdicts on modern poets, delivered in the lecture "Fifty Years of American Poetry": the speech, and the conference, coincided with the Cuban missile crisis. Other late prose includes essays on Kipling and Frost and a long introduction to Christina Stead's *The Man Who Loved Children*, a novel that "knows as few books have ever known—knows specifically, profoundly, exhaustively—what a family is" (*Third* 3). 1963 began auspiciously, with plenty of new poems and plans for a summer in Europe: Jarrell had probably finished his last book of poems, *The Lost World*, by the time he and Mary embarked in June (Pritchard 288). His letters from England, Germany, and Italy to Taylor, di Capua, Lowell, and others record a busy, exuberant season of opera, art galleries, motoring, and sightseeing. Jarrell was also delighted with Adrienne Rich's new poems, which he critiqued in letters to her.

Mary and Randall returned to America in November, and Randall's behavior began to change. Approaching his fiftieth birthday, he seems to have worried deeply about his advancing age—he liked to call his condition *torschlusspanik* (German for "door-closing panic") (*Remembering* 159). After President Kennedy was shot, Randall spent days in front of the television, weeping. Sad to the point of inertia, Randall sought help from a Cinncinnati psychiatrist, who prescribed "a newly marketed mood elevating drug," Elavil: the drug bears much of the blame for what happened next (*Remembering* 159, Pritchard 290–291). By the fall of 1964—after months on Elavil—Jarrell became hyperenergetic, erratic, and sometimes grandiose or irrational. (The psychiatrist, meanwhile, proved disturbingly willing to renew prescriptions by phone.) At Greensboro, Randall alienated the Taylors—and his other friends—as he fought hard for an impracticable scheme to remake the English department. When Hannah Arendt arrived to give a lecture, Jarrell introduced her with a rambling story about the football star Johnny Unitas. Randall also went on a credit-card-fueled flying binge and "tipped a waitress with a $1,500 check" (Pritchard 292). At some point he asked Mary for a divorce; Lowell later told Taylor that Randall had become "involved with a girl at Goucher" College in Maryland (McAlexander 170).

In early 1965 Randall was sent to a North Carolina hospital; he was taken off Elavil immediately and briefly given Thorazine. Unsurprisingly, his elation ceased; depression—perhaps a withdrawal symptom—followed. In April the *New York Times* published a viciously condescending review of *The Lost World*. Soon afterwards, Jarrell slashed a wrist and returned to the hospital. His brief, contrite letters to Mary, to Peter Taylor, and to others written during these months are some of the most moving documents of his life. After a summer with Mary, Randall began teaching his Greensboro classes; he returned to the hospital in October for rehabilitative work on his hand. (The last poem he wrote, an uncharacteristic and haunting near-sonnet, portrays the hospital's "Hand House" ["Previously" 196].)

On the evening of October 11, 1965, Jarrell was sideswiped by a car while walking along a road; he died of the resulting injuries. Mary, the police, the coroner, and ultimately the state of North Carolina judged his death accidental, a verdict made credible by his apparent improvements in health, his rapprochement with her, and the odd, sidelong manner of the collision; medical professionals judged the injuries consistent with an accident and not with suicide. Because initial news reports were ambiguous, because Jarrell had earlier slashed his wrist, and because other poets (such as Sylvia Plath) had ended their lives, some of Jarrell's literary acquaintances had trouble accepting the coroners' report. Taylor seems to have thought the event deliberate; even he, though, wrote to Robert Fitzgerald, "I don't know whether or not his death was suicide . . . Probably no one will ever know" (McAlexander 170).[11]

Jarrell's friends reacted to his sudden death with grief—and with public events. Lowell, Taylor, and Robert Penn Warren organized a day of tributes at Yale, with contributions from (among others) Arendt, Berryman, Bishop, Fitzgerald, Marianne Moore, Ransom, Rich, Tate, and Mary Jarrell herself. These and other essays, poems, and images comprised the memorial volume, *Randall Jarrell 1914–1965*, published by Farrar, Straus and Giroux in 1967. A *Complete Poems*, including much (though not all) of the unpublished work, appeared to broad notice in 1969, followed by several critical books on the poetry; two books of uncollected essays (1969 and 1980); *Faust, Part I* (1976); a volume of *Letters*, with Mary's annotations (1985; revised, 2002); a new selection of essays, *No Other Book*, prepared by Brad Leithauser (1999); and a volume of Mary's own recollections, *Remembering Randall* (1999).

Jarrell has latterly become a popular subject for American poets' elegies: Berryman, Lowell, Shapiro, Phillip Booth, Robert Hass, Richard Howard, Eleanor Ross Taylor, and the critic Eve Kosofky Sedgwick (among others) have all published poems about Jarrell's work or his life. Howard imagines Jarrell as a modern Tiresias—man, woman, and wise elder in one; Booth's quiet poem seeks help from "Saint Jarrell" (6, 159). Berryman's "Op. posth. no. 13" imagines a posthumous meeting where

> all will be as before
> whenas we sought, among the beloved faces,
> eminence and were dissatisfied with that
> and needed more.
>
> (*RJ* 19)

Essayists and reviewers (among them Susan Sontag and Adam Gopnik) continue to admire Jarrell's prose. Gopnik describes "the feeling that his work . . . wasn't just yours but you, the you that you had always intended to be" (92–93). Yet critics have not always known what to make of Jarrell. William Pritchard, whose biography of Jarrell appeared in 1990, was surprised to find himself less than "totally sympathetic" to Jarrell the man: "I have become aware," Pritchard wrote, "of just how strange a phenomenon he was" (6–7). Other academic readers reacted to Pritchard's biography by emphasizing strange aspects Pritchard had neglected, among them Jarrell's difficult mother, his desire to write in the voices of women, and his frequent rejections of adult, academic, and masculine norms.

These debates risk obscuring the virtues to which the memoirs, and the poems, attest. All accounts of the man paint him as immune to social conventions, free of *ressentiment*, and always ready to say what he thought and felt. The first of his several reviews of B. H. Haggin reads like a hopeful self-portrait: Haggin, Jarrell decided, "is more interested in saying precisely what he thinks about a composer or a performer . . . than he is in anything else whatsoever; consequently he is a sort of exemplary monster of independence, of honesty, of scrupulous and merciless frankness" (*KA* 154). Jarrell defined himself by successive enthusiasms—from *Ariadne auf Naxos* to auto racing, from Kafka to Kitten to Kipling—which he did not stint to share. With those enthusiasms, and those wishes, came a deliberate childlikeness, evidenced in his freedom from adult vices and in the affectionate preference for G-rated slang—"Gee," "Gosh," "Baby doll!"—which Berryman lampooned in an unpublished poem ("Roethke's"). He found off-color language and gossip distasteful; Berryman believed Jarrell did not drink, though Mary records his later interest in quality beers (*Remembering* 37). A colleague and friend at Greensboro, Robert Watson, recalls that Jarrell "identified with children and the cozy world of the child. When we asked callers what they would have to drink, he was the only guest who would call for 'milk and cookies' " (*RJ* 264). Jarrell himself wrote to Eisler in 1948: "I am childish in many ways, but this is as much good as bad" (*Letters* 205).

Though Jarrell scared or puzzled some acquaintances, he clearly inspired remarkable loyalty and gratitude, not only from his wife but from his friends. "His voice could express more affection and welcome than anyone," Eleanor Ross Taylor recalled; "His honesty was related to his generosity to students, to me, and . . . to [dead or neglected writers] like Christina Stead and [Tristan] Corbière" (*RJ* 234, 237). "To Randall's friends," Peter Taylor wrote, "there was always the feeling that he was their teacher. To Randall's students, there was always the feeling that he was their friend. And with good reason in both cases" (*RJ* 246). To Lowell, "Randall was the only man . . . who could make other writers feel that their work was more important to him than his own. . . . I have never known anyone" (Lowell continued) "who so connected what his friends wrote with their lives, or their lives with what they wrote" (*RJ* 106).

These connections may be a key to his character. He clearly enjoyed sharing a house with the Taylors, and his happy second marriage meant that he and Mary were never apart. At the same time he complained that Peter Taylor—an inveterate host—"likes too many people" (McAlexander 174). Jarrell retreated from cocktail parties into smaller conversations or fled upstairs to play with the hosts' young children. Though he disliked large social gatherings, he seems to have been perpetually in need of close companionship and emotional alliance—from his four important romantic partners (Amy Breyer, Mackie, Elisabeth Eisler, and Mary); from friends like Arendt, Lowell, the Taylors, and Warren; and in another sense from his favorite books and musical works, on which so much depended. In his months apart from each of his wives, and in his few months of romance with Eisler, he depended as few people could on an intimacy conducted through the mail.

The creatures in his children's books, too—the gingerbread rabbit in flight, the estranged bat-poet, the lonely hunter, stranded mermaid, and orphan boy of *The Animal Family*—are seeking reliable, intimate companions. The bat-poet finds it, or almost does, in the earnest chipmunk, to whom Mary compared herself. For Robert Fitzgerald, Jarrell's "interest in tennis represented an attachment to common life, as later on sports cars did and later still professional football, and . . . he placed a peculiar value on these hobbies"; "he must have known," Fitzgerald continued, "that at times he was not only lonely, but faintly monstrous," and "he wished not to be" (*RJ* 73).[12]

The life displays, then, the virtues Lowell singled out—"wit, pathos and brilliance of intelligence" (*RJ* 103). It suggests, too, a tremendous, needy loneliness and a consequent, constant need for human intimacy and belonging. Jarrell wanted to connect himself with the rest of the human world, partly because he sometimes found it hard to do so. There followed a desire to separate intimacy from anything that might challenge or destroy it: here, perhaps, lies the source of Jarrell's sometimes gleeful, innnocent undecorousness. "I'm a thoroughly dependent person," he confessed to Peter Taylor in 1965, adding that he was "so afraid of being bored and surrounded by empty time" (12 May 1965; Taylor letters).

"The biggest permanent consolation for anything," he wrote Amy twenty-one years earlier, "is that the world's so interesting" (*Letters* 154, 116). Randall Jarrell's poems projected his own needs and the needs he imagined into characters whose lives offered causes, figures, and languages for them. His lifelong preoccupations with loneliness and its remedies, with the self and how it might be changed, gave him his emotional repertoire: expectation, disappointment, pathos, sympathy, nostalgia, half-believed fantasy, mourning and melancholia. It lent him, too, a set of subjects: soldiers, airmen, lonely children, children as readers, girls and girlhood, fairy-tales, the postal service, housewives, hospitals, office workers, illness and old age. The same preoccupations, I argue in chapter 1, gave him a distinctive and valuable style.

Chapter 1

JARRELL'S INTERPERSONAL STYLE

Randall Jarrell's best-known poems are poems about the Second World War, poems about bookish children and childhood, and poems, such as "Next Day," in the voices of aging women. "Next Day" begins in a supermarket, where its lonely shopper puns on brand names:

> Moving from Cheer to Joy, from Joy to All,
> I take a box
> And add it to my wild rice, my Cornish game hens.
> The slacked or shorted, basketed, identical
> Food-gathering flocks
> Are selves I overlook. Wisdom, said William James
>
> Is learning what to overlook. And I am wise
> If that is wisdom.

(CP 279)

If the henlike shoppers amount to "selves [she] overlook[s]," she too feels over-looked, and wishes "That the boy putting groceries in my car / / See me. It be-wilders me he doesn't see me." Feeling less than present to herself, she sees her face in the mirror as alien:

Its plain, lined look

Of gray discovery
Repeats to me: "You're old." That's all, I'm old.

And yet I'm afraid, as I was at the funeral
I went to yesterday.
My friend's cold made-up face, granite among its flowers,
Her undressed, operated-on, dressed body
Were my face and body.
As I think of her I hear her telling me

How young I seem; I *am* exceptional;
I think of all I have.
But really no one is exceptional,
No one has anything, I'm anybody,
I stand beside my grave,
Confused with my life, that is commonplace and solitary.

(CP 280)

Several readers have found the poem representative.[1] Like many of Jarrell's pro-tagonists—among them the "Woman at the Washington Zoo" in her "dull, null" uniform, the depressed child of "The Elementary Scene," and the dead American airmen of "Losses"—the woman in "Next Day" seems confined by circumstance and fate to a deeply troubling typicality. This is the plot many of Jarrell's poems suggest, the story his characters suffer: no one else confirms their unique selfhood, and so they are given occasions to doubt it.

Everyone who reads "Next Day" acquires some idea of the sort of person who speaks and how she feels. It takes longer to see how Jarrell's stanzas contribute to our sense of her frustrations—to see in the poem Jarrell's verse style. Jarrell rhymes "exceptional" with "exceptional," the word with a later instance of itself; the buildup of other repeated words ("wisdom," "wish," "afraid," "body") sug-gests the woman's doubts that such words, for her, retain useful meanings. The rhyming of stressed with unstressed syllables helps produce the self-muffling, self-baffling tone she adopts. And the spaces and pauses the stanza form leaves (as if for replies) help make the poem as affecting as it is.[2]

Jarrell's stylistic particularities have been hard for critics to hear and describe, both because the poems call readers' attention instead to their characters and be-cause Jarrell's particular powers emerge so often from mimesis of speech.[3] Jar-rell's style responds to the alienations it delineates by incorporating or troping speech and conversation, linking emotional events within one person's psyche to speech acts that might take place between persons. This chapter will emphasize those interpersonal elements, which, taken together, create Jarrell's style. I begin by describing an early poem in which Jarrell seems to discover the interpersonal as a goal for his poems. I then show how that goal emerged from Jarrell's readings of modernism, of literary history, and of Wordsworth. These readings, in turn, let us see how his verse style works and what its elements achieve.

Randall Jarrell began to create his style in poems he finished between 1939 and 1942; the best-known among them is "90 North."[4] It is a poem of announcement, discovery, and self-dedication, analogous to other self-dedicatory poems (Keats's "On First Looking into Chapman's Homer," Heaney's "Digging") in which an extraliterary discovery stands for a poet's commitment to his work. The dreamer-explorer says he has reached a goal: "I sailed all night—till at last . . . I stood at the northern pole" (CP 113). Yet the dream quest, remembered from childhood, seems futile to the adult dreamer who completes it:

> The world—my world spins on this final point
> Of cold and wretchedness; all lines, all winds
>
> End in this whirlpool I at last discover.
> And it is meaningless.
>
> (CP 113)

The isolated, adult, his explorations "meaningless," seems to have discovered (to borrow Geoffrey Hartman's words about Wordsworth) "that to heighten consciousness [is] to intensify rather than assuage the sense of isolation" (*Wordsworth's* xvii). Like Wordsworth at Simplon Pass (*Prelude* [1805] 6: 580–585), Jarrell's dreamer expected sublimity, and wisdom, from a summit, but learns instead that he must go back down:

> There in the childish night my companions lay frozen,
> The stiff furs knocked at my starveling throat,
> And I gave my great sigh: the flakes came huddling,
> Were they really my end? In the darkness I turned to my rest.
>
> —Here, the flag snaps in the glare and silence
> Of the unbroken ice. I stand here,
> The dogs bark, my beard is black, and I stare
> At the North Pole . . .
>
>   And now what? Why, go back.

The "huddling" flakes, and the dogs, are plural and alive; only the poet's "I" and his flagpole stand alone. The poem, in fact, pivots on the word "alone"—the only word that ends two lines, and those lines one after the other, as if the poem had then to retrace its steps:

> Here at the actual pole of my existence,
> Where all that I have done is meaningless,
> Where I die or live by accident alone—
>
> Where, living or dying, I am still alone;
> Here where North, the night, the berg of death
> Crowd me out of the ignorant darkness,
> I see at last that all the knowledge
>
> I wrung from the darkness—that the darkness flung me—
> Is worthless as ignorance; nothing comes from nothing,
> The darkness from the darkness. Pain comes from the darkness
> And we call it wisdom. It is pain.

Alan Williamson has written that Jarrell's poems tell a "story of our loneliness in the world" ("Märchen" 283). "90 North" may be said to propose—along with Jarrell's vocation—a dilemma central to that vocation: loneliness, in various guises, constitutes the problem, and the "pain," that the poems wish to remedy.

Jarrell's best critics have often overstated the poems' senses of futility by ignoring the ways in which his style contains and answers them.[5] Jerome Mazzaro has called Jarrell's corpus of poetry "a succession of efforts . . . to get rid of the 'aloneness' which he felt" (*CE* 99). These efforts generate the fictions of speaking and listening with which he created his style. Even as it describes isolation, "90 North" thus imagines a listener. The poem flaunts devices that imply speech and response—deictics ("There," "Here"), rhetorical questions ("Were they really my end?"; "Now what? *Why* . . . "), self-corrections ("The world—my world"), and repetitions. These evocations of listeners became essential components of Jarrell's practice.

Jarrell developed that practice by attending at once to his own emotions and to literary history. "90 North" sets limits to unaided imagination. But its discovered terminus, where "all lines, and winds / End," also tropes a more specific limit—the end, not of wishes or poetry but of modernist poetry, what Jarrell in 1942 dubbed "The End of the Line." "Modernist poetry," he wrote, "appears to be and is generally considered to be a violent break with romanticism; it is actually

. . . an end product in which most of the tendencies of romanticism have been carried to their limits" (*KA* 77). "Poets can go back and repeat the ride," Jarrell continued, or "settle . . . along the railroad"; nevertheless "Modernism As We Knew It . . . is dead" (*KA* 81). William Pritchard writes that " '90 North' is exactly the poem to illustrate the 'fairly solitary individuality' [Jarrell] predicted for the poet of the early 1940s, at the end of the line, just where the man in the poem finds himself" (81). But "90 North" reflects the postmodernist poet's dilemma in more specific ways. The polar explorer who turns back to the real world points the way, not only for modern poetry to rejoin other poetry but also for modern poetry to face, and hence to rejoin, other people, whose speech can be heard and shared.[6]

Modernism can be distinguished *from* romanticism, in Jarrell's view, by its greater "specialization": the modernist poet is much less like nonpoets, modernist poetic language much farther from nonexpert speech and prose, than Romantics and their language were.[7] The early poem "Esthetic Theories: Art as Expression" mocks poems, like medical specimens, "preserved in jars, and certified / By experts" (*CP* 384). Jarrell wrote in 1950 that he intended his poems "for the audience that reads poetry from age to age, I believe, and not for the more specialized audience that reads modern poetry" (*KA* 170). Reviewing *Poetry and the Age*, Delmore Schwartz found that its essays "express the anguish of one who does not feel superior, but lonely; and the dismay of one who does not want to be cut off from other human beings by his love of literature" (*CE* 43). Against the "expert" or "specialist" models he deplored (models that chapter 2 will revisit), Jarrell's work attempts to reduce the distance between poets and the rest of the world.

The explicitly political poems of the thirties and forties sometimes see politics in the same terms in which other poems and letters see literary history and private life. How can Jarrell bring himself closer to the subjects and victims of politics? An unpublished poem, "The Patient Leading the Patient," asks what Jarrell can do for "The poor with their bad manners and bad bones . . . whom I do nothing for / Unless pity is something; and it is something, / Isn't it?" (Berg Collection). Alluding to Christ's "The poor ye have always with ye" (Matthew 26:11), "The Soldier Walks Under the Trees of the University" attacks the gaps in understanding between academia and the war effort, academia and the American poor, academia, and everything "real":

> The poor are always—somewhere, but not here;
> We learn of them where they and Guilt subsist
> With Death and Evil: in books, in books, in books.
> Ah, sweet to contemplate the causes, not the things!

The soul learns fortitude in libraries,
Enduring patience in another's pain,
And pity for the lives we do not change:
All that the world would be, if it were real.

(*CP* 401)

Jarrell's early Marxism (recalled in the later poem "The Tower") looks here like a desire for solidarity with the world outside literature, the contemporary world below the tower and its libraries.

Modernist specialization, modernist remove, were hardly Jarrell's discovery: he inherited (from Edmund Wilson, among others) the idea that poets after Pound and Eliot would have to reconnect themselves to the outside world. Auden's late-thirties work took on just these problems—one reason Jarrell followed it so intently and with such mixed feelings. By 1941 he had reached a judgment on it he was never to retract: "Auden has been successful," Jarrell wrote, "in making his poetry more accessible; but the success has been entirely too expensive. Realizing that the best poetry of the twenties was too inaccessible, we can will our poetry into accessibility—but how much poetry will be left when we finish?" (*Third* 149).

Jarrell shared Auden's early Marxist sympathies, as his thirties and forties essays attest; he even wrote an admiring poem about Friedrich Engels (Berg Collection).[8] But the kind of poetry Jarrell developed did not find its answer to modernist isolation by turning (as Wilson recommended in *Axel's Castle*, as Auden had in poems such as "Spain") from the level of the solitary individual to the level of a whole society. Jarrell's mature poems would describe, and try to alleviate, the isolation of the modern poet, not by addressing a whole society but by recognizing other people one by one—seeking, with and for them, as notes for a 1958 essay put it, a "quiet private place where something can ripen"—whether or not such a place could be had (UNC-Greensboro).

This difference between the level of society (which Jarrell's lonely characters largely reject) and the level of the interpersonal (which Jarrell and his characters seek) might be understood in terms of the differing goods the philosopher Paul Ricoeur names "equality" and "solicitude."[9] For Ricoeur "*Equality . . . is to life in institutions what solicitude is to interpersonal relations.* Solicitude provides to the self another who is a face, in [Levinas's sense]. Equality provides to the self another who is an *each*" (202; italics Ricoeur's). The front pages of the *Nation* pursued "equality"; the poems and book reviews Jarrell published in the back of the same magazine pursued "solicitude" instead. Jarrell's literary-historical problem about modernism, his ethical problem about solidarity, and his more personal problem about loneliness, thus steered him toward the same goal: he

would write poems that describe and alleviate isolation, imagining "other peo-
ple" and their speech.

Jarrell found models for such poems in Wordsworth. From the early forties to
the sixties, his prose constantly invokes Wordsworth as a standard of value and as
a counterweight to current practice. "The End of the Line" mentions many
poets but quotes only Wordsworth: "the very world, which is the world / Of all of
us—the place where, in the end, / We find our happiness or not at all" (*KA* 81).
Jarrell wrote Harry Ford in January 1955: "I'm working hard on Wordsworth
right now—I mean to do four or five long articles, designed from the beginning
to be a book"; the same year Jarrell "spent a month reading nothing but
Wordsworth . . . and like him much better than ever, even" (Berg Collection;
Letters 404).[10] Jarrell told the readers of the *New York Times Book Review* in 1955
that "when I recommend the second book of *The Excursion*, or speak of
Wordsworth as one of the three or four greatest of English poets, I don't mind
having the remark thought either a truism or an absurdity" (*KA* 220). Three
years later he treated the audience at the National Book Awards to quotations
from the preface to *Lyrical Ballads*, from Book 7 of the *Prelude*, and from
Wordsworth's sonnet to Toussaint L'Ouverture ("About Popular Culture" 9–10).

It took originality for a reader trained on New Critical practices to see
Wordsworth as a usable model.[11] Robert Penn Warren wrote in *American Re-
view* in 1934, "I had rather read [Archibald] MacLeish's *Poems, 1924–1933* than
Wordsworth's *Prelude*; and I am prepared to accept whatever damnation that in-
volves" ("Twelve Poets" 218). (The same issue contained Jarrell's first published
poems.) Warren (and Brooks and Ransom and Tate) are the critics Jarrell de-
scribed in 1941, who "have repudiated romanticism so wholeheartedly that they
condemn in their criticism the vices that they exploit in their poetry" (*KA* 62).
Jarrell's 1941 letter to Louise Bogan declares by contrast his own allegiances: "I
was simply charmed by something you said (in *Partisan Review* I think) about
the feel of early romanticism at its best; I feel so, too" (*Letters* 45).

What did Jarrell learn from Wordsworth? Occasionally his poems echo
Wordsworth directly.[12] More often he invoked Wordsworth's example as oblique
authorization for his own projects. Jarrell's poems take seriously Wordsworth's
famous prescription of 1802: "the Poet must descend from [his] supposed height;
and, in order to excite rational sympathy, he must express himself as other men
express themselves" (261). Jarrell's "The One Who Was Different" exclaims (in
lines Elizabeth Bishop admired), "I feel like the first men who read
Wordsworth. / It's so simple I can't understand it" (*CP* 316). "When critics first
read Wordsworth's poetry," Jarrell reminds us in "The Obscurity of the Poet,"
"they felt that it was silly"—though many "*said*, with Byron," that it didn't make
sense (*Age* 8; italics Jarrell's). The disarming flatness, the patches of very simple

(and unironic) diction that have made Jarrell's critics so uncomfortable—these, too, seem learned from Wordsworth. Reviewing Jarrell's *Selected Poems* in 1956, James Dickey imagined a debate between two fictive readers, A and B:

> B. . . . the poems are the most untalentedly sentimental, self-indulgent and insensitive writings I can remember; when I read them I cry and laugh helplessly all night, over the reputation that has come out of such stuff.

> A. I would say, in answer, that you have missed the entire point of Jarrell's contribution, which is that of writing about real things, rather than playing games with words. . . . His world is *the* World, and People, and not the cultivated island of books, theories, and schools.

> (*RJ* 34–35)

Dickey later sided with his "A" character, concluding that "Next Day" (for example) "is convincing as speech before it is convincing—or even felt—as 'Art' " (*Reader* 299).

Jarrell took from Wordsworth the idea that poems had to be "convincing as speech" before they were anything else; to be, for him, "convincing as speech," the poem ordinarily had to imagine a listener. Barbara Schapiro has described Wordsworth's "continual reference to a personal other . . . in his most deeply introspective poems": as William turns to Dorothy in "Tintern Abbey" and to Coleridge throughout the *Prelude*, Jarrell and his personae also invoke projected listeners (31–32). "The Bad Music" asks: "Of those millions, how many know or love at all / You, Anna?" (*CP* 368) "The Player Piano"—written over twenty years later—pivots on imperatives, asking its audience twice to "Look" and once to "Listen" (*CP* 354–355). Both Jarrell and Wordsworth quote other speakers in their poems, and both like to quote children—the children in "The Truth" and "Protocols," numbed and half conscious of death, look like answers to the child of "We Are Seven," who knows nothing of it. Both Jarrell and Wordsworth can turn in mid-poem from one auditor to another; both can treat poems as occasions to resituate oneself in time, to contrast a remembered event with a present occasion.

All these poetic tactics cohere as one overarching project, a project inaugurated in "90 North." David Bromwich has shown how Wordsworthian vocation reappears in Frost and in Stevens stripped of the encounters with other people that Wordsworth requires. What Bromwich finds in Wordsworth's "Resolution and Independence" (but not in its modernist rewritings) is a quality he calls "sympathy," though (he writes), "Sympathy may be a misleading word for what I mean: 'acknowledgement' or 'recognition' might be better. But [sympathy's] very etymology includes what is central to my argument: a feeling that touches some second figure, and that could not come into being without it" (*Choice* 230–231).[13] Sometimes Jarrell's second person is an imagined listener or reader. Sometimes it is a character who is lost, or dead, or beyond hearing. And sometimes the second person appears and responds in the scene of the poem, an occurrence that corresponds to a "happy ending." It is such a turn to the intersubjective — to the quest for "acknowledgement" or "recognition" — that binds Jarrell's work most deeply to Wordsworth's poetry.

Jarrell's Wordsworthian turn towards the interpersonal created his characteristic verse style. Many readers see discontinuities between the war poems and later poems such as "Next Day." The first often feature an omniscient or impersonal narrator; the second tend to be spoken by characters. These differences make it easy to miss the persistence of Jarrell's goals: both the war poems and the later poems seek to establish a nexus of recognition between reader and speaker, speaker and listener, actor and observer.

The poet of the war poems seeks or wishes — often fruitlessly, as he realizes — to individualize soldiers and pilots who risk becoming mute, interchangeable objects. The convalescent serviceman in "The Sick Nought" disturbs Jarrell into heights of rhetoric because he seems not even to know his family:

> Do the wife and baby travelling to see
> Your grey pajamas and sick worried face
> Remind you of something, soldier? I remember
> You convalescing washing plates, or mopping
> The endless corridors your shoes had scuffed;
> And in the crowded rooms you rubbed your cheek
> Against your wife's thin elbow like a pony.
> But you are something there are millions of.
> How can I care about you much, or pick you out
> From all the others other people loved
> And sent away to die for them? You are a ticket
> Someone bought and lost on, a stray animal:
> You have lost even the right to be condemned.

> (CP 174)

As Paul Fussell suggests, this soldier's worn-down bewilderment gives Jarrell an especially vivid example of the facelessness the war poems, in general, fear. The ability to recognize other individuals, and to be recognized by them, seems to Jarrell a (even *the*) test of personhood; to be anonymous is not to have lived.[14]

The soldiers and airmen who are granted some measure of consciousness in the war poems seek (and only occasionally find) a particular, dead or departed or vulnerable individual amid the alienations of the war. The lost flier in "A Front" asks, "*Can't you hear me?*" before his plane crash-lands (CP 13; italics Jarrell's). "A Pilot from the Carrier," falling slowly in his parachute (and perhaps to death by fire) recapitulates the trajectory of the explorer-poet in "90 North": "He is alone; and hangs in knowledge / Slight, separate, estranged: a lonely eye / Reading a child's first scrawl" (CP 153). Another poem about a pilot, "The Dead Wingman," deserves more attention than it has received. Its protagonist circles, in dreams, the space where his wingman died:

> Seen on the sea, no sign; no sign, no sign
> In the black firs and terraces of hills
> Ragged in mist. The cone narrows, snow
> Glares from the bleak walls of a crater. No.
> Again the houses jerk like paper, turn,
> And the surf streams by; a port of toys
> Is starred with its fires and faces; but no sign.
>
> In the level light, over the fiery shores,
> The plane circles stubbornly: the eyes distending
> With hatred and misery and longing, stare
> Over the blackening ocean for a corpse.
> The fires are guttering; the dials fall,
> A long dry shudder climbs along his spine,
> His fingers tremble; but his hard unchanging stare
> Moves unacceptingly: *I have a friend.*
>
> The fires are grey; no star, no sign
> Winks from the breathing darkness of the carrier
> Where the pilot circles for his wingman; where,
> Gliding about the cities' shells, a stubborn eye
> Among the ashen nations, achingly
> Tracing the circles of that worn, unchanging No—
> The lives' long war, lost war—the pilot sleeps.

(CP 157)

Shifts in caesura placement and line length graph the feel of a moving airplane: lines seem to yaw, bank, turn. Jarrell's speaker seems at once a pilot bereaved of his companion and a poet looking for readers, sadly confined to his unstable aerial view. The horribly distant houses look like paper—it would be better to live in them than to see them from afar. By the same token, it would be better to see the faces as faces than as toys, but Jarrell's weary pilot can see no one face-to-face: no one answers or looks back.

Jarrell liked to define literature (following Freud's definition of a dream) as "a wish modified by a truth."[15] The description gains special force in "The Dead Wingman," where the poem's false or avoided endings represent the pilot's wish ("I have a friend") and the actual end of the poem the truth (*SH* 140–141). Key words grow multivalent through repetition: the poem describes a *stare* in search of a *sign* that turns out to be a recurring *no*. The poem begins as a rescue mission, gives us to understand that the mission has failed, and ends as a dream of that mission: when the pilot's dream ends, the poem does too. The words "sign" and "no" and the rhyme on "stare" all return: nothing *will* change, no listener, no audience, no friend can ever be found.

Suzanne Ferguson has described "The Dead Wingman" as a poem of unrelieved fatalism: its final "no," she writes, "expands from the simple negation of the individual's search for his 'little friend' to [a] universal negation" (*Poetry* 96). Its attitudes become more complex, and more generous, once the pilot's actions are seen as models for reading and writing. Over the length of the poem the aerial remove of the poet-pilot-dreamer, the distance of the land, the inaccessibility of the missing partner, remain insistently "unaccepted," a hypothesis persisted in despite contrary evidence. The pilot and his chronicler end the poem without renouncing their desire to close the distance, to find the one person they mean to hear or see—they trace the circles of their ache even in sleep and give up only when exhausted. Jarrell's poem, circling its *no*, thus imagines a bereaved pilot to whom Jarrell offers his own poem in partial consolation, even solidarity: "The Dead Wingman" aches and strives, and sounds as if it aches and strives, to be a speech to and for its pilot, to become itself the sign of recognition he can't see.

Seen this way, the pilot of "The Dead Wingman" can look very much like the woman of "Next Day," who also mourns her best, or only, "friend." Both poems seem to allegorize models of poetic reading like Allen Grossman's, in which poems model intersubjective relations. For Grossman, poems make their readers fictively intimate with persons who (by the end of the poem) have said to us all they can ever say: "the poem," he writes, "is, therefore, the dead friend" (319).[16] Like "The Dead Wingman," "Next Day" tries to pick out its nameless speaker and to alleviate her loneliness by individuating her to us, making for her a responsive poem (even a stanza form) of her own. And the graveside scene near the end of "Next Day," like the pilot's dream in "The Dead Wingman," gives us a model of "care" (as Grossman would put it) in that now-solitary speaker's memory, a model to which she wishes to return. As Jarrell offers his third-person poem to the pilot who mourns "The Dead Wingman," the woman of poems such as "Next Day" offers her speech to us: in both, a reader may recognize the speaker and thus take the place of the absent friend.

"The Dead Wingman" and "Next Day" show how the wartime Jarrell and the author of his last poems shared stylistic devices and deeper goals. We have seen how those goals arose: the rest of this chapter will show how his style enacts them. Jarrell's 1948 letter to William Carlos Williams describes some of his favorite formal devices:

> the regular way I write now—forms I use, that is—is that in "Lady Bates," "Moving," and the new poem ["The Night Before the Night Before Christmas"] I'm sending with this letter. I find that by having irregular line lengths, a good deal of irregularity of scansion, and lots of rhyming, not just perfect regular rhymes, musical forms, repetitions, "paragraphing," speech-like effects, and so on, you can make a long poem seem a lot shorter and liver. But of course you know this better than I do.
>
> (*Letters* 191)

These are all "speech-like effects," nor does Jarrell confine them to long poems: they are essential elements in his sometimes hopeful, sometimes desperate simulations of speaking and listening.

Though many nineteenth- and twentieth-century poets may be said to trope speech, Jarrell's speechlikeness far exceeds the norms of his era. Jarrell's meters (as Stephen Spender noticed) tend to evoke, but also to violate, accentual-syllabic pentameter norms in the name of varying kinds of speech.[17] Karl Shapiro had those metrics in mind when he wrote that Jarrell "advanced beyond Frost in using . . . the actual rhythms of our speech" (*RJ* 215). Jarrell told Allen Tate that his 1940 poem "The Christmas Roses" "is supposed to be *said* (like a speech from a play) with expression, emotion and long pauses" (*Letters* 26).[18] Its speaker's desperate garrulity belies her loneliness; the terminal patient speaks to her absent friend (or romantic partner), whose absence has made her feel unreal (and made her want to die):

> Why don't you write to me? . . . The day nurse sits and holds
> The glass for me, but yesterday I cried
> I looked so white. I looked like paper.
> Whiter. I dreamt about the pole and bears
> And I see snow and sheets and my two nurses and the chart . . .
>
> (*CP* 392)

The images' logic overlaps with that of "90 North": seeing oneself, and only oneself, in the mirror resembles a visit to the cold, deathly North Pole.

The poem—probably Jarrell's first with a female speaker—has become a locus for discussion of Jarrell and gender.[19] If "The Christmas Roses" was the first of Jarrell's poems to link speechlikeness and the feminine, it was also the first one to show how thoroughly speechlikeness could demonstrate loneliness, how much poems that sounded like speech could represent a speaker's need for response. The end of the poem leaves the hospital settings behind entirely, becoming a protest and plea to the absent beloved: "Touch me and I won't die, I'll look at you / And I won't die, I'll look at you, I'll look at you" (*CP* 393). That closure amounts to a tonal gamble, a bawl: either we react almost as if to a real acquaintance dying or we dismiss her pleas as sentimental, as failures of art.

Jarrell's craft—so involved in troping speech—required that he risk such sentimentality.[20] These risks turn up, often, in his endings, which can rely on tone, inflection, and the force of a speech act almost to the exclusion of images. If the poems begin (like "Next Day") in concrete situations, they are often situations from which the recognized speakers wish to escape. The poems can thus end on abstract adjectives ("commonplace," "solitary"), as in "Next Day," or in bizarre, affecting, abstract illocution, as in "The Venetian Blind," whose speaker finds that inside or around him "something calls, as it has called, / 'But where am I? But where am I?'" (*CP* 55). Jarrell's revealing notes for a talk on his own poems show that he knew the risks his work was taking: "poetry," the notes assert, is

> a process of decades not a craft: craftsmanship useless except as accompaniment, concomitant, ancillary: craftsmanship, technique useful for everything except what is essential and the great and original poets technique, craftsmanship, often look to the first generations like clumsiness, lack of technique, bad craftsmanship: Whitman, Wordsworth, Hardy, so many more—

> (UNC-Greensboro)

Early in his career Jarrell began a lengthy essay called "Why Particulars Are So Much More Effective Than Generalities" (Berg Collection). In choosing generalities for his endings so often, Jarrell knew what he was doing. And what he was doing was choosing intonation, persona, pace—all the aspects of poems that make them like speech—over consistent symbols, proportions, and descriptions—the aspects of poems that make them like craft objects.

In many of the war poems the awkwardness of real speech becomes the chief stylistic goal. The child who speaks "The Truth" (Jarrell's note tells us) "has had his father, his sister and his dog killed in one of the early fire-raids on London" (CP 11):

> I used to live in London till they burnt it.
> What was it like? It was just like here.
> No, that's the truth.
> My mother would come here, some, but she would cry.
> She said to Miss Elise, "He's not himself";
> She said, "Don't you love me any more at all?"
> I was *my*self.
> Finally she wouldn't come at all.
> She never said one thing my father said, or Sister.
> Sometimes she did,
> Sometimes she was the same, but that was when I dreamt it.
> I could tell I was dreaming, she was just the same.
>
> (CP 195)

Comparison of these lines with their source (Anna Freud and Dorothy Burlingame's *War and Children*) will demonstrate how far they are from mere transcription.[21] What matters in them is not raw verisimilitude but the sense of speaking and listening—the interpersonal nexus wished or hoped into being—for which realism in speech serves Jarrell as a proxy. In this case that nexus joins the mother and the shell-shocked boy; she returns at the end, when "she put her arms around me and we cried." As with "The Christmas Roses," the apparent artlessness of "The Truth," Jarrell's elimination from it of most kinds of specifically poetic organization, makes the devices peculiar to *his* work—the interruptions, the repetitions, the open spaces—clearer.[22]

All these devices ask us to imagine a speaker's vocalized, demonstrated need for others. Charles Taylor writes that "the self's interpretations [of itself] can never be fully explicit" since those interpretations are "part of, internal to, or constitutive of the 'object' studied" (34). If Taylor is right, poetic language should approach inarticulacy as it tries harder to distinguish the self (or the inner self, or interiority) from its social surround. And this is exactly what happens in Jarrell, whose hesitations, evasions, ellipses, and stutters (all present in "The Truth") enact the difficulty of making one's own interiority present to others. His rhetorical questions, and the spaces his poems leave for answers, contribute to the same project, since, as Taylor also writes, "One is a self only among other selves. . . . My self-definition is understood as an answer to the question Who I am. And this question finds its original sense in the interchange of speakers" (35).

Jarrell often incorporates "interchange of speakers" in subgenres of poetry (such as the meditative or scenic lyric) that normally exhibit only one speaker.

When he observes people with nothing to say, their silence (as in "The Sick Nought") becomes the poem's subject; happier figures in Jarrell's war poems find themselves amid some sort of verbal interchange. His most accomplished war poem along these lines must be the intricately awkward "Transient Barracks," which describes a gunnery instructor's return to America. "Transient Barracks" sets itself to make several overheard speakers, and their overlapping phrases, contribute to the creation of one lyric subject. Here is the first half:

> Summer. Sunset. Someone is playing
> The ocarina in the latrine:
> You Are My Sunshine. A man shaving
> Sees—past the day-room, past the night K.P.'s
> Bent over a G.I. can of beets
> In the yard of the mess—the red and green
> Lights of a runway full of '24's.
> The first night flight goes over with a roar
> And disappears, a star, among mountains.
>
> The day-room radio, switched on next door,
> Says, "The thing about you is, you're *real*."
> The man sees his own face, black against lather,
> In the steamed, starred mirror: it is real.
> And the others—the boy in underwear
> Hunting for something in his barracks-bags
> With a money-belt around his middle—
> The voice from the doorway: "Where's the C.Q.?"
> "Who wants to know?" "He's gone to the movies."
> "Tell him Red wants him to sign his clearance."
> These are. Are what? Are.

(CP 147)

With their quick scene-setting, their self-deprecating narrator and their reliance on the soldiers they quote, the lines mimic the chitchat we might overhear in an actual barracks. They owe much to the war reporter Ernie Pyle, whose columns about ordinary soldiers Jarrell admired unreservedly.[23] For Pyle, he wrote, the speaking soldiers' "scraps—jobs, families and states . . . are a bridge pushed back shakily to their real lives; and [Pyle] understands and puts down what they tell him, always; and the foolish think it a silly habit of his" (KA 116).

As in the dispatches, so in the poem, the soldiers and flyers' lives, their continued being, matter more than any point an observer-author could make *about* them. It is in this populated, talky, milieu that the shaving soldier knows and claims himself as a speaking subject. The poem began when he looked at his face and can end when (answering somebody else's question) he realizes that he is "home for good":

> The man
> Puts down his razor, leans to the window
> And looks out into the pattern of the field,
> Of light and of darkness. His throat tightens,
> His lips stretch into a blinded smile.
> He thinks, *The times I've dreamed that I was back . . .*
> The hairs on the back of his neck stand up straight.
>
> He only yawns, and finishes shaving.
> When the gunner asks him, "When you leaving?"
> He says, "I just got in. This is my field."
> And thinks: *I'm back for good. The States, the States!*
> He puts out his hand to touch it—
> And the thing about it is, it's *real*.

(CP 148)

The instructor feels "real" and knows he is "back for good" when he can join in the conversation, answering a direct question: "This is my field." Repeated words at line endings (*field*, *real*), with their chiming long *e*, frame the key lines, almost all of them reported speech. Jarrell's ending thus makes a particular structural principle out of what for Grossman is a general rule: Grossman writes, "The achievement of that state of sociability in which interhuman acknowledgement is adequate to human need extinguishes lyric by putting an end to the trouble which gives rise to lyric" (277). This interhuman acknowledgement becomes the effect produced by Jarrell's closing phrases. The sick woman of "The Christmas Roses" dreamt of being listened to, of being heard: the conversation of the Stateside dayroom confirms the flyer's new safety, which seems to him a dream come true.

"For the confirmation of my identity," Hannah Arendt wrote in *The Origins of Totalitarianism*, "I depend entirely upon other people; and it is the great saving grace of companionship for solitary men that it makes them 'whole' again" (476).[24] The shaving man in "Transient Barracks" recognizes himself in the mirror because he is surrounded by companions who can speak to him. More usually, people in Jarrell's poems, like the patient of "The Christmas Roses," try but fail to recognize themselves in mirrors, attempt to claim their faces as theirs.[25] Mary remembers Randall as playfully obsessed with mirrors: "He had favorite and unfavorite mirrors but I believe he looked into all he ever saw" (*Remembering* 136). The fourteen-year-old girl in "The Night Before the Night Before Christmas" "looks at herself in the mirror / And thinks; 'Do I really look like *that*?' . . . 'What do I *really* look like? / I don't know" (*CP* 42). The woman in "Next Day" is "afraid, this morning, of my face," which "Repeats to me, 'You're old.' " Christopher Benfey has looked at Jarrell's poems and seen "a man seeing himself as a woman in the mirror"; for him, Jarrell's "mirror poems . . . mak[e] male narcissism and male identity relatively self-contained and self-justifying, while condemning women to exhibitionism, dependent on the gaze of others" (123, 128). If to be "feminine" in Jarrell's time and place meant depending on others to confirm one's own identity, then almost everyone in Jarrell's poems seems "feminine": not only the lonely woman of "Next Day" but also the soldier in "Transient Barracks," "The Lonely Man" in the poem of the same name, and the bearded Jarrell of "Thinking of the Lost World":

> I hear a boy call, now that my beard's gray:
> "Santa Claus! Hi, Santa Claus!" It *is* miraculous
> To have the children call you Santa Claus.
> I wave back. When my hand drops to the wheel,
> It is brown and spotted, and its nails are ridged
> Like Mama's. Where's my own hand? My smooth
> White bitten-fingernailed one?
>
> (CP 338)

Jarrell is not really Santa Claus, nor is he the boy he remembers being. But he is glad when the boys call him "Santa Claus"—glad but also disturbed, since (like the boy in "The Truth") he doesn't seem to others to be himself. As in "Transient Barracks," the seed of the "miraculous" lies in others' speech. Encounters with mirrors, attempts to establish visual identity, end in anxiety; aural interchange has better results. And the poems' many exclamations and rhetorical questions—exclamations such as "Hi, Santa Claus!" or "The States!"; questions such as "Where's my own hand?"—thus become the simplest and most consistent of the many devices with which Jarrell imagines speech as interchange, testing or confirming the presence of somebody else.[26]

Fictions of imagined or real companions, of listeners answering and being answered, console Jarrell and his characters whenever anything can. These fictions of shared space, response, interchange extend outside Jarrell's own poems into their relations with other texts. When Mark Jarman writes that "Jarrell's characters seem to speak in quotations," he means not that they quote one another—though they do—but that they quote or allude to books they have read (573). Thus the squirrels in "The Night Before the Night Before Christmas" "have nothing to lose but their lives" because the girl in the poem has read the Communist Manifesto, and the snow-loaded boughs near the end of the poem seem to read *"To End Hopefully / Is a Better Thing—/ A Far, Far Better Thing"* because the girl, falling asleep, conflates Sydney Carton's words with a motto from her father's office (CP 50). The woman in "Next Day" takes refuge in William James; the hermitlike painter of "The End of the Rainbow," living alone on a California beach, quotes Goethe and Beddoes to her dog and rehearses, to herself,

> Proverbs of the night
> With the night's inconsequence, or consequence,
> Sufficient unto the night . . . *Every maid her own*
> *Merman*—and she has left lonely forever,
> Lonely forever, the kings of the marsh.
>
> (CP 221)

These chains of quotations and allusions might remind us of the chains of speakers in poems such as "Transient Barracks"—they trope them, in a sense.[27] Quotations connect Jarrell's stranded characters to a world more populous and more hospitable than one beach cottage or apartment or bedroom. In the logic of Jarrell's quotations, the more we can use or reuse others' words, the more we feel our world is theirs too, and the less lonely we become.

Jarrell's exchanges and quotations interact with his frequent forms of aposiopesis—trailing off, interruption, and self-interruption. All create moments and instances where (as Pritchard puts it) "words fail him, or just about"; these moments "implicitly ask . . . to be understood by the sympathetic reader as proof of true feeling" (198). These devices, too, evoke the intersubjective—the play between one speaker and the possibility of another. Jarrell's broken-off lines can imply that a conversation should have taken place but cannot: they indicate—sometimes quite literally—distress calls. The climactic speech act in "A Front," a flier's "Over—," goes unanswered. His controllers "beg, order, are not heard; and hear the darker / Voice rising: *Can't you hear me? Over. Over—* / All the air quivers, and the east sky glows" (CP 173). "A Perfectly Free Association" also ends on a distress call: its air traffic controller

> hears, from the homing fighter,
> The fairly scared, the fairly gay
> Voice saying, *Mayday! Mayday!*

Then there is a position, static,
And the voice ends on *May*—

(CP 452)

Jarrell closes other poems with similar calls for assistance. More often, though
(as in "The Dead Wingman"), he ends poems by following broken-off utterance
with a brief closural gesture—mentioning, for instance, sleep or death. Evoking
(in Barbara Herrnstein Smith's term) "nonliterary experiences" of closure, such
devices allow the poems to end while leaving their problems of human com-
munication unsolved (121).

If (as Grossman claims) a whole or integral line of poetry represents a whole
speaking subject, Jarrell's interdependent, incomplete speech acts, his broken-
up sentences, and his cut-off or wavering pentameter-based lines represent
interdependent, relational selves. So often afraid they are "commonplace" and
"solitary," the people in his poems are no more whole nor self-sufficient than
their utterances: they say things such as "That I—That I—But anything will
do," or "These are valued at—some value I forget, / Which I learned from—I
cannot remember the source" (CP 306). These phrases make no sense, convey
no information, until we have learned to hear the characters behind them. The
characters, in turn, elicit our sympathy by trying and failing to say things: an un-
sympathetic character in Jarrell's novel "seemed very human and attractive"
when, for once, "he lost his way in his sentence" (49–50).

The discipline known as sociolinguistics has devoted much attention to
forms and devices of conversation, among them interruption, repetition, and in-
completion. These devices often signal a change of speaker; they also distin-
guish conversation from recitation and scripted performance. As the sociolin-
guist Robin Lakoff explains,

ordinary conversation makes much use of devices that signal, "I'm making
this up as I go along": repetitions, corrections, hesitations, and "fillers" that
play for time to compose one's thoughts. In part, these are literally neces-
sary because speakers are constructing their talk as they go along; but they
also figuratively signal, "This talk is spontaneous: you can trust me."

(43)

These "conversational" features are those Jarrell's poems flaunt and depend on.
The style of such "private discourse," Lakoff continues, implies

at least the conventional expectation of parity among participants—if not
social real-world equality at least equality of linguistic opportunity . . . a

discourse type that is reciprocal is likely to be spontaneous, and one that is public, to be formal as well. . . . Power goes along with formality, non-spontaneity and nonreciprocity.

(44)

Jarrell's talky, stuttery style could therefore mark his verse as informal and distant from public power.

It could also mark his verse as feminine. The same devices that mark speech as conversational, spontaneous, or shared can also mark particular speakers as women. Lakoff lists habits observers take to characterize women's spoken English as against men's: most of the features in her list also characterize Jarrell's poetry as against the work of his peers. One such habit is the use of "adjectives . . . expressing emotional not intellectual evaluation" (such as *lovely)*"; another involves "Forms that convey impreciseness: *so, such,*" "hedges of all kinds" (204). Jarrell's poetry make copious use of these features: he writes, in one late poem, "It's so— / So *agreeable,*" and in another, "I saw that he resembled— / That he *was*— // I didn't see it" (*CP* 305, 287). Lakoff also describes "Intonation patterns that resemble questions, indicating uncertainty or need for approval" as stereotypically feminine; Pamela Fishman's empirical studies have in fact found that "women use tags and declarative questions much more often than men" (204, 254). Jarrell uses these patterns at key points in his poems: "Don't signs, don't roads know any more than boys?"; "If things could happen so, and you not know / What you could do, why, what is there you could do?" (*CP* 132, 262). Other examples of feminine speech patterns include *being* interrupted (examples of which multiply above) and being indirect.[28]

All these "linguistic traits," Lakoff explains, "are directly connected not with their speakers' actual lack of power, but with their feelings about the possession of power. Women's language becomes a symbolic expression of distance from power, or lack of interest in power" (207). Jarrell took advantage of these associations, and his contemporaries noticed. Karl Shapiro's prose poem to Jarrell contrasts his "prose sentences—like Bernini graves, staggeringly expensive, Italianate, warm, sentences once-and-for-all" with "the verses you leave half-finished in mid-air—I once knew a woman who never finished a sentence" (*Bourgeois* 91). Shapiro seems to have mapped the difference between Jarrell's prose and verse onto purported masculine and feminine "sides"; later critics divided his work up in similar ways.[29]

If men tend to interrupt, and women to be interrupted, it is no wonder the poet who wrote of himself, " 'Woman,' men said of him, and women, 'Man' " should tend to interrupt himself (*CP* 471).[30] At the same time Jarrell's linguistic habits—from his subjective adjectives to his abstract endings—emphasize "rapport" (in Lakoff's terms) over "facts," acknowledgement of persons over the sharing of information. (The final lines in both stanzas of "Transient Barracks," for example, provide no concrete details, no "brute facts," at all: nor do the closing phrases of "90 North.") The apparent femininity of Jarrell's style (which led him to redraft a few poems by making their speakers clearly women) appears, at least in some poems, as a consequence of his concern to represent our need for the intersubjective. Langdon Hammer and James Longenbach have both shown how Jarrell's "semifeminine" tones and attitudes help him (in Hammer's phrase) "disengage literature from power" (*Letters* 19; "Who" 392). His speech patterns and syntactical choices perform this separation in order to imagine selves and speakers who need one another—they imagine the interpersonal.

To evoke the interpersonal is in Jarrell's poems to fulfill a wish. The alienated modern man in "Jamestown" who asks a witch to "make me what I am" has been absorbed into the social and institutional, as against the interpersonal; he cannot assimilate difference, cannot change, and his imperviousness to enchantment reflects his lack of imagination (CP 257). But the man in the later "A Man Meets a Woman in the Street" who wishes to stay as he is describes an ideal condition, since he already has the intimacy he needs. His wish fulfillment is very literally a mutual recognition; at the end of the poem, the man's wife turns to see him catching up to her:

> A wish, come true, is life. I have my life.
> When you turn just slide your eyes across my eyes
> And show in a look flickering across your face
> As lightly as a leaf's shade, a bird's wing,
> That there is no one in the world quite like me,
> That if only . . . If only. . . .
> > That will be enough.
> . . . .

> Our first bewildered, transcending recognition
> Is pure acceptance. We can't tell our life
> From our wish. Really I began the day
> Not with a man's wish: "May this day be different,"
> But with the birds' wish: "May this day
> Be the same day, the day of my life."

> > > > > > (CP 353)

The end of this poem (among the last Jarrell wrote) deploys all his stylistic devices in order to present a wish fulfilled—the wish for "recognition," which justifies a life and lets the poem end. The man's satisfaction consists in a series of equivalences: his wish is his life, his wife is the wife, his day the day, for which he had hoped. Jarrell's play among ordinary words establishes just those equivalences.

"Recognition" became in Jarrell's last poems his own word for what his characters seek. For the psychoanalytic thinker Jessica Benjamin, erotic love (as distinct from sexual desire) constitutes precisely an achievement of recognition, a fulfilled wish to be known and changed by another: "the desire for erotic union with another person who is endowed with the capacity to transform the self can be seen as the most intense version of the desire for recognition . . . the point is to contact and be contacted by the other—*apprehended as such*" (*Like* 184). Such a desire creates the whole form of a much shorter, earlier love poem. After Jarrell met Mary von Schrader in 1951, he wrote this poem, "The Meteorite," for her:

> Star, that looked so long among the stones
> And picked from them, half iron and half dirt,
> One; and bent, and put it to its lips
> And breathed upon it till at last it burned
> Uncertainly among the stars its sisters—
> Breathe on me still, star, sister.
>
> (CP 264)

The poem depends on the fiction it builds of a singular listener—her attentions, at first as unlikely and distant as starlight and then as close as the breath in a kiss, cue the whole speech. The poet-lover-stone called "One" rests solitary in the middle, until the female star and the noun "star" return in the last lines to elevate and embrace it.[31] Stars in love poems normally keep their distance (Keats's "Bright Star," Auden's "The More Loving One"); this star comes close enough to heed a request. Like "A Man Meets a Woman in the Street," "The Meteorite" imagines the relation between lovers as creating its own—in this case, extraterrestrial—shared space, a space as distinct as possible from the ordinary and alienating social world. Randall told Mary von Schrader, in a letter written soon after the poem's composition, "I'll be glad to move away from this society into Ours" (*Letters* 323). The experience of falling in love, of being loved, *meant* for Jarrell the creation of terms of intimate recognition, terms that set him (as they would set any lover) apart from the crowd, the larger "society," of stars or stones.

If the love poems embody recognition at its most joyful, its clearest instance has to be "In Galleries." The American museum guard at the start of this poem "has a right to despair"; in the sculpture he watches,

> The lines and hollows of the piece of stone
> Are human to people: their hearts go out to it.
> But the guard has no one to make him human —
> They walk through him as if he were a reflection.
>
> (CP 298)

Nor does the guard see the visitors — he "stands / Blind, silent, among the people who go by / Indistinguishably," like the sad shopper in the supermarket or the soldier waiting in line. The Italian museum guard in the second verse-paragraph "speaks and smiles / And whether or not you understand Italian, / You understand he is human and still hopes": he evokes a minimal recognition (and gets a minimal tip). But the best kind of museum guard (also Italian) is piously enthusiastic. When he

> takes a magnifying glass
> From the shiny pocket of his uniform
> And shows you that in the painting of a woman
> Who holds in her arms the death of the world
> The something on the man's arm is the woman's
> Tear, you and the man and the woman and the guard
> Are dumbly one. You say *Bellissima!*
> *Bellissima!* and give him his own rapt,
> Dumb, human smile, convinced he guards
> A miracle. Leaving, you hand the man
> A quarter's worth of nickel and aluminum.
>
> (CP 299)

The coins with which the American tips the guard are inadequate, as any recompense would be inadequate, to the experience of empathy the guard makes possible. He has, moreover, given the tourist that experience by showing him or her another depiction of empathy: a painted tear on a painted arm. "The visitor as well as the guard," Suzanne Ferguson writes, "must come alive to make the miracle happen" (*Poetry* 195). Jarrell highlights the pity involved in Christian religious awe in order to redescribe its virtues in human, secular terms. That guard's "gestures," the poem says, "are full of faith in — of faith"; but the painting (according to Mary Jarrell, a Verona *Pietá* — she does not say which one) inspires in Jarrell not an assent to religious faith but an experience of human community.[32]

If "In Galleries" and "A Man Meets a Woman" demonstrate the recognitions the poems seek, "Seele im Raum" presents their more usual dilemma: a protagonist who can't be recognized or individuated by the other people she sees. Given pride of place in *The Seven-League Crutches* (1951, "Seele im Raum" describes a woman who for years had seen, or hallucinated, a friendly eland at her dinner table. The speaker's breakings- and trailings-off announce the reality of the eland, even if "they" — her family — cannot see it. The eland seems present inasmuch as it resists words:

> Many times
> When it breathed heavily (when it had tried
> A long useless time to speak) and reached to me
> So that I touched it — of a different size
> And order of being, like the live hard side
> Of a horse's neck when you pat the horse —
> And looked with its great melting tearless eyes
> Fringed with a few coarse wire-like lashes
> Into my eyes, and whispered to me
> So that my eyes turned backward in their sockets
> And they said nothing —
>   many times
> I have known, when they said nothing,
> That it did not exist. If they had heard
> They *could* not have been silent. And yet they heard . . .
>
>   (CP 37)

Jarrell's woman felt overlooked by her husband or children: the eland seemed to know her as they could not. (She learns later that "elend" in German means "wretched.") The eland comes into being in response to the state of mind Nancy Chodorow later named "lack of self, or emptiness. This happens especially when a person who has this feeling is with others who read the social and emotional setting differently but do not recognize this, nor recognize that the person herself is in a different world." Chodorow suggests, following the psychoanalyst Enid Balint, "that women are more likely to experience themselves this way. Women who feel empty of themselves feel that they are not being accorded a separate reality nor the agency to interpret the world their own way" (*Mothering* 100).

It would be almost right to say (as other commentators have said) that the eland represents imagination, or the woman's "separate reality."[33] It would be truer to say that the eland is the companion, even the listener, the imagination creates so that it may be recognized: when the eland tried "a long useless time to speak" and "looked with its great melting tearless eyes . . . Into my eyes, and whispered to me," it acts out a desperate approximation of exchanges like the one at the end of "In Galleries." The woman suggests, and no one argues otherwise, that if the eland isn't real, isn't compatible with "real life," then real life may not be worth living. Later she asks, in lines rich with self-interruptions,

> Is my voice the voice
> Of that skin of being—of what owns, is owned
> In honor or dishonor, that is borne and bears—
> Or of that raw thing, the being inside it
> That has neither a wife, a husband, nor a child
> But goes at last as naked from this world
> As it was born into it—
>
> And the eland comes and grazes on its grave.

(CP 39)

The "thing" that can be shown and remembered but not directly described is something like a soul; it is the part of her left over after she fulfills her social role. This soul or "thing" has summoned up (hallucinated, or created) the eland because souls require acknowledgement and do not get it: "And yet when it was, I *was*—[. . .] Yet how can I believe it?" As Hammer puts it, "The eland is the embodiment of her will to imagine another life, a full sensual life in which one's desire need not be postponed or dismissed as make-believe" ("Who" 405).

This desire can appear more specifically as a desire for interpersonal channels, a companionable remedy for her "lack of self." A husband who saw the eland would therefore see how wretched, *elend*, the woman has been. Part of "Seele im Raum" adapts Rilke's "The Unicorn," which Jarrell translated; Rilke's unicorn, like the housewife's eland, becomes real because human beings require its company:

> because they loved it
> One became an animal. They always left a space.
> And in the space they had hollowed for it, lightly
> It would lift its head, and hardly need

To exist. They nourished it, not with grain
But only, always, with the possibility
It might be.

(CP 482)

The eland, too, is summoned into being: it represents not the woman's soul but her soul mate, not the inner self but the companion whose presence makes innerness knowable. The eland becomes the occupant "of a different size / And order of being" who establishes the space ("raum") in which her soul ("seele") can know itself.[34]

And this is why we see the eland at dinner. In *Pictures from an Institution* a succession of dinner parties and household scenes offer models for good and bad kinds of sociability. One bad kind appears in the novelist Gertrude Johnson, who lacks empathetic imagination: Gertrude sees everyone, save her husband Sidney, as "material"—"she listened only As A Novelist" (131). Desperate for recognition and empathy, the woman of "Seele im Raum" imagines the eland as her friend and companion. Gertrude reverses "Seele im Raum" exactly, since she sees all her companions as elands: " 'It's nice not to have to lie out at some water-hole with a flash-bulb,' I heard her say once, 'but just to be able to ask your eland home to dinner.' The listening elands laughed and swallowed" (35).

Like many of Jarrell's poems, "Seele im Raum" addresses interiority with the syntax proper to conversation: it depends on the tension it maintains between the diction and forms of conversation (dinner conversation, say) and the abstract, "higher" language traditionally associated with lyric poems (such as Rilke's "Unicorn"). That tension becomes another way to imagine Jarrell's intersubjective project. Often Jarrell's most lyrical passages ask whether the voices they project can ever be manifest in the real, shared world. Such questions drive several mysterious poems from the 1950s, among them "The Orient Express":

Outside me there were a few shapes
Of chairs and tables, things from a primer;
Outside the window
There were the chairs and tables of the world . . .
I saw that the world
That had seemed to me the plain
Gray mask of all that was strange
Behind it—of all that *was*—was all.

(CP 65)

Here, as in "Seele im Raum," a desire to present plausible speakers, to create characters who seem like "other people" and show their need to relate—a desire we might call novelistic, or (following Bakhtin) dialogic—exists in tension with lyric's drive to present an inner being separate from social circumstance, an "I" both more specific and more universal than the social types and representatives of the novel. In the terms of "The Orient Express," the novelistic presents the facts, the "gray mask" of the external world, the lyric the "some thing / Behind everything." And in the terms of "Seele im Raum," the novelistic presents only "the skin of being"; pure lyric presents the "raw thing" within. It is when the two versions of persons—the novelistic and the lyric, the exterior and the interior— are given shared ground, shared words, that intersubjective recognitions can take place.

The tangled-up, self-interrupting syntax in "Seele im Raum" thus suggests that if the woman—if anyone—has a "naked" being, an interior or imagining self apart from her roles, that interior self has to be understood through hard-to-share speech. Once deprived of her eland, she can "be" only when explaining it to others: "Being is being old / And saying . . . 'To own an eland: that's what I call life!' " Like many repeated terms in Jarrell's poetry ("wish," for example, in "Next Day" and "A Man Meets a Woman . . . "), "being" becomes what William Empson called a Complex Word and makes a Statement in Words; it includes the noun "human being"; "being" as existence; "being" as the carrier of an adjective (being married, being tall, being American—having the qualities by which others know us); and "being inside" (having a psyche).[35] These versions of being prove hard to reconcile; their incompatibility requires lonely people to invent companions like elands—or like the readers implied by certain poems.

Jarrell has been praised for his mastery of the dramatic monologue, or of forms allied to it.[36] Robert Langbaum argues in a well-known study that dramatic monologue aims "to establish the speaker's existence, not his moral worth but his sheer existence" (*Experience* 200). Herbert Tucker has shown how modern readers have learned to see all poems *as if they were* dramatic monologues: for Tucker (who disapproves of it) this modern practice satisfies our "thirst for intersubjective confirmation of the self" (242).[37] Jarrell's characters seek precisely what Tucker claims modern readers seek. And this is why Jarrell—who in some poems (such as "A Conversation with the Devil") speaks explicitly as a modern author—can make characters in other poems epitomize frustrated modern readers. "The Woman at the Washington Zoo" brings this conjunction to its zenith. The woman is an ordinary, sublunary self, excluded from the demesnes of imagination (foreign countries, beast fables, science fiction), which taunt her with unapproachable proximity:

The saris go by me from the embassies.

Cloth from the moon. Cloth from another planet.
They look back at the leopard like the leopard.

(CP 215)

The Woman sees an exotic world, whose denizens—from leopards to diplomats'
wives—seem individuated. But she does not and cannot belong to that world: it
won't look at her or return her gaze. She expects to go

To my bed, so to my grave, with no
Complaints, no comment: neither from my chief,
The Deputy Chief Assistant, nor his chief—
Only I complain . . . this serviceable
Body that no sunlight dyes, no hand suffuses . . .

Shakespeare's "dyer's hand," "almost subdued / To th'element it works in" is a
well-known trope for artistic creation.[38] But when Jarrell reused the allusion in
the 1960 essay "A Sad Heart at the Supermarket," he was complaining that con-
formism, capitalism, consumer culture, subdue our individual natures: he
wrote there that "mass culture's"

values are business values: money, success, celebrity. If we are representa-
tive members of our society, [those] values are ours; and even if we are
unrepresentative, non-conforming, our hands are—too often—subdued
to the element they work in, and our unconscious expectations are all that
we consciously reject.

(SH 71)

This Washingtonian seems all too "representative," one of the "poor unknown
failures" Jarrell's essay later invokes; Jarrell described her elsewhere as "a kind of
aging machine part," "a distant relation" to the housewife in "Seele im Raum"
(SH 71; KA 320). Both women (in D. W. Winnicott's words) have "become one
of the many who do not feel that they exist in their own right as whole human
beings" (29).

The woman at the zoo addresses a vulture, with perverse hope, as her "wild
brother." Crying out to him, in quintessentially Jarrellian repetitions, "You
know what I was, / You see what I am: change me, change me!," she seeks from
the vulture-brother-fantasy-companion (as the readers in Jarrell's poems about

libraries sought from books) an individuating recognition that both permits, and constitutes, being "changed" (*CP* 216).[39] The colorless woman at the zoo has been taken to complain of sexual loneliness.[40] But as much as she thrills at, and dreads, the sexuality of the vulture image, the Woman also seems here to be complaining that she has no part in imaginative creation. If the woman's invisibility is her problem, a change in who she is will either make possible, or constitute, the solution.

Several of Jarrell's other protagonists also cry out for "change"; the children in "Children Selecting Books in a Library," for example, seek "CHANGE, dear to all things not to themselves endeared" (*CP* 107). These characters want at once to dispose of their familiar selves and to reveal those selves to someone else: for them being changed amounts to being recognized, and the problem the Woman faces is that each seems a prerequisite for the other. She has to be different in order to be noticed and has to be noticed to seem individuated, different. Jessica Benjamin equates the wish for psychic change with the wish for recognition and both with the wish for confirmation of selfhood: for her the self "is reciprocally constituted in relation to the other, dependent on the other's recognition, which it cannot have without being negated, acted on by the other, in a way that changes the self, making it nonidentical" (*Shadow* 79). Finding no such recognition in life, the Woman at the Washington Zoo seeks it in fantasy, just as readers seek it in literature. We therefore recognize *her*; as readers of modern literature, we understand her dilemma as the animals and the diplomats cannot. And it may indicate the Woman's success as a model of reading that Jarrell wrote his own essay about this poem at the request of Cleanth Brooks and Robert Penn Warren, who printed it in the third edition of *Understanding Poetry*.

I have argued that Jarrell's style pivots on his sense of loneliness and on the intersubjectivity he sought as a response. Loneliness, the social psychologist Linda Wood argues, "is failed intersubjectivity"; as such, she continues, it is "paradoxically the most social" of imputed emotions (188–190). To come from the explorer of "90 North" to the Woman at the Washington Zoo and the shopper of "Next Day" is to see how Jarrell's psychological interests prompt sociological ones. The people in poems such as "The Woman at the Washington Zoo," or "Next Day," or "The Sick Nought" risk and fear becoming mere social types: the (or any) new soldier, the (or any) housewife, the (or any) bored student, "anybody." Jarrell's drafts of "Next Day" include a prose sketch that summarizes the poem's concerns about personal distinction, bound up as they are with concerns about mortality:

My friends talk as if I were an exception, and I've always been one, have seemed to myself so truly exceptional, but with age, being old, there are no exceptions, everyone has same commonplace typical representative ending, as if you'd been transformed into woman in street, Everywoman, makes complicated life simple, single, a lonely solitary passive process.

(Berg Collection)

Is she "typical" just because she is aging? Will that process erase her "complicated life," which separates her from "anybody" else? Critics who find the woman unrealistic (because she reads William James) exhibit just the stereotyped reactions she fears, overlooking *her* and seeing only the social group to which she belongs.[41] Jarrell's fictive housewife, looked at askance for her reading, thus resembles the real "upper-middlebrow" housewife in William H. Whyte's *The Organization Man*, who surprised her neighbors by reading Plato and told Whyte, "Now all of them are sure I'm strange" (365).[42]

Just as the poems' speakers feel in danger of fading into indistinguishability, the classes they represent threaten to become the poems' topics, to make them unimaginable as individuals. "Next Day"—a representation of one lonely woman, distinguished from others by Jarrell's language – has looked to many readers like a poem about commodity culture, whose typical victim can buy Cheer and Joy but never cheer or joy.[43] The poem, as we have seen, depends on repeated words—"all," "wise," "wish," "see," "flesh," "imagining," "now," "change," "face," "old," "body," "exceptional." If these words sketch the woman's problems, they also trope the identical commodities at the start of the poem. Lined up on "shelves," these are notionally various but fundamentally indistinguishable—just like the "selves" who buy them, in whose ranks the woman of "Next Day" fears she belongs. Jarrell elsewhere encouraged such a reading; he asked in the essay "A Sad Heart at the Supermarket,"

Reader, isn't buying or fantasy-buying an important part of your and my emotional life? . . . It is a standard joke that when a woman is bored or sad she buys something to cheer herself up; but in this respect we are all women together, and can hear complacently the reminder of how feminine this consumer-world of ours has become.

(SH 68)

"Next Day" is hardly the only poem whose story of loneliness, selfhood, and failed intersubjectivity also leads to a kind of social criticism. If Jarrell's focus on loneliness led him out toward other, "ordinary," people, his interest in social and cultural threats to individuality, and to its recognition, led him to portray those threats in his works. Jarrell depicts particulars of wartime life; makes poems out of changes in American reading, viewing, and listening habits; and notices changes in the built environment, education, and consumption (from the supermarket to the elementary classroom and the postal service). Later chapters will view more of those social and historical phenomena as they affected Jarrell's verse. The next chapter, however, will show how, and why, they inform his prose.

Chapter 2

INSTITUTIONS, PROFESSIONS, CRITICISM

Recent years have seen an impassioned debate about academic institutions and the profession of letters. Bruce Robbins has shown how some literary intellectuals "manufacture vocations for themselves . . . in speaking in public, of the public, to the public, and to some extent for the public" (21). Stanley Fish, however, has argued that "literary criticism is *only*, today, an academic discipline [whose] specialized language . . . is the mark of its distinctiveness" (*Professional* 43). Responding to Robbins, to Fish, and to David Simpson, Timothy Peltason asks that contemporary critics learn from Victorian thinkers how to make "complex characterizations of the experiences . . . offered by written texts"; to do so, we must "believ[e] that *literary* experience is a distinct and valuable kind" (985). These debates might benefit from attention to Jarrell, whose famously entertaining essays, along with his comic novel, reject both professional *and* public concerns, professional and public institutions, in favor of other kinds of experience. They do so in order to resist what Jarrell saw as a mid-century trend toward the erasure of private life—a trend his prose goes out of its way to resist.

Recent critics have focused—as I have in chapter 1—on Jarrell's interaction with his poetic colleagues. He also, however, reacted—and contributed—to mid-century social criticism. During the years of Jarrell's artistic maturity, thinkers as disparate as Theodor Adorno, Hannah Arendt, R. P. Blackmur, Erik

Erikson, Erich Fromm, Leslie Fiedler, Leo Lowenthal, Mary McCarthy, Dwight Macdonald, David Riesman, Bernard Rosenberg, Lionel Trilling, Ernest van den Haag, and William H. Whyte described with dismay societies, schools, and universities dominated by "scientific management," by markets, and by a conformist social life. They feared the reduction of vocation and avocation to institution and discipline; they feared, also, the eclipse of aesthetic experience, even of private life.

The most important social theorist for thinking about Jarrell must be his close friend Hannah Arendt. Jarrell met Arendt during 1946, when he lived in New York City and edited the book reviews in the *Nation*. He called Arendt's *The Origins of Totalitarianism* (1950) "one of the best historical books I've ever read" and told Arendt she was his closest possible ally[1] (*Letters* 245). She seems to have returned the compliment. Arendt wrote after his death, "Whatever I know of English poetry, and perhaps of the genius of the language, I owe to him" (*RJ* 4). Though their personal friendship is well known, critics have thus far failed to connect his works to hers.[2]

Such connections may be found in broad fears about modern society. That "society," Arendt argued, "introduces between the private and the public a social sphere in which the private is made public and vice versa" (*Between* 188). *Origins* attacks the "perversion of equality from a political into a social concept": this perversion risks creating a society where "every individual . . . is 'normal' if he is like everybody else and 'abnormal' if he happens to be different" (54). Jarrell shared Arendt's fear of the social, a fear that inspired the political theorist Hanna Pitkin's recent monograph. Pitkin (who distrusts the concept) explains, " 'Society' [to Arendt] means a leveling of people into uniformity, the destruction of individuality. . . . Arendt insists explicitly that the social threatens and ultimately destroys privacy, just as much as it threatens and ultimately destroys public life"(14).[3]

Arendt explored these ideas before *Origins*, in essays Jarrell would have read: her brief piece on "French Existentialism" ran in the *Nation* in February 1946, a few months before Jarrell took charge of its book reviews. In Arendt's thumbnail sketch, French existentialism aims to disentangle people from institutions: it opposes the *esprit sérieux*, the attitude that leads a man to "think of himself *as* president of his business, *as* a member of the Legion of Honor, *as* a member of the faculty, but also *as* father, *as* husband, or as any other half-natural, half-social function" (172).[4] Individual taste became, for Arendt, a way of resisting, not only conformism but instrumentalization, the conversion of people into their social functions: "We can rise above specialization and philistinism of all sorts," she later wrote, "to the extent that we learn how to exercise our taste freely" (*Between* 225).

Arguments about, and against, conformity also pervaded David Riesman's *The Lonely Crowd* (1950). Riesman and his coauthors Nathan Glazer and Reuel Denney describe "other-direction," a character type newly prevalent in America. A child growing up "other-directed" "learns . . . that nothing in his character, no possession he owns, no inheritance of name or talent, no work he has done is valued for itself, but only for its effect on others" (49). Though Riesman is careful not to condemn other-direction per se, he ends with a grave warning: "The idea that men are created free and equal is both true and misleading: men are created different: they lose their social freedom and their individual autonomy in seeking to become like each other" (373).[5] Other-directed adults may create a bland, purposeless society, one that seeks cohesion at the expense of all other virtues. The sociologist Dennis Wrong recalls the "ubiquitous anathematizations of conformity in the 1950s to which Riesman's diagnosis of the changing American character was so readily assimilated" (167).[6] Arguments modeled on Riesman's and on Arendt's suffused the social criticism of the fifties, producing a stream of essays in such journals as *Partisan Review*, and such well-known later books as William H. Whyte's *The Organization Man* (1957).

These conceptions of public and private, taste and conformity and individuality, pervade Jarrell's literary essays. He complained in "The Obscurity of the Poet" (1951) that in modern America, "The truth that all men are politically equal, the recognition of the injustice of fictitious differences, becomes a belief in the fictitiousness of differences, a conviction that it is reaction or snobbishness or Fascism to believe that any individual differences of real importance can exist" (*Age* 17). Both Riesman and Jarrell would contrast Eisenhower, a mass-marketed product and hence a successful candidate, to Adlai Stevenson, a bad candidate but an individual.[7] Jarrell struck a paragraph on this theme from a late draft of his essay "The Taste of the Age":

> When at the end of the last presidential campaign I saw the final telecasts of the two candidates, I was struck by the difference between the programs. Governor Stevenson made a speech, an old-fashioned speech, one that he had written himself; his sons were there to add Human Interest, but after all, Gladstone had sons, too. But the other program was, in comparison, like a well-run factory, and all President Eisenhower had to do was smile and watch it produce.
>
> (Berg Collection)

Ike is the supreme product of Riesman's new America, where "*the product now in demand is neither a staple nor a machine: it is a personality*" (italics in original) (*Lonely* 46). Jarrell shared Arendt's tendency to conflate (in Pitkin's words), "disciplinary normalization, oppressive conformity to mainstream values, [and] the obliteration of individuality" (17). As Arendt sought to save public life, what she termed (honorifically) "politics," from its bleak counterpart in the social, and as Riesman examined "other-direction," Jarrell's poetry, criticism and fiction tried to imagine ways to save *private* life, individual experience.[8] Jarrell's defenses of individuality against institutional or professional interests thus cast themselves as defenses of taste.

How can mere reading, mere taste, combat other-direction? The coming society, Jarrell complains in a notebook, is "trying to reach [a] situation where everybody doing anything is archetypical—stands for everybody"; its enemy, and Jarrell's hope, is a "17 year old sitting alone reading ~~George Herb~~ Wordsworth" (Berg Collection; strikethrough in original). He outlined, in 1955, his fears about a well-managed, conformist future:

> Sometimes when I can't go to sleep at night I see the family of the future. Dressed in three-tone shorts-and-shirt sets of disposable Papersilk, they sit before the television wall of their apartment, only their eyes moving. After I've looked a while I always see—otherwise I'd die—a pigheaded soul over in the corner with a book; only his eyes are moving, but in them there is a different look.
>
> Usually it's Homer he's holding—this week it's Elizabeth Bishop.
>
> (KA 244–245)

"Silent reading," Sven Birkerts has claimed, "is the very signature—the emblem of subjectivity": Jarrell here puts its emblematic aspects to use (*Readings* 105). That reader of Bishop, and his seventeen-year-old cousin immersed in Wordsworth, are enjoying a kind of intimacy with the authors of *The Prelude* and of *A Cold Spring*, though it is intimacy mediated by print. Such intimacy often seemed to Jarrell the only way to retain an inner life.[9]

Like many mid-century thinkers, Jarrell derived his concerns about postwar conformity from his experience of the Second World War. Paul Fussell writes that to many observers the army "boys turned by training into quasi-interchangeable parts . . . seemed even more anonymous and bereft of significant individual personality than their counterparts in the Great War" (66). Jarrell's wartime poems and prose registered those effects. He wrote in one review that "when one considers the mechanisms of the contemporary states—from the advertising agencies that turn out their principles to the aircraft factories that turn out their practice," one despairs: "it is we who wither away, not the state"

(*Age* 157). A wartime letter to Lowell decides that "most of the soldiers are, if not completely, at least virtually, ignorant of the nature and conditions of the choices they make; besides this, they are pretty well determined in the passive sense" (*Letters* 150–151). Nonliterary observers described, and decried, the same passivity: according to the historian Ellen Herman, psychological researchers "discovered that U.S. soldiers had no meaningful understanding of why they were fighting or what the war was actually about. Worse, they did not seem to care" (69).

Jarrell's wartime letters confirm such alarming findings; his war poems dramatize them. The people in them are his first victims of the hypostatized social: the army and the war have made them, to quote Pitkin, "product[s] or victim[s] of historical forces" rather than "free autonomous agent[s]" (20). (Several of the denser, more abstract poems experiment with Marxist explanations for those forces.)[10] Even those who "determine / Men's last obedience," who hold powers of life and death, seem themselves "determined" (CP 183). In "Prisoners," the laboring captives, each with a "white P on their backs," "Go on all day being punished," "loading, unloading"; they

> look unexpectedly
> At the big guard, dark in his khaki, at the dust of the blazing plain,
> At the running or crawling soldiers in their soiled and shapeless green.
>
> The prisoners, the guards, the soldiers—they are all, in their way, being
>   trained.
> From these moments, repeated forever, our own new world will be
>   made.
>
> (CP 165)

The poem grew from a scene Jarrell observed at Chanute Field in Illinois: he wrote to Mackie about "two prisoners who load on the [garbage] cans and an MP who does nothing but guard the prisoners—the MP *always* looks much more criminal than the prisoners, who are dressed in conspicuous blue clothes, are in, generally, for minor offenses, and have no possible way of getting out of the field, and need guarding about as much as I do" (Berg Collection). In the poem, the ungainly, half-rhymed hexameters (anapestic with spondaic substitutions) mimic the prisoners' rhythm as they work; the same meter works to set the prisoners' labor against earlier, heroic wars, since it resembles the dactylic hexameter (with spondaic substitutions) of the *Iliad*. Standing at the end of the history of Western individuals (as Achilles stood at its beginning) prisoners and guard make literal the collective coercion that will soon be "our" fate.

A spectacle of power without agency, in which everyone seemed under compulsion and nobody seemed in charge, was exactly what many soldiers saw in the Army and the war.[11] Arendt feared a similar fate for the whole postwar world. The foreword to *Origins* explained that the globe, in the late 1940s, looked "as though mankind had divided itself between those who believe in human omnipotence (who think that everything is possible if one knows how to organize masses for it) and those for whom powerlessness has become the major experience of our lives" (vii). That experience of powerlessness unites almost all the people in Jarrell's war poems: the orphans, the gunners, MPs, POWs, refugees.

Arendt considered totalitarian societies the final and worst symbol and. in certain senses the result, of human loneliness. Old tyrannies destroyed public life; totalitarianism, however, "destroys private life as well," since it "bases itself on loneliness, on the experience of not belonging to the world at all, which is among the most radical and desperate experiences of man" (*Origins* 475). Totalitarianism thus amounts to "organized loneliness," "a principle destructive for all human living-together" (*Origins* 478). The loneliness on which totalitarian modes of social reorganization rely, and which they exacerbate, is the isolation Jarrell's poems evoke, the isolation described in the previous chapter: it is the state of affairs (confronted by the Dead Wingman and the Woman at the Washington Zoo) in which no other person confirms my identity.

To say that Arendt can help us read Jarrell is hardly to say that Jarrell considers fifties—or forties—America totalitarian. Yet Jarrell's later works, like Arendt's later thought, reflect both writers' attention to the world war and to the conditions that preceded it. Arendt writes that

> total domination, which strives to organize the infinite plurality and differentiation of human beings as if all of humanity were just one individual, is possible only if each and every person can be reduced to a never-changing identity of reactions, so that each of these bundles of reactions can be exchanged at random for any other.
>
> (*Origins* 438)

Loss of individuality, for Arendt, meant the reduction of people not only to lonely isolates but also to predictable, interchangeable machines, so that behaviorist accounts of them become true. Jarrell thought he saw just that phenomenon taking place in the army; so did the sociologists Maurice Stein and Arthur Vidich, who argued that after the Second World War the military became a "model for . . . the 'social system' as a whole," and for "the pervasive manipulation of identity that suffuses mass society" (493, 27). Karl Shapiro's eulogy for

Jarrell put the same finding in more dramatic terms: "our army never melted away. . . . Our poetry, from the forties on, records the helplessness we felt in the face of the impersonal character of the age" (*RJ* 222). Jarrell's prose not only records that sense but tries to counteract it.

Jarrell's defenses of individuality begin with his war poems and extend into the later poems' lonely lives. The same defenses shape his essays, which draw on the ideas of his peers and teachers, some of whom were the writers we now call New Critics. Sentence by sentence, however, Jarrell rarely sounds much like the peers he admired. His distinctive prose style goes out of its way to reject the professional, disciplinary conventions upon which most literary critics (then and now) relied; these conventions, Jarrell implies, might be part of "the social," enemies of private life and of art.

Whatever its subjects, Jarrell's critical prose consistently makes, through its style, two arguments about literature in general. The first of these overarching arguments concerns the status of words and speech acts in poems. As against Allen Tate, Cleanth Brooks, and others, Jarrell liked to insist that we regard poems not as heterocosms but as troped speech among and about persons. This view let Jarrell use his reviews to offer general truths, not about the poems under discussion but about the human affairs they describe. Elizabeth Bishop's poetry "understands . . . that the wickedness and confusion of the age can explain and extenuate other people's wickedness and confusion, but not, for you, your own" (*Age* 235). A very long reading of Robert Frost's "Home Burial" gave Jarrell occasion to suggest that "there are no long peacemaking speeches in a quarrel: after a few sentences the speaker always has begun to blame the other again" (*Third* 206). John Guillory has claimed provocatively that Cleanth Brooks's description of good poems as "paradoctrinal" nondiscursive objects served to empower professional critics, to whom readers appealed for explanations (166). Jarrell liked to insist instead that poems presented persons and their lives; words in poems therefore had the same status as words in fiction, prose, and conversation.[12]

This insistence is not simply a direction for reading poems. It is also, in Langdon Hammer's phrase, another of Jarrell's "attacks on the professionalism of the literary culture at large" ("Who" 392). The problem of poets' entry into universities, like the problem of critics captured by disciplines, struck Jarrell as a specially salient case of a general dilemma: the capture of aesthetic and private experience by institutions, interests, and rules. For "many young poets," Jarrell quipped in 1955, "poetry is a game like court tennis or squash racquets—one they learned at college—and they play it with propriety, as part of their social and academic existence. . . . Wasn't it one of these poets who said, the other day,

'I accept the university'? And wasn't it a Professor of Poetry who replied 'By God, he'd better!'?" (*KA* 231) Jarrell rewrites Emerson's famous exchange with Margaret Fuller by replacing "universe" with "university." His problem is not that the poets are too scholarly but that they have become servants of institutions.

The parallel with the *esprit sérieux* is exact. To the extent that critics judge literature as specialists, they are not reading it *as* literature at all. "A critical method can help us neither to read nor to judge; still, it is sometimes useful in pointing out to the reader a few gross discrete reasons for thinking a good poem good—and it is invaluable, almost indispensable, in convincing a reader that a good poem is bad, or a bad one good" (*Age* 88). This sentence and dozens of others like it position Jarrell as a reader like other readers, but one so familiar with the techniques and impostures of merely professional criticism that he can convince readers to trust their own tastes.

Here, then, is the second overarching argument Jarrell's critical essays contain: literary reading requires readers to distance themselves from institutions, professions, and disciplines. He wrote in "The Age of Criticism":

> Critics have a wonderfully imposing look, but this is only because they are in a certain sense impostors: the judges' black gowns, their positions and degrees and qualifications, their professional accomplishments, methods, styles, distinctions—all this institutional magnificence hides from us the naked human beings who do the judging.
>
> (*Age* 87)

The impostures, here, consist of the pretense that literary criticism can be a profession like business or law, with formalized methods and standard qualifications. By contrast, real "criticism demands of the critic a terrible nakedness: a real critic has no one but himself to depend on" (*Age* 90).

Such appeals to intuition against method prove themselves by *sounding* as little as possible like value-neutral or "academic" writing. They sound more often like the language of journalism and "reviewing." Jarrell is, however, careful to avoid the representative or unobtrusively general voice common to journalistic reviewing. A brace of tactics—from extravagant similes and emblems to exceptionally lengthy sentences and exclamations—makes Jarrell's critical prose more recognizable, more idiosyncratic, and more personal than the prose of the other journalistic or essayistic critics of his era.[13] Through "rhetorical devices not usually found in literary criticism," as Keith Monroe has put it, "Jarrell attempted to create a personal criticism," analogous to "conversation among friends" (262).[14] His elaborately unmannerly sentences work to describe com-

plex reactions to single poems but also record the affective power of more ab-
stract arguments, as in this peroration from "The Obscurity of the Poet":

> When you begin to read a poem you are entering a foreign country whose
> laws and language and life are a kind of translation of your own; but to ac-
> cept it because its stews taste exactly like your old mother's hash, or to re-
> ject it because the owl-headed goddess of wisdom in its temple is fatter
> than the Statue of Liberty, is an equal mark of that want of imagination,
> that inaccessibility to experience, of which each of us who dies a natural
> death will die.
>
> (*Age* 12)

The tone, at first peremptory, grows extravagantly energetic as Jarrell warms to
the works he is defending, then grave as he draws away from them. The sen-
tence begins as something a teacher might say in a classroom, and ends more
like a Protestant sermon.

Akin to such demonstrations of personal feeling are Jarrell's refusals to offer
long, overt, step-by-step arguments. (His early collection of aphorisms includes
the simple, gloomy warning *"Don't argue"* [7].) Figurative passages disguise
their nature as arguments by seeming to be (mere) metaphors or impressions.
Describing, in 1945, Auden's changing ideas of Original Sin, Jarrell writes:

> Auden first slipped into this dark realm of Faërie . . . on the furtive excur-
> sions of the unbeliever who needs some faked photographs of the Little
> People for use as illustrations to a new edition of *Peter Pan*, but who ends
> up as a cook's boy helping the gloomier dwarfs boil toads and snails for the
> love feast that celebrates the consummation of their mysteries. Thus in
> *New Year Letter* many things [e.g. the Devil] are used as mere metaphors
> or conceits which a few months later are accepted as dogmatic and eter-
> nal truths.
>
> (*Third* 177–178)

These sentences offer a compact account of Auden's development. Yet, Jarrell's
method of disguising, or leaving implicit, the arguments his sentences contain
has led some readers to conclude that Jarrell does not make arguments at all.
One recent reviewer complains that "excellent turns of phrase do not make a
good critic" and that "Jarrell's writing" fails to be "real criticism." Jarrell's figura-
tive and synthetic language contains precisely what this reviewer says it lacks,
new insights for "an audience already interested and somewhat knowledgeable"
about the writers in question (Kirsch 24). What it does not contain are explicit,

connected, literal, discursive, arguments: we are invited to furnish those for our-
selves, by interpreting the figurative language.

Jarrell's stance and its verbal correlates set themselves against the course of
criticism during his lifetime—developments that seemed to him to collude
with the threat of the social. While Jarrell was developing his critical practice,
eminent mid-century critics such as Ransom, I. A. Richards, Northrop Frye,
and Kenneth Burke hoped, each in his own way, to systematize criticism, to
provide "principles," "anatomies," "grammars," "rhetorics," or prolegomenas
for the near future's literary analysts.[15] Ransom in *The World's Body* (1938) fa-
mously called for a "Criticism, Inc. or Criticism, Ltd.," which might "become
more scientific, or precise and systematic" when "taken in hand by profession-
als" (329). Later system-building critics even warned against personal involve-
ment: Frye, for example, began his *Anatomy of Criticism* (1957) by asking that
criticism achieve "some measure of independence" from its literary objects
(10–11).

T. S. Eliot declared, in words Jarrell later quoted, "There is no method ex-
cept to be very intelligent" (*Age* 87).[16] But (as Hammer has shown at length) the
author of "Tradition and the Individual Talent" presented to advocates like Tate
"a view of the 'literary' that rigorously and categorically excludes 'the personal
values' (moral, social, religious) of poet and critic alike," conceiving of literature
as "an autonomous—and an oddly *corporate*—entity" (*Janus-Faced* 69). Seeking
a demesne distinct from that of the sciences, Eliot-inspired "orthodoxy" looks to
acknowledge and sometimes to imitate the impersonal, received authority of
nonscientific institutions—in particular (as Guillory has argued) of religious in-
stitutions.[17] Ransom appears to say outright that his brand of professional analy-
sis aims to create a secular priesthood. He declared in his 1951 preface to *The
Kenyon Critics*, "the one authority which is still universally reputable is litera-
ture. But literature is cryptic . . . the greater our faith in its authority, the more
hidden is likely to be its rule of life and way of salvation. . . . It is the critic who
must teach us to find the thing truly authoritative but hidden" (ix).

To such authoritative aspirations, Jarrell (though he admired Ransom's
poems) objected with humor and force. In Jarrell's way of thinking—the one his
prose implies—particular works may indeed be authoritative, as for him
Wordsworth and Rilke and Proust surely were. Yet their authority exists only in
private, proved on the pulse of the reader. As literature, the *Prelude* and the *Son-
nets to Orpheus* do not and cannot have the kind of authority that can be so-
cially enforced or embodied in an institution. Their power depends on psychol-
ogy rather than on exegesis—on sympathy rather than on interpretation. Jarrell
wrote to Robert Penn Warren as early as 1935, "the majority of my tendencies
are not at all Eliot-ish and didactic" (*Letters* 5). "Eliot-ish" aspirations and atti-

tudes, no less than social-scientific ones, represented for Jarrell a subordination of unpredictable individual response to institutional or disciplinary canons of value.

Jarrell's divergence from his mentors can be overstated: as early as 1940 Allen Tate, in "The Present Function of Criticism," warned that "professional 'educationists' and . . . sociologists . . . have taught the present generation that . . . the greatest thing is adjustment to Society (not to a good society)" (*Essays* 199). Tate and Jarrell both posit literature as a force against "social adjustment."[18] Yet Tate is defending an intellectual and a moral elite, as well as a specific (ultimately religious) ideal of a "good society," and doing so with a moralized hauteur. For Tate and for Ransom, as for their utilitarian enemies, that good society is to be imagined by a cadre of professionals—the difference is simply that for Tate and Ransom the right professionals are experts in literature.[19] Though his teachers worried about specialization, Jarrell attended more carefully than they could to its workings within the postwar world and within the demesne of literature: he concludes "The Age of Criticism" in hope that "a few people . . . pay no attention to what the most systematic and definitive critic says against some work of art they love" (*Age* 95).[20]

The project Jarrell's critical essays share, the project his "undisciplined" sentences demonstrate, is thus not simply, as William Pritchard writes, "to put criticism in its proper, subordinate place" (213). We can say more specifically that Jarrell's tactics in his critical prose seek to subordinate criticism as an institution, as a profession requiring specialist training, to a prior experience of private reading. One of Jarrell's unpublished lectures on Auden drew explicitly the distinction so much of his published prose implies:

> Somebody said, at one of our lectures early this fall: 'Anybody can *read* poems: the difficult thing is to make discursive statements about them.' She and I have been living in different worlds. Anybody *can* make discursive statements about poems—half the people I know start making discursive statements a block and a half before they reach the poems. But to read the poems, really to read them—that *is* difficult.
>
> (Berg Collection; underscore in original)

What makes literature worthwhile, Jarrell implies here—what we care about in literature—may be susceptible to cognitive analysis but is never reducible to that analysis. The reasons we read literary books, and the reactions that lead us to want to call some books good and other books bad, cannot be reduced to the reasons nor to the evidence professional critics can use in discursive arguments.[21] "The best critic who ever lived could not *prove* that the *Iliad* is better than *Trees*: the critic can only state his belief persuasively, and hope that the reader of the poem will agree—but *persuasively* covers everything from a sneer to statistics" (*Age* 88).

These most basic, most difficult to describe reactions, which motivate the rhetoric of persuasion but cannot accommodate objective evidence, are the reactions that establish the possibility of human interiority and intersubjective relations, even amid intrusive institutions. Charles Altieri calls such reactions "first-person commitments" and contrasts them with attempts at impersonal analyses: "when the 'I' [considers] the singular 'you,' it seeks a relationship defined not by general rules but by specific conditions . . . ranging from intimate companionship to internalized tribunals" (*Canons* 305, 306). A "real critic" Jarrell wrote, speaks from just such conditions: he "can never forget that all he has to go by, finally, is his own response, the self that makes and is made up of such responses—and yet he must regard that self as no more than the instrument through which the work of art is seen" (*Age* 90).

Such a declaration transforms Eliot's famous impersonality into a vehicle for first-person commitments, commitments on the part of one naked self (the critic's) to another (that embodied in the work of art). Allen Grossman has argued that poetry "is . . . the kind of utterance that makes the person present" to the reader, in the [philosophical] sense of "person" as a "value-bearing" entity "which has rights" (20). It is the aim of all poetry, for Grossman, to make value-bearing, honored "persons" from what were initially dishonored "selves": "The disposition to honor selves, awakened by poetry, must be responded to if poetry can be said to be truly read" (19–20). Jarrell's program for critical feeling (it might be better to say *readerly* feeling) works out, in its tone, assumptions, and attitudes, precisely this disposition, which might also be called a willingness to enter into first-person commitments or (following Stanley Cavell) a readiness to acknowledge.[22]

Jarrell's largest distinction as a critic does not lie in the *idea* that acknowledgements of persons underlie literary experience. That idea existed before him and has been pursued since without reference to him. Jarrell's distinction as a critic, rather, is that he made the process of acknowledging persons in poems, of being personally affected by what one reads, continually manifest in his prose style. That style—along with the arguments it encodes—resists demands that criticism be "systematic," demands that it produce objective knowledge rather than acknowledgement, because such demands turn what would otherwise be ends (readings, reactions, literary experience) into means for the production of more criticism. Such demands thus convert readers into mere instruments, into machines of sorts, as "The Age of Criticism" implies:

Some of [the criticism in the quarterlies of the 1940s and 1950s] is as good as anyone could wish: several of the best critics alive print most of their work in such magazines as these. Some more of this criticism is intelligent and useful—it sounds as if it had been written by a reader for readers, by a human being for human beings. But a great deal of this criticism might just as well have been written by a syndicate of encyclopedias for an audience of International Business Machines. It is not only bad or mediocre, it is *dull*; it is, often, an astonishingly graceless, joyless, humorless, long-winded, niggling, blinkered, methodical, self-important, cliché-ridden, prestige-obsessed, almost-autonomous criticism.

(*Age* 72–73)

The figurative language explains the emotional force: literary reading and writing have here become a factory managed by mechanical organization men, who superintend what they ought to combat—"the specialization, the dividing into categories, of people's unlucky lives" (*Age* 77).[23]

Stanley Edgar Hyman described mid-century critics in his 1948 study *The Armed Vision* (1948): Hyman's ideal critic, Jarrell quipped, would "resemble one of those robots you meet in science-fiction stories, with a microscope for one eye, a telescope for the other, and the mechanical brain at Harvard for a heart" (*Age* 89). Mechanical, professional, powerful, insensitive, institution-bound critics deserve professional, powerful, insensitive, institutional-bound poets. They get what they deserve in the Auden of the forties and fifties, as one Princeton lecture imagined:

There is a book called *The Armed Vision* which gives a most impressive picture of what the ideal critic would know: it can be summed up briefly, in the word, *everything*. *The Age of Anxiety* is the sort of poem such a critic would write. . . . In Auden's later poems one finds everything that money can buy, i.e. everything that the most extensive information, the most laborious ingenuity, and the most professional [penciled in: technological] production know-how (hindered, adulterated or occasionally transfigured by that obstinate survivor, genius) can manage to produce. The poems are the work of a real Man of Letters. (It is those Letters that kill.)

(Berg Collection)

The Age of Anxiety struck Jarrell not only as a bad poem by a great poet but also as a stimulus to his fears about "technique," about the dominance of methods and groups.[24] The menace includes "the social" in all its forms, from institutional role-playing to behaviorist predictability to economic efficiency; it recalls

Jarrell's earlier verdict that "Auden . . . has bureaucratized his method about as completely—and consequently as disastrously—as any efficiency expert could wish" (*Third* 143).

When New Critical thought was newer, Jarrell defended it against both commercial book reviewing and historical scholarship. He wrote in 1941 that "Universities . . . produce good criticism . . . at best . . . only as federal prisons produce counterfeit money—a few hardened prisoners are more or less surreptitiously continuing their real vocations" (*KA* 62). The jargon of bad mid-century critics, Jarrell explained in "The Age of Criticism," developed in "fifteen or twenty years"; as New Critical practice came to dominate the academy, its reduction to replicable method moved some of its practitioners to protest (*Age* 83). Gerald Graff calls "The Age of Criticism" "the most celebrated" among several such protests (228). Graff's *Professing Literature* views such alarms over "routinization" as a recurring phenomenon in the history of critical methods. He blames, in part, the structure of universities, whose "institutional arrangements do not require [competing] discourses to confront one another" (240, 243). Each new critical school can thus denounce its predecessor as routinized; later the same school, if its adherents acquire enough power, will harden into routine itself. Allen Tate's "Miss Emily and the Bibliographer" (attacking biographical and philological scholarship) thus occupies the same position for one stage in the history of English departments as "The Age of Criticism" occupies for the next.[25]

Declaring "New critic is but old scholar writ large," "The Age of Criticism" anticipates Graff's argument. But rather than suggesting, as Graff does, different institutional arrangements, Jarrell views institutions themselves as the problem. If Graff's problem is with the ways in which literary studies have been constructed as a discipline, Jarrell's problem seems to be *that* they have been too completely constructed as one—that not enough energy, time, or resources remain (in or outside the academy) for the enjoyment of literature in ways that do not produce measurable (critical) results. Conscious that institutions, methods, techniques in some form will always be with us, Jarrell attacks particular institutions and methods when the threat they pose to individual, unprofessional activity becomes especially great.

"The Age of Criticism" thus belongs not only to the history of the discipline of literary criticism but also to a continuing argument about the meanings and uses of disciplines. What does it mean to call criticism a discipline? Mark Bauerlein contends (citing Talcott Parsons):

Each discipline achieves its own knowledge through distinct and fixed 'modes of implementation.' The requirement of cognitive rationality means that disciplinary knowledge must be cognizable in systematic, re-peatable ways. (This is why something like the writing of poetry, which may have its own goals and methods, still can never be a discipline in this sense, since cognitive rationality is not necessarily part of its creative domain. Only when the experience of poetry is broached on a cognitive rational basis, namely through criticism, can poetry become a discipli-nary object.)

(49)

For Jarrell, both Bauerlein and his opponents have mistaken means for ends: criticism should never be *entirely* "systematic" or "repeatable," since it requires subjective, one-of-a-kind personal elements in order to construe its object of study at all. The criticism that dominates the Age of Criticism (Jarrell believed) might squeeze out just those crucial aspects. Its faults resemble the faults Jarrell found in André Malraux's art criticism, which also relied too much on general models: "If the methods of some discipline deal only with, say, what is quantita-tively measurable, and something is not quantitatively measurable, then the thing does not exist for that discipline—after a while the lower right-hand cor-ner of the inscription gets broken off, and it reads *does not exist*" (KA 181).

"The Age of Criticism" is no more a call to abolish academic literary criti-cism (and the review of Malraux no more a call to abolish art history) than a predecessor such as Tate's "Miss Emily and the Bibliographer" is a call to abol-ish scholarship. It is instead (to adapt Bauerlein's terms) a warning against mis-taking the disciplinary object construed by one or another kind of criticism for the more complex, more unpredictable, and emotionally richer literary object as it is available to a range of (initially) amateur readers, the object from which "disciplinary objects" must then be derived.[26] Jarrell's antidisciplinary position and idiosyncratic critical practice thus support, perhaps unexpectedly, Geoffrey Hartman's famous argument that criticism when it is worthy of itself is always also a genre of imaginative literature.[27] Hartman warns that the impulse to de-fend individual creativity against "institutional or commercial forces" can bol-ster "the prejudice that separates the creative from the interpretive"—a preju-dice (Hartman writes) we ought to resist, since "a critical essay, a legal opinion, an interpretation of Scripture, a biography can be as inspiring and nurturing as poem, novel or painting" (*Journey* 43).

To be useful to literary reading (in Jarrell's model) criticism must be subjec-tive, hence creative. "The work of criticism is rooted in the unconscious of the critic, just as the poem is rooted in the unconscious of the poet," he concluded in "Poets, Critics and Readers" (KA 314). Critical creativity will, though, have to manifest itself in a special and self-subordinating relation to other creative work. As against the work products of a professional discipline, which an attorney or chemist sets out to produce (and to which life outside the laboratory may be irrelevant) "true criticism . . . must always be, in some sense, a by-product . . . of a private poetry-workshop or a private reading-room" (*SH* 103). Jarrell appeals self-consciously (as his frequent rhetorical questions suggest) to his readers' feelings. It is precisely such feelings that we bracket when we are trying to interpret a culture from outside, to consider cultural forms as "third-person," disciplinary objects.

Jarrell's prose thus begins in an abreaction to careerism and ends as a (Wordsworthian) ethics of reading.[28] The peroration to "Poets, Critics and Readers" describes "an unusually humane and intelligent critic" who has declared " 'All the reading I do is in order to write or teach' "—all, that is, with one exception: a yearly rereading of Rudyard Kipling's *Kim* (*KA* 317). It is in that rereading of *Kim*, and not in reading "in order to" do something else, that Jarrell locates the value of literature. When he reads *Kim* that anonymous critic

> read it, as Kipling wrote it, just because he liked to, wanted to, couldn't help himself. To him it wasn't a means to a lecture or an article, it was an end: he read it not for anything he could get out of it, but for itself. And isn't this what the work of art demands of us? . . . It demands of us that we too see things as ends, not as means—that we too know them and love them for their own sake.
>
> (*KA* 317–318)

This Kantian vocabulary is Jarrell's usual one for moral judgments. The malevolent Sam, in *The Man Who Loved Children*, "has made the beings of this world, who are the ends of this world, means" (*Third* 41). The same vocabulary marks Jarrell's asides on how to read: "When one reads as a linguist, a scholar, a New or Old or High or Low critic, when one reads the poem *as a means to an end*, one is no longer a pure reader but an applied one" (*KA* 307). A reader who can't treat a work of art as an end may be unable to treat a person as an end, especially when neither seems important. This analogy between the treatment of poems and the treatment of persons emerges near the end of "The Obscurity of the Poet":

> People always ask: *For whom does the poet write?* He needs only to answer, *For whom do you do good? Are you kind to your daughter because in the end someone will pay you for being?* . . . The poet writes his poem for its own sake, for the sake of that order of things in which the poem takes the place that has awaited it.
>
> (*Age* 26; italics in original)

Implicit here, as in "The Age of Criticism," are two different (but not contradictory) theses about the relation of aesthetic goodness in literature and the other arts to ethical goodness in human action. In the first model, the aesthetic and the ethical are linked by analogy: both are served when the objects in their domain (works of art; persons) are treated as ends, traduced when those objects are treated as means. As David Haney puts it (following Emmanuel Lévinas), "the structure of the reader's relationship to a literary text has affinities with a person's ethical relationships to others": "Because the art work unites means and ends . . . one's relation to it resembles an ethical relation to another person" (38, 39). Jarrell thus sees something not only depressing but dangerous about the sort of reader who "knows what he likes, but is uncomfortable when other people do not read it or do not like it—for what people read and like is good: that is what *good* means" (*Age* 71). Someone who cannot distinguish artistic goodness from popular success may not be able to tell good from evil.

In the second idea about art and ethics, our potentially shared or similar responses to good works of art reveal the shared basis of our moral personhood. As we are obliged, for Jarrell, to treat works of art first of all as ends, so are we obliged to consider everyone as *potentially* receptive to art. Jarrell told an audience at Harvard that "Proust and Chekhov, Hardy and Yeats and Rilke . . . demand to be shared: if we are satisfied to know these things ourselves, and to look with superiority or indifference on those who do not have that knowledge, we have made a refusal that corrupts us as surely as anything can" (*Age* 22). That which "demands to be shared," the noncognitive remainder in literary experience, the knowledge-of potentially available to anyone (in contrast to technical, specialized knowledge-about), makes such a demand felt by anyone who *can* share it. The aesthetic in general, in Jarrell's account, does some of the same work Wordsworth proposes for his own poetry in his 1802 preface to *Lyrical Ballads*: it "binds together . . . the vast empire of human society," drawing on "sympathies" that may exist in all of us "without any other discipline than that of our daily life" (258–259).

Guillory's influential *Cultural Capital* shows (drawing on the sociologist Pierre Bourdieu) how literary works and doctrines about them function as sources of social power and thus of class distinction. If we identify (as Jarrell often did) *disciplinary, specialized* reading and writing with the *professional* practice of literary criticism and with the socioeconomic rewards of that practice, we can see that the unprofessional, potentially universal grounds for aesthetic experience Jarrell believes liberals are obliged to imagine resemble not only Wordsworth's goal for his poems but also Guillory's idea of "remainder." Guillory asks, "Is it possible to translate the (false) philosophical problem of 'aesthetic value' into the sociological problem of 'cultural capital'?" He answers, finally, that it is possible—"with the qualification that the translation always has a remainder, which is nothing other than aesthetic experience" (327).

"From the sociological point of view," Guillory continues, "the experience of any 'pure' aesthetic pleasure is of no interest at all"; "aesthetic pleasure simply falls outside the sociological field . . . incapable of articulation in the game of distinction, except as the pretext of the game." But "it is only by taking the *articulation* of aesthetic discourse as identical to aesthetic experience" that Bourdieu and others can ascribe formal innovation to high culture and *haut bourgeois* discourse alone (333). Through the idiosyncrasies of his prose style, and through the argument it entails, Jarrell seeks to highlight just that "remainder," the part of reading that would be left if there were no consideration of "cultural capital," of social position, professional reward, and social difference, involved in reading (especially in reading poetry). Jarrell's style of criticism thus seeks to rescue his own and our experience of works of literary art from those works' status as both disciplinary objects and repositories of cultural capital.

The threat Bourdieuian sociology poses, in theory, to the possibility of aesthetic experience, in theory, duplicates the threat the Age of Criticism posed to aesthetic experience in practice: the threat that it might be a deceptive name for material interests.[29] One way to demonstrate that aesthetic experience is not simply a pretext for demonstrations of mastery, that we *can* treat art works as ends and not means, might be to describe one's own experience of particular texts while stretching or flouting the conventions by which high-status disciplines "articulate" that experience. Such demonstrations are, as I hope I have already shown, exactly what Jarrell's prose style aims to provide.[30] A critic with such goals would take care to advocate supposedly minor or unimportant works, works without potential for cultural prominence. Jarrell did exactly that, over and over, furnishing a long list of such works in "The Age of Criticism" (*Age* 79). When discussing a canonical author, a critic with these goals would remind readers that any canonical poem was enjoyed before it entered syllabi and textbooks and that all works of art, even overwhelmingly powerful ones, were once unknown. Jarrell begins a long essay on Stevens with exactly these reminders.[31] Finally, such a critic would bring up—as we have seen Jarrell do—the (alterable, though not alterable at will) social position of the works discussed and the doctrines about them, in order to distinguish (in principle) social position and fact from personal reactions—though they may never, in practice, be entirely disentangled.[32]

Jarrell's prose thus shows us critical reading vanishing asymptotically into personal experience and vice versa: the personal seems to emerge in Jarrell's writing exactly in so far as the text under discussion calls it forth. We will see this mode of reaction, personal yet impersonal, described and defended at the end

of Jarrell's campus novel. That novel finds among its characters the virtue his es-
says imagined: it—and they—imagine a space where works of art produce not
disciplinary knowledge but individuating acknowledgement. This space allows
us, in turn, to recognize persons distinct from the institutions, professions, social
roles, and public controversies among which they—and we—will always live.

Jarrell did not restrict his engagement with postwar social thought to his essays
and poems. The same concerns about art, individuals, and "the social" inform
Jarrell's one work of prose fiction for adults, the comic novel *Pictures from an In-
stitution*. *Pictures* describes an academic year at Benton College, a progressive
women's college modeled on Sarah Lawrence, where Jarrell taught in 1946–47.
The narrator spends the year there as a visiting professor; another visiting teacher
is Gertrude Johnson, a successful, witty, malevolent novelist. As Jarrell's narrator
gathers information for his book on Benton, Gertrude gathers material for her
novel based on life at the college. For all its comedy, *Pictures from an Institution*
may be called the most Arendtian of Jarrell's productions, both because it is most
fully occupied by Arendtian concerns about "the social" and because it dates
from Jarrell and Arendt's closest association. Jarrell even kept the successive
drafts of his novel in a binder Arendt had given him, left over from the produc-
tion of *Origins of Totalitarianism*.[33] Benton and its characters contain almost
every aspect of "the social" as Jarrell's essays and poems up to 1952 imagined it:
readers encounter bureaucracy, "adjustment," narrowly economic thinking, con-
formism, and norm-worship, reductionist accounts of human behavior, sub-
servience to institutional interests, narrowly disciplinary approaches, false public-
spiritedness, snobbery, inverse snobbery, falsely democratic attacks on taste, and
hostility to individuation. Gertrude's novel, *Pictures* supposes, will illuminate
Benton's faults mercilessly, as if it were a totally predictable, self-enclosed socio-
cultural system. Jarrell's own novel, however, shows not only the bad aspects of
Benton's institutions but also the ways in which even the most predictable of its
individuals, and the least promising of its works of art, can escape their sway.

Benton's President Robbins identifies his own interests entirely with those of
Benton College: "President Robbins was so well adjusted to his environment
that sometimes you could not tell which was the environment and which was
President Robbins" (10–11). He attends not to people but to social formations:
"There was a part of Gatsby that his bank, the company that insured him, and
other institutions knew—a part that was in love not with Daisy but with the
bank; and this part of Gatsby President Robbins shared with Gatsby" (17). Presi-
dent Robbins, in love with institutions, acts out what Whyte would later dub the
"social ethic," which promises "an equilibrium in which society's needs and the
needs of the individual are one and the same" (7). Though Robbins heads a rel-

atively innocuous institution, his traits remind Jarrell's narrator of other, more dangerous ones—President Robbins "had the morals of a State; had, almost, the morals of an Army" (72). Robbins fits *almost* perfectly into a social system, in Parsons's sense of that term: the sociologist Chris Jenks writes that in a "social system the social norms . . . diminish the potential distinction between the self and the collectivity by engendering a coinciding set of interests for both" (16).

Each of Jarrell's unflattering "pictures" functions on the one hand to caricature such "social" behavior as Robbins's, and on the other to undercut reductively sociological accounts of human life. The people of Benton come close to being explicable in the terms those accounts offer but are never wholly so: "Had it not been for Mrs. Robbins, President Robbins' life would have been explicable down to the last detail. . . . But why had he married Mrs. Robbins? It was a question to which there could not be an answer" (11). The most venomous attacks on Benton's predictable behavior are consistently shunted to Gertrude, who believes that everyone (not just President Robbins) obeys material interests and social scripts all the time (whereas, in truth, not even the Robbinses do).

Gertrude's style of explanation does not even account for all of Gertrude: in her rare moments of self-doubt, she is entitled (as the characters in Jarrell's poems are entitled) to repetitions, rhetorical questions, grammatical breakdown: "away from their laughter, their held breath, their widening repudiating eyes, Gertrude felt: *Am I*—was she what? She felt: *Am I? Am I?*" (255). Gertrude even displays, without an ulterior motive, real affection for her husband, Sidney, bringing him lemonade when he is sick. Normally she is surprised that "people, ordinary people, could take themselves seriously. . . . But as she watched Sidney drink the lemonade she did not see how ridiculous he was, but watched seriously and with interest, taking him on his own terms" (207). "Sidney was what Gertrude could be good to"; as for everyone else, Gertrude really believes that "People just aren't *loveable*" (207; italics in original).

What is wrong with Gertrude in Jarrell's novel seems closely akin to what is wrong with literary criticism in Jarrell's essays. Here is the rest of the passage in which Gertrude offers Sidney lemonade:

> From the black steel of Gertrude's armored side there opened a kind of door, and from it a hand emerged and held out to Sidney a glass of lemonade—cold, and with sugar in it, even if it was bad for him—and the hand, seriously and with interest, watched Sidney drink the lemonade. Then the door closed; but still, it had been open for that long: for that long there had been nothing between the world and Gertrude but a hand holding a glass of lemonade.
>
> (206)

The steel-armored, tanklike Gertrude, defended by her theories of human mo-
tivation and human depravity, resembles the invulnerable, mechanical reader
of "The Age of Criticism," with his armed vision and computerized heart. And
the nearly mechanical Gertrude, who can be humanized and softened by ex-
actly one person, Sidney, resembles the harassed, overprogrammed professor in
"Poets, Critics and Readers," who can be a human being, rather than a profes-
sional interpreter, with exactly one book, *Kim*.

Is *Pictures* a roman à clef? Jarrell taught at Sarah Lawrence when Mary Mc-
Carthy did, and many readers took Gertrude for McCarthy.[34] Gertrude's own
novel about Benton suggests McCarthy's *The Groves of Academe* (1952), which
mentions Jarrell by name.[35] An unpublished lecture about *Pictures* has Jarrell
defending his novel against the charge that it was disguised nonfiction:

> During the last year people's conversations with me, literary conversa-
> tions, have got in a rut. This is the rut: Who's President Robbins? Who's
> Gertrude Johnson? Where's Benton? Some of the time, though, people
> don't ask me, they tell me. I've got used to delivering a little two-minute
> speech that could be entitled: 59 *Overwhelming Differences Between
> Gertrude Johnson and* — oh, say Senator McCarthy. I'm perfectly willing
> to have people think Gertrude Johnson me, or part of me — the book's de-
> signed to make them do that; but I'm not willing to have them think my
> poor dear ugly mouse of a Gertrude Johnson a pretty actual lady novelist.
> Nor am I willing to have you think that the president of your college is re-
> ally President Robbins — the last few months it's begun to seem to me that
> man is a featherless biped who thinks that the president of his college is
> really Dwight Robbins.
>
> (Berg Collection)

Pictures refuses to become, prides itself on never quite becoming, simply a
chronicle of the mechanical interests it mocks, exactly as it prides itself on not
being simply a portrait of the real people who happen to resemble its characters.
(Riesman's admiring comments on Jarrell's novel emphasize just such ethno-
graphic scruples.[36])

Whether or not we see McCarthy in Gertrude, the president of Sarah
Lawrence in President Robbins, or the professional anthologist Oscar Williams
in the professional anthologist Charles Daudier, we believe the novel Gertrude
is writing will resemble *Groves* more than it resembles the one we are reading.
When Gertrude complains about Benton, she is usually right; she does not see
how her complaints (about systematization, predictability, interests) apply also
to her, nor does she see how the same complaints can only be *mostly* or *usually*

true of any individual, even the most conformist—even herself. "Gertrude said about Benton, in the voice of a digital computer nagging at cash-registers: 'Americans are so conformist that even their dissident groups exhibit the most abject conformity. . . . There was some truth in what she said; I had felt its truth, I know, At Home On Bleecker Street," where Gertrude lives (104–105). Jarrell's narrator, in a rare peroration, tells Gertrude flatly, "People aren't like anything, there are too many of them" (98). Later in the novel,

> Gertrude had impressed me by talking about a "definition by ostenta-
> tion"; she said . . . that it was just the thing for me. "How do you do it?" I
> asked. She answered: "you simply point."
>   "That *is* just the thing for me," I admitted. I felt that a definition by os-
> tentation was almost as good as none. (178)

Gertrude's conversation is better (and funnier) than her books, because the books are more systematic, "crushed down into method" (132). The purely sociological novels she writes exhibit a kind of Pharisaism:

> She made her characters, held them, to the letter of the law. If one of
> Gertrude's heroines, running to snatch from the lips of her little daughter
> a half-emptied bottle of furniture polish, fell and tore her skirt, Gertrude
> knew the name of the dressmaker who had made the skirt—and it was the
> right one for a woman of that class, at that date; she knew the brand of the
> furniture-polish. . . . But how the child felt as it seized and drank the pol-
> ish, how the mother felt as she caught the child to her breast—about such
> things as these, which have neither brand nor date, Gertrude was less
> knowing, would have said impatiently, "Everybody knows *that!*"
>
> (133)

This passage has an exact antecedent in Virginia Woolf's famous 1924 lecture, "Mr. Bennett and Mrs. Brown." Seeing a Mrs. Brown in a train, Woolf writes, Arnold Bennett would notice "how Mrs. Brown wore a brooch which had cost three-and-ten-three at Whitworth's bazaar; and had mended both gloves . . . and . . . had been left a little copyhold, not freehold, property at Datchet" (106–107). Woolf argued that modern art had to extricate character as such from external, social facts like those Bennett's novels gathered.

If Bennett believed that he could illuminate character by describing such things, Gertrude does not believe in character at all—instead, "know[ing] why everything is as it is," she believes in a kind of social determinism. Those who offer deterministic social explanations, however, are unpredictable persons themselves, and Jarrell emphasizes their eccentricities. Jerrold Whittaker, for example, is "every inch a sociologist": "Everything, to Jerrold, was the illustration of a principle" (49, 57). Jerrold and his wife, Flo, believe that they are entirely rational, committed to criteria of utility and public good. In fact, they are the strangest, most purely amusing people in the novel. Visiting their house is "like going to the zoo": they

> had a bulletin board for the children, and pinned to it, like butterflies, their children's schedules, their doctor's telephone number, their senator's telephone number, the dates you could see the Perseids and the Leonids, and the first red leaf; the food they ate when they were well, the medicine they took when they were ill, the clothes they wore when they were dressed, the sheets they lay under when they were undressed, all had been recommended by Consumers Union.
>
> (52)

The Whittakers also collect craft objects and folk art—this (the descriptions suggest) is how the human need for art, for *useless* experience, expresses itself in people who believe they are rational calculators of utility: "Jeremy Bentham's stuffed body would not have been ill at ease in their house," though he would have had to share it with "pepper-mills, needle-point footstools, barometers, chess-tables, candle-molds" (53).

Jerrold explains everything in the too-rational terms of academic social science. Flo combines her belief in social analysis with a commitment to public virtue: "she . . . dealt with primroses in lots of a hundred thousand, and remained on macroscropic or molar terms with her universe—she oversaw it with systematic benevolence" (58). "Almost everything that happened to Flo and her family and friends was, after all, only private; and to her real life was public, what you voted at or gave for or read about in the *Nation*. Life seemed to Flo so petty, compared to real life"[37] (58–59). Jarrell refuses to make Flo a Mrs. Jellyby; she is ridiculous, and unpleasant, but neither hypocritical nor deluded: "if I were a town, there is no one I should rather have by me in a disaster" (58). Flo represents the dominance of public interest, of political interpretation, over private life—and she represents that dominance at its least harmful and most sincere; she has to, since Jarrell's point is to critique exclusively political thinking *as such*, rather than any particular political outlook.

The Whittakers' artlessly public rationality thus becomes the most benign possible version of the theories for which President Robbins's life is the practice—theories that account for all human choices in terms of groups and interests. Gertrude's novels are in turn the art form that corresponds to the theory and practice of Benton, since she chronicles sociological people, giving them plots by manipulating them: "she looked at [the narrator's wife] the way you'd look at a chessman if it made its own move" (36). A novel that took sociological, or interest-based, explanations for all behavior as seriously as Gertrude, or Jerrold, or Flo took them, but more thoroughly and consistently, would indeed resemble a chess game, denying its characters even the semblance of agency. Such a novel would refuse to produce, in Woolf's sense of the word, "characters" and would therefore disaffiliate itself from psychology, allying its explanatory methods instead to anthropology and sociology and interpreting what seem to be human decisions as workings-out of cultural rules.

Christopher Herbert has claimed that Anthony Trollope wrote just such novels. In Trollope's *Doctor Thorne*, Herbert writes, "personality is presented . . . as a sociological phenomenon through and through," "a nexus of institutional forces," and "the unconscious . . . produced in effect by a calculus of institutions" (293). For Herbert this is a demonstration made again and again, rather anxiously, by social theory from the late nineteenth century on, a demonstration whose force post-Romantic literature struggles to escape. The antipsychological implications of such thinking, Herbert explains, rule out not only character but plot, in any strong sense of either word: "To incorporate into fiction in any concerted, explicit way the ethnographic thesis that individual personality is parasitic upon standardized or stereotyped cultural patterns . . . would undo at its root the vital principle of novelistic imagination." Should that thesis "come into ascendancy in a novel, it could only do so . . . in an anomalous fictional type"—like Trollope's—"marked not only by dramatic inertia and by shallowness, but by . . . affective privation" (259, 260).

At Benton the "ethnographic thesis" *almost* explains how people behave. It is for this reason, Jarrell suggests, that Benton could not host the plot of a conventional novel: "it was a world in which *almost* nothing happened, a kind of steady state" (221; italics in original). Gertrude nevertheless gives her book a "Real Plot. It could have happened anywhere—anywhere except, perhaps, Benton" (214). Jarrell remarked by contrast in an unpublished lecture that his own "book has no plot" (Berg Collection).[38] Flo and Jerrold and the rest of Benton conform *closely enough* to systematizing ideas of social behavior, make up such a nearly predictable system, as to rule out a plot, which would require them to act on one another with cumulative unpredictability. As individuals, though, each has a saving oddity, which rules out the "affective privation" Herbert describes, replacing it with humor. A book about Benton has anecdotes, but no plot, because it has persons, but none of them is in charge:

Is an institution always a man's shadow shortened in the sun, the lowest common denominator of everybody in it? Benton was: the soldiers, as always, were better than the army in which they served, the superficial consenting nexus of their lives that was Benton. The people of Benton, like the rest of us, were born, fell, in love, married and died, lay sleepless . . . won lotteries and wept for joy. But not at Benton.

(222)

(Note, once more, an analogy with the army.)[39] Benton conforms both to a social ethic and to an "ethnographic thesis" as much as any milieu, for Jarrell, can: one result is that people, insofar as they belong at Benton, do not change.

Against the institutions and the disciplines of the Age of Criticism, Jarrell's essays demonstrated his own, wilfully personal, reading practice. In the same way, against its Bentonian caricatures, *Pictures* sets a range of admirable minor characters devoted to private life and, always, to art. All of them, and only they, appreciate (what is now called) classical music. Flo and Jerrold Whittaker "loved folk ballads," though "they knew that they should like Classical Music" (67). Gertrude's insistence on seeing people socially, as congeries of interests, prevents her from understanding music at all; instead she appreciates architecture (67–68). The latter is the most public of art forms; the former the least reducible to discursive meaning and instrumental use.[40] By contrast, the most sympathetic characters in *Pictures* are a composer and a singer, Gottfried and Irene Rosenbaum.

Jarrell manages to associate Gottfried with everything in art that individualizes or acknowledges, not so much in Gottfried's own compositions as in his responses to others' work. A former student remarks that Gottfried "goes over your piece as if he were you, and the next girls' piece as if he were her—she" (137). Gottfried's status as an ideal listener is guaranteed by his unpredictability—a feature Jarrell cherished in literary reading: "You say, after you have listened to someone talking for a while about music, or painting, or literature, 'I see the line you're taking.' It was impossible to say this about Gottfried . . . where music was concerned" (137). "To say that someone is typically anything," *Pictures* declares, "is an unfavorable judgment"; "when Gottfried was least his kind he was most Gottfried" (175, 173). Gottfried's hard-won freedom from public demands, his sensitivity to individuality in people, his alertness to individuality in music, and his own freedom from confinement to type make up not four virtues but one. As the ideal (music) critic, he is the ideally individuated, encyclopedically knowledgeable but un-professional listener Jarrell's literary criticism envisions for novels and poems.

Refugees from Nazi Europe, the Rosenbaums are models not only of right relations to art but of domestic life, "like Baucis and Philemon" (125). Both have chosen private life over the public world; their disillusion with the latter seems complete. (Here, of course, as Jarrell told Arendt, neither one seems anything like her [*Letters* 392].) Gottfried Rosenbaum's "speech was a pilgrimage toward some *lingua franca* of the far future — 'vot ve all speak ven de Shtate hass viderdt away,' as he would have put it" (13). *"Ven de Shtate hass videredt avay* was one of his favorite phrases — he seemed to find it inexhaustibly humorous" (137). Repeating that phrase, Rosenbaum dismisses the failed hopes of European radicals; he also enacts a dream of private life freed from political demands. He has the personal and moral advantages of statelessness — advantages this refugee composer has achieved at incalculable costs.

Gottfried "had once ended a long half-hour's political lecture — conversation, the speaker would have called it — by saying to the speaker, 'Nijinsky said, *Politics is Death.* Is that right?' " (162). Jarrell endorsed the same quotation earlier, in an unfinished essay on the award of the 1948 Bollingen Prize to Ezra Pound:

> Most people felt so extraordinary an interest in Pound's case because here at last was an aesthetic question, a matter of art, from which the art could be almost wholly excluded, leaving nothing but politics and public morality. . . . "Politics is death," said Nijinsky — who was insane; "Politics is destiny," said Napoleon to Goethe, and his statement has been admiringly repeated every since, to end in Mann's monumental-statuary paraphrase: "In our time the destiny of man finds its expression in political terms." What a destiny! what an expression! For the artist, for a "private man" — and in what matters most to us we are necessarily private men — Napoleon's statement is more insane than Nijinsky's; and today who has not begun to see in Nijinsky's words a certain elementary empirical truth?
>
> ("Pound" 11–12)

Questions of public life and conduct, brought improperly into the sphere of private aesthetic response, become not political but "social" questions, encouraging not debate but conformist sectarianism. The Rosenbaums, like "The Pound Affair," identify the aesthetic, the private, and the authentic; their admirable lives suggest that authentic individuals, authentic response, can be found *only* in private life — the public sphere seems, for these speakers, at this moment, irrevocably compromised. If the aesthetic is the private (as against the reductively public), it is also the interpersonal (as against the social): the art works Jarrell most admires, in *Pictures* as everywhere else, let individuals recognize one another. Irene Rosenbaum had been an opera singer, but her voice now suits only small-scale performance. When she sings *lieder*, her failures become virtues, since they lend "importance" to private lives: "of all the singers I have ever heard she was the most essentially dramatic: she could not have sung a scale without making it seem a part of someone's life, a thing of human importance" (164).

Such a virtue is certainly not incompatible with the novel as a genre, but it seems incompatible with the kind of novel *Pictures* most resembles, which is a satire of types. How can a satirical novel attack people's tendency to treat one another as self-interested predictable groups—that is, as satires of its own sort treat them? One solution is to build in a satirist (Gertrude) who remains unsparing and unforgiving and then show how her views (satire's views) cannot account for all of human behavior (thus satirizing her). Another solution is to write sentences in which the narrator turns on himself, as when he remarks that Flo

> had learned to think of people only in hundred-thousand lots, but she couldn't help feeling for them, sometimes, one at a time—so that I thought once more, in uneasy perplexity: how shall I feel about Flo? That figure of fun, that pillar of righteousness, that type of the age, that index of the limitations of the human being, that human being? Flo was so sharply delimited, her bounds were so harshly and narrowly set, that you were aware as you seldom were of your own limitations, and said to yourself, "To someone I am Flo."
>
> (115)

Jarrell's satire (unlike Gertrude's) seems designed not only to justify his readers in their individual likings but also to humble them as Flo humbles the narrator. Flo reminds him of "the limits of the human being"; Gertrude "did not know—or rather did not believe—what it was like to be a human being" (189). Reminded that groups, institutional interests, and caricatures cannot entirely predict human behavior, we (and the novel) are recalled to the humanity of the people we are likely to caricature.[41]

Pictures from an Institution, then, explores the limits of institutional, social, and professional explanations for human behavior, as well as the challenges "the social" poses to private life and aesthetic experience. Its fears and denials that sociology might really explain human conduct allow it to address the fears about mechanical people that later commentators have described in 1950s movies.[42] The fortunately imperfect likeness between Bentonians and machines, between persons and the roles into which they fit, takes its own science-fictional turn in Jarrell's last chapter.[43] The narrator has been conversing with John Whittaker, the son of Flo and Jerrold, "who has read science-fiction since he was seven" (271). John asks, apropos of all the adults at Benton,

"Haven't you noticed how they talk just the same, and dress just alike, and read the same books, and—and leave the same day and come back the same day? And I've never talked to a one of them that didn't say to me, 'What grade are you in this year?' And do you know why?"

"Why?"

"They're androids."

I too had read science-fiction, and I knew that androids are synthetic human beings, robots who look just like you and me. I laughed delightedly, but said: "You're kidding me." He laughed too, and said, "Yes. When I was younger I believed it, though. It explained a lot of things to me."

(271–272)

The specialized critics, institutional poets, and utilitarian educators in Jarrell's essays all seem depressingly close to machines, their function divided between the public and the professional. Being not quite predictable, not quite programmable, the people of Benton seem to a reader of science fiction not quite androids. It becomes Jarrell's task, in the last scene of the novel, to drive home that *not quite*, to demonstrate for good the interior life of some nearly robotic Bentonian. As we might expect, that demonstration comes through a work of art.

Jarrell's narrator has mocked Benton's sculpture teacher, Sona Rasmussen, and her theories of art throughout the novel. In its final pages, after an absurd collegiate social event called "Art Night," the narrator encounters Rasmussen's newest work, made from a railroad tie:

"He's the East Wind," Miss Rasmussen said. She was right: he was the East Wind. . . . I told Miss Rasmussen over and over again what a wonderful statue it was; my shame at having misjudged her so—for to me she not only had looked like, but also had been, a potato bug . . . made me more voluble than I should otherwise have been. . . . She talked to me about the statue for a while, and I saw, not in dismay but in awe, that to appreciate what she said you still would have had to be an imbecile: she said about the East Wind exactly what she had always said about those welded root-systems of alfalfa plants that the storeroom of the studio was full of. . . . As long as her work had been bad she had been a visible fool, and now that her work was good she had disappeared into it. This was an unjust fate; and yet she wouldn't have thought it unjust, I didn't think it unjust—I would have vanished willingly into the words of the East Wind.

(275–276)

Recall here that the art Jarrell exalts most, from Frost's real poetry to Irene's fictive singing, gives importance to a particular human being. This sculpture, which the narrator calls not a sculpture but a *statue*, fits that paradigm entirely.

The version of aesthetic experience at the end of *Pictures* thus gives an ethical dimension and an emotional weight to often-caricatured New Critical theories of impersonality. Here, again, Jarrell seems to enact a hypothesis Allen Grossman describes. For Grossman "poetic reading . . . is a case of the inscription of the value of the person . . . the willing of the presence of a person." He adds that "the possibility of the assertion of the presence of the person is established only if the natural author of the poem, the author in history," can be distinguished from the person in the poem: "*No merely natural person is perceptible*" (344; italics in original). For Sona Rasmussen's East Wind, the work as manifestation of a person, to a particular, responsive, viewer or reader, can and should occlude the circumstances, institutions, and "natural persons" through which the work came into being. Sona's disappearance into her East Wind is just the same as Jarrell's recognition of personhood *in* the East Wind and, by extension, in Sona herself. This recognition takes place when and because he looks at the sculpture and not at Sona, nor at her aesthetic theories, nor at Benton itself.

Such contemplation is what Jarrell's critical essays promote and what "the social" by definition threatens. To acknowledge the (fictive) person manifest in the East Wind, the passage suggests, after knowing Sona Rasmussen, is to contemplate Guillory's "remainder," the part of a work not predictable from any theory of making, knowledge of the maker, or knowledge about the potential audience. "Criticism's dependence on institutions," Altieri reminds us, "does not entail devotion to analyzing those dependencies" (*Canons* 44). Jarrell, in *Pictures* as in his reviews and essays, indeed analyzes institutions—but he does so mostly in order to help readers see past those institutions into the persons imagined in works of art. In doing so Jarrell suggests that readers and critics (even academic critics) can examine art with goals neither public nor professional, goals derived instead from personal and unpredictable reactions to individual works.

John Burt has described recognitions of personhood as they emerge from persuasion: "if we take anyone seriously," Burt writes, "we recognize in that person the power to become" (14). To learn to see or hear art is to learn to recognize persons in a certain way: it is "to become," to be changed by them. If the narrator's discovery of the East Wind is one instance of such change, another is his discovery, thanks to the youthful character, Constance, of twelve-tone music he once dismissed: "so far as the *Lyric Suite* is concerned, we had been foolish and young and Constance old and clever; and we were grateful to her for that best of gifts, a change in one's own self" (151). Such changes, which also prove that one *has* a self to change, are the sort Jarrell's critical essays seek to produce; "institutions," "professions," and "the social" are finally names for what blocks their way.

Jarrell's last prose forays into social criticism were his most overt and his least thoughtful. While he continued to write about literature, after 1955 he became more concerned about the mass media, which he dubbed the Medium: "The Medium is half life and half art, and competes with both life and art. It spoils its audience for both; spoils both for its audience" (*SH* 81). This composite Medium attacked in Jarrell's late essays encompasses celebrities and photo-heavy magazines, television programs of all sorts, popular music, and especially advertising. Though it appears to exempt escapist genre fiction, it certainly includes the popular fiction Jarrell dubbed "Instant Literature: the words are short, easy, instantly recognizable words, the thoughts are easy, familiar, instantly recognizable thoughts" (*KA* 295). This Medium destroys the individuated tastes, and thus the deeper individuality, real art nourishes and preserves; instead it supposedly makes us less sensitive, more passive, and more alike. "The Medium shows its people what life is, what people are, and its people believe it: expect people to be that, try themselves to be that . . . and if what you see in *Life* is different from what you see in life, which of the two are you to believe?" (*SH* 78).

Jarrell announced his campaign against popular culture in a 1958 speech at the National Book Awards and carried it out in the essays of *A Sad Heart at the Supermarket* (1962). In doing so he was far from alone: his stylishly presented theses against "the Medium" continue arguments against "mass culture" and the mass media advanced before the Second World War by (among others) Wordsworth, Arnold, Eliot, Adorno, Lionel Trilling, and Dwight Macdonald. Late-fifties and early-sixties intellectuals found it hard to avoid "the mass culture debate" (as two anthologies named it); Karl Shapiro recalled that "Jarrell's generation, my generation, inherited the question of Culture—Mass Culture versus True Culture. It is our *pons asinorum* and we all had to cross it" (*RJ* 206).[44]

The critiques of advertising, pop music, and television in *A Sad Heart* rely explicitly on the psychoanalyst and social critic Ernest van den Haag, who saw in the rise of "mass culture" the end of individuality. According to van den Haag, "Producers and consumers [of mass-produced cultural objects] go through the mass production mill to come out homogenized and de-characterized"; in a passage Jarrell liked to quote, "the production of standardized things by persons demands also the production of standardized persons" (*MC* 513). Those arguments seem to emerge from the rule that governed Jarrell's earlier prose: *advocate whatever might hinder "the social"*—whatever might mitigate the taste of "this age in which each is like his sibling" and in which everything must have a use (*Third* 71). Such a rule stands behind his defenses of taste as such, his defense of privacy, his interest in nineteenth-century education, his devotion to folktales and to the folk culture of the past, even his attraction to the pure and nonconformist escapes provided by science fiction and by sports.

The same confidence in his own emotive responses that energizes Jarrell's literary criticism can make his vivid essays about mass culture seem, now, insensitive, dated, or shallow. Rather than attacking particular aspects of institutions, mistaken ideas about professions and disciplines, or counterproductive approaches to reading and teaching, these essays attack whole sectors of culture, as if nothing good could ever come from them. Rejecting so many popular cultural forms, Jarrell also gave up a powerful argument he might have used (one Leslie Fiedler *did* use) in defending poems, novels, and plays from professionalization: if we seek aesthetic experience that *cannot* become cultural capital, wouldn't comic books make a good place to look?

Jarrell's late attacks on mass culture matter, however, because they are intertwined with his earlier thoughts on other parts of society. They matter, as well, for the poems they helped him write. Relations between the poems and the late essays emerge in his notebooks, where some pages read, in part:

The permissive society: you may do anything [you please] as long as it's what we all do [pleases us all]. (Jarrell's brackets)

38–22–38 MEASUREMENT NUMBERS

STEAK—THE PLATONIC IDEAL

Entertainers as ideal—and politicians more like entertainers—people with private lives that are themselves public lives—our ideals don't have private lives—those too are an exhibit

Fabian—the entertainer—ideal as your own reflection in the mirror—somebody who identifies himself with you rather than reverse—you breaking the bank at Monte Carlo, without exceptional qualities to make identification difficult; Old surviving movie stars so much more individual, Rock Hudson, Tab Hunter etc. seem as composite photograph, invented stat. norms, as names—not only do you confuse, you feel the confusion doesn't matter.

(Berg Collection)[45]

Some of the poems linked to Jarrell's mass-culture critique (notably "Next Day") entered anthologies. Others, such as "The Wild Birds," remain nearly unknown. In that poem "our" complicity with advertisements, our comfort in the world, represents our deeper willingness to tolerate what we are given, our inability to imagine change. The poem breaks cleanly into two halves. The first, which examines the comforts the Medium offers, breaks up into easily parsed short lines:

> In the clear atmosphere
> Of our wishes, of our interests, the advertisers
> Of the commodities of their and our
> Existence express their clear interests, the clear
> Wishes, clearly, year after year.
> What they say, as they say,
> Is in our interest, in theirs . . .
>
> (CP 486–87)

The relentless abstractions of these opening sentences suggest the abstract, general "interests" of the advertisers, who seem to rob us of particularities. The advertisements are always "darkly there" for all of us because they have nothing to do with the (unique) truths that distinguish us from one another: their satisfactions remain the same from place to place, "year after year"—"Regardless of life, regardless of death, / Regardless."

The rest of the poem introduces the advertisers' opposites, the "wild birds" of the title, who come to us "from the atmosphere, dream-cleared, dream-darkened, / In which they live their dark lives." These "others" must represent both genuine art and truth, since they "call death death, life life, / The unendurable what we endure"; but what can they offer that advertisements cannot? These "wild birds" become at last

> Those who beat all night at our bars, and drop at morning
> Into our tame, stained beaks, the poison berry—
> O dark companions,
> You bring us the truth of love: the caged bird loves its bars.
>
> (CP 487)

From one perspective, the wild birds' true art offers us cognitive and affective freedom, a chance to learn and to be surprised. But this freedom can also look like death, because we have accustomed ourselves to the ads' promises of caged happiness. The caged birds—as the analogy works itself out—are not advertisers but us, their audience: the choice art offers us—the escape from the cage—may destroy the selves we know as ours. In *Pictures* and in Jarrell's essays art brings change, change growth, and both imply pleasure. This poem prompted by the pleasure of advertising confronts another hypothesis: what if the "change" art offers will ruin our lives? The poem draws on Jarrell's other obsessions—on his interest in Rilkean abstractions, on his late desire to try out wildly varying line lengths, and Freud's idea of the death wish. At the same time the poem could not exist had Jarrell not written *A Sad Heart*.

This chapter has examined the concerns—often thoughtful, sometimes merely reflexive—about conformity, about institutional systems and roles, and latterly about the rise of "mass culture" that informed Jarrell's most characteristic prose and some of his best poems. The same concerns have occupied some psychoanalysts. Christopher Bollas, for example, diagnoses in some contemporary patients a "particular drive to be normal, one that is typified by the numbing and eventual erasure of subjectivity in favor of a self that is conceived as a material object among other man-made products in the object world" (135). In one of Bollas's examples, a "female patient wanders from one store to another. . . . She might find herself in a supermarket for an hour or more, not because she is in particular need of any food or other items but because the material aesthetic of the supermarket, resplendent with its vegetables, cereals, and canned goods, is soothing" (139). The patient moves, we might say, joylessly from Cheer to Joy, from Joy to All.

Devised in the early 1980s, Bollas's category of "normosis" would not have been available to Jarrell. Its surprising congruence with his work shows instead that Jarrell's cultural and historical interests cannot be fully separated from his own engagements with psychoanalysis. Jarrell made a conscious study of psychoanalysis and of other branches and kinds of psychology; these modes of thought ramify throughout Jarrell's work and it is to them that chapter 3 will turn.

Chapter 3

PSYCHOLOGY AND PSYCHOANALYSIS

It has become commonplace to claim that mid-century literature owed much to Freud. The social theorist Eli Zaretsky explains that "For many [fifties intellectuals] Freud was at the center of [an] antirationalizing return to the personal" ("Charisma" 347).[1] Helen Vendler suggests that "the most inclusive rubric, perhaps" for "the lyric poetry written in America immediately after World War II is 'Freudian lyric' " (*Given* 31). Alan Williamson calls Jarrell, rightly, "the most consciously psychoanalytic even of the poets of the 'confessional' generation" ("Märchen" 283). Jarrell's interests in psychoanalysis differed from those of his poetic contemporaries (Lowell, Berryman, Bishop, Schwartz) not just in degree but in kind. These interests can help reveal his poetic powers; the poems, in turn, anticipate recent directions for psychoanalytic thought.

Where other professions and disciplines seemed to him to threaten private life, Jarrell found in psychology, and especially in psychoanalysis, ideas that inform his interpersonal style. Jarrell's handwritten notes for a talk about his own poems include the directions, "Gestalt psychology for form of art, Freud for content (and form as well)"; his manuscripts include attempts at very technical psychoanalytic criticism (UNC-Greensboro).[2] He later told an interviewer, "I would rather be wrong with Freud than right with most other people" ("Interview" 10).[3] Nancy Chodorow writes that psychoanalysis shows how selfhood, while always shaped by culture, "is equally shaped and constituted from inner life" (*Power* 5). This process finds examples and forms in Jarrell's poems, which rely on concepts of the unconscious; on gestalt theories of perception; on the pre-oedipal dyad of baby and mother; on Freudian eros and thanatos; and especially on dream work. If some of his poems rely on familiar models of pre-oedipal and oedipal sexuality, others anticipate feminist revisions of Freud, focusing on transference and the analytic process to depict their interpersonally needy selves.

Of Jarrell's many uses of psychoanalysis, the earliest—and the easiest to spot—are his interest in the unconscious and in the death wish. Jarrell's critical prose likes to insist on unconscious desires, not (as in Freud) as motives to artistic creation but as the chief sources of literary value.[4] His first long essay on Auden, published in 1941, asks, "How conscious, rational, controlled is poetry? can poetry afford to be?" Jarrell answered (alluding to Wordsworth), "The sources of poetry—which I, like you, don't know much about, except that they are delicate and inexplicable, and open or close for no reason we can see—are not merely checked, but dried up, by too rigorous supervision" (*Third* 148–149). Jarrell's critiques of the later Auden argue repeatedly that Auden has moved too far from the unconscious roots of his best, and of all the best, poetry.[5] The argument grows explicit in unpublished lectures:

> Many of the early poems give the reader the impression that they have been produced by Auden's whole being, are as much unconscious as conscious. . . . Wherever we look, from the *Iliad* to [Thomas Hardy's] "During Wind and Rain," we can see that the rational intelligence guides and selects, but that it does not produce and impose: we make our poetry, but we make it what we can, not what we wish.
>
> (Berg Collection)[6]

During Jarrell's student days, he spent a month on a South Carolina island with Hanns Sachs, "Freud's friend and disciple" (as Jarrell called him), who edited the psychoanalytic journal *American Imago*; Sachs later became a model for Gottfried Rosenbaum in *Pictures* (*Letters* 392). Jarrell's ideas about the unconscious revise ideas in Sachs' 1942 book *The Creative Unconscious*, much of which appeared in psychoanalytic journals during the late thirties. "The Unconscious" for Sachs, as for Freud, "underl[ies] dreams, daydreams, and poetic creation; but it works in a different way with each of them" (13). Sachs elaborates on Freud's explanation (from "Creative Writers and Daydreaming") of why "high art" seems to avoid direct wish fulfillment: it conceals traces of unconscious wishes more thoroughly than popular art can. This concealment, for Sachs, proves that the desires behind works of high art must be our deepest and most hidden.

This argument that the best art retains the deepest unconscious traces became in Jarrell's criticism an argument that the best art has to leave those traces visible: it must address a reader's own unconscious. Inexplicable, noncognitive responses are the best and highest responses (he sometimes implies). They are, at least, not *instrumentalizing* responses— they do not serve any visible, external end. The opposite of a psychoanalytic poetics would thus be for Jarrell a rhetoric, a way of consciously using poems to get people to *do* something, as Auden did in "Spain 1937":

> *The inevitable increase in the chances of death* sounds like an insurance company's remark on the change in the climate, not a *bit* like "You've got a good chance of getting killed if you enlist with the Loyalists." . . . How much better off Auden would have been if he'd said he-knew-not-quite-what to an audience that couldn't quite make out what he meant.
>
> (Berg Collection; underscore in original)

Jarrell stuck with this position for as long as he kept reviewing poetry. For all the merit of *The Shield of Achilles*, he decided in 1955, Auden would never write "quite so well as he was writing at the beginning of the thirties. . . . When old men, dying in their beds, mumble something unintelligible to the nurse, it is some of those lines that they will be repeating" (KA 230).

Jarrell's later judgments of other authors also made the detectable presence of the unconscious one, even *the*, source of value in poetry. "Poems begin in the unconscious," he declared in 1956 (KA 268). In writing about his own poem "The Woman at the Washington Zoo," Jarrell explains,

> I tried to give a fairly good idea of the objective process of writing the poem. You may say, "But isn't a poem a kind of subjective process, like a dream? Doesn't it come out of unconscious wishes of yours, childhood memories, parts of your own private emotional life?" It certainly does: part of them I don't know about and the rest I didn't write about. . . . If after reading this essay the reader should say: "You did all that you could to the things, but the things just came," he would feel about it as I do.
>
> (KA 319)

The general idea that real poetry, or good art, had to draw on "the unconscious" obviously leaves room for many programs, depending on what the unconscious is and what it wants. In poems of the thirties and forties, writing out of the unconscious often meant writing about the death wish, the thanatos that emerged in *Beyond the Pleasure Principle* and came to prominence in Freud's later work. When Jarrell's earliest poems are more than simply derivative (of

Auden), it is often because they contain arguments about thanatos. "The Refugees" (1942) sticks closely to current events until its last stanza:

> What else are their lives but a journey to the vacant
>   Satisfaction of death? And the mask
>   They wear tonight through their waste
> Is death's rehearsal. Is it really extravagant
>   To read in their faces: What is there that we possessed
>   That we were unwilling to trade for this?

(CP 370–371)

A never-completed poem about Amy Breyer's work in pediatric intensive care (entitled in drafts "A 12 Year Old" and "An Intern in Pediatrics") decides that "Our rejection of the world, "the wish for death," is "Not really a wish, only the absurd / And touching response of our unhappiness, our helplessness" (Berg Collection.

Sachs had argued that true art must acknowledge "the influence of the death instinct" (238). Freud's own thanatos, "the assumption of the existence of an instinct of death or destruction," makes its most famous appearance in *Civilization and Its Discontents* (1929–30), where it turns outward and becomes aggression (21:119). But the death instincts Jarrell prefers to depict are those in Freud's essays of the teens and twenties, which sometimes wonder if "the aim of all life is death" (18:38). As several critics have noticed, Jarrell could follow Freud in identifying a wish to die with an "oceanic feeling" and a return to the womb.[7] One of the aphorisms in the early "Sayings of the Bloksberg *Post*" reads, "Some of us want to return to the womb and some of us want to be God; but everybody wants to die" (4). According to "The Difficult Resolution" (1941), all of us

> learn to think,
> "My wish unsatisfied, my need unknown;
> My intent, and the world's, incommensurable;
> And happiness, if there is happiness, inaccessible—
> Let me sleep, let me perish!" In the warm darkness
> The sleeper whispers at last: "The grave is my mother."[8]

(CP 399)

Later notes on Eliot continue the interest in thanatos, asking "Freud? What is it that is the satisfaction of the oldest wish of all, the really archaic (?) sleep, then death; those satisfy it" (Berg Collection).[9]

In the fifties and sixties, Jarrell's interest in depicting a putative death wish became an interest in potential absorption into a mother, or into an inescapable, enveloping family. This way of thinking derives from Melanie Klein, for whom, in Joseph Smith's summary, "the ultimate desires . . . are the desire for remerger with the mother, on the one hand, and the desire for individuation and separateness, on the other. . . . Whatever goes in the direction of remerger with the mother goes in the direction of regressive loss of subjecthood; whatever goes in the direction of separateness portends finitude and death" (114). As Alan Williamson has demonstrated, this is how *some* of Jarrell's later poems proceed. The virtually suicidal protagonists of poems such as "Sleeping Beauty: Variation on the Prince" and "Windows" wish to enter a pair bond or a family unit so tight that it leaves them neither the need nor the possibility for self-consciousness. Reunion with the ideal mother becomes, in these poems, a source of dread but also a goal.[10]

Other poems seek new, more compact forms appropriate to *thanatos*. One such poem is "A Prayer at Morning," a moving, uncanny lyric whose year of composition remains unknown:

Cold, slow, silent, but returning after so many hours.
The sight of something outside me, the day is breaking.
May salt, this one day, be sharp upon my tongue;
May I sleep, this one night, without waking.

(CP 490)

The poet seems to pray at once for an exciting ("sharp") life and for permanent relief from it. Its single quatrain holds ideas about the engulfing, comforting womb, with its salt water, and contrasting ideas about adventure and fortitude. Does the last line ask for relief from insomnia or for irreversible unconsciousness? Its strikingly counterpointed wish for tranquility may or may not be a wish for death.

Jarrell's interest in the death wish found common ground with his interest in child psychology. The much-glossed "A Quilt-Pattern" explores the Oedipal dreams, fears and fantasies of a sick American child: he dreams of a threatening gingerbread house, like the one in *Hansel and Gretel*, and realizes (though he cannot quite admit it) that the house tastes like his mother.[11] Jarrell's most formally satisfying poem about Freudian versions of children's dreams is not "A Quilt Pattern," but "A Hunt in the Black Forest," published (as "The King's Hunt") in 1948 and revised much later for *The Lost World*.[12] "A Hunt in the Black Forest" begins with a frightened boy curled up in bed. He has been reading Grimms' tales, or else they have been read to him:

After the door shuts and the footsteps die,
He calls out: "Mother?"
The wind roars in the leaves: his cold hands, curled
Within his curled, cold body, his blurred head
Are warmed and tremble; and the red leaves flow
Like cells across the spectral, veined
Whorled darkness of his vision.

(CP 319)

Like *The Taming of the Shrew,* "A Hunt in the Black Forest" has a prologue but no epilogue— the rest of the poem constitutes the boy's dream. In the dream a hunter—the king in disguise—finds a forest cottage whose residents are a mute and a dwarf. The mute has had his tongue cut out as punishment for some crime and has been branded with a crown to show it. The king asks for food and "ladles from the pot / Into a wooden bowl" the mute's "shining stew." Meanwhile "the mute / Counts spoonfuls on his fingers. Come to ten, / The last finger, he laughs out in joy"; the stew is poisoned or magicked and kills the king quickly and painfully. By this time the mute has gone outdoors in order to help the dwarf see the dead king:

A little voice
Says, "Let *me!* Let *me!*" The mute
Puts his arms around the dwarf and raises him.

The pane is clouded with their soft slow breaths,
The mute's arms tire; but they gaze on and on,
Like children watching something wrong.
Their blurred faces, caught up in one wish,
Are blurred into one face: a child's set face.

What is impressive about "A Hunt in the Black Forest" (besides the accomplished fluency of its narration) is how thoroughly, comprehensively, even reductively Freudian and oedipal Jarrell has managed to make it. For Sister Bernetta Quinn, "The murder in the dream ... is equivalent to the child's passionate wish to destroy some part of the grown-up world" (RJ 148). To Suzanne Ferguson the poem "represents the child's desire for revenge on authority" and the dwarf and the mute are the child's good and bad sides (*Poetry* 198). If anything both critics understate the oedipal allegory.[13] The father appears as a king, the mother as a house and a nourishing pot. The talking dwarf (the child's conscious mind; his ego; his immature phallus) cannot get into the house (mother), where food (nurture, sex) is kept in a fiery pot, in order to take revenge on the king (father), who feeds from the pot with his ladle. The mute (the child's unconscious or his id) feels the wound the father has inflicted and enacts a long-sought revenge. (The mark of the crown, and the loss of the tongue, suggest that the mute is a secret heir to the throne; he is in some sense the king's son.) When the mute can count to ten (when the child grows old enough), his father dies. After the murder of the father, the parts of the child can come together: watching the dead father/king they have the same face (since they are really the same person). Moreover the pair of them look "like children watching something wrong"; the ending suggests Freud's myth from *Totem and Taboo* about the origin of culture in a plot by brothers against a father.

"A Hunt" comprehends so many aspects of classical Freudianism that it may seem predictable to contemporary readers (though Bruno Bettelheim's *The Uses of Enchantment*, which made popular in America the psychoanalytic interpretation of fairy tales, only appeared eleven years after Jarrell's death). The poem shows how thoroughly and programmatically Freudian Jarrell could be when he wanted to be: it authorizes us to read divergences and omissions in other psychoanalytic poems as *conscious* differences from Freudian accounts— if not quarrels with the founder, then attempts to explore other aspects of psychology and psychoanalysis.

We will return to Freud with other poems about dreams—few of them so unambiguous, or so strongly narrative, as "A Hunt." First, though, it will help to see how Jarrell used the experimental psychology he learned at Vanderbilt. A 1939 letter to Allen Tate explains: "Before I quit [psychology as a discipline] the psychology I was much the most interested in was Gestalt psychology, which is all mixed up with philosophy and very non-positivistic in attitude" (*Letters* 19). Known today for their research into perception, the gestalt psychologists (notably Wolfgang Köhler and Kurt Koffka) also undertook more abstract projects. Jarrell's adjective "antipositivistic" probably refers to Köhler's 1938 *The Place of Value in a World of Facts*. Köhler's volume sets out to show, in secular, scientific terms, the reality of the self: "the 'subjective' part of the phenomenal field, including the emotional life, the kinaesthetic and the visual components of the self, represents under normal conditions a unit which as such has commerce with the 'objective' world" (354). Köhler aimed to resolve the supposed conflict between scientific and subjective, or phenomenological, views of human life. "It is a bad habit," Köhler concluded, "to believe that in the nature of the psychophysical problem there is contained a threat to the characteristics of our mental processes" (410). Whenever—as in "The School of Summer"—Jarrell finds himself showing (as if to scientists) that subjective experience is not nothing, or that "the emotional life" can affect the outside world, he is drawing on what he learned from gestalt psychologists.[14]

Jarrell also used Köhler's and Koffka's work on perception. He remarked in 1953, reviewing Malraux's *The Voices of Silence*, "Of the quasi-aesthetic organization of visual perception itself—an organization that is at the root of aesthetic organization—Malraux is ignorant: for him Koffka, Köhler, Gombrich and the rest might never have existed" (*KA* 187). In his 1942 lecture "Levels and Opposites," Jarrell had explained:

> Figure and ground, all the perceptual forces which fight to produce the strongest organization, the best possible gestalt out of the weaker organizations of the actual stimuli, should remind anyone of the structural forces that operate in poetry. (Koffka's *Principles of Gestalt Psychology* is indispensable reading for anyone interested in the organization of poetry.)
>
> (700)

The cumulative perception Jarrell describes is explained in the 1935 textbook he recommends. The same textbook shows how gestalt rules apply to aural and temporal art forms, like music (or, by extension, poetry):

> A melody is a whole organized in time. . . . The earlier notes of the melody have an effect upon the later ones, because they have started a process which demands a definite continuation. A melody, a rhythm, a spoken sentence, are not analogous to beads on a string . . . but they are continuous processes . . . very soon these events have their own shape, which demands a proper continuation.
>
> (437)

Koffka's law of "good continuation" in turn generates his "law of reproduction," by which "a part of a trace tends to establish the whole process that gave rise to the whole trace" (568). ("CDE," for example, brings to mind the rest of the alphabet, especially "AB" and "FGH.") These ideas of traces, unities, and completions may have helped Jarrell develop his speechlike style, which so often gives suggestions, fragments, and parts of utterances, leaving us to infer their proper completion. Koffka's perceptual laws even anticipate Jarrell's later themes of autobiographical memory, since those laws may apply to our own pasts (which also come to us in perceptual "traces") as much as they do to a symphony or a drawing.

Gestalt terms and Freudian theories together gave Jarrell a critical vocabulary in which he could discuss at once perception and desire, form and feeling, as he did in the essays on Auden: "In Auden's work the elements of *anxiety, guilt, isolation, sexuality* and *authority* make up a true Gestalt, a connected and meaningful whole" (*Third* 162). Auden's pairings of abstract adjective with concrete noun "depend on . . . the fact that the context of the poem (*ground* in relation to the expression's *figure*) is still concrete" (*Third* 136). Köhler and Freud join hands in an essay on Robert Graves: "living with" a particular poem by Graves "is like being haunted by a Gestalt diagram, changing from figure to ground, ground to figure, there in the silent darkness, until we get up and turn on the light and look at it, and go back to sleep with it ringing—high, hollow, sinister, yet somehow lyric and living—in our dream-enlarged ears" (*Third* 85–86). Here as elsewhere Jarrell merges gestalt terms with dreams; together, he suggests, they can explain both the form of a poem and the wishes and motives the poem contains.

"The originality of *The Interpretation of Dreams*," John Hollander has written, "lay not so much in its . . . enabling of criticism to treat poems as if they were as personal . . . as dreams—but in its discovery that dreams were as powerfully and obsessively organized, and as serious in their mimesis, as poems" (*Work* 201). Neither Jarrell nor Freud was the first to liken dreams and poems.[15] But the dream analogy did far more work, and more kinds of work, for Jarrell than for most other poets, in part because his gestalt psychology let him think about the kind of formal unity dreams could attain, and in part because his other psychological and psychoanalytic interests lent themselves well to oneiric modes.[16] Jarrell wrote to Peter Taylor in 1958 that he had "plans for a book showing dreams and poems have same structure, roots, etc" (Collection of Mary Jarrell). Jarrellian characters who must choose between the privacies of sleep and dreaming and the harsh, impersonal world of the army (or even of the consumer) face exactly the choice between isolation and social immersion to which Jarrell's interpersonal style reacts and from which it seeks to imagine a refuge.[17]

The contrast between dream and the world we wake to, the wish we construct and the world that refutes the wish, gave many of Jarrell's poems their emotional centers. The tormented insomniac in the posthumously published "City, City!" is invited to "Still, dream," since "all these somethings" in the world he wakes to "add to nothing" (*CP* 475). The Rilkean speaker of another late unpublished poem, "Dreams," wants to join the beloved he calls "sister" in a mutual dream (*CP* 477). And the wry, pathetic, "one-armed, one-legged and one-headed" veteran in "Terms," waiting for his pension checks and killing time in his yard, finds that his dreams express both his wish for a new life and his wish to die. He wakes from an extravagant dream in which he is crucified and resurrected, sees "the toaster / on its rack over the waffle-iron," and tells himself " 'It's all a dream . . . I am a grave dreaming / That it is a living man' " (*CP* 210–211).

To borrow another distinction from Hollander, Jarrell's poetry appropriates dreams both as trope and as scheme.[18] Sometimes the poems have the sorts of meanings we find in dreams (encapsulating secret wishes, for example, or manifesting the child within the adult). Sometimes the poems try to work structurally and perceptually as dreams do (making abstractions concrete, jumping among scenes, perspectives, and people, or blurring them together).[19] And sometimes, as in "Terms," one poem uses dreams in all these ways. Dream as trope and dream as scheme both drive Jarrell's most famous poem, "The Death of the Ball Turret Gunner":

> From my mother's sleep I fell into the State,
> And I hunched in its belly till my wet fur froze.
> Six miles from earth, loosed from its dream of life,
> I woke to black flak and the nightmare fighters.
> When I died they washed me out of the turret with a hose.

> (CP 144)

Barrels of printer's ink have been used on this poem, and thousands of undergraduates have memorized it. Its popularity owes something to the violence that makes it memorable, something to its verbal economy (not usually one of Jarrell's special strengths), something to the *unheimlich* tone of its posthumous speaker, and something to its ease of interpretation: it can be quickly decoded to yield many symbols, "meanings," and "themes."[20] The poem describes the fracture under fire of "a plexiglass sphere set into the belly of a B-17 or B-24," as Jarrell's note put it (*CP* 8). It also describes the familiar concept of birth trauma (elaborated by Freud's former ally Otto Rank).[21] "The Death of the Ball Turret Gunner" takes literally two further dicta from the *Interpretation of Dreams* the first, that the dream's condensation produces "no more than *fragments* of reproductions (of waking experience)", the second that "dreaming is on the whole an example of regression to the dreamer's earliest condition," a return not only to the child's state but to the infant's (54, 587; italics in original).[22]

The poem's genuine cruxes—matters of contradictory or unresolvable literal meanings rather than of polyvalent symbols—occur where it invokes oneiric processes. "Dream of life" (as Leven Dawson notes) is a phrase from Shelley's "Adonais" (*CE* 238). Is the gunner's "dream of life" a Shelleyan flight to pantheistic peace? Is it a dream of civilian life? Or does he dream of life in the womb, "loosed" from it to wake and die in the bomber? Are the "nightmare fighters" monsters, persons, or the fighter escorts ("little friends") that accompany bombers? Do they fight against nightmares, emerge from, or resemble them? The poem becomes at once an attempt to encapsulate some basic wishes dreams can reprise and an attempt to replicate in a very short poem the particular overdetermination and unresolvable ambiguities we take to characterize both dreams and accounts of them.[23]

If (like a Freudian dream) the poem conflates and equates symbolic fragments of experience, it also conflates and equates disparate ways of regarding and marking time.[24] We can imagine minutes of aerial combat and minutes of hosing out afterwards; bad dreams that might last all night; the gestation and birth, or abortion, of a fetus (nine months or less); the gestation, birth, and death of a human being old enough to serve in a war; and even (if ontogeny recapitulates phylogeny) the (painful or futile) evolution of the human species. The poem's techniques of condensation and displacement allow it to contain all those time scales within what could be either an elegy or a description of a dream.

Dreams as schemes and as tropes inform many of Jarrell's war poems, among them his best known, his longest, and his most formally elegant. "A Field Hospital" keeps its three stanzas focused on a single wounded soldier:

He stirs, beginning to awake.
A kind of ache
Of knowing troubles his blind warmth; he moans,
And the high hammering drone
Of the first crossing fighters shakes
His sleep to pieces, rakes
The darkness with its skidding bursts, is done.
All that he has known

Floods in upon him . . .

(CP 199)

In the two eight-line stanzas that follow, the soldier remembers the dream he has had, receives an injection, and "then, alone, / He neither knows, remembers—but instead / Sleeps, comforted."[25] Describing a dream, the poem seeks formal, aural devices for the ambiguous status of dreamt experience in a half-awake dreamer. One such device is the intricate rhyme scheme: Jarrell's twenty-four lines use only three, loud, monosyllabic rhymes— *-ake, -own, -ead*—and restrict themselves further to two per stanza. The result is an unusually intense sense of one soldier's consciousness and a remarkably blurred, ambiguous view of the real states of his body and of the battlefield. "Blind warmth" sounds like a description of prenatal sleep. But this soldier with a bandage over his eyes may also be literally blind: he cannot know (yet), and so neither can we.

As with the ball-turret gunner, the bloody war constitutes both an unwelcome maturation and a recapitulation of birth trauma. Yet the middle of the poem explores not the womb but a peacetime memory. The guns overhead enter his dream as sounds of American hunters:

> "The great drake
> Flutters to the icy lake—
> The shotguns stammer in my head.
> I lie in my own bed,"
> He whispers, "dreaming"; and he thinks to wake.
> The old mistake.

For dangerous gunshots, the dreamer substitutes the familiar, comforting shots he heard at home; for air-to-ground fire from enemy airplanes, the dreamer substitutes ground-to-air shots that kill only wildfowl. The dream machinery negotiates between wish and fact, the place the dreamer wants to occupy and the sensory inputs around him, until the two collide (at the word "mistake"). The secondary elaboration, recasting the noise of the external world, has failed to keep the dreamer asleep: he will need pharmaceutical help instead.

Jarrell expanded his use of dreams in postwar poems that focused on children's experience. Mary Kinzie has written that Jarrell's "main business is dreamwork, which translates the experience of the childhood self into the language of the adult" (70). This combining or shuttling into and out of dream life delineates spaces of interiority, since it cannot take place in a social or external world. Such transitions govern "The Black Swan," one of Jarrell's most appealing poems about dreams and one of his most shapely. Its semantic and formal ambiguities mimic the operation of the dream work; they also help the poem embody concerns about loneliness and companionship. Here is the whole poem:

> When the swans turned my sister into a swan
>   I would go to the lake, at night, from milking:
> The sun would look out through the reeds like a swan,
>   A swan's red beak; and the beak would open
> And inside there was darkness, the stars and the moon.
>
> Out on the lake a girl would laugh.
>   "Sister, here is your porridge, sister,"

I would call; and the reeds would whisper,
    "Go to sleep, go to sleep, little swan."
My legs were all hard and webbed, and the silky

Hairs of my wings sank away like stars
    In the ripples that ran in and out of the reeds:
I heard through the lap and hiss of water
    Someone's "Sister . . . sister," far away on the shore,
And then as I opened my beak to answer

I heard my harsh laugh go out to the shore
    And saw—saw at last, swimming up from the green
Low mounds of the lake—the white stone swans:
    The white, named swans . . . "It is all a dream,"
I whispered, and reached from the down of the pallet

To the lap and hiss of the floor.
    And "Sleep, little sister," the swans all sang
From the moon and stars and frogs of the floor.
    But the swan my sister called "Sleep at last, little sister,"
And stroked all night, with a black wing, my wings.

                                             (CP 54)

The poem never leaves the girl's voice nor the girl's fantasy: we are even farther inside her consciousness than we were with the soldier of "A Field Hospital." The girl's food, house, and work— "porridge," a "pallet," "milking"—identify her with the villagers of Northern European fairy tales.[26] Attentive readers figure out that the girl's sister has died, and Jarrell's one-sentence note confirms that the "sister is buried under the white stones of the green churchyard" (*CP* 6). The "black swan" envisioned at the lake embodies the girl's fantasies that she can rejoin her sister, first by becoming a swan herself and then simply by refusing to wake from her dream.[27]

"The Black Swan" is not quite a fairy tale, but its narrator speaks with the voice of a fairy tale; it sounds almost as if a girl from a European folktale had walked into an analyst's office to narrate her dream. Yet the wish at the center of this intricate dream is not the programmatically oedipal wish of "A Hunt" nor the infantile merging of other poems. Instead it is a bereaved child's wish for intimate companionship. The great comfort the dream provides in its various manifestations, stanza by stanza, is not just that of bringing the dead sister back but that of bringing the two sisters into some relation where they can

care for each other. The speaker brings the sister/swan her porridge, then be-
comes a swan herself, and finally accepts comfort from the black-winged
swan.

The girl's dream thus fits a Freudian model of how dreams work without re-
stricting itself to an orthodox reading of what they ultimately mean. A dream is
the fulfillment of a wish but disguised and transformed, with abstractions turned
into symbols. When the dream threatens to become so implausible as to wake
the girl up, the secondary elaboration revises it in the direction of plausibility,
bringing the dreamer in from the "green mounds of the lake" to the house
where she lies on her pallet. In the second stanza the girl enters the swan's beak
and becomes a swan. But the dream obeys a sort of law of conservation of girls:
if the figure of a girl simply vanished, the dream would have to admit that a girl
had disappeared, letting death into a dream meant to keep it away. Jarrell's (that
is, the girl's, the dream work's) solution is to retain a girl in the poem but to
disidentify her with *this* girl, the "I" of the poem, who is now a swan. Thus the
personae in the poem seem to switch places:

> Out on the lake *a girl* would laugh.
>   "*Sister,* here is your porridge, sister,"
> I would call; and the reeds would whisper,
>   "Go to sleep, go to sleep, *little swan.*"
> *My* legs were all hard and webbed . . .

The girl wishes to join her sister: the wish is granted through a general blurring
of people with one another and with swans.

Unusual verbal effects bring those blurs about. The poem comprises many
interlaced patterns of repetition (sonic, grammatical, and imagistic), almost
none of them perfectly synchronized: a gap in one pattern is filled in smoothly
by others. Except for the first and (inevitably) the last, none of the stanza-ends
coincides with a sentence-end. Where repetitions in other poems give the effect
of conversation and interruption, these are arranged instead for an effect of
seamlessness, even perhaps of a rocking lullaby. Such effects grow more audible
the more one considers the rhythms: the poem begins in anapestic tetrameter,
ends in pentameter, and shuttles smoothly between the two meters throughout.
Even more important are repeated single words—*whisper, sister, wing, beak,
hiss, swan.* Their patterns approximate the chain-linking effects of terza rima, as
when "swan" and "shore" and "floor" recur in *aba* patterns.

Other repeated noun phrases weave together lines and stanzas. The reeds
"whisper, / 'Go to sleep, go to sleep' "; "the lap and hiss of water" reappears two
stanzas later as "the lap and hiss of the floor." Swans sing "Sleep, little sister";

two lines later "the swan my sister called 'Sleep at last, little sister,' / And stroked all night, with a black wing, my wings." These beautiful concluding lines also mark the first place in the poem where sister swan and speaker swan actually touch. The process of rereading "The Black Swan" is a process of discovering these and other repetitions, of finding patterns in what sounds at first like smooth improvisation, of taking apart narratives about metamorphosis, of finding secret needs in a naive and sympathetic speaker's account of irrational action. In other words, reading this poem is like interpreting dreams.

The later dream poem "Field and Forest" brings Jarrell's thinking about psychoanalysis together with his thought about social roles and professions.[28] Jarrell explained in a letter to Sister Bernetta Quinn that the poem is "about the unconscious and conscious in man—I use the fields to stand for the conscious and the forest to stand for the unconscious" (Berg Collection). A reader of Jarrell's essays might add that the fields are also professional "fields," "lines" of work that can harden into "ruts":

When you look down from the airplane you see lines,
Roads, ruts, braided into a net or web—
Where people go, what people do: the ways of life.

Heaven says to the farmer: "What's your field?"
And he answers: "Farming," with a field,
Or "Dairy-farming," with a herd of cows.

(CP 334)

"Dairy-farming" is a "field" in the sense that "Romanticism" or "crystallography" is a field: "Seen from on high / The fields have a terrible monotony." "Fields" in this sense had also turned up in *Pictures*, where President Robbins espoused a "Field Theory of Conversation": "He always found out what your field was . . . and then talked to you about it" (43).[29]

What makes us distinct from others who share our "fields" are the differing forms and wishes in each person's unconscious. The unconscious (since we all have one) thus both guarantees individuality and gives us our sturdiest form of human commonality: in the terms of the allegory,

A farmer is separated from a farmer
By what farmers have in common: forests,
Those dark things—what the fields were to begin with.
At night a fox comes out of the forest, eats his chickens.
At night the deer come out of the forest, eat his crops.

The unconscious (forest) harbors destructive impulses but also contains our childhood. The representative "farmer" can ignore or contain it, but cannot obliterate it:

> If he could he'd make farm out of all the forest,
> But it isn't worth it: some of it's marsh, some rocks,
> There are things there you couldn't get rid of
> With a bulldozer, even—not with dynamite.
> Besides, he likes it. He had a cave there, as a boy;
> He hunts there now. It's a waste of land,
> But it would be a waste of time, a waste of money,
> To make it into anything but what it is.

The unconscious, on this reading, not only differentiates people from one another and prevents us from becoming our professional roles; it is also the preserve of our past identities and the source of gratuity, impulse, play. And the "waste" here is exactly the "waste" invoked earlier by "A Girl in a Library," where "The soul has no assignments, neither cooks / Nor referees; it wastes its time" (CP 16).

"The unconscious" for the Jarrell of "Field and Forest" looks in fact very like a soul; it is what remains of the farmer when at night he removes, first his artificial accoutrements— clothes, "false teeth," "spectacles"—and then the physical and mental features we might otherwise think define him. At night, in bed,

> he's taken out his tongue: he doesn't talk.
> His arms and legs: at least, he doesn't move them.
> They are knotted together, curled up, like a child's.
> And after he has taken off the thoughts
> It has taken him his life to learn
> He takes off, last of all, the world.

(CP 335)

Jarrell here adapts some sentences of Freud's; Meredith Skura identifies these same sentences both as central to Freudian dream theory and as a barrier to theories of literature as dream. I quote Skura, who in turn quotes (and translates) Freud:

> The contrast between waking and dreaming, Freud says, is the contrast between our mature, civilized selves and our infantile selves. The

dreamer, Freud explains, removes his civilized extensions one by one, like a man taking out his false teeth and removing his eyeglasses before he goes to bed, and regresses to his infantile wishes and his infantile forms of expression, visual hallucinations and concrete thinking.[30]

(136)

Jarrell makes this passage describe not the dream work, exactly, nor the creation of a work of art but the service both dreams and (the right sorts of) art can perform for dreamers and for readers. Stripping off our "civilized extensions," reverting to the nighttime dark of the forest, dreams and (certain) art works can reveal the human subject as a subject. And if the unconscious is the feature that distinguishes our real selves from our mere social roles, and if "dreams are the royal road to the unconscious," then we can look forward in the rest of "Field and Forest" to a dream that tells us in general (paradoxically) what individuality is.

When you take off everything what's left? A wish,
A blind wish; and yet the wish isn't blind,
What the wish wants to see, it sees.

There in the middle of the forest is the cave
And there, curled up inside it, is the fox.

He stands looking at it.
Around him the fields are sleeping: the fields dream.
At night there are no more farmers, no more farms.
At night the fields dream, the fields *are* the forest.
The boy stands looking at the fox
As if, if he looked long enough—
                    he looks at it.
Or is it the fox that's looking at the boy?
The trees can't tell the two of them apart.

These final lines allegorize a metapsychology, one that animates all of Jarrell's style. "Who we are," the self distinct from social roles, (a) concerns hidden desire and its potential fulfillment; (b) emerges from childhood; and (c) seems relational—it involves being able to look at something that looks back at you. Jarrell may be remembering Frost's "The Most of It," whose intruding buck stands for the animate unknowable (338). Yet where Frost keeps his buck utterly alien, Jarrell makes the fox almost boylike, the boy almost foxlike: communication is neither insisted on nor ruled out. The fox boy the final lines create is a merger of identities, like the merger in "The Black Swan." This picture of "what the wish wants to see" is a picture of interchange, mutuality, as what the unconscious wants. It is also a picture of the unconscious as a boy old enough to explore a wood and not (though it might be better to say not *only*) as a murderous mute or an infant.

In "Field and Forest," then, adult desires emerge from a creative child who is a source of interest and individuality, not from the predictably oedipal child of "A Hunt" nor from the pre-oedipal (Kleinian) infant of other poems. "Inside" the professional with his instruments is a boy who wants mutuality, discovery, and play: not only is his destructiveness attenuated, but his *sexual* desire seems not to be there at all. We might say that this boy here is a boy of the latency phase; we might say that Jarrell softens the harsh truths of Freudian doctrine. But we might say instead that the poem, alternating anxiety and ease and combining sociological worries with notions of child development, has found a delicately credible version of childhood, dream life, and the unconscious, a version more open-ended and more attuned to other people than the version most frequent in Freud. The boy in "Field and Forest" has as much to do with Wordsworth as with Freud; he is the child described, within psychology, most fully by object-relations models.

This chapter has shown the special depth and breadth of Jarrell's interest in psychoanalysis; his special interest in perceptual psychology; and his various uses of dreams. Chapter 1 suggested that Jarrell's poems fit models of intersubjectivity drawn from object-relations theory. Yet Jarrell did not make frequent reference to object-relations theorists: some began writing only after his death. (Winnicott's foundational "Transitional Objects" paper only appeared in 1953.) One could maintain, with Alan Williamson, that Jarrell simply "intuited much that object-relations theory" would later grasp or that Jarrell's early life predisposed him to represent object loss (285).[31] But Jarrell's conscious involvement with psychoanalysis *can* provide a link to his intersubjective concerns. We can find this link in clinical practice—in the relations between analyst and patient and in the mutable bonds that develop between them. Jarrell could attend to these aspects because—unlike his peers—he considered psychoanalysis both from the position of the patient and from the position of the analyst.

Though many mid-century writers identified poetry with psychoanalysis, few identified personally, as Jarrell did, with psychoanalysts. Mary Jarrell recalls that "psychoanalysts *interested* Randall. We met about one a year wherever we were and got to know them from Cincinnati to San Diego to Amsterdam. . . . Many times he wished aloud he could *be* an analyst" (*Remembering* 33). "Poets, Critics and Readers" had instructed "real readers" to behave like psychoanalysts:

Freud talks of the "free-floating" or "evenly-hovering" attention with which the analyst must listen to the patient. Concentration, note-taking, listening with a set—a set of pigeonholes—makes it difficult or impossible for the analyst's unconscious to respond to the patient's; takes away from the analyst the possibility of learning from the patient what the analyst doesn't already know; takes away from him all those random guesses or intuitions or inspirations which come out of nowhere—and come, too, out of the truth of the patient's being. But this is quite as true of critics and the poems that are *their* patients.[32]

(*SH* 96)

Listening like a psychoanalyst—for Jarrell—means treating people humanely; listening to poems is identified with both.[33]

Jarrell's identification with analysts helps solve the recurrent problem of how to imagine the listener or putative interlocutor for those of his poems that are (or are like) dramatic monologues. Charlotte Beck distinguishes Jarrell's persona poems from the Browning monologue: they "are not, like Browning's, said aloud to a listener"; as "utterances of a mind looking inward," they instead "resemble Shakespearean soliloquies, wherein the speaker puts into words those unutterable truths he or she would tell no one" ("Personae" 69). Poems such as "Seele im Raum," "Next Day," "The Orient Express," "Hohensalzburg," and even "The Truth" imagine more precisely what their characters would say *if there were* some speech situation in which they could tell, were expected to tell—expected, even, to help someone else interpret—what Beck calls their "unutterable truths."

One such situation is that of psychoanalysis. Associating, remembering, and drawing fragmentary, swift conclusions, Jarrell's speakers seem to obey what psychoanalysts call the Fundamental Rule, by which analysands must speak all their thoughts. To whom do Jarrell's lonely people speak? If one answer is *to themselves* (since the poems work like soliloquies), other answers include *to their future selves* (who will understand them better), *to their past selves* (whose hopes they address), and finally *to an analyst*. Jarrell's poems imagine listeners who behave like psychoanalysts; these listeners are identified at once with the poet (who creates a character and transcribes his or her speech) and with the reader (who listens and interprets). Psychoanalysis thus becomes one name for "the realism which pursues 'unreal' experience" that Hammer finds in "Seele im Raum": where but in psychoanalysis would we expect to hear someone say, "Shall I make sense or shall I tell the truth? / Choose either—I cannot do both" ("Who" 404; *CP* 39).

The poems' imaginations of speaking and listening thus recall analysts' transcripts and case studies. "The written case-study," Carolyn Steedman explains, "allows . . . the dream, the wish or the fantasy of the past to shape current time, and treats them as evidence in their own right"—as we are encouraged to do in Jarrell's poems, from "90 North" on (*Landscape* 20–21). The tentativeness of Jarrell's mature style, with its hesitations and repetitions and deliberately vague passages, also finds analogues in what psychoanalysts do. The analyst, Roy Schafer writes, must "tolerate ambiguity or incomplete closure over extended periods of time . . . and bear and contain . . . experiences of helplessness, confusion and aloneness" (7).

Analysands' complaints can also be famously vague: Freud describes "a woman patient who introduced herself with these words: 'I have a sort of feeling as though I had injured or wanted to injure some living creature—a child?—no, more like a dog—as though I may have thrown it off a bridge, or something else'" (15:85). Two sorts of vagueness emerge in such a statement. One is a periphrastic approach to some eventually disclosed content. Another is vagueness about the content itself (which indicates its unconscious origins). Jarrell's mature style appropriates both sorts of vagueness. In "The One Who Was Different," a man attending a funeral decides,

> This is the sort of thing that could happen to anyone
> Except—
>   except—
>
> Just now, behind the not-yet-drawn
> Curtain (the curtain that in a moment will disclose
> The immediate family sitting there in chairs)
> I made out—off-stage looking on-stage,
> Black under a white hat from Best's—
> A pair of eyes. Too young to have learned yet
> What's seen and what's obscene, they look in eagerly
> For this secret that the grown-ups have, the secret
> That, shared, makes one a grown-up.
> They look without sympathy or empathy,
> With interest.
>
>   Without me.
>
> It is as if in a moment,
> In the twinkling of an eye,
> I were old enough to have made up my mind
> What not to look at, ever . . .

(CP 317–318)

"What not to look at" (what the hidden child wants to see) is the corpse that waits at the end of every life: the rambling, associating speaker uses the vagueness of analytic speech to testify to his own difficulties in comprehending his own adulthood and death. (Richard Flynn notes that drafts read "except—except Randall" [*Lost* 125].) These difficulties emerge through the poem's anxious pauses. Readers are asked to participate in a sort of dialogue, to solve the riddles the speaker's evasions present.

What goes on in the analytic hour thus resembles, *in its manner of proceeding*, what we hear in a Jarrell poem, whether or not the poem seems psychoanalytic in content. Meredith Skura has likened the analytic process to literary interpretation in general: a "study of the minute changes which take place during the analytic hour," she writes, "can not only suggest new meanings for texts but can also suggest how *any* meaning is created within and between people" (202). Skura offers prescriptions for critics, not for poets. And yet Jarrell's mature poetics adopt those features of analysis that Skura recommends. In temporally unfolding, pieced together monologues and dialogues, their characters move from problems about defining the self (the "where am I?" of "The Venetian Blind"; the sick child's "Think of me!") to problems about reliance on others' presence ("and yet when it was, I was" from "Seele im Raum") to problems of "exchange" that are both at once.

A key poem here is the funny, profound "A Game at Salzburg," in which an existential affirmation of selfhood becomes an affirmation of (always frustrating, never quite discursive) "exchanges."[34] The poem describes a game German-speaking adults play with small children: "a girl of three . . . says to me, softly: *Hier bin'i*. / I answer: *Da bist du*."[35] Later,

> the sun comes out, and the sky
> Is for an instant the first rain-washed blue
> Of becoming: and my look falls
> Through falling leaves, through the statues'
> Broken, encircling arms
> To the lives of the withered grass,
> To the drops the sun drinks up like dew.
>
> In anguish, in expectant acceptance,
> The world whispers: *Hier bin'i*.
>
> (CP 68)

The children's game here constitutes phatic communication, establishing preconditions for later exchange by establishing that an "I" can speak to a "you." Such phatic communication amounts to a search for acknowledgement, one the breathless daring of the close seems ready to attribute to all life and all art, from the neglected statues of postwar Austria to its "ragged" children and "withered" grass. All these objects, and the people who view them "have in common," as Kinzie has put it, "their compatible need of the other in order to be" (85). To return from Salzburg to the consulting room, and from this poem to Jarrell's work in general: if psychoanalysis resembles the reading, and also resembles the writing, of literature, both may be special cases of more general truths about intersubjectivity, intimacy, and selfhood. These general truths are the truths to which Jarrell's poems attend: that we know and recognize our own interiorities only in imaginatively intimate relations.

Jarrell's poems can embody those truths because they imagine both patient and analyst, and (therefore) the space between them. Jarrell's identification with analysts in general (and thus with Freud in particular) controls the strange short poem "The Sphinx's Riddle to Oedipus." With its Rilkeanisms and faux antiquity, the poem would be unintelligible as a comment on Sophocles: it has to be, since it is, in fact, a comment on Freud. Lionel Trilling's summary of the relevant anecdote cannot be improved:

> As a student [Freud] stood in the great Aula of the University of Vienna, where were set up the busts of the famous men of the University, and he dreamed of the day when he should be similarly honored. He knew exactly what inscription he wanted on the pedestal, a line from *Oedipus Tyrannus*, "Who divined the riddle of the Sphinx and was a man most mighty"—the story is told by his biographer that he turned pale, as if he had seen a ghost, when, on his fiftieth birthday, he was presented by his friends and admirers with a medallion on which these very words were inscribed.
>
> (31)

Here is Jarrell's poem:

> Not to have guessed is better: what is, ends,
> But among fellows, with reluctance,
> Clasped by the Woman-Breasted, Lion-Pawed.
>
> To have clasped in one's own arms a mother,
> To have killed with one's own hands a father
> —Is not this, Lame One, to have been alone?

The seer is doomed for seeing; and to understand
Is to pluck out one's own eyes with one's own hands.
But speak: what has a woman's breasts, a lion's paws?

You stand at midday in the marketplace
Before your life: to see is to have spoken.
—Yet to see, Blind One, is to be alone.

(CP 270)

Certainly the "Oedipus" here is Freud, "discoverer" of the Oedipus complex, of the death drive, and (in the poem) of the self-alienation that Jarrell's poems try to diagnose, if not to cure.[36] The "fellows" are the male inhabitants of an academic common room, the members of a psychoanalytic institute. And the Sphinx is both an id and a potent, ancient mother figure. Declamatory in tone, yet semantically evasive, the poem seems uneasily stuck between couplets and terza rima, unable to end satisfactorily in either. It is a poem about anxiety, about not being able to stop working, and about the ambiguous "satisfactions" that cap a successful career.

In *The Woman at the Washington Zoo* (1960) "The Sphinx's Riddle" is placed just before—and thus serves to introduce—a longer, more hopeful consideration of poets and psychoanalysts, "Jerome." The eponymous protagonist in "Jerome" is a psychoanalyst who sees patients all day. At night he dreams of the saint who shares his name; the next morning he visits the felids at the Washington Zoo. Mary Jarrell regards Jerome as Randall's representative (*Remembering* 33). Exploring the fissures between dreaming and waking life, and the professional role of analyst and analysand, "Jerome" also becomes an *ars poetica*: the psychoanalyst who dreams of the saint considers what the secular poet can do.[37]

"Jerome" begins by identifying the wishes, instincts, dream creatures the patients present and those the analyst sees in himself: "Each day brings its toad, each night its dragon."[38] Throughout the day the psychoanalyst-saint

Listens, listens. All the long, soft, summer day
Dreams affright his couch, the deep boils like a pot.
As the sun sets, the last patient rises,
Says to him, *Father;* trembles, turns away.

(CP 271)

After dinner, the analyst-poet-saint-interpreter will be analyzed by his own dream visions:[39]

The old man boils an egg. When he has eaten
He listens a while. The patients have not stopped.
At midnight, he lies down where his patients lay.

All night the old man whispers to the night.
It listens evenly. The great armored paws
Of its forelegs put together in reflection,
It thinks: *Where Ego was, there Id shall be.*

The "old man" (Jerome) dreams of telling his own dreams to a nocturnal
sphinx-lion-dragon (in drafts, an angel) who behaves like a training analyst and
whose thought consists of torqued, reversible Freudian slogans. It makes sense
that in this *ars poetica* the analyst-poet should undergo a dream that is also an
analysis; it makes sense also that the dream should be one *about* transference.
But the dragon-lion-father-interpreter also becomes an aspect of Jerome him-
self, and the dream recognizes this transformation by describing one of Jerome's
imagined selves, the saint, from the viewpoint of another, the companion-lion.
As in James Merrill's *The Changing Light at Sandover*, the human protagonist
speaks and thinks in pentameters, his supernatural counterpart in longer lines:

The dragon

Listens as the old man says, at dawn: *I see*
—There is an old man, naked, in a desert, by a cliff.
He has set out his books, his hat, his ink, his shears
Among scorpions, toads, the wild beasts of the desert.
I lie beside him—I am a lion.

At this point in the poem a reader may lose track of who speaks to whom, of
which of the speakers and alternate selves "is" Jerome. But this confusion—it-
self a kind of transference—is (as in "The Black Swan") part of the point. For
Jarrell our relations to others, when they are intimate enough, actually consti-
tute our relations to ourselves.

A dream that has this truth among its themes will of course mix up speaker
and listener, self and other, the speaking subject and its internalized "objects."
And this secular truth about the human psyche comes to replace the divine
truths dictated to the first, saintly Jerome. This latter-day psychiatrist-Jerome
wishes to be divinely inspired (hence influential and unerring) in his interpre-
tive work, as was the Saint Jerome who wrote the Vulgate; he too wants to take

dictation from an angel.[40] But the angel who arrives refuses to bring any heavenly dicta, leaving Jerome instead to seek earthly help: the psychoanalyst

> *kneels listening. He holds in his left hand*

> *The stone with which he beats his breast, and holds*
> *In his right hand, the pen with which he puts*
> *Into his book, the words of the angel:*
> *The angel up into whose face he looks.*
> *But the angel does not speak.* He looks into the face
> Of the night, and the night says—but the night is gone.

> He has slept. . . . At morning, when man's flesh is young
> And man's soul thankful for it knows not what,
> The air is washed and smells of boiling coffee,
> And the sun lights it. The old man walks placidly
> To the grocer's; walks on, under leaves, in light,
> To a lynx, a leopard—he has come:

> The man holds out a lump of liver to the lion,
> And the lion licks the man's hand with his tongue.

> (CP 271–272)

The poem sounds (though the worksheets show otherwise) as though Jarrell had set out to write a sestina, then changed his mind. Its formal armature has been, for five six-line stanzas, its repeated words: "listens," "lion," "patient," "night," "old man." But the repetitions recede at the end of the night. After the analyst's dream ends, in the morning, rhyme and assonance become as important as repetition to the poem's aural patterning. "Young" rhymes with "tongue," "placidly" half rhymes with "coffee," and a final pattern of *l*'s and *n*'s suggests that the activity of "listening" with which the poem began has diffused through the rest of Jerome's life. It is as if Jerome has worked through some pattern of frustration and can again enjoy (secular) company. The intimacy between Jerome and his lion, and the work Jerome can do with his patients, together replace the sacred relation the saint may have had to the angel.[41]

The lion seems to know Jerome, just as the fox of "Field and Forest" knew his boy. The lion also recalls the companion animals in other poems—the housecat in "Moving," for example, and the MGM lion, Tawny, in "The Lost World," to whom the young Jarrell says, "You're my real friend" (CP 94, 288). What do these gentle animals have to do with the analytic process, and why are they usually felids? Cats in Jarrell—whether lions or kittens—return human affections: they lick our hands or consent to be held. At the same time, as Katharine Rogers points out, cats make no "attempt to conform to our standards. . . . Seeing them as essentially different from ourselves, we . . . idealize them for the self-assured independence and the freedom from inhibitions that we feel we should restrain in ourselves" (3).

Jarrell folded such sentiments into a 1941 poem that ends by asking a domestic cat: "Men aren't happy: why are you?" (*CP* 468). Companion animals, and especially cats, seem to have given Jarrell—in his life as in some of his poems—models or standards for human care. As the psychologist Gail Melson points out, "caring for pets, unlike caring for babies, young children, or other people, is free of the gender-role associations that typecast nurture as . . . essentially feminine" (55). Companion animals (as Melson also argues) offer both "unthreatening intimacy" and a "distinct subjectivity," one we cannot mistake for part of ourselves; "psychological separation from one's pet," moreover, "is never a prerequisite for maturity" (17, 49). Cats, in particular, seem both to want or need us and to have a psychic life that is not parasitic on ours—they seem neither helpless nor predatory but, rather, adapted for coexistence. In this sense we might even say that psychoanalysis aims to make its patients more like cats! This line of thought, of course, describes a serious overinvestment in cats. Jarrell nourished just such an investment—memorial essays, the letters, and the biography all offer tales of Kitten, "the Persian cat responsible for all the cats in my poems" (*Letters* 158).[42] His poems find ways to link cats to his other concerns. If "Jerome" is the poem that most fully represents the way Jarrell saw his work as an adult poet, it is no wonder the poem ends with a surprisingly gentle lion, a big cat.[43]

Even without its leopard, lynx, and lion, "Jerome" pursues the analogy between the unfolding of selfhood in a poem and the "analytic process" (as Skura would put it) about as far as Jarrell can make it go. If poetry can be a profession in any good sense, it would have to be a profession whose ideal of itself is like that of psychoanalysis, a profession oriented toward private life. But if this is to say that the analyst's *professional* role redeems the idea of poetry *as a profession*, it should not be said without qualification. The analyst's happiness comes not in his consulting hours but in his morning without patients. The lion, the lynx could not want the analyst's professional services: they want the lump of liver and the chance to nuzzle Jerome's hand. Even the poet as analyst, in other words, has to escape (the poem shows how he escapes) from too narrowly professional, technical versions of his own activity.

"Jerome" (like "The Wild Birds") grew from drafts of "The Woman at the Washington Zoo." Jerome's friendly offer of liver to lion and lynx derives from the Jarrells' own visits to the National Zoo, where "We had made friends with a lynx that was very like our cat that had died in the spring before" (*KA* 323). Mary quotes Randall's worksheets from *his* essay on "The Woman at the Washington Zoo":

> What was coming to me was the ending of another poem a poem that was a kind of opposite/other side obverse of this poem/ By the time I finished "The Woman at the Washington Zoo" I had the first line of a new poem: *Each day brings its toad, each night its dragon....* I said to my wife I'm going to write a poem about St. Jerome now, he's a psychoanalyst—His lion is at the zoo.
>
> (*Jerome* 9)

Just as Jerome is both poet and psychoanalyst, the Woman at the Zoo is both a modern reader and an analyst's patient. Beside the Woman's plea—"You know what I was, you see what I am: change me! change me!"—we can set (for example) Freud's conclusion: "At the end of an analytic treatment the transference must itself be cleared away; and if success is then obtained or continues, it rests ... on the internal change that has been brought about in the patient" (26:453).[44] Such exchanges are at the same time felt as work *between* people and as searches *inside*, stripping off inessential roles to reveal some previously invisible core.

Such a search becomes visible in "The Woman" when we divide the poem up into sections: each one, compared to the former, moves further (as it seems to the woman) "inside." The first section concerns *clothes*—in contrast to the colorful garments elsewhere, the woman's own outfit presents only a "dull, null / Navy," one that attracts "no / Complaints, no comment," not much of anything (as the break on "no" confirms).[45] The woman appeals from external to internal, which means, in the second part of the poem, her body. This "serviceable / Body" seems drab and unsatisfactory too: she has kept it from contacts with others, inside her drab clothes ("no sunlight dyes" it); worse yet, it is sexually inexperienced ("no hand suffuses" it either). Worst of all, it is destined to age and die: "Oh bars of my own body, open, open!"

The third part of the poem must evoke some aspect of the woman that would stand to her body as her body stands to her clothes: a more interior, less contingent, harder to see aspect, something like a "soul." Like Jerome, and like "Jerome," she can do so only by reference to the imaginary others, the anthropomorphized animals at the end of the poem, who humanize first one another ("The wild brother at whose feet the white wolves fawn") and then the woman herself. Even such hallucinated interchange beats being left alone. And this is what makes "The Woman at the Washington Zoo" such an important example both of Jarrell's interpersonal style (as I have shown in chapter 1) and of his particular debts to analysis. Christopher Bollas writes of many adults' "search for an object that is identified with the metamorphosis of the self" (15—16).[46] The woman's utterance "Change me!"; characters' hopes in "The Märchen" "to change, to change!"; and Jarrell's own declaration, "I've always had a passion for changing myself as much as I can" all seem like examples of the transformational quests Bollas describes, quests that are always also searches for other subjects (*CP* 85; *Letters* 154). The interaction and "change" the woman seeks, the fantasy she describes, and even the verbal unfolding of that fantasy—sometimes rapid, sometimes hesitant, tracked by repetitions— arrive in the manner of a patient describing a dream.

How do Jarrell's psychoanalytic poems diverge from those of his contemporaries? The best-known Freudian poems from the era of "Freudian lyric" are those of Jarrell's close friend Robert Lowell, in particular the poems in Lowell's *Life Studies* (1959).[47] We can say that the differences between the analytic poetics of *Life Studies* and the analytic poetics of Jarrell in the fifties and sixties reflect the differences between thinking about undergoing analysis and thinking about how one might conduct it. Lawrence Kramer has considered how Lowell's "apostrophes set beloved, intimate others in the place of the silent, anonymous Other"—the oedipal mother—"to whom the poetry of *Life Studies* is really addressed" (84). Kramer describes Lowell's consistent occupation of the place of the patient, offering up the memories from which *Life Studies* arose.[48] We see in *Life Studies* Lowell's interest in the emotional life of the analysand, with its overlays of defenses and shames. And we do not see in Lowell the technical and cognitive interests that distinguish Jarrell's best uses of psychoanalysis. We do not see in Lowell, in other words, the wishful or hopeful attention to a present interlocutor that characterizes "Seele im Raum." Nor do we see the self-consciousness about transference and dream work that distinguishes poems as different as "The Dead Wingman," "Field and Forest," "The Black Swan," and "Jerome." Lowell's "I" always seems to address his own past; in Jarrell some listener (whether present or merely yearned for) affects how the poem unfolds.

One pair of poems might show these differences. In "Dunbarton" (1956–58) Lowell examines his younger self, his odd behaviors and his hidden (masochistic, identificatory, homoerotic, vaguely oedipal) motives:

> I borrowed Grandfather's cane
> carved with the names and altitudes
> of Norwegian mountains he had scaled—

more a weapon than a crutch.
I lanced it in the fauve ooze for newts. [. . .]
I saw myself as a young newt,
neurasthenic, scarlet,
and wild in the wild coffee-colored water.
In the mornings I cuddled like a paramour
in my Grandfather's bed
while he scouted about the chattering greenwood stove.

(LS/FUD 65–66)

Only one person is speaking, and he speaks both to and about a real person who is not there: he is absorbed in the work of memory almost to the exclusion of anything else. Jarrell's "The End of the Rainbow" (1954), by contrast, presents a landscape painter named Content, raised in New England and living in California, who sometimes blames her Puritan mores for her social and sexual dissatisfaction. She, or Jarrell's narrator, describes herself as

> set upon the path, a detour of the path
> Of righteousness; her unaccommodating eyes'
> Flat blue, matt blue
> Or grey, depending on the point of view—
> On whether one looks from here or from New England—
> All these go unobserved, are unobservable:
> She is old enough to be invisible.
>
> Opening the belled door
> She turns once more to her new-framed, new-glassed
> Landscape of a tree beside the sea.
> It is light-struck.
>
> If you look at a picture the wrong way
> You see yourself instead.
>   —The wrong way?

(CP 222–223)

Here and in the lines that follow we see the woman as she sees herself, as her friend could have seen her, as an analyst might see her, and as she might see one of her paintings.[49] We also "see" how and why she feels suppressed, unseen. We see hypotheses, both Jarrell's and hers, about what or whom to blame (New England "puritanism"? "frigidity"? shyness? ill luck?). Moreover we hear both her attitude (bewildered but sometimes defiant) and Jarrell's own (regretful and perhaps superior) toward the ways in which her life has worked out.

For Lowell the poem's center will be "I saw myself"—the finding of forms for the analysand's own recovery of material about his life. (Grandfather exists always as the young Lowell saw him.) But the accomplishment of lines like Jarrell's emerges from the ways in which they accommodate movements in and out of a single consciousness. Opening up metrically and grammatically to admit contrasting tones and perspectives on the subject ("Content") whom they barely contain, Jarrell's lines are like the glassed-over picture in which a viewer can see someone else or "yourself instead." To be influenced by the psychoanalytic goals of Jarrell's poems— as few writers (Frank Bidart, perhaps) have been—is not to invent a poetics appropriate to one's particular traumas, or life history, but to seek instead a poetics of psychoanalytic process—one appropriate to the step-by-step disclosure of a self with help from an imagined listener.

We can say now that Jarrell has at least two "psychoanalytic" programs for poetry. The first program is one Jarrell shares with the other Freudian poets of his era—with Lowell and Berryman and Delmore Schwartz; it relies on enactments of basic Freudian doctrines, doctrines more important to the literature of the fifties than to poetry or fiction since.[50] These doctrines include, for Jarrell, oedipal desire and hostility, repression, the idea that libido explains most if not all of our hidden motives, and the idea that the interesting differences between men and women are biological. Though we now have an easy time calling these axioms sexist, they informed poetry as good as Berryman's *Dream Songs*, along with honorable cultural criticism: Trilling even considered Freud's biologizing tendencies a guarantor of human freedom.[51]

This program, however, almost demanded that poems acknowledge and portray (heterosexual) male desire, either in its originary sexual form or as aggression. Lowell's succession of styles has been seen as a series of forms for depicting such aggressions, directed, in the course of his poetry, first at the cosmos and at society, then at the family, then at Lowell himself.[52] Lowell found, also, a language appropriate to the energies and frustrations of heterosexual, adult masculinity over decades during which those energies ceased to seem natural or inevitable analogues for poetic power. Similar arguments could be made about Berryman's poetry of the 1960s. Jarrell, by contrast, almost never depicts aggressive, or consciously sexual, adult men: readers (their tastes formed in part by Lowell) who want psychoanalytic poems to depict libidinal energies usually come away from Jarrell disappointed.[53]

We might identify this libidinal absence with Jarrell's frequent occupation of the position of analyst, *listening to* the speakers he imagines. At least for heterosexual men in Anglo-American cultures, part of being a good analyst—and part of being a sympathetic listener—has involved refusing to acknowledge sexual desires, which would disrupt established channels of confidence and wreck the analytic process.[54] Such refusals both aid Jarrell's identification with such a listener and constitute part (though only part) of what Hammer calls Jarrell's choice not to "write like a man" ("Who" 403). The sexual feelings, and the anger, of the adult poet, have in this reading the same status as the countertransference, whose promptings the analyst ought not to obey.

The choices and interests that made it impossible for Jarrell to write well about adult anger and libidinal energy were the choices and interests that created Jarrell's poetics of speaking and listening and gave him the second of his two psychoanalytic programs. This second program takes up the interpersonal aspects of analysis; the ways in which it is a process of speaking and listening; and the positions of both patient and analyst. Readers may ask whether this program—which emphasizes intersubjective exchange rather than libidinal energy—can be called psychoanalytic at all. An important answer here is that Jarrell's analytic poetics—in what I have called their second program—anticipate what many practicing analysts, and some Anglo-American feminists, have done with Freud. Writing in 1983, Ethel Person described

> a growing consensus that libido theory, taken alone, provides an inadequate explanation of human development. While the basic constructs of psychoanalysis (motivations, the importance of childhood experiences, unconscious mental processes, and so forth) are still viable and are almost universally accepted, some tenets of metapsychology have been challenged. . . . Sexuality is considered one independent variable among others, although it is still regarded as the leading one by some theorists. Object relations theory attempts to formulate those ways in which the experience of the external world is internalized, not just in the organization of perception and affective relationships, but in the very creation of subjectivity.
>
> (86)

The paradigm shift Person outlines both countered certain kinds of sexism and helped psychoanalytic traditions develop better accounts of how adults come to be who they are. And the contrast Person describes between libidinal and object-relations models is precisely the contrast between what I have called the first and the second psychoanalytic programs in Jarrell. Object-relations models' gaps and failures—the parts of psychic life they avoid—even resemble Jarrell's gaps and omissions: as Jane Flax attests, an "emphasis on object-relatedness entails . . . an obscuring of the non-object related aspects of sexuality and desire"

(110). Jarrell's love poems, with their "dream of a wholly nonsexual tenderness" (as Vendler has put it) leave just these aspects out (*Part* 112).

These first and second psychoanalytic programs can exist in entire separation: both, moreover, lend themselves well to poems about dreams. The first program dictates "A Hunt in the Black Forest"; the second suffuses "The Black Swan." The programs can also compete inside a poem. It seems to me that the intricacies of "The Woman at the Washington Zoo" are best heard if we take the male vulture-buzzard as above all a companion, the woman's problem as above all isolation. But the poem can also be taken in overtly sexual ways: perhaps it depicts a kind of "frigidity" which cries out for extreme, even violent, "cure." (Someone who read the poem in that way now would be debunking it; someone who read it that way in 1960 might claim to appreciate its sympathy.)

The two programs can also collide, as they do in the late poem "Gleaning."[55] Its speaker remembers "Coming home from Sunday picnics in the canyons," "when I was a girl in Los Angeles":

> Driving through orange groves, we would stop at fields
> Of lima beans, already harvested, and glean.
> We children would pick a few lima beans in play,
> But the old ones, bending to them, gleaned seriously
> Like a picture in my Bible story book.
>
> (CP 343)

Now she gleans figuratively instead, sifting her past for moments like that one. The rapid triple rhythms of the beginning reverberate like isolated memories through the slower succeeding lines.

At the poem's emotional center is the woman's admission that something has been lost—and perhaps nothing gained—in the transition from playful to serious "gleaning." Experience, age, adulthood, have brought her no real rewards: "If my heart is heavy, / It is with the weight of all I've held." She is willing to embarrass herself (as if following the Fundamental Rule) before her reader-auditor by admitting that her memories of "play" still feed her hopeful fantasies: she wants to be like Ruth, and if being like Ruth means finding a new husband, a "lord," it means, too, hoping for new, exciting experience. In her fantasy,

> At noon the lord of the field has spread his skirt
> Over me, his handmaid. "What else do you want?"
> I ask myself, exasperated at myself.
> But inside me something hopeful and insatiable—
> A girl, a grown-up, giggling, gray-haired girl—
> Gasps: "More, more!"

Thus far she resembles the men and women of other poems we have seen, evoking—with gasps, periphrases, pauses— a "something inside me" to be heard and sought. Like the speaker of "Next Day," this woman wants to be noticed, to be desired, to find a *younger* self inside her, and to discover further intimacy. Exclaiming "more! more!" as its rhythms speed up again, "Gleaning" arranges different formal indicators around the same psychic need.

Specifically libidinal wishes then take over the poem. The man whom the gleaning "gray-haired girl" seeks conforms not to biblical types of husbands and redeemers but to American stereotypes about African American male potency:

> I can't help *expecting*
> A last man, black, gleaning,
> To come to me, at sunset, in the field.
> In the last light we lie there alone:
> My hands spill the last things they hold,
> The days are crushed beneath my dying body
> By the body crushing me. As I bend
> To my soup spoon, here at the fireside, I can feel
> And not feel the body crushing me, as I go gleaning.

This rough sex, which had seemed to her like "more" life, may really be a kind of "dying," a wish for a final severance between the self and its weight of "things" and "days": sex, for her, might be indistinguishable from death. "Gleaning" combines two modes of "confessional" poetry, one focused on shocking (libidinal, aggressive) desire, the other on retrospect and self-discovery. Its uneasy, perhaps unsatisfactory, task is to accommodate both modes of turning psychoanalytic insights into poetic forms.

"Gleaning" raises obvious questions about gender, questions that must wait for chapter 6. If the poem makes a good terminus for a discussion of Jarrell's two psychoanalytic programs, it also introduces a third program that informs Jarrell's poems—a program variously indebted to psychoanalysis, to Wordsworth, and to Proust. That program concerns not hidden desires, nor "the unconscious" as such, nor dreams, but the persistence of the self through time: it lets Jarrell's characters ask why and whether they are the same people they were. Such questions and their formal correlates inform his style as well; they deserve a chapter—the next one—all to themselves.

Chapter 4

TIME AND MEMORY

"In order to have a sense of who we are," writes Charles Taylor, "we have to have a notion of how we have become, and of where we are going" (47). The unconscious (in psychoanalytic terms) bears traces of early experience; clinical practice moves from present experience to its roots in the recent or distant past. For these reasons and others, Jarrell's poems often seek a past self within present experience, or a child within an adult. With help from concepts central to psychoanalysis, and from literary sources such as Wordsworth and Proust, his characters try to understand themselves as agents with inner lives by understanding how their present selves have emerged from their pasts. While Jarrell's other stylistic signatures imagine how people (try to) relate to other people, Jarrell's verbal repetitions bear on how his personae understand time and on how they relate to their own histories. No account of his poems can stand without an account of those repetitions and of how they help him imagine time.

I have argued that Jarrell's poems draw on psychoanalysis and that they often focus on transference and on object-relations. An "account of psychic life," Nancy Chodorow explains, based on "transference, projection and introjection" places its actors "in a relational world—both internally object-relational and interpersonally intersubjective" (*Power* 17). Such accounts (of which "Gleaning" is one) constitute a self through present others, through internal memories of those others, *and* through our memories of our past selves. Sophisticated descriptions of transference (Chodorow singles out Hans Loewald's) coin compound terms that evoke both the actual past and the past as we remember it: these

> formulations—"the past in the present," "alive past," "past unconscious" and "present unconscious," "what was is, and what is, was," "unconscious living past"—represent an attempt to resolve two apparently contradictory views: on the one hand, that psychic reality is created subjectively and intersubjectively in the here and now; on the other hand, that psychic reality . . . was created in the there-and-then past.
>
> (*Power* 45)

These "apparently contradictory views" create some of the tensions—between helplessness and agency, between past and present—that drive Jarrell's poems. Meredith Skura, too, credits psychoanalysis with insights into how past and present work together, concluding "that analysts are . . . not looking for the past but for all the ways in which the past affects the present without being recognized as doing so" (209). To seek recognition—to seek ways of being seen—is, from such points of view, to seek some way of having seen, in oneself, one's own past. Hence come the formulae—so frequent in Jarrell—of children and young people "inside" older ones and of a felt "soul" "inside" the visible person.

Geoffrey Hartman has also written of "ghostly" feelings, feelings of nonexistence, "of being an outsider to life"; seeking cures for such feelings, "I want to know myself, not only my processes of knowing" (*Fateful* 21). I might have such feelings if I believed (as so many of Jarrell's characters do) that nobody else saw or heard me as a being in my own right. I might have such feelings, too, if I believed I no longer had much in common with my younger selves—that they had authentic being, while I (my present self) did not. Object-relations theorists show how these sorts of alienation produce each other, and set out to treat both. Transference, in the models of analysis that Skura and Chodorow endorse, helps us imagine interiority by helping analysands relate past to present (and thereby "inside" to "outside"). The experience of therapy thus helps cure the feeling that one is not a person, not real, not an agent, not (or no longer) oneself.

These senses of ghostliness, self-alienation, and nonexistence, for which Jarrell's personae seek cures, have parallels in both Anglo-American and continental philosophy, where they become problems and paradoxes about personal identity. In one sense "personal identity" means something like "psyche" or "soul"—it is the answer to the question "Who am I?" and it is meaningful to the extent that such a question can be answered, that we can conceive of someone who imagines or discovers an answer. This sense of "identity" (call it *synchronic*) dominates many poems we have already seen, from "Next Day" to "The Venetian Blind" to "The Sick Nought," with their animating fear that the questions "Who is this person? What makes her unlike all others?" might not have any answer. The answers they do have may always involve our relations to other persons. For Jessica Benjamin, as we have seen, these questions can only be answered if we can imagine other persons answering them about us and ourselves answering such questions about other people.

Another kind of identity seems to depend on our past, on who we and other people have thought we were, and of how those previous entities create the people we have become. Call this identity *diachronic*. Richard Wolheim asks us to imagine

the conditions under which, say, a boy who once stole apples from a particular orchard and some general who, years later, won renown on a famous battlefield would be one and the same persons, and likewise, those conditions under which the boy and the general would be two different persons. That which tells us whether a and b, both f, are the very same f, that which tells us whether the boy and the general, both persons, are the very same person, are criteria of identity: every criterion of identity is relative to a particular concept—say, the concept f, the concept *person*—in that it fixes identity under this concept: and the philosophical intuition is that concept and criterion of identity relative to it are essentially linked. The former determines the latter.

(300)

"Concept of person" here has to do with what I have just called "synchronic identity"; "criterion of identity" has to do with "diachronic" identity. To put the same insight another way: if I want to know what makes me a person, or what makes me myself, I may well ask what makes me the same person I was ten minutes or ten years ago. And if I want to know whether I am still the person I was, I will have to decide what I mean by "person" in order to find out.

It may be intuitive, but it cannot be beyond dispute, that questions about personal identity in the sense of attribution and agency must be questions about identity in the sense of sameness over time. Paul Ricoeur distinguishes sameness in time, space, or meaning (for which he uses the term *idem*) from selfhood and agency (for which he adopts the term *ipse*). He then addresses the ways in which these concepts can be differentiated or conjoined. Ricoeur describes (with reference to *idem*-identity) a criterion . . . of *uninterrupted continuity* between the first and the last stage in the development of what we consider to be the same individual. This criterion is predominant whenever growth or aging operate as factors of dissemblance. . . . The demonstration of this continuity functions as a supplementary or a substitutive criterion to similitude; the demonstration rests upon the ordered series of small changes which, taken one by one, threaten resemblance without destroying it. This is how we see photos of ourselves at successive ages of our life.

(117)

For some of Jarrell's protagonists, the "uninterrupted continuity" tying their past to their present manifestations seems to them simply absent, disrupted beyond recall: they do not feel they have anything left in common with the boy or the girl they were. For other protagonists, that "continuity," though felt, seems to them inadequate for a robust sense of self.

In these matters Jarrell's ambitious early unpublished fragments (rather than his first, Audenesque, publications) pursue interests that would shape his later work. Fragments about his 1938 breakup with Amy Breyer already show a concern with time and duration; their pentameters struggle to represent his feeling of a life stalled or reversed. One fragment asks its "you" (evidently Breyer),

> But did you care
> How it would end? Wish that it could end
> Except as it was, as it was, as it was? the snake
> Curled tail in mouth within the rubber egg,
> Living and about to live, yolk-yellow, Time
> That's stopped becoming, in the end found how to be.
> As I sit here in my cooling room, alone
> For a little, if I am ever, now, alone,
> I think, you are here, just as you were—*are*, yesterday,
> Are tomorrow, not always. Time—
> What use are you to us? We *are* Time.

(Berg Collection)

How could a person "be" without "becoming"? How can we go on being the same people we were? If we change, who will miss us?

These same questions animate the characters in Jarrell's poems of the fifties and sixties, who feel cut off from their past selves almost as frequently as (and sometimes because) they feel excluded from a life with other people. The woman in "Gleaning" insisted that somewhere inside her she could locate the girl she had been, though she had to resort to a violent fantasy life to do so. In "Thinking of the Lost World" Jarrell asks whether by growing old he has become a different person or acquired a body somehow no longer his own: "Where's my own hand? My smooth / White bitten-fingernailed one?" (*CP* 338). "Women on a Bus" begins with its speaker's repelled astonishment that "These sacks of flesh piled in a pile" could ever have been "a girl" (*CP* 489). That speaker, herself an aging woman, has displaced onto other passengers her fears about her own dying body. All these poems' speakers ask how they can be the same people they were: in each, troubles with diachronic identity generate troubles with synchronic identity, and seem to preclude synchronic recognition.

To see how Jarrell's poems work these problems out, we need to look at one more philosophical treatment. Responding to Derek Parfit's famous thesis that "identity is not what matters," Marya Schechtman distinguishes "the reidentification question and the characterization question. The former is the question of what makes a person at time t2 the same person as a person at time t1; the latter the question of which beliefs, values, desires and other psychological features make someone the person she is" (245; 1–2). (These seem very like Ricoeur's *idem* and *ipse*.) The reidentification question has nothing to do with the special status, or the imputed uniqueness, of *persons* (it could be asked about figs, for example, or flags). The characterization question addresses that uniqueness directly: it asks not "about 'identity' understood as 'the relation which every object bears to itself and to nothing else,' but rather as 'the set of characteristics that make a person who she is' " (75–76). And yet, Schechtman sees, "The question of whether action A is attributable to person P is obviously intimately connected to the question of whether person P is the same person as the person who performed A" (77). If I lost my ability to see my past, present, and future as all in some sense belonging to *me*, as the continuous experiences of one subject, I might lose my sense of personhood as well.

That ability, Schechtman shows, depends upon my relation to other people. "The very concept of personhood is inherently connected to the capacity to take one's pace in a certain complex web of social institutions and interactions" (95). And "in order to do this, one needs . . . a self-concept that is basically in synch with the views of one held by others"; "one's self-conception must cohere with . . . the story that those around her would tell" (95). This congruence of course admits of degrees—I can be closer or farther from the story those around me would tell of my life, just as they can disagree somewhat with one another. But our stories cannot be entirely disjunct. The philosophical definitions and the subjective, felt senses of personhood (*ipse*-identity) both become problematic or incoherent for people with a sufficiently extreme difference between their notions of their own experience—including their "inner lives"—and the notions others around them can have. Obvious examples of this sort of problem (the ones Schechtman gives) include people who are psychotic. Other examples are people who feel robbed of character, "empty of self " (in Enid Balint's phrase) or struck by a "ghostly feeling" (in Hartman's), because others' stories about them are nothing like theirs; their inner lives have no interpersonal confirmation.

This is of course the problem of the housewife in "Seele im Raum," of the Woman at the Zoo, of the instrumentalized soldiers standing in their lines. In Jarrell's most intricate poems, the query "What makes me a person at all?" turns out to be inextricable from the other queries "What makes me the same person I have been, and how can I know if nobody else can tell?" Jarrell explored those links as early as the war poem "Mail Call," where soldiers' letters from other people constitute links to their past, hence to their senses of personhood:

> Surely the past from which the letters rise
> Is waiting in the future, past the graves?
> The soldiers are all haunted by their lives.
>
> Their claims upon their kind are paid in paper
> That establishes a presence, like a smell.
> In letters and in dreams they see the world.
> They are waiting: and the years contract
> To an empty hand, to one unuttered sound—
>
> The soldier simply wishes for his name.
>
> (CP 170)

To get a letter is to be rightly named, fixed in one's personal history; not to get a letter is to lack "presence," to feel like a ghost. Jarrell's single-file, end-stopped stack of pentameters suggests the troops' stiff, interminable wait. The poem also seems fixated on nouns that denote time: *past, future, lives, years.* The soldiers wish to be recognized by others, and *thereby* to seem continuous with the selves they have been.

As an investigator of personal identity—of Ricoeur's *idem* and *ipse,* of the self with others and the self with its own past—Jarrell has no parallel among modern poets. His masters in such investigations were sometimes Freud and Rilke, sometimes Wordsworth and Proust. The difference between one person at one time and "the same" person at another—a difference that can make them seem like separate people—became a topic for all Jarrell's postwar long poems. The same topic suffuses "The Elementary Scene," a short poem Jarrell began in 1935 and finished in 1960.[1] The poem presents itself as a dream, or a memory of a dream, which could be a child's or an adult's:

> Looking back in my mind I can see
> The white sun like a tin plate
> Over the wooden turning of the weeds;
> The street jerking—a wet swing—
> To end by the wall the children sang.
>
> The thin grass by the girl's door,
> Trodden on, straggling, yellow and rotten,
> And the gaunt field with its one tied cow—
> The dead land waking sadly to my life—
> Stir, and curl deeper in the eyes of time.
>
> The rotting pumpkin under the stairs
> Bundled with switches and the cold ashes
> Still holds for me, in its unwavering eyes,
> The stinking shapes of cranes and witches,
> Their path slanting down the pumpkin's sky.

(CP 231)

Rhythmic unevenness, frequent spondees, and clangorous half rhymes (swing/sang, ashes/witches) testify to the hardship the child felt. The vivid "scene" (a travesty of the "primal scene") is a primary school from the early twentieth century, for this child a place of unrelieved misery: the other children seem to be singing without him, the tied-up cow to have been somehow *like* him, Halloween an occasion for bullying.

Thus far the poem has remained descriptive, testifying to the persistence of these images in "my mind." As the poem rises away from the elementary school, its field and stairs and vague horrors, we see how hard it is for Jarrell to say *how* this memory informed an older self—and how hard it was for the child to imagine a future. Above the school (and in longer, much more fluid, lines),

> Its stars beckon through the frost like cottages
> (Homes of the Bear, the Hunter—of that absent star,
> The dark where the flushed child struggles into sleep)
> Till, leaning a lifetime to the comforter,
> I float above the small limbs like their dream:
>
> I, I, the future that mends everything.

Is the dreamer child or adult? Does the tormented young Jarrell dream that the older Jarrell will justify his sufferings? Or does the older Jarrell reexamine that dream?

An earlier version of the poem (with the same title) appeared in the first issue of *Southern Review*, in 1935. The earlier poem joined the same first three stanzas to an entirely different concluding sentence:

> And even here, the patched comforter,
> The white iron bed,—creak to me,
> Their forms contorted, waiting, still,—
> That world, silent, drowned in time,
>
> Regret turning, Grief with its nails.
>
> ("Two Poems" 86)

This ending is less ambiguous (and less powerful) because it places the poem securely in the adult's dream. There the adult in his (too small) bed remembers the child's misery, now "drowned in time"; the elementary-school world acquires the aspect of a recurring bad dream.

The later poem thus complicates the earlier, refusing to solve the problem at its center: is the child the adult remembers "the same" as the adult the child once hoped to become? Drafts of the poem from the 1950s give it the working title "The Child's Dream/Sleep" (UNC-Greensboro). Mary Kinzie argues that the later version of the poem "rejects the child's point of view to speak from the adult's" in the last two lines (84). The point of view they create, in which Jarrell speaks of himself as his own future, becomes remarkable partly for its merging of the child's remembered point of view and the adult's newer, less agonized, take on the same images. A reader who knew both the old and the new versions might even liken the ambiguities between adult and child consciousness to the partial merger Jarrell has accomplished between the old and the new poem. With its altered, "mended" ending, is "The Elementary Scene" of 1960 a new, mature poem? Or is it "the same" as a work by a much younger poet, who gives it a different ending now that he has become his own "future"? In the 1960 poem the adult has "mend[ed] everything," yet the adult relates to the child only as our separable emotions and memories relate to us. He has in a sense been created by the child. Yet he is helpless to confer on the child the skills and defenses he has acquired, because he is no longer that person: they may not seem the same even in dreams.

These matters of memory, identity, and growth are Wordsworthian, philosophical, and psychoanalytic, but above all they are Proustian. Jarrell labeled Proust in 1951 "the greatest of the writers of this century"; later poems refer to him by name and imply that Jarrell reread him often (*Age* 26).[2] The hard to fathom links between past and present, child and grownup, in "The Elementary Scene" appear through the temporal ambiguities of a dream. Such "extraordinary effects which [dreams] achieve with Time" are experiences Marcel considers:

> Have we not often seen in a single night, in a single minute of a night, remote periods, relegated to those enormous distances at which we can no longer distinguish anything of the sentiments which we felt in them, come rushing upon us with almost the speed of light as though they were giant aeroplanes instead of the pale stars which we had supposed them to be, blinding us with their brilliance and bringing back to our vision all that they had once contained for us, giving us the emotion, the shock, the brilliance of their immediate proximity, only, once we are awake, to resume their position on the far side of the gulf which they had miraculously traversed, so that we are tempted to believe—wrongly, however—that they are one of the modes of rediscovering Lost Time?
>
> (3:950)

"The Elementary Scene" seeks just the effects Proust claims to reject: Proust's stars may even be the stars in the 1960 poem. The unity of past and present, outer and inner, selfhood that dreams and spoken exchanges (for Jarrell) create is famously reserved, in Proust, for the coincidental triggering "impressions" (such as the madeleine dipped in lime-leaf tea) by which selfhood may begin to be salvaged from Time. Marcel decides in the last volume of *A la recherche* that such "diverse happy impressions" had

> this in common, that I experienced them at the present moment and at the same time in the context of a distant moment, so that the past was made to encroach upon the present and I was made to doubt whether I was in the one or the other. The truth surely was that the being within me which had enjoyed these impressions had enjoyed them because they had in them something that was common to a day long past and to the present, because in some way they were extra-temporal, and this being made its appearance only when, through one of these identifications of the present with the past, it was likely to find itself in the one and only medium in which it could exist and enjoy the essence of things, that is to say: outside time.
>
> (3:904)

Though he might not call them "outside time," such experiences are just those Wolheim invokes as tests of identity. Jarrell would use his own memory triggers of taste and smell in his longest autobiographical poem, *The Lost World*.

If "90 North" began Jarrell's investigations of intersubjective recognition, "The Elementary Scene" inaugurated his explorations of diachronic identity. Those explorations included poems about adults' memories of childhood, as well as other poems about aging and old age. Jarrell's line of poems about aging begins in the early forties, with "The Christmas Roses": it becomes newly visible with "The Face" (1948), a poem written (Jarrell told Elisabeth Eisler) in "a style quite different from my usual style"—one derived from his new interest in Rilke (*Letters* 206).[3] Its nameless speaker says her face is

> Not good any more, not beautiful—
> Not even young.
> This isn't mine.
> Where is the old one, the old ones?
> Those were mine.
>
> (CP 23)

Old and young have somehow been reversed: her younger face has become "the old one" in the sense that it is her *former* face, and her new face, since it looks old, seems to her not hers.[4] The woman continues:

> It's so: I have pictures,
> Not such old ones; people behaved
> Differently then . . . When they meet me they say:
> You haven't changed.
> I want to say: You haven't looked.

It is as if her aging body had moved forward into the present moment, while her psyche had stayed behind. The people who say to her "you haven't changed" make her feel even worse, since it is not something we say to the young. An exact precedent is the party where Madame de Guermantes reëncounters Marcel:

> "As for you," she continued, "you are always the same, you never seem to change." And this remark I found almost more painful than if she had told me that I had changed, for it proved—if it was so extraordinary that there was so little sign of change in me—that a long time had elapsed. "Yes," she said, "you are astonishing, you look as young as ever," another

melancholy remark, which can only mean that in fact, if not in appear-
ance, we have grown old.

(3:970.)

Jarrell's speaker feels that she has changed radically, has become a different
person, merely because she has aged. This feeling is by no means unique to the
old: children can think of themselves that way, too, though children (as in "The
Elementary Scene") often believe their future selves will *improve* on the pres-
ent. "The Face" recalls such beliefs with raw regret:

> This is what happens to everyone.
> At first you get bigger, you know more,
> Then something goes wrong.
> You are, and you say: I am—
> And you were . . . I've been too long.

Rilke's "Faded," which Jarrell translated, resembles "The Face" but ends on a
different note: its old woman tidies her room because "the very same young girl"
she was "May be, after all, still living there" (CP 480). Jarrell's woman feels that
she cannot possibly be, or be seen as, "the very same" in *any* sense. She feels, as
she sounds, hollowed out, helpless, anomic: "I'll point to myself," she promises
or remembers, "and say: I'm not like this. / I'm the same as always inside. / And
even that's not so."

Like "Next Day," but more obviously so, "The Face" is what Laura Quinney
has termed a poem of disappointment (as opposed to disillusion): the loss it de-
scribes cannot possibly be recuperated or compensated by psychic reinvest-
ment or symbolic consolation, because what is lost is a sense of the worth of the
self that can be consoled. Quinney writes that in such a poem, "the disap-
pointed subject is panicked by the barren prospect of time, but also feels sub-
ject to time because the self stripped of ontological grandeur—and therefore of
the assumption that it is a permanent essence—no longer expects to transcend
time, but sees itself as agglutinated, dissolved, and rearranged in time" (8).
Time itself seems to the woman in "The Face" to have deprived her of most of
her interiority, leaving her room only for abstract complaint. The poem is so
thoroughly disappointed, so deprived of objects and points of reference, that it
has to conclude somewhat blankly and anticlimactically: "If just living can do
this, / Living is more dangerous than anything: // It is terrible to be alive." Sim-
ply because her *face* has grown old, she feels she has lost the continuity of per-
sonal identity that made her meaningful to others, thence to herself.

Something similar but more complicated has happened in "A Ghost, a Real Ghost," which Jarrell called "one of the most personal poems I ever wrote" (*Letters* 305). Here the speaker is far less developed in terms of specific biography, social context, physical features. We do not even know if the "I" of the poem is dead or alive, a man or a woman. (I call the speaker "she" for convenience.) Yet this speaker tells us far more about herself and her preoccupations than the operagoer of "The Face" could. She lives in a world of remembered songs and places but can no longer belong to a present moment. She cannot even see herself in the mirror, as she tells us late in the poem:

> The first night I looked into the mirror
> And saw the room empty, I could not believe
>
> That it was possible to keep existing
> In such pain: I have existed.
>
> (CP 262–263)

Perhaps she is now a "real ghost" or even a vampire (like the vampire in Jarrell's "Hohensalzburg"); perhaps, instead, a beloved partner has left (the bedroom mirror shows an empty room). Most plausibly, the sentence may mean that because this speaker has grown old, when she looks into the mirror she no longer sees *herself*, only a face that seems not to belong to her.[5]

In all these interpretations the poem investigates criteria of identity; it shows how we know we exist by knowing that whoever we were is still who we are. When those criteria are removed, the result is an unassimilable shock to the self, in which interiority, imagination, and desire seem to have become segregated from the person who is feeling them. To search for oneself in a mirror is a commonsense response, but it is one that cannot rescue the lost self. Jarrell's "Ghost" behaves like another of Winnicott's patients, of whom Winnicott writes:

> We discussed the way in which talking *to oneself* does not reflect back (on one's sense of self) unless this is a carry-over of such talking having been reflected back by *someone not oneself*.
> She said: "I've been trying to show you *me being alone* . . . that's the way I go on when alone, though without words at all, as I don't let myself start talking to myself" (that would be madness).
> She went on to talk of her use of a lot of mirrors in her room, involving for the self a search by the mirrors for some person to reflect back. (She

had been showing me, though I was there, that no person reflects back.) So now I said: "*It was yourself that was searching.*" . . . I meant that she exists in the searching rather than in finding or being found.

She said, "I'd like to stop searching and just BE. Yes, looking-for is evidence that there is a self."

(63; italics in original)

Winnicott's studies show, and Jarrell's poems enact, the ways in which problems about imperiled selfhood are problems about interaction: in order to be sure we have selves, we require that others notice the links between who we are now and who we were.

Problems of "evidence that there is a self"—of its continuity across time, and of its presence for others—are perhaps Jarrell's central subject, from "90 North" through "Jerome" to his very last poems. Where they lack both solutions and etiologies, they are difficult experiences (as "The Face" showed) to render vivid or concrete in a short poem, because they involve a speaker cut off from the physical world of objects and details. Jarrell surmounted that difficulty in "The Face" by borrowing a generalizing, terse style from the early Rilke. His more original solution in "A Ghost" is to devote three-fifths of the poem to an analogy, the story of an (or another) "old woman," who also loses her criterion of identity. The "I" who begins the poem does nothing except "think," react, and "know" for the first three stanzas of the five-stanza poem, since she is concentrating on that analogy:

> I think of that old woman in the song
> Who could not know herself without the skirt
> They cut off while she slept beside a stile.
> Her dog jumped at the unaccustomed legs
> And barked till she turned slowly from her gate
> And went—I never asked them where she went.

(CP 262)

The old woman cannot "know herself" because she has been deprived of the criteria (visual similitude over time, and recognition by a companion) that established her continuity in time. Since "that old woman" is a figure from a tale, the criteria are simplistically physical (a skirt), the companion a dog, the exile geographic rather than psychic.

This self-exile again suggests the experiences of children, who also seem to trade one self for another:

The child is hopeful and unhappy in a world
Whose future is his recourse: she kept walking
Until the skirt grew, cleared her head and dog—
Surely I thought so when I laughed. If skirts don't grow,
If things can happen so, and you not know
What you could do, why, what is there you could do?

I know now she went nowhere; went to wait
In the bare night of the fields, to whisper:
"I'll sit and wish that it was never so."
I see her sitting on the ground and wishing,
The wind jumps like a dog against her legs,
And she keeps thinking: "This is all a dream."

This wishful old woman (like the woman in "Gleaning") behaves like a travesty of the biblical Ruth: she will sit out in the cold fields, skirtless, forever, because she has lost what makes her herself, and nobody will arrive to redeem her. And as dog is to wind, so is this old woman to the "ghost" who speaks the poem, of whose loss that woman is only the symbol. The poem ends:

Was the old woman dead? What does it matter?
—Am I dead? A ghost, a real ghost
Has no need to die: what is he except
A being without access to the universe
That he has not yet managed to forget?

(CP 263)

This poem finds (as several of Jarrell's most affecting poems fail to find) a formally effective, convincing way to end a poem of disappointment without betraying its central pessimism: it ends with a unanswerable question, not about the solutions for this sort of disappointment (there are none) but about its causes and how to interpret them. Under what circumstances might I ask whether I were "dead"? I might be "undead," a "real ghost," zombie, or vampire. I might also experience stigma, "social death." The soldiers in "Mail Call" felt like ghosts because, in the army, they felt cut off from their lives. But the invisible deadness this "real ghost" feels does not stop there: what horrifies her at last is that she remembers the "universe" where she felt alive.

To feel thus is to be a ghost. And to feel shut out of a universe that we remember, a universe that defined us as persons in irretrievable ways, is not an experience as unusual as its supernatural analogues may make it seem: all adults are "ghosts" in this sense as regards childhood, and each of us is a ghost with respect to whatever phase of life we no longer occupy, can no longer fit. The adolescent who wishes to remain a presexual child, the teacher who wants to fit in with her students, the old man who wishes to regain his youthful prestige, will all feel like ghosts when they realize they cannot do so. Again, Jarrell finds poetic form for an emotional dilemma described in Proust:

> just as one has difficulty in thinking that a dead person was once alive or that a person who was alive is now dead, so one has difficulty, almost as great and of the same kind (for the extinction of youth, the destruction of a person full of energy and high spirits is already a kind of annihilation) in conceiving that she who was once a girl is now an old woman ... so that one might well refuse to believe that *this* can ever have been *that* ... that it is the same matter incorporated in the same body, were it not for the evidence of the similar name and the corroborative testimony of friends, to which an appearance of verisimilitude is given only by the pink upon the cheeks, once a small patch surrounded by the golden corn of fair hair, now a broad expanse beneath the snow.[6]
>
> (3:983)

If we were defined by our present social roles we would never feel like ghosts, nor would we feel others had become ghostly or alien, because we would never remain attached to persons who were no longer part of our everyday lives. What we had "no access to" we *would* "manage to forget." But (Jarrell has maintained—has demonstrated—all along) we are not so defined: because our past selves and roles pervade present memory and imagination, we can come to identify our real selves so thoroughly with now unavailable persons, roles, behaviors as to feel stranded, unknowable, unreal. Where Marcel wants to rescue interiority from Time, the people Jarrell depicts want not to live outside time but to live with others in it. And what Jarrell does for these Proustian concerns is what lyric does with all concerns: fears about diachronic identity acquire in "A Ghost, a Real Ghost," with its analogies, sharp breaks, and unanswered questions, not only another character to enact them but formal correlatives with which they make themselves felt.

One of those correlatives is repetition. As with "Next Day," "The Black Swan," and "Jerome," one can reread the poem many times without noticing its repeated words: in the first three-and-a-half stanzas, "went" (lines 6, 12), "skirt" (lines 2, 9, 10), "so" (lines 11, 15, 20, 21), "ghost" (the title and line 22). Not only the repetitions but the six-line stanzas suggest that the poem works (as did "Jerome") rather like a sestina. James Cummins has claimed that the repeated words in a sestina "are signposts—each time you come around to them you are aware (one of their very important functions is to *make* you aware) of the passage of time: this word is the 'same,' but only in the sense [that] a human being is the same at different ages" (156). In a true sestina the cycle of words marks time with some regularity: their felt continuity may stand for the continuity of a life. Here, however, between "The first night" and the second "existed," no key word recurs. "A Ghost, A Real Ghost" presents a human being who feels she may *not* be the same, simply because she has aged. In consequence the repeated-word signposts, different and yet the same, drop out of the poem when that alienated human being enters. When the armature of repetitions returns ("existing . . . existed," "dead . . . dead," "ghost . . . ghost"), the question they suggest is the question the speaker asks: in what sense, if any, am I the same person I was? Jarrell may have learned to use these effects by writing sestinas early in his career. He would use other effects of repetition for other poems about the passage of time in a life.

Jarrell's many uses of repetition were the one element of his verse style not discussed at length in chapter 1, because they so often depend on the ways—reserved for this chapter—in which Jarrell's poems address the passage of time. We can now look again at Jarrell's repetitions and at other poems they control. Those poems will lead us, in turn, back to the lessons he took from psychoanalysis. Joseph Frank has shown how modernist writers such as Eliot and Joyce used words as if they existed in space, not in time: the "meaning-relationship" in *The Waste Land* "is completed only by the simultaneous perception in space of word-groups that have no comprehensible relation to each other when read consecutively in time" (15). Against such high modernist concepts of literary works as spatial wholes, Jarrell insisted in "Levels and Opposites" that

> the poem is completely temporal, about as static as an explosion; there are no things in a poem only processes. Even its score on the page is not, really, either spatial or static; we might call that, parodying the old definition of matter, the permanent possibility of a certain temporal series of perceptions.
>
> .   (697)

The lecture anticipates Stanley Fish's later insistence that we hear a poem as "no longer an object, a thing-in-itself, but an *event*" (*Text* 27).

Jarrell's own poems depend on the properties they possess as events in time. "Speech rhythms," George Steiner writes, "punctuate our sensation of time-flow"; "the current of language passing through the mind" can thus "contribute

. . . to the definition of 'interior time' " (136–137). Every meaningful concept of time, Norbert Elias argues, depends on the use of one sequence of events to measure another: "timing operations connect . . . two or more different se-quences of continuous changes, one of which serves as a timing standard for the other (or others)" (72). Iterable events in works of art can both mark, and stand for (because they mark) time, just like the ticks of a watch or the bursts of a geyser. In the war poem "O My Name It Is Sam Hall," a group of prisoners and their guard measure time by the military music, the stop-and-go pace of a pris-oners' march, and the slower pace of the song that gives the poem its name. The poem's military prisoners and their guard know that they resemble one another (since they are all subordinated to the army) more than they differ (as captives and captor): all four men roam a landscape that anticipates the plain in Auden's "Shield of Achilles," and all experience time's passage in the same way. They and the rest of their detachment say nothing, and all hear the same grating, pub-lic, predictable music:

> They listen once more to the band
>
> Whose marches crackle each day at this hour
> > From the speakers of the post.
> The planes drone over; the clouds of summer
> > Blow by and are lost
>
> In the air that they and the crews have conquered—
> > But the prisoners still stand
> Listening a little after the marches.
> > Then they trudge through the sand . . .
> . . . .
>
> They graze a while for scraps; one is whistling.
> > When the guard begins
> *Sam Hall* in his slow mountain voice
> > They all stop and grin.

(CP 166)

Against the marches and the PA system, predictable messages from a remote au-thority, Jarrell sets first a prisoner's isolate "whistling" and then the song the guard sings. Jarrell's note preserves the words to the song: "*O my name it is Sam Hall / And I hate you one and all / Yes I hate you one and all / God damn your eyes*" (CP 9–10). Guard and prisoners hear the same public music, obey the same authorities, and finally resent them in the same way, setting their own private music against those impositions: the guard's song, crystallizing a shared resentment, seems to give him the power to stop time.[7]

The significant "timing standards" in Jarrell's poems include not only speech rhythms and rhythmic breaks, interpolated songs, and narrated events but also repeated phrases and words.[8] And these standards can in turn raise questions, or evoke emotions, about the flow and shape of time. In Jarrell's early sestina "A Story," verbal repetitions mimic the frustrated impatience of a schoolchild:

> What do the students talk about all day?
> Today the dean said: "There's a new boy lost."
> He said it to the matron, I could hear their
> Footsteps in the corridor, but it was empty.
> I must tell them what I heard those people say.
> When I get up I'll tell the other boys.[9]
>
> (CP 131)

Jarrell invented other forms with repetends for other poems about World War II; in these ("Goodbye, Wendover; Goodbye, Mountain Home," for example) the cycling words and phrases usually depict the repetitiveness of army life. In the postwar poem "Hope" (the first of two with that title) repetitions also track the unsatisfying passage of time:

> The week is dealt out like a hand
> That children pick up card by card.
> One keeps getting the same hand.
> One keeps getting the same card.
>
> (CP 111)

The repeated words here, the repeated, too similar days, make unsatisfactory substitutes for the new letters children hope to find in the post.

Using irregular repetitions of word and phrase as governing principles, later poems scrutinize our experience of speech, companionship, selfhood, and time. The near-sonnet "Well Water" is one such poem:

> What a girl called "the dailiness of life"
> (Adding an errand to your errand. Saying,
> "Since you're up . . . " Making you a means to
> A means to a means to) is well water

Pumped from an old well at the bottom of the world.
The pump you pump the water from is rusty
And hard to move and absurd, a squirrel-wheel
A sick squirrel turns slowly, through the sunny
Inexorable hours. And yet sometimes
The wheel turns of its own weight, the rusty
Pump pumps over your sweating face the clear
Water, cold, so cold! you cup your hands
And gulp from them the dailiness of life.

(CP 300)

In the poem's two versions of time (of "the dailiness of life") the first leaves us feeling treated solely as means (as "a means to / A means to a means"); the second lets us feel recognized as ends. The first involves our limbs but not our faces, and it seems solitary even when it is not. The second feels like nourishment, like refreshment, like having something touch and revive our faces, and it permits interjections ("so cold!") as if it brought us into a speaking relation with another human being. "Well Water" divides neatly at "And yet," where the mode of experience, the pace, and the rhetoric change; drafts of the poem even place asterisks there (Berg Collection). (In Bishop's "At the Fishhouses" and Frost's trochaic near-sonnet "For Once, Then, Something"—two precedents for "Well Water"—the cold, clear water refuses the poets exactly the human companionship, the sense of common purpose, Jarrell describes.)

The bisected poem imagines a difference between being treated as a means and feeling recognized as an end. This difference is also a difference between two ways of experiencing time—one Jarrell names as "inexorable hours," another he describes by portraying a single instant. These alternatives emerge through patterns of repeated words—"errand," "means," "well," "pump," "squirrel." Jarrell's second sentence ends in vowels of long quantity (*squirrel, through, sunny, inexorable*) and in consonant clusters that slow the lines down as the errands Jarrell imagines grow more draining. When the poem shifts to the kind of experience, the kind of time, that seems to be its own reward, the lines speed up; those clusters give way to strings of r's and l's. When the phrase "the dailiness of life" returns, it refers not to the first (unsatisfying) kind of experience but to the second (summed up in the exclamation): its sense and thus its affect have been transformed.

Allen Grossman has argued that time scales in poems always figure the human lifespan: "the first words of every poem locate the speaker in the poem at a point of recurrence . . . or of recognition of synchronicity (the all-at-onceness of experience)" (257). From this aoristic point the poem unfolds in time: at the end of a poem "all the elements are unexchangeable and have come to the end of all their histories" (275). Moreover (Grossman continues) "time asymmetry opens out the possibility, which is fundamental to the usefulness of poetry, of experimenting with the situation of *having chosen* or *having no more choices*" (275–276; italics in original). Reaching the end of a poem is like having lived all one's life.

That analogy, available in principle to all poems, does symbolic work in Jarrell's poems, because his style takes advantage of it. Many of Jarrell's speakers, many of his poems, declare themselves to be about "having no more choices": their adulthood and their inability to "get themselves changed" (as Kinzie puts it) seem inseparable (70). Even as they describe such feelings, poems such as "Well Water" present other, more hopeful or less frustrating ways to experience time. The fluid present tense of dreams offers one such scale; the moment-by-moment time of conversation, of interpersonal exchange, amounts to another. We have seen in "A Ghost, A Real Ghost" Jarrell's uses of time scales and repetitions to imagine the course of a life. Jarrell's last word on these subjects, and his most elaborate use of time scales and repetitions, is "The Player Piano." The poem deserves to be quoted whole:

I ate pancakes one night in a Pancake House
Run by a lady my age. She was gay.
When I told her that I came from Pasadena
She laughed and said "I lived in Pasadena
When Fatty Arbuckle drove the El Molino bus."

I felt that I had met someone from home.
No, not Pasadena, Fatty Arbuckle.
Who's that? Oh, something that we had in common
Like—like—the false armistice. Piano rolls.
She told me her house was the first Pancake House

East of the Mississippi, and I showed her
A picture of my grandson. Going home—
Home to the hotel—I began to hum,
"Smile a while, I bid you sad adieu,
When the clouds roll back I'll come to you."

Let's brush our hair before we go to bed,
I say to the old friend who lives in my mirror.

I remember how I'd brush my mother's hair
Before she bobbed it. How long has it been
Since I hit my funnybone? had a scab on my knee?

Here are Mother and Father in a photograph,
Father's holding me. . . . They both look so *young*.
I'm so much older than they are. Look at them,
Two babies with their baby. I don't blame you,
You weren't old enough to know any better;

If I could I'd go back, sit down by you both,
And sign our true armistice: you weren't to blame.
I shut my eyes and there's our living room.
The piano's playing something by Chopin,
And Mother and Father and their little girl

Listen. Look, the keys go down by themselves!
I go over, hold my hands out, play I play—
If only, somehow, I had learned to live!
The three of us sit watching, as my waltz
Plays itself out a half-inch from my fingers.

                                        (*CP* 354–355)

One of Jarrell's last and best poems about the life course, "The Player Piano" is also one of his last and best poems built around repetitions. Jarrell's recapitulating speaker returns to "Pancake House," "home," "brush," "baby," "blame," "look," and finally "play," which garners new meanings with each occurrence. The speaker no longer plays (is no longer a child; no longer entertains fictions) except in memory. She used to pretend (play) to play the piano. And her playing (the player piano) bears the same relation to playing (a musical instrument) that children's playing and wishing (about the shape and meanings of their adult lives) has to the lives adults actually live. The waltz, "played" by the piano itself, "plays itself out," comes to an end, literally *unrolls*, as the speaker's life approaches its end and as the poem approaches its own. (The word *play* with all its available meanings, takes on similar roles in a late fragment: "Play me again to show that I was played," Jarrell writes there, "Really played once. / Was I really?" [*CP* 490])

Why does the encounter in the Pancake House spark the retrospect that takes over "The Player Piano"? One answer is that the particular memories speaker and proprietor share remind the speaker of other memories: Fatty Arbuckle serves as her madeleine, her lime-leaf tea. Another answer, I think, is that the Pancake House proprietor resembles Jarrell's woman, knows the history they share, enough to be able to understand her, and that this act of understanding provokes her to try to describe herself. Successfully recognizing oneself in the mirror—seeing one's own continuity with past versions of oneself—is for Jarrell like being recognized by others (for example, like "meeting someone from home").

"Well Water" presented two kinds of time. "The Player Piano" has three: the narrative time of a life, the instant a photograph captures (and in which we view it), and the moment-by-moment time in which a performance or conversation takes place. Photographs—"a picture of my grandson," the photographs of parents the woman considers later in the poem—preserve likenesses at given points in time: they are not temporal art forms. Our photographed images do not change at all, but we may no longer recognize them as *us*. We feel linked to our own pasts ("The Player Piano" contends) neither in the instantaneous photograph nor in a sense of our lives as continuous narratives (a sense we can rarely achieve). We have to think on a shorter time scale instead—one defined by a kind of performance. The poem's constructions invite readers to join its scene of listening, notably at the last stanza break: "Look, the keys go down by themselves!" The exclamation seems to identify the poem's readers, or listeners, with the woman's mother and father, listening to their little girl. In both cases what is performed—what we, or Mother and Father, listen to—seems to have been under her control but is not. We as readers have come to take the place of the woman's (girl's) mother and father, lending her agency by listening.

Another name for this substitution is transference. "The Player Piano" thus becomes not only Jarrell's last word on repetition and time scales but also his last use of psychoanalysis: without the analytic hour as model for readers' and listeners' experience, the poem would not exist. To relive one's early experience *with a listener* is to work through transference, hence to understand one's life as a whole. The three time scales at work in the poem thus resemble the three senses of time that, for Julia Kristeva, operate during an analysis. There is "the linear time of the patient's narrative: a time belonging to memory." There is "the zero time of silence," the suspension in the present moment "that marks the patient's discourse at the same time as the analyst's listening." Finally there is "the time of interpretation: to give a meaning to memory, but also to the suspension of memory." As all three time scales intersect, Kristeva writes, "temporality is multiplied, and analysts live several lives within one life" (285–286). These three simultaneously experienced time scales reappear in "The Player Piano": the multiple sense of "play" in the closing phrases contains them all.

The poem recalls the common dream or wish to find a moment when one's life first went wrong. For Jarrell no such moment of choice, no fall, can be found, nor could it have been averted had there been one. To be "old enough to know any better" is just to have realized that nothing we do makes a difference: it is to see one's life as a script laid out in advance like a piano roll, to regard one's life story as always already written, hence as pathetically separate from one's consciousness, one's wishes and acts of will. Citing both Erikson and Winnicott, Chodorow identifies the feeling of confirmation in one's own identity with tragic acceptance: "At the end of an analysis, just as at the end of a life, a person, if all goes well, comes to recognize herself for who she is and has been" (*Power* 255). She even suggests that the sense of self that analysis gives us depends not only on our seeing our lives as a plot but also on our seeing them as the only possible plot: "Although all lives are contingent and all lives, in some sense, could have been other than they are, ego integrity requires seeing this as not the case" (*Power* 258). And this is just what happens at the end of "The Player Piano"; selfhood, individual identity, seems to come for this woman from her and our realization that she could not have become other than who she is.

The figure of the piano roll, sounding as parents and child hear its music, reconciles this woman to her "played out" life because it gives her a feeling of recognition and thus of continuous identity, which can survive her sense of helplessness. She has been to her own life as the player piano is to its score—the instrument of its unique expression, yet powerless to alter its plan. That ending (Elizabeth Bishop called it "marvelous") invites us to help Jarrell's woman recognize herself, to situate ourselves in her scene of listening and to experience time and inevitability along with her (*One Art* 433). Pritchard says rightly that in the conclusion an "as-if moment of play [has] occurred" (312). Yet the source of its power is not the "magical piano" but the situation in which we imagine we listen, in which she seems—by all manner of conscious fictions and rather as in an analysis—to have been heard (312).

A less attentive poet—or one who remembered his childhood less well—might relegate considerations of personal identity, continuity, and memory only to poems about adulthood and old age (like "A Real Ghost"), or about adults remembering childhood (like "The Player Piano"). Children in Jarrell, however, share the adults' concerns about past and lost time, about how they can hold on to their identity absent the circumstances that helped create it. If I become a different person in different places, with different companions, in a changing body, who can I say I am? And if I remain the same in new environs, how will I stand the ensuing isolation?

These are the questions the girl in "Moving" asks. The progress of the poem—measured by a moving truck's departure from her former home—

amounts to her discovery that such questions can only be answered collaboratively, with help from other people—or from cats.[10] Here is the first stanza:

> Some of the sky is grey and some of it is white.
> The leaves have lost their heads
> And are dancing round the tree in circles, dead;
> The cat is in it.
> A smeared, banged, tow-headed
> Girl in a flowered, flour-sack print
> Sniffles and holds up her last bite
> Of bread and butter and brown sugar to the wind.
>
> (CP 93)

As the lines shrink and expand, they focus on the girl at the poem's center; the poem moves from third person to first-person plural to first-person singular. The girl is like the cat in not wanting to move, and Jarrell adopts her voice and her fears:

> Butter the cat's paws
> And bread the wind. We are moving.
> I shall never again sing
> Good morning, Dear Teacher, to my own dear teacher.
> Never again
> Will Augusta be the capital of Maine.
> The dew has rusted the catch of the strap of my satchel
> And the sun has fallen from the place where it was chained
> With a blue construction-paper chain. . . .

The verses focus on their shortest line, "Never again," and follow it up with a Forties schoolgirl's apocalypse: Maine disappears, the sun falls into the blue sea, and

> Never again will Orion
> Fall on my speller through the star
> Taped on the broken window by my cot.
> My knee is ridged like corn
> And the scab peels off it.

The knee scab (and the tree-climbing elsewhere in the poem) are hints of "tomboyism": the girl in the poem has not yet had to assume any kind of adult sexual role. Judith Halberstam has claimed that in "popular cinema . . . tomboy-ism represents a resistance to adulthood itself rather than to adult femininity" (6). Like the movies Halberstam summarizes, "Moving" uses childhood an-drogyny as a way of thinking less about gender than about age. Girlhood seems to serve Jarrell as a double foil for adulthood and for masculinity—in this sense tomboys make the best girls. The girl's knee scab links her to the older woman of "The Player Piano" who asks "How long has it been since I . . . got a scab on my knee?" (CP 354) Like the girl in "Moving," Jarrell's adults fear that growing older will mean the end of their world.

Adults, however, can usually distinguish among brute facts (seven stars can be seen in the night sky), social or consensual facts (we call those stars, in En-glish, "Orion"), and fictions (Orion is a hunter with a bow). Adults also know what sort of statements depend for their truth on who utters them ("I live in Au-gusta," "My knee hurts") and what sorts of statement are not contingent in that way ("Augusta is the capital of Maine"). The girl's charm, and the poem's, lies in her failure to hew to these distinctions. This inability lets her thoughts and fears illustrate a more general anxiety about growing up and moving from one phase of life or one role to another.

Everyone in Jarrell who feels this anxiety responds in at least one of three modes. They embrace fictions that simulate intimacy. They seek intimacy (with other people and with cats). Finally, they try desperately to link current selves to past selves, to establish an interior continuity between past and present experi-ence—a continuity that mitigates their altered social roles. The girl in "Moving" tries all three mental strategies, for which the poem finds forms. First she makes up a fairy-tale destination continuous with the tales she knows: "We are going to live in a new pumpkin," she decides, "Under a gold star." As her house re-cedes—and along with it the fictions of witches and stars—Jarrell returns to the third person, mapping the girl's seeming distance from her old self:

> The cat is dragged from the limb.
> The little girl
> Looks over the shoulders of the moving-men
> At her own street;
> And, yard by lot, it changes.
> Never again.
> But she feels her tea-set with her elbow
> And inches closer to her mother;
> Then she shuts her eyes, and sits there, and squashed red
> Circles and leaves like colored chalk
> Come on in her dark head

And are darkened, and float farther
And farther and farther from the stretched-out hands
That float out from her in her broody trance:
She hears her own heart and her cat's heart beating.

She holds the cat so close to her he pants.

(CP 94)

Here the girl behaves like a subject of Winnicott's, clutching "significant others" and "transitional objects" in order to know she is still the same person she was.[11] (To listen to one's own heartbeat is to look for a measure of self and time independent from place: her heart is the same heart and beats in the same chest, no matter where she lives—though it also beats faster and louder the more apprehensive she becomes.) As the moving truck rolls farther away from the house, the lines stretch "farther and farther" too, moving inside the truck and then inside the girl's imagination. The same lines pick up echoes and half rhymes that suggest (without resolving into) terza rima: *mother/ red/ chalk/ head/ farther/ hands/ trance/ beating/ pants* (which rhyme *abcbadded*). A child's valediction to her house has become a poem about a perilous—even a purgatorial—symbolic journey. The girl moves toward understanding herself as a being who persists in time—a knowledge that creates a terrible ("broody") loneliness when others fail to confirm it.

The child's problem in "Moving" vis-à-vis her earlier child-self duplicates the adults' problems in other Jarrell poems: how do I establish my continuity with earlier versions of myself? If I cannot establish that continuity, what am I? And if I can so establish a self, how can I avoid the awful loneliness that comes when nobody else will recognize and confirm that self? Jarrell's techniques in "Moving," as in "The Elementary Scene" and "A Ghost"—with their shifting pronouns and speakers, their moves away from and toward the protagonist's consciousness—adapt themselves to these Proustian questions. They do so in part by borrowing from the theory and practice of psychoanalysis, which helps them depict fluctuations between conscious thought, hypnogogic drift, and dream states. And the lines' continuities from figure to figure, phrase to phrase, scene to scene come to suggest the larger questions about the continuity of personal identity—what we can "hold ... close to us," what will come "Never again"—raised by Jarrell's fears and dreams.

This chapter has examined some psychoanalytic and philosophical bases on which Jarrell's poems considered the identities of persons, both their status as agents and their continuity over time. The next two chapters view Jarrell's use of *kinds* of persons. We have seen how Jarrell's children resemble his adults, how his women resemble his men, and how his poems dramatize problems any human subject might have. How are the children in Jarrell unlike adults? How are women, for him, unlike men? Jarrell's poetry can imagine them as different and their differences, sometimes, as socially constructed. He depicts both natural families—which he tends to regard as dangerously rigid—and adoptive or simulated families, in which (as Mary Jarrell and Richard Flynn have insisted) he tends to rejoice. These kinds of persons and the families they form will lead us back to Jarrell's dealings with selfhood—how it comes about, what it requires, and why it matters after all.

Chapter 5

CHILDHOOD AND YOUTH

A "person's self," Christopher Bollas writes, "is the history of many internal relations": "infant, child, adolescent and adult" (9). These relations link us to our pasts but also to the classes in which others place us—to ideas about youth and adulthood, men and women, parents and children. Richard Flynn writes that Jarrell "fused his theory of child development with a theory of poetic development" (*Lost* 102). Childhood becomes for Jarrell a symbol of the kinds of value he found in the self: those kinds of value can appear as "play," as creativity, and as ways of resisting fixed institutions and roles. Jarrell's once well-known poem "A Girl in a Library" considers the new, and threatening, category of teenagers. Other poems—in particular the underrated long poem "The Night Before the Night Before Christmas"—show how the values Jarrell found in *childhood* led him to identify his literary projects with *adolescence*, a self-conscious state between childhood and maturity. Flynn has painted Jarrell as a defender of childhood innocence and of the nuclear family: these views are there, but they are not the whole story. This chapter shows what other values Jarrell found in childhood and in adolescence; the next will show how his imagined families, with their adults and their young people, fail or succeed.

William Empson famously traced to the Romantic period "the doubt as to whether this man or that was 'grown-up,' which has ever since occupied so

deeply the minds of those interested in their friends" (*Seven* 21). Jarrell encour-
aged his readers and his friends to ask that question about him and about his
work.[1] We have seen already how Jarrell's mannerisms—his abstemiousness, his
physical enthusiasms, his enthusiastic disregard of social norms—encouraged
his acquaintances to consider him childlike; Maurice Sendak, Jarrell's collabora-
tor on *The Bat-Poet* and two other children's books, called the poet he knew in
the sixties "not a grown-up in the conventional sense" (quoted in *Remembering*
114). Detractors called Jarrell's poems puerile.[2] David Kalstone, an admirer, saw
in the poetry "baffled American innocents who refuse to become adults" and de-
tected in Jarrell's prose "the child's privilege to be tactlessly true" ("Critic" 32).

How did these ideas serve Jarrell's work? Peter Coveney's 1957 study of liter-
ary children explains how, for Wordsworth, Blake, and their heirs, "the child
could become the symbol of Imagination and Sensibility, a symbol of Nature
set against the forces abroad in society actively de-naturing humanity" (xi–xii).
We have already seen the tormented child of "The Elementary Scene," the
timid, reflective child of "Moving," and the phantasmal boy of "Field and For-
est," who represents an adult's deepest being. Hints of all three children flit
through Rilke's "Childhood," which Jarrell translated. Rilke's child sees himself
as helpless and useless: "The time of school drags by with waiting. And dread,
with nothing but dreary things. / O loneliness . . . " (*CP* 242). Nonetheless the
adult whom that child became sees the child as a lost hope, a "Face that shone
up from the water, sinking: / O childhood, O images gliding from us / Some-
where. But where? But where?" (*CP* 243) The children in Jarrell's own poems
incorporate both halves of Rilke's binary: they are self-conscious, anxious indi-
viduals, but they are also figures in the minds of nostalgic adults.[3]

Carolyn Steedman has explored the rise of the child as cultural symbol,
showing how grown-up writers came to "embody . . . what is lost and gone in
the shape and form of a child" (*Strange* viii). In the kind of account that Steed-
man labels "Wordsworthian,"

> a self was formed by . . . bits and pieces of a personal history, and this de-
> tritus, these little portions of the past, most readily assumed the shape of a
> child when reverie and memory restored them to the adult. The child
> within was always both immanent—ready to be drawn on in various
> ways—and, at the same time, always representative of a lost realm, lost in
> the individual past, and in the past of the culture.
>
> (*Strange* 10)

Just such a "child within" looks up at the adult in Rilke's "Childhood," and just
such a child animates "The Grown-Up" in Rilke's poem of that name, which

Jarrell also translated: the poem's symbolic veil offers its grown woman "one vague answer: / In thee, thou once a child, in thee" (*CP* 239).

Jarrell, James Atlas decided, "resented the necessity of becoming socialized," which is to say of growing up (27). His poems and indeed his life set the concept—both Rilkean and Wordsworthian—of the child as (in Steedman's phrase) "something *inside*: an interiority" against the concept of "the social" (*Strange* 20). Arendt, too, thought "the social" the enemy of children: "The more completely modern society . . . introduces between the public and the private a social sphere in which the public is made private and vice versa, the harder it makes things for its children" (*Between* 188). The sociologist Chris Jenks explains how children might threaten "the social" in theory and practice. "Whenever a social world is assembled in theorizing," she writes, "it is traditionally populated and articulated through 'normal' 'natural' and 'rational' models of human conduct"; such a model "personifies adulthood." By definition, then, "childhood constitutes a way of conduct that cannot properly be evaluated and routinely incorporated within the grammar of existing social systems" (11–12). Any such "system is fed by the compliant personalities of its members and must, perforce, consume children" (19). The more grown-ups feel that they themselves (or adults in general) have been "socialized," or "consumed" by a "social system," the more attractive children's relative freedom becomes.

Pictures from an Institution illustrates just this manner of thinking with President Robbins' preschool-aged son, Derek. In contrast to his glad-handing father, Derek cannot talk to adults at all. Instead he growls, which makes him instantly likable:

> Derek did growl at you—he had a wonderful growl, an astonishingly deep growl for so young a child—and unless you had a heart of stone you growled back. Not even Lotte Lehman has made sounds that have bewitched me like that growl: when I heard it I not only believed in the Golden Age, I was in it—I felt for a moment that life was too good for me.
>
> (19)

When Derek grows up enough to start talking, he remains charmingly antisocial, developing an obsessive interest in snakes. It would, Jarrell thinks, be better to be Derek than to be President Robbins, though even Derek will have to give ground when older:

> The nursery school teacher asked me despairingly: "Now what, may I ask you, is the prognosis for a child like that?" The growls and snakes—and Derek—had made me like Derek so much that I hated to say it, but I

replied: "I guess he'll turn into a grown-up in the end, one just like you and me." The teacher said, "But I'm not joking"; and I said to myself, "But I'm not joking." But what both of us meant to say was, I think: "Poor little boy! poor little boy!"

(21)

Derek's unselfconscious innocence and his unconscious aggression are inseparable, and, compared to Benton's adults, the novel finds both charming.[4]

If the young child Derek represents childhood as an antidote to "the social," the youthful-seeming Constance—and the narrator's memory of a younger Constance—evokes immaturity as potential. Constance's "father had said to me, when she was twelve or thirteen, 'She doesn't want to grow up'; and had concluded, after a pause, soberly, 'But she'll have to.' I felt that she didn't have to—many people don't; but I was surprised that he knew she didn't want to" (142). Though she has already finished college, Constance still seems strikingly young: she "was growing up—no, not growing up, she was about to be ready to grow up" (37). Constance seems, moreover, to know that she represents potential and even to represent it visually: "Constance's face was a question mark that you looked at and did not want to find an answer for" (146).[5] An answer, of course, would be an adulthood; and an adult, in the world of Jarrell's novel, is someone who has a social place, a known status in the small society of Benton. By contrast, "Constance was of no importance, and people—usually without meaning to—showed her that they knew this" (146).

Constance resembles other young women in Jarrell's life and writing. She may have had a real-life model in Jarrell's younger friend Sara Starr, who attended Sarah Lawrence and whom he regarded as a "niece" (*Letters* 250, 297).[6] Christina Stead's twelve-year-old Louie (an "ugly duckling") also represents, for Jarrell, both interiority and potential: "Louie is a potentiality still sure that what awaits it in the world is potentiality, not actuality" (*Third* 26). Reading about her (Jarrell continued), we are reminded of our own youth, and such "memories are deeply humiliating in two ways: they remind the adult that he once was more ignorant and gullible than he is; and they remind him that he once *was*, potentially, far more than he is" (*Third* 19).

If young people such as Louie represent both interiority and "potentiality," they also represent the grim chance that interiority and potentiality might be the same thing—that whatever constitutes our inner lives might simply be used up as we get older, "become socialized," become less than we could have been. Jarrell's 1946 review of Walter de la Mare showed deep ambivalence about the "unreality" in de la Mare's verse. And yet when we read the whole review it is hard not to see in de la Mare's literary children the poems Jarrell himself would write. De la Mare, Jarrell wrote in the *Nation*, "grieves . . . over Man and the Present and what Is, these terrible crippling actualizations of the Child and the Past and what Might Have Been. This world of potentiality that he loves and needs is the world of the child *as it seems to the grown-up*" (*Age* 151). A later essay portrays "the country of [John Crowe] Ransom's poems"; here, too, children stand for potential and for the aesthetic, as against the practical, adult, and actual:

> Children are playing in the vacant lots, animals are playing in the forest. Everything that the machine at the center could not attract or transform it has forced out into the suburbs, the country, the wilderness, the past: out there are the fairy tales and nursery rhymes, chances and choices, dreams and sentiments and intrinsic aesthetic goods—everything that doesn't pay and doesn't care.
>
> (*Age* 110)

Jarrell appreciates, but mocks, Ransom's streamlined, pastoral youths. At the same time the passage summarizes the ideas of childhood on which Jarrell would draw and against which he would set the particular children, and the familial environments, his own poems and stories depict.

If Jarrell's children have poetic ancestors, they also have cousins in fifties social criticism, where "play" became a key term. Riesman declared that "play may prove to be the sphere in which there is still some room left for the would-be autonomous man to reclaim his individual character from the demands of his social character" (*Lonely* 325, 327). Erik Erikson opined that "To the working adult, play . . . permits a periodical stepping out from those forms of defined limitation which are his social reality" (*Childhood* 213). For these and other social thinkers, "play" became the opposite at once of other-direction and of alienated labor. The word retained all these meanings for Jarrell, in "The Player Piano" and in many other poems. Content, the painter in "The End of the Rainbow," envisions two kinds of human activity. One is the child's play she has left behind, valuable in itself but perhaps restricted to children. The other is the grown-up "work" her art becomes when viewed as a job or a craft. Play (and the presence of children) seem to her to be life, work (and adulthood) to invite Death:

> At home in Massachusetts, gold, red gold
> Gushes about the Frog-Prince, Princess, all the Princelets
> Digging with sand-pails, tiny shovels, spoons, a porringer
> Planned, ages since, by Paul Revere. They call:

> "Come play! Come play!"
> Death breaks the ice
> On her Hopi jar and washes out the brushes;
> Says, as he hands her them: *Life's work. It's work.*

> (*CP* 227)

Content resembles the women Jarrell saw in Eleanor Ross Taylor's poetry, where "everything is work for mortal stakes, and harder because of the memory of play, now that nothing is play" (*SH* 197). It can be hard to tell, from "The End of the Rainbow," whether (or when) Content wishes she had become a mother or whether she wishes she were again a child. In either case, her problem is that she feels too completely grown-up, too far from childhood—stranded without "play" in a world of "work."

If children—in particular children playing—give adults proof of human interiority, grown-ups might confirm their own interiority by showing what they have in common with children. Jarrell likes to show just that about certain authors. "One of the most obvious things about [ordinary] grownups, to a child," he wrote, "is that they have forgotten what it is like to be a child." Christina Stead, by contrast, understands how "any grownup" is an "ordinary monster . . . to you if you weight thirty or forty pounds and have your eyes two feet from the floor" (*Third* 31). Robert Graves "has never forgotten the child's incommensurable joys; nor has he forgotten the child's and the man's incommensurable, irreducible agonies" (*Third* 81).

Jarrell's own poems also seek similarities between children and adults. In "The Orient Express," "One looks from the train / Almost as one looked as a child"; in "The Memoirs of Glückel of Hameln," "We are all children to the past" (*CP* 65, 78). David Walker writes that "Many of Jarrell's adults are perpetually moving from innocence to experience. . . . The result, particularly in the late poems, is that the distinction between childhood and adulthood dissolves, both as a dramatic element in the poem and in the reading experience" (64). Readers who have explored Jarrell's themes of childhood have rarely seen how these affect his style. Jarrell praised Stead's knowledge of "Children's speechways—their senseless iteration, joyous nonsense, incremental variation, entreaties and insults, family games, rhymes, rituals, proverbs with the force of law, magical mistakes, occasional uncannily penetrating descriptive phrases" (*Third* 29). Some of those speechways animate "Deutsch Durch Freud," a digressive scherzo of a poem that describes Jarrell's childlike nonmastery of German:

> *My* favorite style is Leupold von Lerchenau's.
> I've memorized his *da und da und da und da*

And whisper it when Life is dark and Death is dark.
There was someone who knew how to speak
To us poor *Kinder* here *im Fremde*.

(CP 267)

The different "incremental variation," heavy rhyme, and obtrusive repetition in poems such as "Variations" and "Hope" (indebted to Auden and to Mac-Neice) attempt to impart to their grown-up subjects the energy of children's songs and games. Parodying lines from Pope's "Essay on Man," "Hope" (the earlier of two poems by that name) contrasts the frustrations of adult life with the unlimited potential (like that of childhood) symbolized by unopened letters:

Woe's me! woe's me! In Folly's mailbox
Still laughs the postcard, Hope:
Your uncle in Australia
Has died and you are Pope.
For many a soul has entertained
A Mailman unawares—
And as you cry, Impossible,
A step is on the stairs.

(CP 111; italics in original)

Jarrell glossed the poem, in a letter by remarking, "I can never see a mailman without thinking he's mine, or an envelope without thinking 'Maybe it's addressed to me' " (*Letters* 215). "A Sick Child" has similar hopes for his postman and expresses them in a winsomely limited diction, in lines marked as "childish" by identical rhyme:

The postman comes when I am still in bed.
"Postman, what do you have for me today?"
I say to him. (But really I'm in bed.)
Then he says—what shall I have him say?

(CP 53)

Later the child imagines the postman mispronouncing a word. For Wendy Lesser that "very clever poetic joke" identifies boy and poet all too closely (12). But the precocious child's amusing, disturbing likeness to the adult poet—and to poets in general—is the point:

If I can think of it, it isn't what I want.
I want . . . I want a ship from some near star

To land in the yard, and beings to come out
And think to me: "So this is where you are!

Come." Except that they won't do,
I thought of them . . . .

Jarrell expressed similar sentiments to Eleanor Ross Taylor: "I'd like nothing better than for some creature from outer space to come and make me its pet!" (*RJ* 236)[7] What the child seeks, what imaginative literature (insofar as it recalls childhood) might promise, is a new form of life miraculously continuous with his old one. Imagination seeks to overcome the limits of experience—the limits that keep a child in his house, a sick child in bed, human beings trapped on Earth, or a poet confined to his one adult life.[8]

Jarrell's most disturbing use of children's speechways shapes the haunting 1965 poem placed last in the *Complete Poems*, "What's the Riddle . . . ":

"What's the riddle that they ask you
When you're young and you say, 'I don't know,'
But that later on you will know—
The riddle that they ask you
When you're old and you say, 'I don't know,'
And that's the answer?"

"I don't know."

(*CP* 491)

The question is perhaps *What is life for?* or *What's it good for?* or the Wordsworthian question, *Was it for this?* The poem returns to the existential situation of "A Game at Salzburg," where all feeling and all discourse take the primordial form of a dialogue between the young and the old. Helplessness before death, verbal gamesmanship, and a need to speak *to* and *for* someone—to ask and be answered—appear in this brief poem as Jarrell's last word on what grown-ups and children can share.

One way to demonstrate what adults share with children is simply to write sensitively about childhood. Another might be to incorporate children's linguistic habits into (adult) verse style. We have just seen how Jarrell did both. A firmer demonstration that adults and children can share experiences might be to write for an audience both of children and of adults, a project U. C. Knoepflmacher and Mitzi Myers call "cross-writing." Knoepflmacher and

Myers (whose own examples come from Victorian magazines) explain that in "cross-writing" "a dialogic mix of older and younger [authorial] voices . . . occurs. . . . Authors who write for children inevitably create a colloquy between past and present selves [in which] we stress creative cooperation" (vii). Successful cross-writing becomes of itself a proof that adults and young readers can share particular tastes.

Some of Jarrell's more surprising recommendations among modern authors amount to praise for their cross-writing. The Irish poet James Stephens, Jarrell told readers of the *New York Times Book Review*, writes "poems in which a child or an angel speaks easily enough for children and hard enough for grown-ups" (*KA* 193). If adults ought to enjoy work aimed at children, young readers deserve access to grown-up books. Jarrell's essay "The Schools of Yesteryear" reminds us that nineteenth-century fifth graders read Milton and Goethe (*SH* 49–52). A 1955 essay decides that "articles written for those dead children who read the [mid-nineteenth-century] *Youth's Companion* were usually more thoughtful and demanding, and of more literary merit, than the articles written for the grown-ups who read the [*Saturday Evening*] *Post* today" (*KA* 212). Jarrell wrote more pointedly in a 1957 letter that

> What children's books don't ordinarily have now, and occasionally used to have, is imagination, inspiration. Nowadays they're made so easy in vocabulary and thought, aimed so directly at some imaginary normal (or normally feeble-minded) child of some narrow specific 'age-group' that neither the writer nor the reader really enjoys them."
> (To R. Maxwell-Willeson, December 16, 1957; Library of Congress)

Children's books should resemble imaginative literature for adults; these bad examples recall, instead, the Organization Man.[9]

Jarrell did not simply praise cross-writing; he practiced it, most notably in the best-known of his four children's books, *The Bat-Poet*. In the story the book tells, a young bat begins flying in the daytime, while other bats sleep. He begins making up poems about what he sees and tries to recite them to a suitable audience. The bat-poet encounters other animals in the woods—the predatory owl, the friendly chipmunk, the haughty mockingbird—and makes up poems about them. Finally he makes up a poem about bats; returning to his cave to recite the poem, he forgets it and goes back to sleep:

> He tried to think of what came next, but he couldn't remember. It was about fur, but he couldn't remember the words that went with it. He went back to the beginning. He said,

A bat is born
Naked and blind—

but before he could get any further he thought, "I wish I'd said we sleep
all winter." His eyes were closed; he yawned, and screwed his face up, and
snuggled closer to the others.

(43)

Jerome Griswold has noticed the book's "diverse constituencies": "struggling
artists," "critics," "literary gossips," and the sixth graders who once encountered
it in a "Junior Great Books" program (52). Jarrell explained in a radio interview
that he wrote *The Bat-Poet* "half for children, half for grown-ups. . . . And a cou-
ple of the poems were pretty much like grown-up poems. Anyway, *The New
Yorker* printed them" (quoted in *Remembering* 101, 124 and Griswold 61). Even
as it appeals to the *New Yorker*, *The Bat-Poet* advertises its suitability for reading
aloud, with formulae children might expect or demand: "Once upon a time
there was a bat" (1). All its images remain both carefully homely, and carefully
explicit: "Sometimes one of [the bats] would wake up for a minute and get in a
more comfortable position, and then the others would wriggle around in their
sleep till they'd got more comfortable too; when they all moved it looked as if a
fur wave went over them" (1).

Mary Jarrell explains (in terms other critics have echoed) that "this book 'half
for children and half for grown-ups' is really for artists: that is, the book tells the
rest of the world what it is like for a tiny percentage to want to be part of the
whole—not isolated" (*Remembering* 102). Poets and poems, the plot suggests—
like children and adults and humanized bats—want company, and cannot go
on creating in isolation: poets with poems want "somebody to say them to" (25).
Since "The End of the Line" Jarrell had been wondering how a postmodern
poet—and himself in particular—might come closer to "other people." *The
Bat-Poet* seems to answer that he cannot. Though there is the occasional
friendly listener (the chipmunk), to rejoin the wider society is to give up one's
chance to make art.[10] The bat-poet, in fact, faces the choice Alan Williamson
finds in many of Jarrell's poems for adults: isolation or engulfment, articulate
loneliness or wordless maternal absorption.[11]

But this is the "adult" reading of the book. Perry Nodelman has read the book
instead as a way to introduce children to the ideas "poem" and "poet": for Nodel-
man, the volume demonstrates that poetry "depends on the hard work of finding
the right words" rather than on innate inspiration (470). And if *The Bat-Poet* de-
scribes not a grown-up poet but a child venturing out of the home, its point be-
comes not that poetry is nearly impossible but that one can leave home and

safely return: it bears, in fact, the theme—familiar from object-relations psychol-ogy—that a life alternating between risk and safety, venture and return, is not only rewarding but natural. "Ordinary experiences of separation and reunion, anger and resolution," writes Jessica Benjamin, "go with the territory of infancy and childhood; working these experiences through is vastly more productive than never experiencing them at all" (*Bonds* 212). In this reading, the bat goes back to sleep among his relatives not because his projects have failed but simply because all bats hibernate and because children must go to sleep at night.

To read *The Bat-Poet* with attention to its cross-writing is thus to see how a not quite allegorical layer of meanings for adults coexists with the story and style of a book for young children. This effect of cross-writing extends to portraits of individual animals. Jarrell's Mockingbird is a "peremptory, authoritative," and conceited figure who recites magnificent poems about himself. Most commen-tators recognize the Mockingbird as a version of Robert Frost, a resemblance Jarrell certainly intended: "On his good days he didn't pay so much attention to the world, but just sang" (8–9).[12] If he is Frost, he is also any Bloomian "Strong Poet" whose power reduces others to spectators: "When the mockingbird had finished, the bat thought: 'No, I just can't say him mine. Still, though—' He said to the mockingbird: 'It's wonderful to get to hear you. I could listen to you forever'" (10). But though the mockingbird represents kinds of poets, he is also a personality type not confined to the world of poetry: children may recognize a gifted, arrogant classmate or sibling, or even a teacher who shows off his own talents rather than helping his students build theirs.

Another exchange introduces young readers to more abstract problems. The book's owl preys on small mammals such as chipmunks: after the bat recites a poem about him,

> The chipmunk said: "It makes me shiver. Why do I like it if it makes me shiver?"
>
> "I don't know. [said the bat] I see why the owl would like it, but I don't see why we like it."
>
> (22)

This is of course a traditional problem of philosophical aesthetics: why can rep-resentations of pain and danger give pleasure?[13] If one strand of *The Bat-Poet* re-members how adults such as Frost could be "childish," another strand reminds adults how many sophisticated "grown-up" topics children might understand. And these conjunctions of meanings carry their own point, or metapoint. The actual similarity Jarrell's prose demonstrates between the feelings a sixth grader might have about a teacher, and the feelings grown-up poets did have about Frost, suggests the more general affective congruences between children and adults.

We have seen the importance Jarrell assigned to the category called "childhood"; we will see more of it when we consider families. What of the related category called youth? The American historian John Demos writes of an early-twentieth-century "broad-gauge standardization of youthful experience" and of "the appearance of a true 'youth subculture' " "around the turn of the century" (105–106).[14] By the 1920s, when Jarrell himself entered his teens, "to be an adolescent was to share with others of a similar age not only a developmental position but also a social status . . . young people began to claim certain things *because* they were young" (106; italics Demos's). Lucy Rollin finds in the twenties an "increasing involvement of teens in their own social sphere, where adults were neither invited nor welcome" (45). Jarrell's lifetime, in other words, saw the evolution of a category of young persons distinct from "child" and "childhood," like it in some ways and unlike it in others. This category, too, informs much of his work.

The soldiers in Jarrell's war poems are among his first portrayals of adolescence: their immaturity, as many readers have noticed, contributes to the pathos of the most successful poems. For Paul Fussell, "a notable feature of the Second World War is the youth of most who fought it. The soldiers played not just at being killers but at being grown-ups" (51). One of Jarrell's first army jobs involved testing and classifying new soldiers: he remarked in a letter to Mackie that "about 1 in 20" of the men he classified was older than twenty-one (Berg Collection). Wounded young soldiers in Jarrell, cry out for, or dream of, their childhood lives and homes; the dying soldier in "The Dream of Waking" even envisions a schoolteacher, cat, and nurse (CP 395). In "Losses," the American airmen "died like aunts or pets or foreigners. / (When we left high school nothing else had died / For us to figure we had died like)" (CP 145). In "Second Air Force," a mother who visits an air base "thinks heavily: My son is grown," though neither her son nor his colleagues nor even their Flying Fortress bombers seem fully grown: "their Fortresses, all tail, / Stand wrong and flimsy on their skinny legs, / And the crews climb toward them clumsily as bears" (CP 177).[15]

Such soldiers are at once adults and children, which is to say they fit wholly in neither category: they represent adolescence. "Jarrell's soldiers," Flynn writes, "exist in a kind of developmental limbo between childhood and adulthood, and often act childishly in order to evade their adult fear of dying and their adult guilt over being murderers" (*Lost* 35). Their unease about responsibility, guilt, maturity, identity becomes an unease Jarrell shares; its essentially personal and pathetic character balances the public, political, moral gravity the war poems, because of their subjects, tend to seek. "Eighth Air Force" (as Flynn has seen) is the key poem here. Its speaker seems at first a sort of war reporter, an observer:

> If, in an odd angle of the hutment,
> A puppy laps the water from a can
> Of flowers, and the drunk sergeant shaving
> Whistles O *Paradiso!*—shall I say that man
> Is not as men have said: a wolf to man?

> (CP 143)

This first stanza introduces the first of the poem's unanswerable questions: is Plautus' famous *Homo homini lupus a* truth about "man," or is it *the* truth?[16] What is a "man"? Can "man" change over time—from the first to the fourth of Jarrell's stanzas, from peacetime to wartime, from Roman times to ours? The poem continues:

> O *murderers!* . . . Still, this is how it's done:

> This is a war. . . . But since these play, before they die,
> Like puppies, with their puppy; since, a man,
> I did as these have done, but did not die—
> I will content the people as I can
> And give up these to them: Behold the man!

> I have suffered in a dream, because of him,
> Many things; for this last saviour, man,
> I have lied as I lie now. But what is lying?
> Men wash their hands, in blood, as best they can:
> I find no fault in this just man.

Forms of "man" occur eight times, six in line endings: the word comes to mean, or suggest, scapegoat, "saviour," observer, villain, Everyman, "wolf," Pilate, and Christ. "Eighth Air Force" thus takes perhaps as far as it can go in one poem Empson's seventh type of ambiguity, where undecidably clashing "opposite meanings . . . show a fundamental division in the writer's mind" (*Seven* 192).[17]

The same ambiguities govern Jarrell's biblical analogies (Matthew 27:19, 24–25). Jarrell's own note tells us that his allusions "compare such criminals and scapegoats as these with that earlier criminal and scapegoat about whom the Gospels were written" (*CP* 8). The words in the final stanza could identify their speaker with Pontius Pilate, or with Pilate's wife, or his audience with the crowd who demands Jesus's death.[18] The sergeant and his crew are Pilatelike, too, part of a system whose outcome is murder. But they are also Christlike, because they are victims a government chooses to sacrifice. No final judgment can be made of these soldiers, because the "I" who speaks the poem has, in wartime, no stable place or set of standards from which to make the judgment. And this is perhaps what the speaker shares with Pontius Pilate, whom Jarrell called in 1945 "the only regular subscriber to *The Nation* in all Palestine" (*Third* 161).[19]

Such interpretive cruxes attracted New Critical admiration. For Cleanth Brooks,

> the speaker (presumably the young airman who cried "O murderers!") is himself the confessed murderer under judgment, and also the Pilate who judges, and, at least as a representative of Man, the savior whom the mob would condemn. He is even Pilate's better nature, his wife. . . . None of these meanings . . . quite cancels out the others.
>
> (*RJ* 29–30)

These mixed reactions resemble those Jarrell admired in Ernie Pyle: nobody but Pyle "makes you feel so intensely *sorry*" for the soldiers of the Second World War. "For Pyle, to the end, killing was murder, but he saw the murderers die themselves" (*KA* 116–117).[20] Writing from an army base in Tucson, Jarrell told Amy Breyer, "My two subjects are bombing Hamburg and bombing crews. I feel sympathetic and sorry for both of them" (*Letters* 116). Jarrell wrote to Margaret Marshall that the American pilots "died for us just the sort of atoning death, a death not for their own sins but for ours (after all most of them were kids just out of high schools . . . too young to vote) that Christ is supposed to have died" (*Letters* 134). To exculpate them is to lie, to condemn them is wrong, and to conclude simply that "man is a wolf to man" is to wrong the part of "man"—identified with childhood—that prefers not to kill but to play with a puppy.

We know why the airmen observed seem young, but why is Brooks sure the observer is young too? One reason might be that the poem's unsettling, unanswered questions—"personalizing" questions about guilt and innocence—are questions we associate with adolescence. And what "Eighth Air Force" tries to do, and finds it cannot do, is exactly what later thinkers wanted adolescents to do: to protest against the impersonal, amoral, instrumental nature of any and all social systems by trying to live and explain life in personal terms. Winnicott explained that the adolescent, or the boy and girl who are still in process of growing, cannot yet take responsibility for the cruelty and the suffering, for the killing and the being killed, that the world scene offers. This saves the individual at this stage from the extreme reaction against personal latent aggression, namely suicide (a pathological acceptance of responsibility for all the evil that is, or that can be thought of).

(148)

From this perspective "Eighth Air Force," quite as much as "Losses," becomes a poem about youth, which tries and fails to stand far enough off from adult society to judge it all at once or else tries and fails to blame itself for everything.

As such, the poem may address the young, headstrong Robert Lowell. Aged twenty-six, Lowell—"a fire-breathing Catholic C.O."—spent parts of 1943–44 in jail for refusing induction (*LS/FUD* 85). Lowell's open letter to President Roosevelt denounced the bombing of European cities—the task the Eighth Air Force carried out. Jarrell wrote Lowell in 1945 describing

> not only the way I feel about people in the war [but] the way I judge. Including German prisoners and former air-crew members, pilots, navigators, etc. I've met thousands of people who've killed great quantities of other people and had great quantities of their companions killed; and there's not one out of a hundred who *knows* enough about it to kill a fly or be stung by a fly. Talking about a slaughter of the innocents! And those are the *soldiers*, not the civilians.
>
> (*Letters* 129; italics in original)

The same letter expresses Jarrell's enthusiastic and partly "anthropological" interest in Lowell's adopted religion. Though "Eighth Air Force" can be (with some strain) read as a Christian poem, it makes more sense if we imagine it mediating between the unsophisticated airmen and the angry, educated Lowell—all of whom seem in different ways too young, too committed to a single perspective, to be able to judge.[21]

Patricia Meyer Spacks opens her important study of adolescence in prose fiction by listing qualities adults ascribe to youth. Among these are "exploration, becoming, growth and pain"; authenticity or genuineness; choice and experiment; emotional extremes; awkwardness, enthusiasm, and volatility; and a focus on the changing self. Neither our era nor any other, Spacks stresses, "invented" adolescence *ex nihilo*. On the other hand, twentieth-century institutions, at least in the United States, have raised it to a new prominence: "The young person's absorption with his or her own growth, discovery and pain are reason enough for proclaiming ours the century of the adolescent" (9).

Such proclamations reached new heights in the 1950s. The sociologist Reuel Denney credited Dwight Macdonald with observing "that the United States had been the first to develop the concept of the 'teenager.' " America's "subculture of youth," Denney continued, has produced "agreement that American young people constitute something of a new social type, even while there is disagreement as to what that type is" (*Youth* 155–156). The sociologist Kaspar Naegele identified adolescence with the personal, adulthood with "the social": "adults are expected to have a knowledge of the impersonal character of many important human arrangements. . . . In contrast, youth still stands for spontaneous, free and unselfconscious activities" (57). Surveying two centuries of novels, Spacks draws a similar, if qualified, conclusion: "What we now call 'adolescent narcissism' guarantees youthful attention to inner experience; it constitutes one of youth's challenges to age" (18).

Jarrell's tireless stress on "inner experience," on the self and its capacity to change, and his opposition to impersonal institutions, are in Spacks' terms (as in Naegele's) characteristically "adolescent" preoccupations. A reader of Spacks (or of Erik Erikson) might say that adult life consists in losing, or recognizing as impossible, expectations acquired early in life about personal fulfillment, or power, or even aesthetic experience. Frost's Oven Bird, who "says the leaves are old," is in these terms the voice of adulthood: "The question that he frames in all but words / Is what to make of a diminished thing" (119–120). Some of Jarrell's poems embody his suspicions that such questions have no good answer: the "adolescent" project of self-definition can have no satisfying end. This is part of the point of the late poem "Aging," which answers Frost's query with cascades of Rilkean challenges:

> I need to find again, to make a life,
> A child's Sunday afternoon, the Pleasure Drive
> Where everything went by but time; the Study Hour
> Spent at a desk, with folded hands, in waiting.

> In those I could make. Did I not make in them
> Myself? The Grown One whose time shortens,
> Breath quickens, heart beats faster, till at last
> It catches, skips. . . . Yet those hours that seemed, were endless
> Were still not long enough to have remade
> My childish heart: the heart that must have, always,
> To make anything of anything, not time,

Not time but—
  but, alas! eternity.

(CP 234)

As Jarrell loads down the last lines with consonant-heavy abstractions, the time the lines describe seems to slow down too. Our uncertainty as to the poem's rhythms—as to its moment-by-moment uses of time—tracks the speaker's uncertainty about the use he has made of his life. And the adult Jarrell the poem presents considers himself a "Grown One" with a "childish heart": he seems to himself to contain all ages at once and to belong to none. Like Content in "The End of the Rainbow," he finds himself unable to become what not only his culture but he himself considers grown-up.[22]

Stanley Cavell asks (apropos the film *Bringing Up Baby*): "If adulthood is the price of sexual happiness, is the price fair? If the grown-ups we see around us represent the future in store for us, why should we ever leave childhood?" (*Pursuits* 124). These are questions Jarrell's poems frequently raise: they are questions about liminal or transitional states, states whose inhabitants (like Katharine Hepburn with her leopards) locate themselves between childhood and adulthood, belonging to neither. This is to say they are questions about adolescence—but questions one asks, as it were, from within it: questions that characterize not social critics considering youth but young people describing themselves. Such questions enter some of Jarrell's lyric poetry and all of his longest poems.

The same questions also explain why some of Jarrell's closest friends liked to imagine him as an adolescent. The key texts here are Robert Lowell's sonnets about him.[23] Adolescence in Lowell can mean many different things; often it means male oedipal violence. But Lowell imagined Jarrell as another sort of adolescent—compellingly personal, awkward, and given to ultimate questions. The first of Lowell's three memorial sonnets runs the sequence of "Aging" in reverse, from Jarrell's unachieved old age ("*Sixty, seventy, eighty:* I see you mellow . . . ") back to Jarrell's and Lowell's shared Kenyon years, as "Students waiting for Europe and spring term to end" (*Notebook* 50). The second sonnet portrays Jarrell as uniquely suspended in time, uniquely attuned to "our first intoxicating disenchantments":

dipping our hands once, twice, in the same river,
entrained for college on the Ohio local;
the scene shifts, middle distance, back and foreground,
things changing position like chessmen on a wheel,
drawn by a water buffalo, perhaps
blue with true space before the dawn of days—

then the night of the caged squirrel on its wheel:
lights, eyes, peering at you from the overpass;
black-gloved, black-coated, you plod out stubbornly,
as if asleep, Child Randall, as if in chainstep,
meeting the cars, and approving; a harsh luminosity,
as you clasp the blank coin at the foot of the tunnel.

(*Notebook* 50–51)

Lowell's phrase "Child Randall" makes him a grownup with a "childish heart" but also a young knight or candidate for knighthood, like Childe Harold or Browning's Childe Roland. Lowell then places him among images of time passing—a Heraclitean river, a series of wheels (like the "sick squirrel's" wheel in "Well Water"), and a highway whose contours merge river and wheel with the road on which Jarrell died. "Child Randall's" death seems, in Lowell's poem, neither a suicide nor an accident but a fate—the metaphysically requisite outcome of a quest not to grow up.

We can find in Jarrell's work, and in his private life, other characteristics Americans identify with youth. One thinks here of his attraction to fast cars: among the many photographs of Jarrell, those in which he looks happiest usually place him behind the wheel.[24] Other parts of Jarrell's later work, however, attack the importance adolescence assumed within his lifetime. Jarrell complained in his notebooks for *Sad Heart*:

Norm now is:
     younger, more adolescent
     to become grown-up faster, the quasi-grown-up category of teenagers is created, that can be *reached fast*—but grown-ups become more like teenagers, less adult (have women of 70 who'll die without ever having worn anything unsuitable for a woman of 25)
(Berg Collection; underscore in original)

The notebooks cite *Seventeen* magazine's advice that "*Boys feel uncomfortable with anyone who is ultra, extra, super, hyper*"; Jarrell quips, "*Paris says to Helen, 'You make me feel uncomfortable'* " (Berg Collection; underscore in original). Encouraged by *Seventeen*, these teens substitute peer-group alikeness for families and for private experience.

Here as elsewhere Jarrell found the rise of mass culture inextricable from the rise of the teenager. *A Sad Heart at the Supermarket* complained that

Children of three or four can ask for a brand of cereal, sing some soap's commercial; by the time that they are twelve or thirteen they are not children but teenage consumers, interviewed, graphed, analyzed. They are well on their way to becoming that ideal figure of our time, the knowledgeable consumer. Let me define him: the knowledgeable consumer is someone who, when he comes to Weimar, knows how to buy a Weimaraner.

(*SH* 67)

"Knowledgeable consumers," who buy Weimaraners instead of reading Goethe, are flat, predictable travesties of adults, and "teenage consumers" are travesties of children. Led by such passages, some critics have seen Jarrell opposed, or else oblivious, to the concerns of "youth." For Mary Kinzie, Jarrell's poems depict only "latency" and "maturity," never adolescence, since in her (somewhat Freudian) framework, adolescence means overt sexuality or violence (70). To Richard Flynn, Content in "The End of the Rainbow" is "a grown-up who has not, in fact, grown up, but is an arrested adolescent" (*Lost* 93). But Content also resembles her creator. She feels, as many of his protagonists do, "old enough to be invisible" (*CP* 224). And she has thoughts that might have come from his essays: "Life, though, is not lived in trust? . . . True, true—but how few live!" (*CP* 226). What Flynn does see is that Content—never married, and having outlived four pet dogs—has not had a normative life course. She has not found a husband nor started a family, and part of her poem records her regrets about it. "There is no [musical] piece," she decides, "just tuning": her life seems to her, as Yeats's once seemed to him, "a preparation for something that never happens" (70).[25]

To understand these ideas and tropes of young people, we need to distinguish, as Rollin does, "teenagers" from "youth": she writes,

we have always had the archetype of the *youth*, the fresh, innocent young person untainted by the culture around him (and the archetype is usually male). The *teenager* is the young person, male or female, who is completely immersed in the surrounding culture—its music, its gadgets, its fashions and fads and slang. On the one hand, *youth* are the shining hope of the future, unspoiled, energetic and ready for the task ahead. On the other hand, *teenagers* are the eager consumers of everything consumable, and for some they are the curse of the modern world.

(ix)

Postwar social critics considered the rise of the teenager part of a general trend toward "other-direction." Riesman had written that the "other-directed" child "never experiences adolescence, moving as he does uninterruptedly with the peer-group. . . . He does not face, as adolescent, the need to choose between his family's world and that of his own generation or between his dreams and a world he never made" (*Lonely* 281). To Riesman as to other commentators, *teens* seemed to pose a growing threat to *youth*.

Jarrell's vivid essays can present just such arguments. In his 1956 "Love and Poetry" what has gone wrong with modern teenagers in love is just what has gone wrong with modern adults:

> Eros, builder and destroyer of cities . . . is for these not joy, not necessity, but only the policy of the firm. O Future, here around me now, in which junior high-school girls go steady with junior-high-school boys, marry in high school and repent at college! . . . Romeo and Juliet's parents sit with a social worker and a marriage broker—ah no, marriage counselor—until the well-counseled Montagues, the well-worked-over Capulets ship the children off to the University of Padua, where, with part-time jobs, allowances from both families and a freezer full of TV Dinners, they live in bliss with their babies.
>
> (KA 251)

Such happy teenagers (so ready to make new families) have made the genuine adolescent impossible: "And love, which is nourished on difficulties and prohibitions . . . how does love thrive on this bland, salt-free, even-caloried diet, the diet of a good invalid?" (KA 252) Complaints like these seem especially close to the once well-known ideas of Edgar Z. Friedenberg, who argued in *The Vanishing Adolescent* (1959) that

> the emphasis on cooperation and group adjustment characteristic of modern life interferes specifically with the central developmental task of adolescence itself. *This task is self-definition. Adolescence is the period during which a young person learns who he is, and what he really feels. It is the time during which he differentiates himself from his culture, though on the culture's terms. It is the age at which, by becoming a person in his own right, he becomes capable of deeply felt relationships to other individuals perceived clearly as such.*
>
> (29; italics in original)

Though invented years before Friedenberg's book, the Benton College of *Pictures* has the characteristics Friedenberg would attack. Encouraging group adjustment, Benton hinders the personal, unpredictable change that should be the special province of the young. Riesman, too, feared that contemporary schools, teaching "skills of getting along isolated from why and to what end," would "produce . . . a sort of permanent prematurity" (*Lonely* 396).

That "prematurity" is the state Benton encourages: "the freshmen of Benton thought the President younger than they" (15). A college president who is like a freshman amounts to a parody of both and makes both learning and rebellion hard; the freshmen think they have nothing to learn, and the adults really have nothing to teach them. Because they are insecure in their adult roles, the teachers of Benton never admit that a student "might be right about something and [faculty] wrong" (82). As a result, Jarrell comments acidly, "the teachers of Benton were *very* grown-up" (86). Flynn decides that "Benton resists whatever threatens to disrupt its complacent, static and perpetual adolescence" (*Lost* 66–67). It would be more exact to say that in *Pictures*, as in the cultural criticism, two concepts of adolescence have come into conflict: Benton favors the wrong one.

Jarrell's positive models of education are not schools or colleges but libraries—or simply young people with books. His unpublished talk for librarians explains: "I rarely feel happier than when I'm in a library—very rarely feel more soothed and calm and secure. . . . If people were like me, libraries and not religion would be the opium of the people" (Berg Collection). Jarrell identified with Christina Stead's Louie, who "reads most of the time—reads, even, while taking a shower. . . . Her life is accompanied, *ostinato*, by *always has her nose stuck in a book*" (*Third* 22). Louie, the young Jarrell of the essay on libraries, and his relatives in poems such as "Children Selecting Books in a Library," resemble the seventeen-year-old reader of Wordsworth whom we met in chapter 2. In each case the *child or youth reading* proves that people in general have intrinsic value and inner lives, lives apart from considerations of use.

Reviewing *Poetry and the Age*, R. W. Flint captured (perhaps without meaning to) the equations Jarrell made between real reading, aesthetic response, and youth: "no modern critic," Flint wrote, "has a more lively respect for that dying species, the general reader. If you don't enjoy this poem, [Jarrell] tells us, *I know a very intelligent little girl who does*" (703). A later essay, "Poets, Critics and Readers," ends "*Read at whim! Read at whim!*" (*KA* 318; italics Jarrell's) Reading "at whim," deriving no material or social benefit, Jarrell's child readers (whose tastes may or may not be ours) become his preeminent examples of interiority. For Jarrell, *adults can understand literature if and only if they can imagine how children read.* If we cannot, we have become like institutions and have made ourselves into means.[26]

The worst things about teenagers, "mass culture" and practical education are therefore the mutually reinforcing threats they pose to private reading—to such reading as the library poems describe. Jarrell complained in "The Age of Criticism":

Some of us write less; all of us, almost, read less—the child at his televi-
sion set, the critic or novelist in the viewplate of the set, grayly answering
questions on topics of general interest. Children have fewer and fewer
empty hours, and the eight-year-old is discouraged from filling them with
the books written for his brother of ten; nor is anyone at his school sur-
prised when he does not read very much or very well—it is only "born
readers" who do that.

(*Age* 76–77)

Riesman, too, denounced schools and school arts programs that functioned as
"agencies for the destruction of fantasy," for "the socialization of taste and inter-
est" (*Lonely* 62).[27] It is this "socialization," at once utilitarian and other-directed,
that Jarrell decried in colleges such as Benton, and in the grade schools later es-
says described. "The Taste of the Age" remembers meeting eighth-grade girls
"who didn't know who Charlemagne was" but who did know how "to conduct a
meeting, to nominate, and to second nominations" and how "to bake a date
pudding, to make a dirndl skirt, and from the remnants of the cloth to make a
drawstring carryall" (*KA* 301). The trouble is not that the girls don't know Euro-
pean history—they may never *need* to know it—but that their education does
not encourage them to learn, or to read, anything they will not need or use.

Chapter 2 showed how Jarrell's sense of the universal dignity of persons de-
pended on his belief in a potentially universal, if often unused, faculty of taste.
Partly as a result, Jarrell found himself deeply dismayed by people who appeared
to have no need or desire for art: "These people who *can't read modern poetry
because it's so*—this or that or the other—why can't they read [Marianne
Moore's] "Propriety" or "The Mind is an Enchanting Thing" or "What Are
Years?" or "The Steeple-Jack'?" (*Age* 188). Jarrell's sense of adults' personhood
depended, as we have also seen, on appeals to ideas about childhood: grown-ups
might lose their interior lives, but youth might be expected to retain them. The
young reader thus became Jarrell's preeminent example of human interiority. A
young person—a *teenager*— who desires no art, no " 'private,' 'inner' values" (in
Spacks's phrase), and who seems happy in her social world, thus challenges
every value Jarrell imagines (18). What could he find to say to such a person?
What if his job required him to teach her? [28]

Such problems animate "A Girl in a Library" (1951), which Jarrell placed at
the front of his 1955 *Selected Poems*. The poem addresses a student Jarrell finds
asleep in a college library; late in the poem the character Tatyana Larina (from
Pushkin's *Eugene Onegin*) joins Jarrell in contemplating the girl. The poem is
one of his wittiest; his contemporaries admired it wholeheartedly—Lowell

compared its "hesitating satire and sympathy" to Pope's (*RJ* 117).[29] Their praise is understandable. "A Girl in A Library" holds some of Jarrell's best aphoristic verse, memorable declarations that help us read the rest of his oeuvre: "The soul has no assignments, neither cooks / Nor referees: it wastes its time" (*CP* 16). "And yet, the ways we miss our lives are life. / Yet . . . yet . . . / to have one's life add up to *yet!*" (*CP* 20). The poem includes allusively clever wordplay, much of it bound up with insults: "This is a waist the spirit breaks its arm on. / The gods themselves, against you, struggle in vain" (*CP* 15). Early in the poem come some rare admissions about how it feels to teach unreceptive students; later come glittering exchanges between Jarrell and Pushkin's wise young Tatyana.

Yet "A Girl in a Library" no longer seems a surefire introduction to Jarrell's poetry. The poem (like the *Sad Heart* prose) invites readers to stand with Jarrell above and against a hapless nonreader; current readers are as likely as not to refuse the invitation, objecting instead to the poem's sense of superiority or to its complex but unmistakable sexism.[30] Suffused by its time's ideas about art and youth, "A Girl in a Library" becomes Jarrell's conflict-laden attempt to deal at once with the emerging idea of the teenager; with the anthropological perspectives explored in *Pictures*; with the troublesome fact that many people of all ages (and many students) do not read for fun; and (at last) with the sexualized human body.[31]

Sleeping, rather than reading, in a library, the girl has rejected literature and imagination and seems genuinely not to miss either. Rather than reading novels or poems or history, she learns (when awake) "Home Economics and Physical Education," "Assignments, recipes, the *Official Rulebook / Of Basketball*" (*CP* 4, 16). When she dreams, she does so "with calm slow factuality," imagining graduation. She wears or has worn a "pink strapless formal"; laughs a "laugh of greeting"; talks ignorantly or ungrammatically, in her own "strange speech"; and goes on (or at least speaks of) "blind dates." Her world of blind dates and formals is, in other words, an early version of the emerging teenage culture—of the "younger, more adolescent" norm of the *Sad Heart* notebooks and of the rebellion-free adolescence Riesman labeled "a time of gregarious, consumption-oriented activity . . . sports, music, dancing, dating" (*Abundance* 118). She fits into her world of peer groups, facts, and practicality just as does the "exceptionally normal" dirndl-making eighth grader, of whom Jarrell sighed: "She was being given an education suitable for the world she was to use it in" (*KA* 303).

To imagine another kind of education would be to imagine other, fictive worlds—just the ability Jarrell associated with childhood and youth, as incarnated by Pushkin's impulsive characters. "Adolescent fire," the *Onegin* narrator declares, "cannot be secret or deceive"; Tatyana herself as a child preferred "imagination" and "fancies" to "games and sport" (2:19, 2:25–26).[32] Entering Jarrell's poem, Tatyana

> Larina (gray eyes nickel with the moonlight
> That falls through the willows onto Lensky's tomb;
> Now young and shy, now old and cold and sure)
> Asks, smiling: "But what is she dreaming of, fat thing?"
> I answer: She's not fat. She isn't dreaming.
>
>   (CP 17)

Even certain animals seem less satisfied, more rebellious and curious, than she: "Many a beast has gnawn a leg off and got free, / Many a dolphin curved up from Necessity— / The trap has closed about you, and you sleep" (CP 16).[33] A student of *physical* education, and an incarnation of the wrong kind of youth, the girl seems happy never to leave her social world nor to escape her physical body.

That body matters more as the poem goes on. The sleeping girl's self-satisfaction and physicality let Jarrell associate her with animals: "She purrs, or laps, or runs, all in her sleep" (CP 17);

>   One sees, in your blurred eyes
> The "uneasy half-soul" Kipling saw in dogs.
> One sees it, in the glass, in one's own eyes.
>
>   (CP 16)

Here the poem begins to alter its tone and to ask what the girl might after all have in common with the man who regards her. She is at least "very human," touchingly fallible; she is also sexualized, and girlish:

> Her sturdy form, in its pink strapless formal,
> Is as if bathed in moonlight—modulated
> Into a form of joy, a Lydian mode;
> This Wooden Mean's a kind, furred animal
> That speaks, in the Wild of things, delighting riddles
> To the soul that listens, trusting . . .
>
>   (CP 17)

The girl is a modern "teenager" who goes on blind dates, but her youth also contributes to her semierotic appeal—though Jarrell can admit it only when Tatyana has left the poem:

You sigh a shuddering sigh. Tatyana murmurs,
"Don't cry, little peasant"; leaves us with a swift
"Good-bye, good-bye . . . Ah, don't think ill of me . . . "
Your eyes open: you sit here thoughtlessly.

I love you—and yet—and yet—I love you.

(CP 18)

The poem ends up as (among other things) a somewhat contorted attempt on the poet's own part to explain to himself why he finds the girl attractive despite his professed contempt for the unimaginative life she represents. Does her igno-rance—reinterpreted as innocence—become sexually exciting? It is hard to judge what sort of "love" is meant—Jarrell himself seems not to know.

However mitigated by Tatyana Larina, the poem finally appeals to familiar gendered binarisms: *man = culture = civilization = authority = experience = knowledge = mind; woman/girl = nature = wilderness = helplessness = inno-cence = ignorance = body*. At the same time it searches for alternatives to these old and troubling pairings. One way to understand the girl—a way the poem considers and rejects—is as pure body, as a kind of animal. A more promising (though still problematic) line of thought comes from anthropology: the girl, and the teens for whom she stands, are really like ancient "peasants." She has, they have, a milieu with its own values and rituals, even "a language of its own / (Different from the books'; worse than the books')" (CP 16). And that milieu sat-isfies her completely.

Jarrell's ending thus identifies the girl's contemporary, practical "culture"— the culture of rule books, Home Ec, and blind dates—with culture as anthro-pologists understand it, as an "array" (in Christopher Herbert's phrase) "of disparate-seeming elements of social life [which] composes a significant *whole.*" This whole can then fall under "an overriding principle of authenticity which one invokes to protest against interference by powerful outsiders in other peo-ples' established social practices" (5, 2; italics Herbert's). Such interference is what the poet refuses, and just such "invocations" end the poem:

Don't cry, little peasant. Sit and dream.
One comes, a finger's width beneath your skin,
To the braided maidens singing as they spin;
There sound the shepherd's pipe, the watchman's rattle
Across the short dark distance of the years.
I am a thought of yours; and yet, you do not think . . .
The firelight of a long, blind, dreaming story

Lingers upon your lips; and I have seen
Firm, fixed forever in your closing eyes,
The Corn King beckoning to his Spring Queen.

(CP 18)

Suzanne Ferguson explains that the girl (still asleep at the end of the poem) "will enact the timeless human ritual of love and suffering represented by the myths" (*Poetry* 140). Warming to her as he goes on, Jarrell also consigns her to an operatic and "timeless ritual" the poet can only watch.

The poem finally registers and explores Jarrell's mixed feelings about the rise of the teenager, about bodies, and about the actual young people he encountered at the Woman's College of North Carolina. All these effects come into sharper focus the more we follow their allusions. Jarrell's own note explains that "the Corn King and the Spring Queen went by many names; in the beginning they were the man and woman who, after ruling for a time, were torn to pieces and scattered over the fields in order that the grain might grow" (CP 4). *The Corn King and the Spring Queen* (1930) is also a historical novel by Naomi Mitchison, which Jarrell had almost certainly read.[34] Mitchison's novel follows Greek contact with the tribal community of Marob, in Scythia: the eponymous protagonists, Erif Der and Tarrik, leave Marob and learn to understand Greek values, among them self-consciousness and individualism. Mitchison's character Hyperides explains in a letter to a Greek friend:

It is natural for men to live in communities and painful to them when these communities break up. . . .Yet as men's minds grow they have to question. And as they question and become different one from another and want to be still more different and to lead each his own separate life, so the community breaks up. The people in it are no longer part of a unity and harmony that includes their friends and their dead and their un-born—a unity in time—and no longer part of the earth and the crops and the festivals of the community—a unity in space. . . . [H]ere in Marob there is and has been a close community in which, I suppose, all were to some extent happy, because all were to some extent in communion with the others. . . . There were two who were the keystone of the community, the Corn King and the Spring Queen.

(416)

The girl in the Greensboro library is not so much like Mitchison's anomalous, willful Spring Queen, Erif Der, as she is like the anonymous, unselfconscious spring queens who came before her. She combines, as they did, youth, sexual power, cultural practices outsiders cannot fathom, and organic belongingness in one community—in this case, perhaps, the community of teenagers, but also the larger community of Americans circa 1950, uninterested in poetry and the past, in Goethe and Pushkin and Wagner, in Europe and libraries. The sleeping girl, and all the young people like her, do not need Pushkin and Goethe (and Jarrell) for the same reason that Marob once needed no Greek: this contemporary teenager will not have the "adolescent" dilemmas of individual, changing selfhood that self-conscious art attempts to solve.

We have seen Jarrell's resistance to "teen culture" and his insistence on the trapped, transitional states of young soldiers. We have also seen Jarrell's own voice identified with qualities purportedly adolescent—with the personal and private, with naïveté, with extremes of guilt and of enthusiasm, and with an uneasy space between childhood and maturity. All these qualities come to the fore in Jarrell's longest poem, "The Night Before the Night Before Christmas" (1948), whose protagonist is a fourteen-year-old girl. "The Night Before The Night Before Christmas" takes place in 1934 (when Jarrell himself turned twenty), over a few hours in the life of its (never named) American girl. She lives in "the Arden Apartments" with her father, aunt, and younger brother; her mother has died, and her brother is ill, perhaps dying (CP 40). The poem consists of her memories, actions, and thoughts as she returns to the family apartment, reads, falls asleep, and dreams. The girl it depicts emerges as the opposite of the girl in the library—she is the most complex, and the most sympathetic, of Jarrell's poetic alter egos.[35]

Jarrell's title tells us to expect a poem organized around notions of "before"—of anticipation, preparation, readiness, and unreadiness. This girl has had to assume the care of her brother, and to contemplate his death, before either could be ready. She stands "before" the rest of her life, and before his death, and stands, too, "before" the belief systems—Marxism, Christianity, the anthropological thinking of folktales—that she explores. Merging sophisticated poetic concerns with typically "girlish" set pieces, the poem is Jarrell's most intricate demonstration of links among "adult" and "youthful" concerns. At the same time it responds (as Longenbach has suggested) to Jarrell's New Critical mentors—and to high modernist long poems.

Broken up like dialogue in a novel, Jarrell's uneven, short lines quote, distort, and incorporate what the girl has read—the Pink and Blue Fairy Books, the New Testament, Marx and Engels, Brecht, Kipling, the Gospels, John Strachey's *The Coming Struggle for Power*. Such density of allusion makes only one aspect of the poem's style. Though much of the poem relies on chains of abstractions, it begins with an image almost filmic; as the girl comes home from school, she

trails toward the house
And stares at her bitten nails, her bare red knees—
And presses her chapped, cold hands together
In a middy blouse. (CP 40)

Some segments incorporate conversation: at home,

she offers to read her brother
Another chapter from *The Iron Heel*.
"No, read me from *Stalky*."
She starts to, but says, "When I was your age
I read it all the time." He answers, "It's not real."

(CP 41)

Other parts of the poem flaunt their open spaces, trailings-off, and associative juxtapositions, which take the place of similes. The vision of squirrels, near the close, is typical:

chattering
From leaf to leaf, as her squirrel chattered:
The Poor, the Poor . . .
They have eaten, rapidly,
From her hand, as though to say:
"But you won't hurt me, will you? *Will you?*"

They have nothing to lose but their lives.

(CP 47)

The poem incorporates so many of Jarrell's techniques—and draws on so many sources—that it is tempting to call it Jarrell's *Waste Land*. Its open spaces, hints, and gaps (already one of Jarrell's signatures) also come to represent "adolescent" potential itself: we do not know, nor does the girl yet know, which if any of the beliefs and fictions she considers can describe her life.

Like Louie, like "A Sick Child," the girl is one of Jarrell's cherished young readers—a role several one-line verse-paragraphs highlight: "She reads." "She is reading a Factory Act, a girl in a room." Her father moves instead in the realm of "the social": he lives amid framed mottoes and belongs to a Moose Lodge. Thus the girl reluctantly wraps

the gloves she has knitted, the tie she has picked
For her father—poor Lion,

Poor Moose.
She'd give him something that means something
But it's no use:
People are so *dumb.*
She thinks with regretful indignation:
"Why, he might as well not be alive . . . "
And sees all the mottoes at his office,
Like *Do It Now*
And *To Travel Hopefully*
Is A Better Thing Than To Arrive.

(CP 43)

The girl's "regretful indignation" recalls the agenda—and describes the tone—of essays such as "The Obscurity of the Poet" and "The Taste of the Age," decrying the gap between a "nonreading" majority and an imaginative minority. The father's liking for slogans and wall placards clinches the analogy: these are what Americans use instead of quoting real poetry.[36] This girl cannot share her intellectual concerns with her father. What she does share with him, she realizes, is affect: "Still, he was sorry when my squirrel . . . / He was sorry as Brother when my squirrel . . . / When the gifts are wrapped she reads" (CP 43).

Reading, the girl identifies individuals and identifies them as helpless sufferers, in everything she reads: she also maps the scenes she imagines onto the Marxist theory she consumes. (In this she resembles the young Jarrell who wrote "The Patient Leading the Patient.") Later the girl sees

    far off, among columns
Of figures, the children laboring:
A figure buried among figures
Looks at her beggingly, a beast in pain.
She puts her hand
Out into the darkness till it touches:
Her flesh freezes, in that instant, to the iron
And pulls away in blood.

(CP 44)

It would be painful to touch iron in the cold weather the girl's town is having; it would be more painful to be the child laborer the girl imagines; and it is painful, in another sense, not to do anything for child laborers other than read about them. The girl is more fortunate than those child workers, than the unlucky adult workers of the Thirties, than her sick brother, and even than her dead pet squirrel. Comparing herself to all of them at once, she "thought, as the living / Think of their life, "Oh, it's not *right!*" (CP 47)

The girl has been worrying, in other words, about distributive justice and obligation, themes that dominate thirties literature: what can she do (and what can poetry do) to help "the poor"? These problems bleed into another, more immediate concern: what can the girl do for her brother? Alan Williamson has written appreciatively of the poem's "adolescent sentimentality . . . which consists in the insistence that everything be special in the sense of precious, included, so that nothing will be . . . cast out" (*Introspection* 123). Christina Stead's Louie charmed Jarrell almost as Jarrell's fourteen-year-old charms Williamson, and for the same, ethically charged, reasons:

> Someone in a story says that when you can't think of anything else to say you say, "Ah, youth, youth!" But sometimes as you read about Louie there *is* nothing else to say: your heart goes out in homesick joy to the marvelous inconsequential improbable reaching-out-to-everything of the duckling's mind, so different from the old swan's mind, that has learned what its interests are and is deaf and blind to the rest of reality.
>
> (*Third* 20)

Remembering the ambiguities of "Eighth Air Force," we can see in this girl's "reaching-out-to-everything" a sense of moral responsibility that does not know where the limits of its powers and obligations might lie. The girl's social liminality, her vertiginous position "before" social and sexual maturity, and her premature responsibility (for her brother) mean that she cannot really identify herself with any one age-grade or social role, and this unmoored status functions for her something like a Rawlsian Original Position, prompting her string of reflections on fortune, and guilt, and desert.

The girl's "reaching-out" to understand her relation to family, state, and class is thus part of a larger (adolescent) project of trying to find out who one is, where one stands among others, and why. We saw in chapter 1 how Jarrell's characters try and fail to do this with mirrors, whose representation of physical resemblances cannot show us our interiority: only our imaginative relations with others, and with our own pasts, can do this. The fourteen-year-old here wants to know both what she's really like (interiority) and what she really looks like (an exact physical image), and she concludes that mirrors can show her neither:

> In her room that night she looks at herself in the mirror
> And thinks: "Do I really look like *that?*"

She stares at her hair;
It's really a beautiful golden — anyway, yellow:
She brushes it with affection
And combs her bang back over so it slants.
How white her teeth are.
A turned-up nose . . .
No, it's no use.
She thinks: What do I *really* look like?

I don't know.
Not really.
  Really.

            (CP 42)

Winnicott describes certain patients' attention to mirrors as searches not for their own but for a mother's face: the girl's "adolescent phase of self-examination in the mirror" (Winnicott's phrase) might in these terms be both a search for her own life as a subject and a search for the motherly caregiver she has had to become (116).

 Shrinking into dimeters, those lines emphasize the girl's frustrated desire to know who she "really" is: why does she feel she cannot? It is not just that mirrors reverse right and left, nor that the girl's face and body have been changing. Nor is the problem solely (as Flynn implies) that she has had to behave like — hence identified herself with — her dead mother. It is also that she cannot know who she is without help *both* from fictions and from real other people. Is she a fairy-tale princess, like the people with "beautiful golden hair" in the Pink and Golden and Blue fairy books in her bedroom? Or are those books "Anachronisms / East of the sun and west of the moon," which she ought to abandon for class struggle? Various fictional modes compete in her mind, and the poem's tableaux bring them into tenderly ironic conflict:

She wraps in white tissue paper
A shiny *Coming Struggle for Power*
For her best friend —
And ties it, one gold, gritty end
Of the string in her mouth, and one in her left hand;
Her right forefinger presses down the knot. . . .

           (CP 42–43)

The charm, and the oddity, come from the juxtapositions — Strachey against gold string and tissue paper — and from the competing stories about the world these competing details represent. The girl's uncertainty about how she looks and who she is seems inseparable from her uncertainty about which symbols fit her life.[37]

The girl and the poem depict her adolescence as a process of self-discovery but also as a progressive discovery of helplessness. As she invokes political and ethical dilemmas much larger than she is, her particular feelings of futility come to look like special cases of general human helplessness—of the helplessness of young people among adults, of everyone before death, of thirties art before capitalism and war, and of literature in general, which for Jarrell may aspire to social efficacy but produces, at best, interpersonal empathy. Of the fictive modes the girl has available, fairy tales are the only ones that promise neither this-worldly nor otherworldly happy endings. The poem thus ends neither with Christ nor with Marx but with the Babes in the Wood:

> Staring, staring
> At the gray squirrel dead in the snow,
> She and her brother float up from the snow—
> The last crumbs of their tears
> Are caught by the birds that are falling
> To strew their leaves on the snow
> That is covering, that has covered
> The play-mound under the snow . . .
> The leaves are the snow, the birds are the snow,
> The boy and the girl in the leaves of their grave
> Are the wings of the bird in the snow.
>
>   (CP 50)

Here (as in the wartime dream poems) Jarrell grafts modernist stream-of-consciousness syntax to the vocabulary of children's stories: the effect is of strained or failed reassurance, of words—repeated, incantatory words—that work as inadequate shields against death. If "a dream is the fulfillment of a wish," part of the wish expressed here (as in "The Black Swan") is that the girl join her sibling in death. Yuletide "snow" thus indicates (like Joyce's snow in "The Dead," like the leaves in the fairy tale) a universal helplessness and mortality. Her brother is dying, and she can no more prevent his death than she can help Victorian laborers, or save the squirrels, or educate "Martha Janitor."[38] She dreams (in a nod to *Peter Pan*) of flying along with her brother and then of returning to the forest to read, to him, gravestones:

There are words on the graves of the snow.
She whispers, "When I was alive,
I read them all the time.
I read them all the time."
And he whispers, sighing:
"When I was alive . . . "

And, moving her licked, chapped, parted lips,
She reads, from the white limbs' vanished leaves:
To End Hopefully
Is A Better Thing—
                    A Far, Far Better Thing—
It is a far, far better thing . . .

She feels, in her hand, her brother's hand.
She is crying.

(CP 51)

The poem ends here, in tears. The girl's imagined posthumous whispers echo what she had said, awake, to her brother: "*When I was your age* I read them all the time." Aging seems, here, hard to tell from dying: the right reactions to dying—the girl's reactions—include both sympathy and fantasy, reading and holding hands.[39]

To be buried in the snow or (like the Babes in the Wood) amid the leaves is one way for the girl to imagine sharing her brother's fate, but it is also a way for her to imagine not growing up. Flynn seems to condemn her for not wanting to grow up, and even for wearing boys' pajamas, with which she "reverts to pre-aware, presexual childhood" (*Lost* 61). There is no reason to think she would be better off without her boys' pajamas, just as there is no reason to wish she were not reading the Fairy Books or the Factory Acts: for her to be more grown-up, farther from fairy tales or more womanly, would only, in the world of the poem, bring her farther from imaginative consolations and closer to death. It seems better to say that for her, as for Jarrell himself, the sources of imaginative power have to do with the consciousness of the child as it is both recollected and recreated in later life. The mind of Jarrell's sort of poet mediates uneasily between the childhood we can no longer have and the adulthood we are obliged to assume. This adolescent protagonist of Jarrell's *ars poetica* thus learns to use tools from children's and from adults' books to interpret, without quite accepting, a world full of tragic "adult" facts: facts like child labor and like the deaths of squirrels, and boys, and mothers.

Refusing compression, masculine "hardness" and "toughness," and surface so-phistication, "The Night Before," Longenbach writes, "represents [Jarrell's] most ambitious effort to write against . . . his teachers['] . . . strategically limited reading of modernism" (62). Alternating humanistic sentiment, realistic detail, fairy-tale pathos, and tactical vagueness, the poem also constitutes Jarrell's im-plicit answer, not just to the Marxian doctrines of his own youth but to mod-ernist long poems.

Introducing William Carlos Williams's 1948 *Selected*, Jarrell compared Williams's extended sympathies to the narrow ones evinced by Eliot's *Four Quartets*; when Williams published the first book of *Paterson* in 1946, Jarrell, de-lighted, called it *in potentia* "the best very long poem that any American has written" (*Age* 241, 233). Between Eliot and Williams stood Ezra Pound, whose *Pisan Cantos* circulated in manuscript as early as the fall of 1946.[40] Jarrell re-acted to Pound's 1948 Bollingen Prize by drafting "The Pound Affair." In April 1948 Jarrell wrote Williams a chatty, admiring letter, announcing his intention to visit Pound at St. Elizabeth's and calling Williams' comments on Jarrell's work "the most interesting thing anybody's ever written about my poetry" (*Let-ters* 190–191). The same letter included a draft of "The Night Before. "

These circumstances suggest, and the poem confirms, that "The Night Before" emerged not only from long thought about childhood and youth but also from Jar-rell's readings of modern long poems. In considering, and in rejecting, both thir-ties left politics and Christian doctrine, Jarrell's first significant long poem amounts to a troubled liberal answer to the ambitious social, philosophical, or theological projects envisioned in Pound and Eliot, more ambiguously in Williams, and in thirties writers from Brecht to the young Jarrell.[41] Like the *Can-tos* and *Paterson* and *Four Quartets*, Jarrell's poem sometimes imagines its protag-onist as the ironically powerless incarnation of premodern culture-heroes (such as Odysseus or Sidney Carton). Much of the "plot" of Jarrell's poem consists of the girl's attempt to apply the ambitious works she has been reading—the Gospels, *Capital*—to her particular waking and dreaming life. As she looks out her window,

> Use, surplus-, and exchange-
> Value (all these and plain
> Value)
> Creak slowly by, the wagon groans—
> Creak by, like rags, like bottles—
> Like rags, like bottles, like old bones . . . .
> The bones of men. Her breath is quickened
> With pitying indignant pain.

> (CP 44)

The girl's attempts to imagine a basis of contact with the "less fortunate"—from the "Martha Janitor" in her building to the squirrels outside her room—recall Eliot's efforts at Little Gidding, Williams' efforts in *Paterson*, and Pound's in confinement at Pisa to find a basis of solidarity stronger than history (CP 46). Readers move, with the girl, *from* grand moral and political frames for making sense of experience *to* the more intimate contexts of the girl's family history, from public "values" to interpersonal ones: as James Atlas put it, the poem's "effect is to localize history" (27).

The poem thus enacts the turn Jarrell's criticism takes, away from large-scale political questions toward the interpersonal. We have seen that turn in essays such as "The Age of Criticism" and in "The Pound Affair": another excerpt from the latter reads:

> The virtuous left, top, good half of our time said to each of us: "You have one responsibility, the world. You must remember to treat each life as an end—wherever it is possible or expedient, that is—*except your own*; your own life is a means by which those other lives, present or future, can be changed for the better—when you yourself have become nothing but a means, a means to that end, you will no longer need to feel to such a degree, the guilt which you feel, and are right to feel, at present."
>
> (12–13; emphasis in original)

"The Night Before" is Jarrell's way of giving such feelings their due—of representing them accurately, and of framing them in the less public concerns that seemed to Jarrell more important. At the same time, "The Night Before" enacts the turn Jarrell's earlier work had suggested, away from modernist isolation and toward "other people." Jarrell had objected that Eliot's "I" in *Four Quartets* never really met or touched anyone else.[42] "The Night Before" responds even to that: "She feels, in her hand, her brother's hand. / She is crying" (CP 51). Moving, with relentless intertextuality, from other people's books and histories to a dream scene where the only speakers are the girl and her brother, "The Night Before" arguably moves from a top-down, deductive ethics based on interpretations of laws, rules, and history to a relational ethics based on immediate sympathy. Sympathetic readers of the *Pisan Cantos* in 1946–49 found themselves making the same move, from Pound as overambitious historical projector to Pound as private artist: Jarrell in "The Pound Affair" became just such a reader.

The poem's search for pathos and for the interpersonal (as against modernist ambition and isolation) finally returns us, and it, not just to Jarrell's use of adolescence but to Jarrell's Wordsworthianism. Its equivocal parallels between historical, socioeconomic deprivation (as represented by *Capital*, by

"Martha Janitor" and "Martha Locomotive-Engineer") and inevitable or natu-
ral loss (the mother's death, the brother's illness) sketch out a position on the
nature and purpose of poetry very close to that of a later Wordsworthian, Geof-
frey Hartman. On the one hand, Hartman writes, "poetry . . . cannot confirm
or disconfirm specific remedies concerning social and political reorganization"
(*Fateful* 62). On the other hand, "art, beginning with romanticism, reflect[s] a
deepening tension between something elegiac . . . a mode of being that is lost
. . . and culture as a creative and contestatory force, helping to cancel old and
form new institutions" (*Fateful* 190). The genius of Jarrell's long poem—and of
the girl he creates—is to side with the elegiac while giving the institutional am-
bitions their due.

The girl's ultimate helplessness to do anything *but* sympathize thus comes to
stand not for the limits of politics but for the limits of poetry. The texts and the-
ories invoked in "The Night Before the Night Before Christmas" offer the girl
in the poem not clear rules for public action but models of sympathy and soli-
darity, analogies and examples for the attention and care poems can provide.
Such care, in turn, seems to belong especially to persons whose place in the
public world is ambiguous, marginal, or powerless—to persons who cannot be
quite be considered children, but who are not full citizens, not adults. The atti-
tudes and ethics recommended by Jarrell's kind of literature—as against those
of high modernist public poems—seem peculiarly the property of adolescence:
if adults cannot share them, so much the worse for adults.

Are these attitudes peculiarly proper, not just to young people but to *girls*?
Freud notoriously assigned women and girls to "the interests of the family," men
to "the work of civilization" (21:103). Nancy Chodorow (citing Juliet Mitchell)
explains that "the social organization of parenting has meant that it is women
who represent the nonsocial . . . and men who unambiguously represent soci-
ety" (*Mothering* 81). The values and ethics I have found in "The Night Before,"
and elsewhere in Jarrell, may also recall the relational ethics Carol Gilligan as-
sociates with women's experience, which "recognize[s] for both sexes the im-
portance throughout life of the connection between self and other, the univer-
sality of the need for compassion and care" (98). Certainly a girl who is
powerless, caring, and crying would be more acceptable to fifties readers, and
perhaps to Jarrell himself, than a boy with the same props, books, and feelings.
(He seems to have turned the speaker in "The Face" from man to woman for
such reasons.) If to be male is (in the words of the song the girl quotes) to be
someone who "must be READy to take POWer," women's and girls' space is by
contrast suited for a poetic defense of private affections (CP 45).

Femininity, in "The Night Before," stands for private as against public life
and values and represents intersubjective affections (and an ethics, and a poet-

ics, based on them) as against political programs. To see this is to see only one of the many ways in which Jarrell used the concept of gender—a category as important to him as age (though no more so) and one no less tied up with family structure. This chapter has shown how Jarrell used ideas and categories that sort individuals by age; the next will show how his work examines, from the perspectives of children and of grown-ups, gender difference and the workings of families. These children and families in turn produce the past that adults can remember: the child's past, emerging from the family, creates the foundation for Jarrell's adult self.

Chapter 6

MEN, WOMEN, CHILDREN, FAMILIES

Every family, John Demos writes, "is (and was) both a system of gender relations *and* a system of age relations" (12). Chapter 5 looked at children and at adolescents in Jarrell's poems and prose; this chapter will examine women and men, mothers and fathers, the families they constitute, and how children fare within them. We have seen already how Jarrell, like his culture, associated femininity with private life and with sympathy—and how he associated himself and his work with all three.[1] Jarrell's later poems depict some men and women who long for private connections and sympathies such as those articulated by the girl of "The Night Before." When those connections work as we would wish, they define intersubjective recognition. When they go wrong, they turn the relations that comprise the family—relations of supposed intimacy—into constricting, obligatory roles.

Jarrell's concerns about mid-century culture moved him to view the family as a refuge from the impersonal, instrumental "social" world. At the same time his psychoanalytic concerns helped him find a vocabulary for pathologies of motherhood, fatherhood, and the nuclear family. In Richard Flynn's apt phrase, Jarrell's "happy families are all invented": these families make space for the imagination Jarrell ascribed to children and for the intersubjective trust all Jarrell's characters seek (*Lost* 99). Jarrell's works explore the relations among childhood, adolescence, and families; among memory, play, reading, imagination, and intersubjective experience. They draw on, and find forms for, all these concepts in their effort to define and defend the self. That self turns out to require—and Jarrell's formal devices turn out to describe—at once attention from others, links to the personal past, and an ability to play.

The closer Jarrell gets to households and mothers, the more important gender seems to become. Some of Jarrell's best poems in the voices of women could almost have been spoken by men. In others, the interesting category is not *woman* but some smaller class.[2] Several poems of the fifties and sixties, however, try to comprehend "woman" as such: in them, as Helen Hagenbuchle put it, "Jarrell is likely to fuse actual women with his idea of Woman" (138). In doing so the poems show what male ideas of Woman are, and (at their best) how those ideas come to be.

Jarrell worked for over a decade on a long and diffuse verse essay called "Woman"—the poem (in all its versions) comprises not so much an argument as an anthology of ideas, short arguments, and quotations concerning women (as such) and femininity. Elizabeth Bishop declared the whole poem "dreadful" when she saw it in *Botteghe Oscure* in 1952; Jarrell excluded the poem from his next book but published a very heavily revised version in *The Lost World* (1965) (*One Art* 242). "Woman" includes essentialist axioms about what "man" and "woman" really are; speculations tracing adult gender differences to early nurture; musings on "your soap operas, your *Home Journals*," and domestic consumption; fragments of a poem on marital love; aphorisms about Man, who "searches for his ideal, / The Good Whore who reminds him of his mother"; and even Freud's declaration that women's " 'superego'—he goes on without hesitation— / "Is never so . . . independent of its emotional / Origins as we require it in a man' " (*CP* 324–329).[3] For Suzanne Ferguson (who admires the poem) "Freud's indictment is itself a form of praise" (*Poetry* 203). The 1952 version anticipates more recent readers' doubts: in it, Jarrell asks, "Have I husbanded uneasily the incarnate / Universal? . . . Or is all this not at all about / Woman, but about myself?" (383, 386). He goes on to identify men with means and women with ends: women "are what all uses / Are made for," while man's "work shall be his life" (389).

The much shorter, later "In Nature There is Neither Right Nor Left Nor Wrong" offers perhaps Jarrell's least convincing female speaker—she begins the finished poem by declaring, "Men are what they do, women are what they are" (*CP* 331). Drafts struggle to articulate something more complicated: one worksheet begins,

Men are valued for what they do, women
For what they are; this I am _____, these _____
are money with which I buy
    men's deeds jut into world

they made like pieces jigsaw
puzzle women emerge from, _____ into ·
The interstices like animals
inhabiting a geometry problem

(Berg Collection)

These lines, and the blanks within them, suggest that women enter the representational system men construct (a system coextensive with society) and find themselves uncomfortable within it. That system also compels women to behave like mothers: as the finished poem has it,

We women sell ourselves for sleep, for flesh,
To those wide-awake, successful spirits, men—
Who, lying each midnight with the sinister
Beings, their dark companions, women,
Suck childhood, beasthood, from a mother's breasts.

(CP 331)

Jarrell's grown woman opines that women are more practical than men—that men have forced them to be. Men, however, see women as "dark," intuitive, bodily, maternal; under the rule of such archetypes, John Brenkman writes, "The real-life mother is misrecognized . . . and the reality she has had for the son is transformed into images of a dreaded oceanic oneness" (183).

Why do men and women, children and mothers, conflate "woman" with "mother," mothers with motherhood, mothers with their families? Vendler finds in Jarrell repeated versions of "the child who was never mothered enough, the mother who wants to keep her children forever" (*Part* 112). Presenting such sentiments, Jarrell's poems also examine them. His clearest prose on the subject introduces Eleanor Ross Taylor's *A Wilderness of Ladies*, a book of poems Jarrell helped Taylor assemble.[4] "No poems can tell you better what it is like to be a woman," Jarrell wrote (with the odd implication that he *knew*); "none come more naturally out of a woman's ordinary existence" (*SH* 205). Taylor's poems, like Jarrell's own Washington Zoo, show how "The world is a cage for women, and inside it the woman is her own cage":

First there were her own family's demands on the girl, and now there are the second family's demands on the woman; and worst of all, hardest of all, are the woman's demands on herself—so that sometimes she longs to be able to return to the demands of the first family, when the immediate world was at least childish and natural, and one still had child allies in the war against the grown-ups. Now the family inside—the conscience, the superego—is a separate, condemning self from which there is no escape except in suicide or fantasies of suicide. . . . And which, really, is the I? The demanding conscience, or the part that tries to meet—tries, even to escape from—its demands?

(SH 197–198)

Adrienne Rich presented her prose work *Of Woman Born* as an attempt to rescue real-life mothers from just such a "family inside": "in the eyes of society," Rich objected, "once having been mothers, what are we if not always mothers?" (*Born* 37). Motherhood under patriarchy, Rich argues, instructs the mother to sculpt her personality into an instrument for the use of the child. If this creates resistance in women with other ambitions, it also creates mothers and former mothers who feel they can be nothing else.[5]

This cultural problem drives Jarrell's poem "The Lost Children." The mother who speaks that poem feels that, with her children dead or grown, nobody can really see who she "is"; she feels adrift or lost with respect to the course of her own life. As she recapitulates Jarrell's other poems on aging, her experience raises the questions Rich would later pursue: how and why did motherhood become a permanent identity, and what can such a concept do to mothers? Of this mother's "Two little girls, one fair, one dark," one has grown up and moved away; one is long dead. In the mother's dream, however, both girls

> are running hand in hand
> Through a sunny house. The two are dressed
> In red and white gingham, with puffed sleeves and sashes.
> They run away from me . . . But I am happy;
> When I wake I feel no sadness, only delight.
> I've seen them again, and I am comforted
> That, somewhere, they still are.

(CP 301)

"The dream of the sunny house," Mary Jarrell wrote, "was a dream I told him, and those were my photographs of my daughters" (*Remembering* 123).[6] Evolving from Mary's account, "The Lost Children" became one of Jarrell's talkiest poems but also one of his most intricately crafted, dependent throughout on repeated phrases and words.

These repetitions offer several ways to read the mother's troubles. The poem could be viewed through Freud's "Mourning and Melancholia," since its mother has failed to give up "the work of mourning in which the ego is absorbed" (14:245). Yet her nostalgic grief focuses less on the "dark one's" death than on the way that both girls grew up and away: "the fair one . . . Is lost just as the dark one, who is dead, is lost." The "objects" (in the psychoanalytic sense) she grieves are not her daughters, exactly, but her daughters-as-children. She thus speaks as if trying to retrieve them, and to understand how they—and she—got "lost." A child reaching her teens (the mother recalls)

> argues with you or ignores you
> Or is kind to you. She who begged to follow you
> Anywhere, just so long as it was you,
> Finds follow the leader no more fun.
> She makes few demands; you are grateful for the few.
>
>   (CP 301–302)

Repetitions portray the woman's reverie through interlocking sets of ordinary words, often at line breaks: *you . . . to you . . . to follow you . . . you . . . follow the leader . . . few . . . you . . . few.* The poem seems, like the aging mother's memories, to double back and repeat itself, as if searching for the vanished girls. Verbs evoke the same concentration on memory: except in the poem's last line, this mother is the subject of action verbs (*braided, was driving*) only when those verbs take the past tense. In the present, and in the recent past ("the other day"), all she can do is contemplate and perceive—*know, look, stare, realize, believe*:

> The girl from next door, the borrowed child,
> Said to me the other day, "You like children so much,
> Don't you want to have some of your own?"
> I couldn't believe that she could say it.
> I thought: "Surely you can look at me and see them."
>
>   (CP 303)

This aging mother seems really to have expected her motherhood and her "lost" children to be visible in her person. (Rich might say that to look at a mother and see, always, her children is exactly the expectation the institution of motherhood creates.) In the same way, the mother expected her "lost" fair-haired child to be visible in her grown daughter: "I stare at her and try to see some sign / Of the child she once was. I can't believe there isn't any" (CP 302). The girl from next door should have seen the children in the mother, she feels, just as the mother should have seen the child in the adult. The family this nameless mother began has recreated her in its image—shouldn't she look like what she is?

In Jarrell's poems, however, nobody looks like the person she feels she is. The borrowed girl's gaze, and the daughter's old photograph, work like more of

Jarrell's unsatisfactory mirrors: people in Jarrell have to be understood, properly recognized, through shared speech—intersubjectively or not at all. And (as in "Seele im Raum") this speaker feels she can be recognized only in the alternate world she remembers, a world of imaginary companions—the lost children of the title. She can be with them—and hence feel like herself—only in the past her dream life recaptures.:

> When I see them in my dreams I feel such joy.
> If I could dream of them every night!
>
> When I think of my dream of the little girls
> It's as if we were playing hide-and-seek.
> The dark one
> Looks at me longingly, and disappears;
> The fair one stays in sight, just out of reach
> No matter where I reach. I am tired
> As a mother who's played all day, some rainy day.
> I don't want to play it any more, I don't want to,
> But the child keeps on playing, so I play.
>
> (CP 303)

The mother, "reaching" back to her dream, says she is *as tired as* a mother, as if to remind us that she only plays at remaining one. In doing so she is playing (as children "play house") at a maternal role—a role in whose absence she feels she has disappeared. "Playing," and playing at being a mother, comprise an alternative not to work but to nonbeing. As in "The Player Piano," when the "play" ends, the poem does too.

"The Lost Children" and "In Nature" explored the conflation of *woman* with *mother*. Other poems and stories see mothers, fathers, and children from other points of view. Jarrell reminded readers of *The Man Who Loved Children* that even a "single separate" "man on a park bench"

> is separated off, not separate—is a later, singular stage of an earlier plural being. All the tongues of men were baby talk to begin with: go back far enough and which of us knew where he ended and Mother and Father and Brother and Sister began? The singular subject in its objective universe has evolved from that original composite entity—half subjective, half objective, having its own ways and laws and language, its own life and its own death—the family.
>
> (Third 3)

Families give Jarrell both psychoanalytic starting points for his thought about childhood and gender and alternatives to the public, "social" world.

Social researchers have found that Americans often attribute to families the characteristics of privacy and care that Jarrell sought in art. The sociologist Chaya Piotrkowski (citing A. Skolnick) asserts that by the 1970s "the family [had] become idealized as the realm of affectivity, intimacy and significant ascribed relations, in contradistinction to the public work world, which is impersonal, competitive, and characterized by the instrumental rather than the expressive" (6). For John Brenkman, Freud's oedipal "household provided a scene of individual male authority distinct from, yet complicit with, the political scene of potential or supposed male equality" (234). Rather than buttressing a public space of male equality, Jarrell's private enclosures—in households, in scenes of reading within those households, even in the stacks of libraries—compete with that public world, providing at their best an alternative space in which intersubjective relations, and "play" in all its meanings, become possible. In Jarrell's time and place, such a space seemed by default or assumption feminine.

Feminine household space also seemed (at that time and place) to hold its own dangers. If "The Lost Children" represents Jarrell's closest approach to later analyses of motherhood, "Windows" links his anxieties about the family to the mass-culture critique of his own time. In this and a few other poems from the 1950s, the nuclear family leaves no room for change or speech: either one stands outside it, painfully lonely, or one enters it and thereby loses individuality and consciousness, falling asleep in a fantasy of incestuous union with a mother or womb. (Jessica Benjamin describes this binary choice as a failure of intersubjective play; Williamson and Kinzie find something like it elsewhere in Jarrell.) One of the achievements of "Windows" is its way of making a complex, Rilkean syntax sound natural and spoken. Another achievement lies in its exploration of maternal and familial fantasies, linking them to the particulars of mid-century geography and technology.[7]

Like "The Lonely Man," "Windows" was written in Princeton in 1951–52. Like that poem, "Windows" begins with a lonely adult on a suburban road, surveying the outdoors, then moving inside, into homes:

Quarried from snow, the dark walks lead to doors
That are dark and closed. The white- and high-roofed houses
Float in the moonlight of the shining sky
As if they slept, the bedclothes pulled around them.
But in some the lights still burn. The lights of others' houses.

Those who live there move seldom, and are silent.

Their movements are the movements of a woman darning,
A man nodding into the pages of the paper,
And are portions of a rite—have kept a meaning—
That I, that they know nothing of.

(CP 232)

In many famous springtime poems, the speaker laments his inaction amid na-
ture's forms of growth. Coleridge complained that in a late-February "dream of
Spring," "I the while, the sole unbusy thing, / Nor honey make, nor pair, nor
build, nor sing" (*Poetical* 1:447). Jarrell torques that tradition by presenting an
active speaker uneasy in the presence of tranquil inaction. Comforting, un-
reachable, and self-contained, the families he sees recall families on television:

> As dead actors, on a rainy afternoon,
> Move in a darkened living-room, for children
> Watching the world that was before they were,
> The windowed ones within their windowy world
> Move past me without doubt and for no reason.
>
> *These* actors, surely have known nothing of today,
> That time of troubles and of me. Of troubles.

Jarrell's lonely speaker wants to join the families he watches. But what he imag-
ines goes on in them is not intimacy (they don't *speak*) but assimilation, uncon-
sciousness:

> If only I were they!
> Could act out, in longing, the impossibility
> That haunts me like happiness!
> Of so many windows, one is always open.
>
> Some morning they will come downstairs and find me.
> They will start to speak, and then smile speechlessly,
> Shifting the plates, and set another place
> At a table shining by a silent fire.
> When I have eaten they will say, "You have not slept."
>
> And from the sofa, mounded in my quilt,
> My face on *their* pillow, that is always cool,
> I will look up speechlessly into a—

It blurs, and there is drawn across my face
As my eyes close, a hand's slow fire-warmed flesh.

It moves so slowly that it does not move.

(*CP* 232–333)

And that is the end of the poem. The lonely man wants to be close to someone else, close enough to feel intimate with them, but cannot imagine himself entering any such relation without joining a family whose attractions return us to infancy and put us to sleep.

Once we enter the house, the poem leaves behind all its abstract nouns and all its reflective verbs: it consists, like a child's story, of people, actions, and things. The poem moves, as the speaker finds his "happiness," from speech to less speech, from reflection to naïve description to no words at all: it moves from ordinary loneliness to what Melanie Klein calls (in "On the Sense of Loneliness") "an unsatisfied longing for an understanding without words—ultimately for the earliest relation with the mother" (301). Chodorow writes that in such a model "the internalized experience of self in the original mother-relation remains seductive and frightening: Unity was bliss, yet meant the loss of self and absolute dependence" (*Mothering* 194). "Windows" thus displays, and knows it displays, a male fantasy or fear in which joining a family becomes the same as engulfment by feminine feeling. The experience that the lonely man in "Windows" imagines is one he wants desperately to have. Yet (as with the Prince in "Variation") we might find it disturbing, even threatening: this particular sleep, in its ultimate immobility, looks much like death.[8]

If the sources here are psychoanalytic, they are also sociological. The poem's lit-up, snowed-under households suggest that a nuclear family—in particular the suburban, middle-class, "Freudian-American family" (Rich's phrase)—can duplicate within itself the "social ethic," the reduction of people to roles, that Jarrell and others saw in the larger society (*Born* 25). The same assimilation of people to roles, which in the workplace is called "professionalization" or "scientific management" or "cooperation," is in the family a submission to roles that look like instincts and that we act out in some fairy tales and dreams. Those satisfactions become in "Windows" a wish for the loss of the self. And yet we do not want to live without roles; most of us do not want to live without some relation to parents, or siblings, or children, if we have them. The poem asks how we can carry on those relations without being programmed by them, and the answer "Windows" gives is that—in the milieu the poem describes—we cannot. That milieu is the postwar American nuclear family, in its own family home: in 1946, writes Elaine Tyler May, "for the first time, a majority of the nation's families lived in homes they owned" (304). The new "suburban home," May continues, "was planned as a self-contained universe. . . . Family members would not need to go out for recreation or amusements, since they had swing sets, playrooms and backyards with barbecues" (305). Jarrell makes that new family environment see all too "self-contained," its enticements at once infantilizing and seductive.

If "Windows" worries about new homes and suburbs, it also introduces social concerns specific to television, whose pictures (unlike stage plays or movies) enter the home. In September 1949 only 13 percent of households in the American Northeast had televisions; by July 1951 the figure was 45 percent, and a year later 59 percent (Bogart 108). The cultural historian Richard Butsch has described an "early 1950s . . . belief that television was very powerful and would turn the worlds of leisure, culture and education upside down" (237). Jarrell likens television (home of the "darkened actors") to picture windows (home of the children who watch them): when this lonely man slips into his comforting fantasy, it is as if he had slipped inside television, whose business, Jarrell thought, was to provide enveloping, passive fantasies. "The Taste of the Age" imagines what such fantasies would have done to Queen Victoria and Albert: they end up

> sitting before the television set, staring into it, silent; and inside the set, there are Victoria and Albert, staring into the television camera, silent, and the master of ceremonies is saying to them: "No, I think you will find that *Bismarck* is the capital of North Dakota!"
>
> (KA 297)

The art critic Thomas Keenan describes "the double incorporation by which television at once contains the world and is then recontained by the home, a home that can then be reintegrated into the world home-system to the extent that 'all' the homes share this new inhabitant—the television light" (130). Jarrell's passage about Prince Albert, and his poem about a snowbound home, imagines just such "recontainment." And such a "world home-system" sounds comforting but also totalizing. If the whole world works as a home, there can be nothing outside to discover: no youth and no growing up. "The ubiquitous TV antenna is a symbol of people seeking—and getting—the identical message," the market researcher Leo Bogart remarked in 1960 (99). Familial roles in Jarrell's poem, too, welcome anyone and obliterate differences—they are roles, the poem suggests, anyone *could* learn to play, if only by giving up what distinguishes him or her from anyone else.

This critique of motherly households and of television recalls many other mid-century portraits of "mass culture" as a threatening maternal Blob.[9] "Windows" does repeat, from a man's point of view, the familiar identification of motherhood with "mass culture" and with a dangerous oceanic oneness. But the poem can also be seen as a prescription. A better family, while secure, would enable its members, and especially its children, to leave and then to return, providing both clear boundaries between outside and inside and a durable alternation of security and adventure, reassurance, and change. Moreover, such a family would not restrict itself to a mother-child dyad: it might admit new members. Such families emerge in the extended household of "The Lost World"; in Jarrell's last children's book, *The Animal Family*; and in "The Owl's Bedtime Story," a poem from another children's book, *Fly by Night*. Jarrell's young owl finds a grown owl dead in the snow, and then rescues an orphaned owlet;

> when he was near
> And stopped, all panting, underneath the nest
> And she gazed down at him, her face looked dear
> As his own sister's, it was the happiest
> Hour of his life. In a little, when the two
> Had made friends, they started home.
>
> (CP 349)

Typically, for Jarrell, the adventure the owl contemplates, and achieves, involves the discovery and rescue of a companion. Less typically, this household maintains itself with a responsible, idealized mother: "All night the mother would appear / And disappear, with good things; and the two / Would eat and eat and eat, and then they'd play" (CP 350).[10]

"The Owl's Bedtime Story" presents an ideal mother in an idealized household, even ending with the maternal rhyme words *nest/ rest/ breast* (CP 350). "Windows" encompasses a period's fears about real mothers and households instead. Personal ideals and social fears interact in the long late poem called "Hope" (the second of two by that name), which follows the thoughts and actions of a young, well-to-do husband. The poem begins when he and his wife return to their Manhattan apartment "at two in the morning / Of Christmas," and tracks his thoughts through the night, until husband, wife, and son eat breakfast. The earlier poem called "Hope" had simply wished something new would come in the mail. Here the narrator's more specific "Hope" (we come to realize) is that he not replicate his own "first family": in particular, he hopes that his wife will not seem to him like his mother. "Hope" considers at length a fear of mothers and what mothers represent—a fear of engulfment and domination. Some readers might see such fears as the subject of the poem (and, hence, the dissolution of those fears as its project). Other readers might emphasize, instead, the poem's varied imaginings of play and childlikeness, or else the ways in which "Hope" shows how its frightening, transferential Mothers have been culturally produced.[11] Sometimes diffuse, sometimes dense, the poem has largely resisted previous critics: to see how it works, and that it works, will require extended attention here.

The poem's provocative opening compares pretended or fictive family "nests" (like the one in "The Owl's Bedtime Story") to actual family dwellings:

> To prefer the nest in the linden
> By Apartment Eleven, the Shoreham
> Arms, to Apartment Eleven
> Would be childish. But we are children.
>
> > (CP 305)

We have to hear the fourth line's stress on "are" to make sense not just of the lines but of the household. To be "children" is to be able to play at adult social roles (like "mother" and "father") without being reduced to them. And yet the lines are as anxious, perhaps as embarrassed, as they are hopeful: can mothers and fathers *want* to be children? Should they? One of Jarrell's many worksheets invokes

HOPE AS CHILDHOOD

> same story but ended differently
> long run one gives up hope of growing up
> marooned on island of childhood FLOE ice castle
> getting smaller and end in water
> but isn't that where one wants to be?
>
> > (Berg Collection)

Do the adults—does this husband—"want to be" in the water or on the ice floe? Ought he try to grow up, or should he resist becoming his parents? The early parts of the finished poem dramatize just such questions: husband and wife

> Walk up the corridor, unlock the door,
> And go down stone steps, past a statue
> To the nest where the father squirrel, and the mother squirrel, and the
> baby squirrel
> Would live, if the baby squirrel could have his way.

Just now he has his way.
Curled round and round in his sleigh
Bed, the child of the apartment
Sleeps, guarded by a lion six feet long.
And, too,
The parents of the apartment fight like lions.
Between us, we are almost twelve feet long.

(CP 305)

The adults have quarreled, this evening, like real lions, but the child hopes they will behave like protective, good fairy-tale lions instead. And the husband seems to share those hopes. He imagines himself and his wife as storybook characters, rather as Jarrell imagined Mary: "Sometimes we were brother and sister 'like Wordsworth and Dorothy' and other times we were twins, Randall pretended. 'The Bobbsey Twins at the Plaza,' he'd say up in our room at the Plaza" (*Remembering* 135). This Jarrellian ideal of marriage is notably and deliberately nonsexual, "childlike": close, in fact, to what Melanie Klein names "the universal phantasy of having a twin" (302).

Once it arrives inside the apartment, "Hope" portrays a multitude of possessions—a "cold / Hill of gifts" under a Christmas tree, Expressionist paintings, and this:

from a province of Norway, a grandfather's
Clock with the waist and bust of a small
But unusually well-developed woman
Is as if invented by Chagall.
Floating on the floor,
It ticks, to no one, interminable proposals.

But, married, I turn into my mother
Is the motto of all such sundials.
The sun, shattering on them,
Says, *Clean, clean, clean*; says, *White, white, white.*
The hours of the night
Bend darkly over them; at midnight a maiden
Pops out, says: *Midnight, and all's white.*

(CP 306)

Something is wrong with this "well-developed" sexualized timekeeper, which makes proposals, marks the passage of time, and dutifully produces, *as if* by na-

ture, maidens devoted to keeping things "clean." It is a kind of parody of repro-
duction — of childbearing and of what Chodorow calls "the reproduction of
mothering." In the clock, the production of maidens and mothers seems to be a
mechanical, lawlike process. Girls "pop out," become "unusually well-developed,"
marry, and "turn into" their mothers; boys grow up to marry those mothers and
eventually become "grandfathers," as if by clockwork.

If this is the way that adults are produced, it might indeed be better not to
grow up. And yet that alternative also makes this husband uncomfortable:

> "A wife is a wife,"
> Some husband said. If only it were true!
> My wife is a girl playing house
> With the girl from next door, a girl called the father.
> And yet I *am* a father, my wife is a mother,
> Oh, every inch a mother; and our son's
> Asleep in a squirrel's nest in a tree.
>
> (CP 307)

Here the man wishes his marriage were *less* like play, more comprehensible or
ordinary. Wanting to feel more grown-up than he does, the man revisits, against
his will, his first family. Asleep, the wife in the poem "resembled a recurrent //
Scene from my childhood. / A scene called Mother Has Fainted" — the anxious
scene all Jarrell's critics read biographically, as a portrait of delicate, difficult
Anna Regan (CP 309). Helpless here, the remembered mother elsewhere in the
poem "governs the happy people of a planet." Such a mother, as several critics
have noted, fits a pattern of narcissistic mothers that Alice Miller (and other an-
alysts) have described: conforming selectively to feminine stereotypes, such
mothers control other people (consciously or not) by alternating helplessness
with stern management. Such mothers constitute, in fact, a type blamed by var-
ious thinkers, especially during the forties and fifties, for all sorts of malaises in
grown-up men.[12] But this mother is also a victim herself, a woman trapped in
the role she has become. If no husband would want her for a wife, no wife
would want to *be* her either. Moreover, no husband would want to mistake his
real wife for such a destructive archetype.

To realize he was making such a mistake, he would first have to understand
how projection and maternal transference had affected him. "Hope" depicts,
slowly, such an understanding; through hints and half-developed fantasies,
readers discover the cosmology of the husband's unconscious, the models of
human development (or regression) that he comes to realize he has held. Can-
celed verse paragraphs from drafts of "Hope" show — more directly than any-

thing in the finished poem—how the husband fears that he (like the man in "Windows") has been absorbed by a family:

> And why pretend
> That I am the husband? I *am* the husband
> And the wife and the child and Apartment Eleven
> I am them all.
>   each other
> We are a way for one another to be
> And cling to each
> a mode of the other's being
>
> 3rd way: wish-fantasy identification with child
> If you aren't your mother or me somehow
> I won't be me

(Berg Collection)

As contemporary readers of "Hope" we may understand the husband but feel for the wife. And the poem seems to anticipate that we will do so. In particular we feel with her what Rich calls "the anxiety of the objectified (woman, mother) who realizes that however much she may *wish* to render herself pleasing and nonthreatening, she will still to some degree partake of the feared aspect of Woman, an abstraction which she feels has nothing to do with her" (*Born* 71; italics Rich's). Much of "Hope" consists of the husband's attempts to characterize his wife. Much of it, too, amounts to his realization that the descriptions, stories, and fantasies he has been unfolding have something to do with his wife's personality but much more to do with his own. Elsewhere in the drafts the wife "hears or dreams that she hears, / Or I dream that she hears / Her father and mother. They are fighting in her sleep": the middle line is the key.

Examining a husband's structure of feeling, the poem asks what that husband might do to alter it. When he saw his newborn son, the husband remembers,

> I saw what I realized I must have seen
> When I saw my wedding picture in the paper:
> My wife resembled—my wife *was*—my mother.
>
> Still, that is how it's done.
> In this house everyone's a mother.
> My wife's a mother, the cook's a mother, the maid's a mother [. . .] (*CP* 310–311)

"Mothers" are threatening, practical, utilitarian, archetypal, sometimes domi-
nating, and sometimes overwhelmed by their responsibilities (so much so that
they faint). But how, "Hope" asks, did all the motherly people in his apartment
come to be as they are?

> Do all men's mothers perish through their sons?
> As the child starts into life, the woman dies
> Into a girl—and, scolding the doll she owns,
> The single scholar of her little school,
> Her task, her plaything, her possession,
> She assumes what is God's alone, responsibility.
>
> (*CP* 311)

Girls are brought up to share, and *men encourage them to share*, their mothers' too
practical, too selfless ethic of maternal responsibility. It is this ethic that creates
frightening, Motherly mothers like Jarrell's own, alternately dominating and help-
less. If these patterns of behavior and thought were passed on by nature and inher-
itance, they would be unbreakable, converting girls into women, wives into moth-
ers, and mothers into domineering archetypes, forever. The grandfather clock
would then be a sufficient symbol for human inheritance. But beside the clock
stands the green fir tree (drafts entitle the poem "The Fir Tree"): under the fir tree
are presents, their contents unknown. If the patterns of parenthood are cultural,
the tree and its gifts imply, we might surprise ourselves by seeing them changed.

Such changes (and here Jarrell stands on firm psychoanalytic ground) will
come when we stop denying our resemblances to our parents, and start under-
standing them.[13] The man in "Hope" finally tries to do just this. The associa-
tions and insistences in "Hope" work like parts of an actual psychoanalysis; we
watch the husband, a sort of analysand, as he tries to teach himself to distinguish
wife and son from mother and self. In its last scene,

> When my son reached into the toaster with a fork
> This morning, and handed me the slice of toast
> So clumsily, dropped it, and looked up at me
> So clumsily, I saw that he resembled—
> That he *was*—
>
>   I didn't see it.
>
> (*CP* 311)

Is the occluded word here "me," or "my father"? Or is it "mother," as it is in "A
Quilt-Pattern"? In that poem of Oedipal fantasy, biology becomes Freudian

truth and psychoanalysis is destiny. The ethical, tonal, and psychological suc-
cess of "Hope" is that it finds credible ways toward other conclusions. Finding
new hope in uncertainty, the allegro concluding lines pivot on their repeated
questions and on the new key words *not, know, new:*

> The next time that they say to me; "He has your eyes,"
> I'll tell them the truth: he has his own eyes.
> My son's eyes look a little like a squirrel's,
> A little like a fir tree's. They don't look like mine,
> They don't look like my wife's.
>   And after all,
> If they don't look like mine, do mine?
>
> You wake up, some fine morning, old.
> And old means changed; changed means you wake up new.
>
> In this house, after all, we're not all mothers.
> I'm not, my son's not, and the fir tree's not.
> And I said the maid was, really I don't know.
>
> The fir tree stands there on its cold
> White hill of gifts, white, cold,
> And yet really it's green; it's evergreen.
>
> Who knows, who knows?
> I'll say to my wife, in the morning:
> "You're not like my mother . . . You're no mother!"
> And my wife will say to me—
>   she'll say to me—
> At first, of course, she may say to me: "You're dreaming."
> But later on, who knows?
>
>   (*CP* 311–312)

Inevitability is for sundials and clocks—the right slogan for people is "Who
knows?" As in a succesful analysis, this husband has talked (to Jarrell's readers)
until he found himself able to change by dissolving a transference. As Suzanne
Ferguson puts it, "If he can convince himself, convince his wife, that she is not
like his mother, not a *Mother*, perhaps . . . they can wake up new" (*Poetry* 208).
That newness may look like "not growing up"; his family will seem to live at
once in a squirrel's nest and at Number Eleven.

"Hope" asks how a family might start to reinvent itself. Such reinventions take idealized, completed forms in Jarrell's children's books, which depict, in Flynn's words, "the need for happy yet improbable families that do not exist in the real world but have to be invented" (*Lost* 101–102). Such an invented, adopted family comes together in Jarrell's last and longest children's book, *The Animal Family*. The book's central figure, a hunter, meets and falls in love with a mermaid, who moves into his house on land; hunter and mermaid adopt and raise a bear, then a lynx, then an orphaned human boy.[14]

The book keeps up a paradoxical attitude toward the nuclear family it models. On one hand, hunter and mermaid duplicate and enjoy the normative family of the early-sixties American child who is Jarrell's imagined reader. Jerome Griswold finds that in the book's "repetition of generations, the hunter's wish is answered"; "things have evolved to the way they used to be, the way families have always been" (102–103). Yet hunter and mermaid form a remarkably odd family, one not only adoptive but playful, fabular. Things have never been *quite* this way, and life on land, the mermaid discovers is unpredictable—parents bring up their children by making up stories, and no one can know quite how things will be.[15]

As in *The Bat-Poet*, the initial problem of *The Animal Family* involves a lonely artist. The hunter would be a storyteller, if only he could find a listener:

> In spring the meadow that ran down from the cliff to the beach was all foam-white and sea-blue with flowers; the hunter looked at it and it was beautiful. But when he came home there was no one to tell what he had seen—and if he picked the flowers and brought them home in his hands, there was no one to give them to.
>
> (8)

With his birth family gone by the start of the book, the hunter needs to construct, or to happen on to, a new family.[16] The hunter dreams of his mother until he hears a mermaid, and then dreams of her. Mermaid and hunter find one another in waking life, and the hunter takes her in. "After the mermaid had lived with the hunter for a while," he tells her another dream:

> "My father was standing by the fire and he was double, like a man and his shadow—I was his shadow. And my mother sat there singing, and she was double too, like a woman and her shadow; and when I looked at it you were her shadow." [. . .]
>
> Finally the mermaid said to him: "I know what your dream means. It means you want a boy to live with us. Then you'll be your father's shadow,

and I'll be your mother's, and the boy will be yourself the way you used to
be—it will all be the way it used to be."

(33, 59–61)

Here the goal of a family seems to be to reproduce itself: a father (but not a
mother) seeks to recreate himself as a boy and thus to become his own father.
Griswold understandably finds the book "a tremendously complicated *male* fan-
tasy" in which "the hunter takes his father's place" (126; italics in original). And
yet the family developed by the hunter and mermaid looks rather different from
the one in his dream—it includes, after all, a mermaid and two wild animals.
Part of the humor, for grown-ups, is the suggestion that the work of raising a first
child is as overwhelming and strange to new parents as raising a bear. And part of
the serious point of this part of the book is the (Jessica) Benjaminesque one that,
with children as with grown-ups, to come to know someone better is not only to
feel closer to them but also to appreciate differences. The lynx's "notions of what
the two of them would find interesting were rather lynxish notions, often ending
in an 'Oh, is *that* all?' from the mermaid or the hunter; but his notions of what
would interest a bear were a bear's—the bear gobbled it up" (118–119).

Part of the work the book leaves for its young reader is thus to figure out ex-
actly how all families are alike and in what respects they can differ. The boy
finds in his new family, as the hunter does, a complete household: "except for
one or two confused, uneasy dreams, all the boy's memories were memories of
the mermaid and the hunter; he *knew* that the hunter was his father and the
mermaid his mother and had always been" (156).[17] A less complex children's
book would end there, with the child's discovery of security and belonging. But
Jarrell's book is more attentive than that: after the boy is adopted, narrative in-
terest returns to the mermaid, who considers the differences between her new
life on land and her old life at sea. To form a family, as hunter and mermaid
have done, is to replicate folkloric archetypes, but it is also to understand differ-
ence and change. Sea people, the mermaid avers, "don't know how to be bored
or miserable. One day is one wave, and the next day the next, for the sea peo-
ple—and whether they're glad or whether they're sorry, the sea washes it away"
(170). Our ability to grow dissatisfied, to want to make a future unlike the pres-
ent, and thereby to change over the course of a life, is what makes "land people"
different and interesting.

To want to be changed is to want to encounter difference; it is also to distin-
guish an outward person (whose attributes might be changed) from an interior
self (which does, and remembers, the changing). The group that the hunter,
mermaid, bear, lynx and boy form together thus represents the hunter's deepest
wish, but it is also a triumph of play and invention. The seemingly inevitable

family bonds formed in the book are also a continuing form of play, a conscious fiction the boy and his new parents share:

> [F]ar along the beach, by the little river, you could see the tiniest lynx there ever was. The boy looked and saw him and said laughing, "That's where he found *me!*"
>
> "Oh, we just told you that," said the hunter, starting their old game. "The very first day your mother and I came to the house, there you were in the corner, fast asleep."
>
> "That's right, fast asleep with *him*," said the boy, giving the bear a push.
>
> "Oh no," said the mermaid, "that was years before the bear came. We've had you always."
>
> (179–180)

Jarrell's last and most admired long poem, the triptych *The Lost World*, imagines another happy, artificial, and unusual family, the extended family of his grandparents and their friends, among whom the young Jarrell lived in Los Angeles in 1926–27, after his parents separated.[18] Jarrell based the poems on his memories, and on the letters he sent his mother during his year there. The poem is full of remembered details, not only from the household of "Mama" and "Pop" (the grandparents) and "Dandeen," (the great-grandmother) but from the Hollywood of the last silent films: among its props are the artificial dinosaurs of the film *The Lost World*, from which the work takes its name.[19] As it imagines its happy family, the poem connects familial relations to almost everything else Jarrell's oeuvre considers: a study of Jarrell's life work would be incomplete without a reading of the whole poem.

The Lost World depicts several kinds of intersubjective exchange—some successful, some frustrated. It experiments with imagined alternatives to a public, instrumental, social world: the poem's household becomes one such alternative, and its various fictive "worlds" become others. As it explores maturation and memory, it recalls the lessons Jarrell learned from psychoanalysis, as well as from Proust and Wordsworth. The poem also responds, in ways critics have not yet noticed, to other poems and to the public events of the Cold War. The poem organizes itself around oppositions and boundaries—adult/child, childhood/adolescence, work/play, fantasy/"real life," past/present, sleep/waking, public/private. Each transition hints at all the others, and all work together to establish at once a theory of "play" and a model of families.

The poem also, implicitly, sets Jarrell's happy year in Los Angeles against both his earlier childhood in California and his subsequent life with his mother in Tennessee. Compared to the families in Jarrell's previous poems, and to Jarrell's mother's household in Tennessee, the *Lost World* household also stands out for what it is not: it does not ask Randall to earn any money, and though it has a busy "Mama," it does not include a mother-and-child dyad. Flynn has implied that Jarrell's defense of the self requires a defense of the family. Yet the poems, and *The Lost World* most of all, do not so much defend as diagnose the particular form called the nuclear family, which had to be reinvented to meet its own goals.[20]

Part 1 of *The Lost World*, "Children's Arms," begins with perhaps the first child in all of Jarrell's poems who seems happy when he is not reading. This is because he lives (even when he is not reading) in a Hollywood replete with imaginative fictions. And this is one reason the poem's terza rima fits its matter: like Dante's *Commedia*, the "Lost World" poems offer a tour of a spectacular other world.[21] The same analogy explains the title. Hollywood is like the underground dinosaur-land of Arthur Conan Doyle's novel, and of the silent film based on it:

> On my way home I pass a cameraman
> On a platform on the bumper of a car
> Inside which, rolling and plunging, a comedian
> Is working: on one white lot I see a star
> Stumble to her igloo through the howling gale
> Of the wind machines. On Melrose a dinosaur
> And pterodactyl, with their immense pale
> Papier-mâché smiles, look over the fence
> Of *The Lost World*.
>   Whispering to myself the tale
> These shout—done with my schoolwork, I commence
> My real life: my arsenal, my workshop
> Opens, and in impotent omnipotence
> I put on the helmet and the breastplate Pop
> Cut out and soldered for me.

(CP 283)

Between fictions and life in L.A. stands not a high wall but a permeable fence. The comedian's "work" is attractive work, since it involves making things up. By the same token the best kind of howling gales are the ones from wind machines, and the best kind of "real life" is a collaborative participation in fictions—Pop makes the armor the boy wears, Homer and Virgil the scripts he follows.

As mock adventurer, mock Aeneas, the "armored" Randall seems to belong to the same class of fictions as papier-mâché dinosaurs and "Arctic" weather. These fictive realms merge with one another: all may seem, to grown-ups, faintly silly. Yet all seem, to the adult poet, collectively better than the world of adult work and power relations. If Jarrell once admired those fictions naïvely, he now admires them for the naïveté they connote and for the harmless powers they attribute to imagination. The poem thus classes together (as the child would not have) the silent movie, the backyard play, the "arms that arm, for a child's wars, the child," and the play the local high school puts on:

> In the black auditorium, my heart at ease,
> I watch the furred castaways (the seniors put
> A play on every spring) tame their wild beasts,
> Erect their tree house. Chatting over their fruit,
> Their coconuts, they relish their stately feasts.
> The family's servant, their magnanimous
> Master now, rules them by right. Nature's priests,
> They worship at Nature's altar; when with decorous
> Affection the Admirable Crichton
> Kisses a girl like a big Wendy, all of us
> Squirm or sit up in our seats . . . Undone
> When an English sail is sighted, the prisoners
> Escape from their Eden to the world: the real one
> Where servants are servants, masters masters,
> And no one's magnanimous. The lights go on
> And we go off, robbed of our fruit, our furs—
> The island that the children ran is gone.
>
> The island sang to me: *Believe! Believe!*
> And didn't I know a lady with a lion?

(CP 284)

One reaction to this passage might stress its comedy: the boys enjoy the play, but not the kissing. A second reaction might see it as a serious defense of children's wish-fulfillment fictions. These fictions constitute equipment that adults salvage for continued use only through memory, by establishing that we are *the same people who* once lived on that island—just as the woman of "The Player Piano" is the same girl who once skinned her knee.[22]

So far "The Lost World" seems to be entirely about fiction and fiction-making—childhood idyll, amateur drama, professional moviemaking, even a mock Shakespearean Green World, with "dried leaves marked THIS IS THE GREENWOOD." The poem then brings those properties into repeated contests with social, physical, and economic fact. Central to those contests will be the relations of children and families, as well as of the words *play, work, belief/believe,* and *habit,* on which the poem pivots:

> Each evening, as the sun sank, didn't I grieve
> To leave *my* tree house for reality?
> There was nothing there for me to disbelieve.
> At peace among my weapons, I sit in my tree
> And feel: *Friday night, then Saturday, then Sunday!*
>
> I'm dreaming of a wolf, as Mama wakes me,
> And a tall girl who is—outside it's gray,
> I can't remember, I jump up and dress.
> We eat in the lighted kitchen. And what is play
> For me, for them is habit. Happiness
> Is a quiet presence, breathless and familiar [. . .]
>
> (CP 284–285)

Here is the second occurrence of "play," and the first of several in rhyming position. These lines also introduce "habit" and "happiness": how to make habit happy, the repeating days of adult life worthwhile?[11] Young Randall and Pop ride a morning bus to

> the dark
> Echoing cavern, where Pop, a worker,
> Works for our living. As he rules a mark,
> A short square pencil in his short square hand,
> On a great sheet of copper, I make some remark
> He doesn't understand. In that hard maze—in that land
> The grown men live in—in the world of work,
> He measures, shears, solders; and I stand
> Empty-handed, watching him.
>
> (CP 285)

"Echoing" beyond what terza rima requires, the iterated sounds (*mark . . . remark, square . . . square, hand . . . understand . . . land . . . stand / Empty-*

handed) mimic factory-floor acoustics; they also suggest (as other repetitions will suggest) the echoes created by memory, which reinterprets "habit," "play," and "work" as it replays them.

The poem leaves Pop's occupation purposely vague, though it is clearly a skilled (and noisy) craft: Pop becomes a Wagnerian "dwarf hammering out the Ring / In the world under the world." Robert Watson writes that here "the child half-nurtured on make-believe tries to understand the habitual, work-a-day world of adults . . . by seeing it in terms of fiction" (*RJ* 268). If the child's world, the tree house, of play is insufficient, the adult world of work is nothing, or mere habit, unless the child's categories redescribe it. And if this "cavern" suggests hell, it is not a Christian hell but a pagan underworld (where all "grown men" eventually go). The problem the child will have to solve is not some dawning sense of sin but a growing awareness that there is a realm, a "world under the world," in which fictions and "children's arms" do not function, in which the relevant powers are not imaginative but industrial. That "world under the world" is what Marxian language calls a base—the secret source of power and structure for the family life it supports. The adult world is distinguished from the child's not by sexuality or disillusion but by its different relation to production and wage labor:

> The sooty thread
> Up which the laborers feel their way into
> Their wives and houses, is money; the fact of life,
> The secret the grown-ups share, is what to do
> To make money. The husband Adam, Eve his wife
> Have learned how not to have to do without
> Till Santa Claus brings them their Boy Scout knife—
> Nor do they find things in dreams, carry a paper route,
> Sell Christmas seals . . .
>
> (CP 285–286)

Jarrell's fifties essays distinguish private (aesthetic) life from the professions; these lines instead distinguish alienated, physical labor from the safer, and feminine, realm of houses and families. Divided (like the poem) into interdependent parts, the Los Angeles of factories, homes, and movie sets becomes a remarkably *benign* demonstration of such binaries as *public/private* and *work/play*—divisions themselves easily mapped onto the binarism *adult/child*.

The child understands Pop both as a Worker (in a world of Work as against Play) and as someone who can bring home real money: the child himself, by contrast, is noneconomic man. But the adult Pop is beloved because (unlike Uncle Howell) he can also participate in the world of children and play:

Starting *his* Saturday, his Sunday,
Pop tells me what I love to hear about,
His boyhood in Shelbyville. I play
What he plays, hunt what he hunts, remember
What he remembers: it seems to me I could stay
In that dark forest, lit by one fading ember
Of his campfire, forever . . . But we're home.
I run in love to each familiar member
Of this little state, clustered about the Dome
Of St. Nicholas—this city in which my rabbit
Depends on me, and I on everyone—this first Rome
Of childhood, so absolute in every habit
That when we hear the world our jailor say:
"Tell me, art thou a Roman?" the time we inhabit
Drops from our shoulders, and we answer: "Yea.
I stand at Caesar's judgment seat, I appeal
Unto Caesar."
              I wash my hands, Pop gives his pay
Envelope to Mama; we sit down to our meal.

                            (CP 286)

Here Pop resembles not a kobold but the hunter boy from "Field and Forest,"
the key to the inner life of the grown man. The remembered attitudes and ways
of childhood serve Jarrell as Roman citizenship served Paul (Acts 22:25–29).
Both represent invisible, permanent membership in a community based on ori-
gins, and both confer rights. Because we are, or have been, children, we may ap-
peal from the judgments and ways of adulthood, of public social life, to the
higher authority of childhood and play. (These rhymes—*day*, *play*, "I could
stay," *say*, *yea*, *pay*— recur at the end of the poem.)

We have seen how often Jarrell's endings feature heightened repetition, mul-
tiple speakers, and verbal interaction; we have also seen how his repetitions
track memory and consider time. All these effects let "Children's Arms" end
with another collaborative idyll. A local lady ("Mrs. Mercer") drives Jarrell to
the library along with "Lucky, / Half wolf, half police-dog":

      "Hello,"
I say to the lady, and hug Lucky . . . In my
Talk with the world, in which it tells me what I know
And I tell it, "I know—" how strange that I
Know nothing, and yet it tells me what I know!—

I appreciate the animals, who stand by
Purring. Or else they sit and pant. It's so—
So *agreeable*. If only people purred and panted!
So, now, Lucky and I sit in our row,
Mrs. Mercer in hers.

(CP 287)

This "talk with the world," in which each reassures the other of his or its bare existence, recapitulates the dialogue of "A Game at Salzburg," but without the earlier poem's resignation: this sort of exchanged confirmation seems fun. The animals here, like the cats in earlier poems, lead a satisfied, purely playful existence. They do not have to work for a living or to enter the public or "social" world at all. Better yet, this idyllic library (unlike the libraries elsewhere in Jarrell) seems relatively continuous with the rest of the city and relatively immune from what would threaten it—from masculine, public, work based on exchange value. Like the island world of the high school play, the car and the world he sees from it represent his "wish," and like it they lack adult men:

> The glass encloses
As glass does, a womanish and childish
And doggish universe. We press our noses
To the glass and wish: the angel- and devilfish
Floating by on Vine, on Sunset, shut their eyes
And press their noses to the glass and wish.

(CP 287)

Robert Lowell's "For the Union Dead" (first published in 1960) also featured a boy with his nose to glass, vanished tropical fish, the lost city of his childhood, automobile traffic, and a "bubble" that holds the past. But in Lowell's poem the child's wishes are bitterly ironized, opposed to the heroic, historical values the adult wishes he could recapture:

> Once my nose crawled like a snail on the glass;
> my hand tingled
> to burst the bubbles
> drifting from the noses of the cowed, compliant fish.

(LS/FUD 70)

If, as Michael Thurston writes, "For the Union Dead" "elaborates a . . . response to historical circumstance," a public role for the personal lyric, *The Lost World* works to remind us that public, national history is never the only circumstance that has shaped us—we answer, also, to the history of a family, of a locality, even of an art form, such as the movies (105). Like Lowell's aquarium, Jarrell's fishy world represents an earlier "kingdom"; like Colonel Shaw's "bubble," Jarrell's enclosed space shows the adult world what it has forgotten. But for Jarrell the "lost" values are not the (masculine) virtues of existential self-sacrifice but the ("womanish" and "childish") virtues of caring, intimacy, and play.

Such play (as Jarrell wrote elsewhere) "demand[s] to be shared" and eventually to be shared outside the family (*Age* 22). Part 2, "A Night With Lions," thus introduces "my aunt" and "my aunt's friend" who owned a lion, "the Metro-Goldwyn-Mayer / lion": "I'd play with him, and he'd pretend / To play with me. I was the real player" (*CP* 288). Aunt, lion, and owner persist in adult memory:

> Now the lion roars
> His slow comfortable roars; I lie beside
> My young, tall, brown aunt, out there in the past
> Or future, and I sleepily confide
> My dream-discovery: my breath comes fast
> Whenever I see someone with your skin,
> Hear someone with your voice.
>
> (*CP* 288)

The passage is as convincingly sexual as Jarrell ever becomes; for Flynn, "the child's confusion is heightened by the sexual confusion of approaching adolescence" (*Lost* 124). But there is nothing menacing, or even chthonically mysterious, about the excited interest Jarrell remembers. It would be at least as right to say that the poem shows how connections made in "play" at one age get preserved in the next, as the people (or "time-slices") we have been become part of the people we grow up to be. These continually changing and cumulative selves resemble the continually changing and accumulating connotations of the repeated complex words—"play" and "work," "wish" and "pretend," "habit" and "happiness"—that keep the old meanings out of which newer ones grow.

As in Jarrell's other poems about the life course, this analogy between repeated words (that accumulate connotations) and growing or aging people (who accumulate experience) drives the words that drive the poem. "A Night With Lions" returns, not just to its initial rhymes but to its opening words, "pretend" and "friend." After Jarrell has "been / Asleep a while,"

> I remember: you
> Are—you, and Tawny was the lion in—

In *Tarzan*. In *Tarzan!* Just as we used to,
I talk to you, you talk to me or pretend
To talk to me as grown-up people do,
Of *Jurgen* and Rupert Hughes, till in the end
I think as a child thinks: "You're my real friend."

(CP 288)

Is it the adult dreamer, or the child he dreams that he is, who thinks "as a child thinks" by the end of the poem? The dreamlike suspended state recalls "The Elementary Scene"; there, as here, grammatical special effects help the poem mull familiar, Proustian questions. How are the adult and the child the same person? The answer the dream provides is that they feel continuous as a web of previous interpersonal relations *and* of previous fictions: a "real friend" is someone with whom one can "pretend."

Part 3 of the poem, "A Street Off Sunset," begins with an olfactory memory trigger, an obvious nod to Proust's madeleine and lime-leaf tea.[24] Smelling the Vicks VapoRub of the old L.A. factory, Jarrell recapitulates his childhood year. This child, Jarrell is delighted to affirm, persists in the adult, where he can be identified as a capacity for intimacy and for fictions—

My lifetime
Got rid of, I sit in a dark blue sedan
Beside my great-grandmother, in Hollywood.
We pass a windmill, a pink sphinx, an Allbran
Billboard; thinking of Salâmmbo, Robin Hood,
The old prospector with his flapjack in the air,
I sit with my hands folded: I am good.

(CP 289)

At the end of the child's day

I go to Mama in her gray
Silk, to Pop, to Dandeen in her black
Silk, I put my arms around them, they
Put their arms around me. Then I go back
To my bedroom; I read as I undress.
The scientist is ready to attack.
Mama calls, "Is your light out?" I call back, "Yes,"
And turn the light out.

(CP 290)

Repeated words—*arms, silk, call, light, out*—show off a verbal exchange, and frame the unusual, end-stopped, one-sentence line: "The scientist is ready to attack."

Randall has been reading the science-fiction magazine *Amazing Stories*, which he finishes in the morning, reading "how the good world wins its victory / Over that bad man." That science fiction will govern the end of the poem. First, however, the poem must give one more example of "play," a game Randall plays with Dandeen:

> Her old face is slow
> In pleasure, slow in doubt, as she sits weighing
> Strategies: patient, equable, and humble,
> She hears what this last child of hers is saying
> In pride or bewilderment; and she will grumble
> Like a child or animal, when, indifferent
> To the reasons of my better self, I mumble:
> "I'd better stop now—the rabbit . . . "
>   I relent
> And play her one more game.
>
>   (CP 291)

The child here, pretending to play, resembles both the mother of "The Lost Children" and Tawny the (adult) lion: we see young Randall growing up.[25]

Dandeen cried, she remembers, during "the War Between the States," when a "captain" put her on a horse. She might have cried again, the adult Jarrell decides, "because I didn't write"—once back in Tennessee, young Randall never answered his grandparents' letters. Turning from his present-day readers to Dandeen, and then back to us, Jarrell exclaims "I *was* a child, I missed them so. But justifying / Hurts too: if only I could play you one more game, / See you all one more time!"[26] Here we are close to the core of the poems—to Jarrell's urgent search for the links connecting memory to family, family to play, childhood to maturation to loss. How are these terms—these experiences—related? One answer might start from the next passage, which describes Randall's pet rabbit:

> His furry
> Long warm soft floppy ears, his crinkling nose
> Are reassuring to a child. They guarantee,
> As so much here does, that the child knows
> Who takes care of him, whom he takes care of.
>
>   (CP 291–292)

This is the promise of "families" in general—one broken where the mother keeps collapsing, or where the mother is impossible to know because she is a destructive archetype. It is a promise kept only in Jarrell's adoptive families, most of all in this one: a promise of reciprocity and of safety, from which shared adventure and imaginative play become possible. But even this "guarantee" is less than certain after Mama enters the chicken coop,

> chooses one,
> Comes out, and wrings its neck. The body hurls
> Itself out—lunging, reeling, it begins to run
> Away from Something, to fly away from Something
> In great flopping circles. Mama stands like a nun
> In the center of each awful, anguished ring.
> The thudding and scrambling go on, go on—then they fade,
> I open my eyes, it's over . . . Could such a thing
> Happen to anything? It could to a rabbit, I'm afraid;
> It could to—
>   "Mama, you won't kill Reddy ever,
> You won't ever, will you?" The farm woman tries to persuade
> The little boy, her grandson, that she'd never
> Kill the boy's rabbit, never even think of it.
> He would like to believe her . . .
>
>   (CP 292)

Here the survival in question (as Flynn notes) is not just the rabbit's, nor the parent's, but Randall's own: a canceled draft of these lines reads, "It could to Randall, I'm afraid" (*Lost* 128). As in Bishop's "In the Waiting Room," to discover who one is—who "takes care of" one, whom one "takes care of"—is also to discover that cared-for and caregivers are separate persons and that all will die. Thomas Travisano has found in Jarrell, Bishop, Lowell, and Berryman "moments of profound loss that are also moments of conscious entry into selfhood" (*Mid-Century* 77).[27] The "selfhood" Jarrell enters into here in this poem, with its climactic moment of loss, looks very like the selfhood that object-relations theorists imagine: it consists largely of the (imagined and real) other people Jarrell has known and of the events and words he has shared with them. He seems in the finished version of the poem to fear more for the rabbit, for Dandeen, for "significant others," than he does for his own mortal body: death is a threat to objects and *hence* to oneself.

To preserve affective objects and fictions is, therefore, to preserve the self, even if this can be done only in memory. The poem ends as just such preservations take place:

> Into the blue wonderland
> Of Hollywood, the sun sinks, past the eucalyptus,
> The sphinx, the windmill, and I watch and read and
> Hold my story tight. And when the bus
> Stops at the corner and Pop—Pop!—steps down
> And I run out to meet him, a blurred nimbus,
> Half-red, half-gold, enchants his sober brown
> Face, his stooped shoulders into the All-Father's.
> He tells me about the work he's done downtown,
> We sit there on the steps. My universe
> Mended almost, I tell him about the scientist. I say
> "He couldn't really, could he, Pop?" My comforter's
> Eyes light up, and he laughs. "No, that's just play,
> Just make believe," he says. The sky is gray,
> We sit there, at the end of our good day.

> (*CP* 292–293)

In effects (and rhyme words) familiar from Jarrell's other work, Pop offers, and the child accepts, a finally false—but credible—reassurance. The world could not end, the rabbit will not die, Pop is Odin (the "All-Father" of Scandinavian legend), and Randall knows, again, who takes care of him, whom he takes care of, and who can share his flights into Greek or Norse myth. Key words recur in a cascade of rhymes on "ay"; as Jarrell recapitulates terms and themes, time seems to contract, as if the triptych had confined itself harmoniously to one day.

That "good day" may remember a crucial day in Jarrell's adult life. A few months before beginning the "Lost World" poems, in November 1962, Jarrell attended a White House-sponsored arts conference in Washington, where he delivered the lecture "Fifty Years of American Poetry." The next day the Cuban missile crisis broke out. Mary remembers that while some writers went home, Jarrell, "inside his poetry bubble, felt no cause for alarm and stayed to the last" (*Letters* 460). A letter suggests, however, how seriously he took the nuclear threat. Jarrell wrote to Adrienne Rich in October 1963,

> It *is* terrible in our time to have the death of the world hanging over you, but, personally, it's something you disregard just as you disregard the regular misery of so much of the world, or your own regular personal aging and death. I get a real consolation out of looking at astronomical pictures. . . . The end of the earth isn't the end of the world but more like the death of a person, or the fall of one leaf. I suppose this is a queer rather pathetic-sounding consolation but I mean it, really feel it strongly. . . . There's

something so inhuman and incommensurable about the likely end of most beings on earth that anything that can cancel it out needs to be inhuman and incommensurable too.

(*Letters* 481)

Jarrell's fragments of an elegy for President Kennedy focus on the president's nuclear responsibilities: they speak of his "Power to end, with a motion of his finger, / The union that he somehow had no share in," and conclude: "Now, when man's power is final / We are grateful to the governors of the world / To be alive—somehow, we are still alive" (Berg Collection). The lines must remember the Cuban crisis, the closest Americans came to a collective end.

The same nuclear fears inform "A Street Off Sunset." The young Jarrell has just finished a tale in which an evil genius plots to blow up the world: "I say, / "He couldn't really, could he, Pop?" My comforter's / Eyes light up, and he laughs. "No, that's just play. . . . " The day is good partly because the boy can end it still close to his extended family. It is good, too, partly because the boy understands that the world could not really end—that fiction and reality can be distinguished. But the nuclear menace of the sixties seemed to dissolve exactly that boundary. Making it really possible for science to create "the end of the earth," the Cuban crisis must have seemed to Jarrell like bad science fiction made real.

Peter Brooks remarks that psychoanalysis, in general, credits "the vast role of fantasy and fiction in our self-conceptions as human beings" (10). The "Lost World" poems credit that role as few autobiographical poets have. And the poem's ideas about that role fit well with object-relations theory. To read the science-fiction story, to imagine the end of the world, and to be reassured that the earth could not really blow up would be to experience the pretended destruction of a cathected object and then to confirm its actual survival. This is the process, Winnicott believed, by which a young child comes to discover the difference between himself and others and thus to learn how to share and to play in the world. In Winnicott's somewhat fanciful summary, "The subject says to the object: 'I destroyed you,' and the object is there to receive the communication. From now on the subject says 'Hullo object!' 'I destroyed you.' 'I love you.' . . . Here fantasy begins for the individual. The subject can now *use* the object that has survived" (90).

This fantasized destruction and reassurance helps the child understand himself as a subject among other subjects, each of whom has both an inside (an inner life) and an outside (composed of appearance and action). For Jessica Benjamin, "this distinction between inner and outer reality—the result of successful destruction—is crucial to perceiving the other as a separate person who does not need to be perfect or ideal" (*Bonds* 213). In Winnicott's own model of child development, this "successful destruction" can be superintended only by one caregiver, normatively the mother. In "The Lost World" the same process relies on a constellation of other caregivers—on Pop and Mama and "my aunt's friend"—and on the agency of printed fiction. This move, or series of moves, from the mother as unique and obligatory caregiver to a potentially reciprocal network of objects—the move Randall made by living with his grandparents—is the move made in feminist revisions of Winnicott, such as Benjamin's.

The chicken does not survive its destruction; the world survives its destruction in science fiction. Which is a better model for Randall's family? To acknowledge one's own eventual destruction (one's mortality), as young Randall cannot quite do, is to accept a reality principle, thus in one sense to cease to be a child. But to accept the reassurance that an object will survive its imagined destruction is to be part of Winnicott's optimistic model of growth. That model—the hen and the Cuban crisis suggest—will not quite take the measure of a world in which "all who love" are hypocrites, no reassurance can be relied on forever, and civilization may indeed come to an end. The model is instead a necessary fiction, like the hunter and mermaid's "we've had you always."

Winnicott maintained that children can learn to play only within an environment of relative responsiveness and security. Such an environment, as *The Lost World* presents it, relies on a complex interplay between trust and fact—between what is seen and what is made up; it relies—as the girl in "The Night Before" had—on a network of fictions. The Los Angeles family (in Jarrell's retrospect) and the Los Angeles cityscape of 1926–27 both represent such environments. To grow up and out of this locale—by returning to Nashville, by becoming an adult—is to experience progressive disillusionment and loss, measured by psychic distance from this "good day." To retain some aspect of its feeling is to be able to trust other people and to trust one's inner life: to live in a world of "work" still able to "play."

This is to say (as we have seen in other poems) that, for Jarrell, to have any sort of satisfying sense of our adult selves, we require both intersubjective confirmation and what we might call autobiographical confirmation, a sense of continuity among past and present, youthful and adult selves. Such a continuity with childhood seems required not only for the philosophers' reasons I discussed in chapter 4 but also because of the special properties (imagination, "play," distance from "the social") Jarrell attributed to childhood—reasons discussed in chapter 5. And these properties render vivid and present not only wishes but also fears. We might even gloss "A Street Off Sunset" with Coleridge's declaration: "If men laugh at the falsehoods that were imposed on themselves during their childhood, it is because they are not good and wise enough to contemplate the Past in the Present, and so to produce . . . that *continuity in their self-consciousness* which nature has made the law of their animal life" (*Works* 4:41; quoted in Coveney 45). The triptych Jarrell called *The Lost World* serves to demonstrate such continuity in its author, not least with its occasional breaks into the present time of writing: "the little girl is crying, here, now / Because I didn't write . . . " Lowell in *Life Studies* rarely presents both child and adult in a single poem; in "The Lost World" their simultaneous presence is part of the point.[28]

In "Thinking of the Lost World" just that continuity seems imperiled. As an inquiry into memory, nostalgia, and time regained, the poem begins from the Proustian realization that the places of our childhood, when we return to them, cannot be the places we remember. When Proust revisits Combray in *Time Regained*, he is "distressed to see how little I relived my early years," even though Combray itself has not much changed (3:709). Revisiting L.A., Jarrell finds objective correlatives for his failure to see his childhood's city:

> Back in Los Angeles, we missed
> Los Angeles. The sunshine of the Land
> Of Sunshine is a gray mist now, the atmosphere
> Of some factory planet: when you stand and look
> You see a block or two, and your eyes water.
> The orange groves are all cut down . . .
>
> (CP 336)

The cut-down trees recall Théodore de Banville's famous *les lauriers sont coupés*, as well as Mignonette's song, in *Wilhelm Meister*: "*Kennst du das Land, wo die Citronen blühm . . .* "[29] "Your eyes water" at smog but also at the absence of the past, as they might smart differently at its presence: "factory planet" tells us that the vocabulary of golden age science fiction has lasted longer than the sets and props of old Hollywood.

If only (the poem muses, as "90 North" had) the science fiction itself, and the adventure stories, retained their former power: "I say to my old self: "I believe. Help thou / My unbelief." The poem brings in for contrast a leonine "mad girl," picked up hitchhiking, who seems to believe entirely in her own fantasies. Jarrell invokes (as if *it* were the land where the orange trees grew) "the undiscovered / Country between California and Arizona / That the mad girl told me she was princess of." Though that country sounds like Hamlet's description of death, the girl's madness nonetheless seems enviable, because it gives her confidence in her own imagination, a confidence the adult Jarrell lacks: "If I could find in some Museum of Cars / Mama's dark blue Buick,

Lucky's electric, / Couldn't I be driven there?" (*CP* 337). To lose one's child-hood commitments to fictions and fantasies is to lose a valuable part of exis-tence, but to retain them unmodified is to go mad.

A subsequent chain of parallel "If only," "If," and "couldn't I . . ." phrases en-acts Jarrell's wish to believe in his childhood's fictions and demonstrates the continuing reality, not of the belief but of the wish. What lasts for the adult Jar-rell (as for Proust) are not the "objects" nor the beliefs of the past but the lan-guage, the interior representations (introjections), and the wishes and fears our commitments to them accrete within us. Of Mama and Lucky and the "tall brown aunt," Jarrell declares,

> All of them are gone
> Except for me; and for me nothing is gone—
> The chicken's body is still going round
> And round in widening circles, a satellite
> From which, as the sun sets, the scientist bends
> A look of evil on the unsuspecting earth.

> (*CP* 337)

After Jarrell has remembered the persons and the fictions of "A Street Off Sun-set," the interactions of Jarrell's past (with Mama, with the late aunt, with a present-day interlocutor) seem to him to be unfolding still:

> Mama and Pop and Dandeen are still there
> In the Gay Twenties.
>   The Gay Twenties! You say
> The Gay Nineties . . . But it's all right: they *were* gay,
> O so gay! A certain number of years after,
> Any time is Gay, to the new ones who ask:
> "Was that the first World War or the second?"

> (*CP* 338)

The "new ones" don't even remember the Second World War: it is not our in-dividual past the present seems to lack, but the past in general, anyone's past. Old people can therefore feel anew their links to their childhoods by listening to one another (as the woman in "The Player Piano" had done) or by telling the right listeners about the past.[30] In doing so, they experience the continuity of their own lives, situating themselves and others in time.

This is why the poem begins with memories of places and other people (Lucky, Dandeen, the "mad girl") but ends with "you" and then with "I"—with

Jarrell's long look at his present-day self. We have seen this part of the poem in chapter 1, where the boys recognize the older Jarrell as Santa Claus: this sort of misrecognition is preferable to looking in the mirror and not recognizing oneself at all. Having seen these two alternatives, readers of *The Lost World* are ready to seek a synthesis of the two, an introspective search that treats not the past recaptured as if it were present but the drive to recover that past and to make it seem present, as the source of continued interiority.

At the end of "Thinking of the Lost World" (and of the volume *The Lost World)* Jarrell thus seeks his child-self and finds himself instead realized in his ability to search for it and to interpret—for us—its absence. Paradoxically, though what he has lost *is* the child he was, the child was like him (and hence remains at his side) because the child, too, experienced loss:

> I seem to see
> A shape in tennis shoes and khaki riding pants
> Standing there empty-handed; I reach out to it
> Empty handed, my hand comes back empty,
> And yet my emptiness is traded for its emptiness,
> I have found that Lost World in the Lost and Found
> Columns whose gray illegible advertisements
> My soul has memorized world after world:
> LOST—NOTHING. STRAYED FROM NOWHERE. NO REWARD.
> I hold in my own hands, in happiness,
> Nothing: the nothing for which there's no reward.
>
> (CP 338)

"Empty-handed . . . emptiness" links the adult to the young Randall, who stood "empty-handed" as he watched Pop at work. (Drafts of the ending emphasize the "shape's" identity: " it is as if I'd handed / Myself? hand something / the boy [. . .] we'd handed each other something" [Berg Collection].) Though "Thinking" is not written in terza rima, its closing lines recall the "Lost World" triptych so closely in part because they echo its rhyming form: *pants* anticipates *advertisements, emptiness- happiness, (no) reward- (no) reward.* In comprehending estrangement, age, and loss, the later poem seems to have grasped, at last, some bits of the triptych's verbal form, just as its speaker finally "hold[s] in my own hands" some form of personal memory itself. The "nothing" on which the poem concludes recalls the "nothing" of "90 North," twenty years earlier—it, too, implies that adulthood, or simply experience, bring with it no new value. Yet this "nothing," unlike the earlier poem, brings with it "happiness" and, along with that happiness, some sense of exchange, of communion, with a childhood self.

Jarrell here, Richard Flynn has written, "wishes (almost desperately) that the child may serve as a symbol of potential, as a redemptive figure to the aging adult, but since the usefulness of the child's perspective for the poet depends on a rejection of such nostalgia, the speaker comes up empty" (" 'Infant Sight' " 115). Flynn sees farther into this poem than do the several readers who consider it a rewriting of Stevens's "Snow Man": "the nothing" here comes not from impersonal nature but from the course of a person's life.[31] Yet Flynn has perhaps missed the tone of Jarrell's "And yet": the difference between "my hand comes back empty" and "my emptiness is traded . . . " is a difference in feeling that allows Jarrell to treat them as opposites. The second independent clause describes a real, beneficial, trade. Adult and ghostly child exchange intangibles that exist only in memory, but their continued existence there yields a kind of ongoing "happiness." The change of mood here allows Jarrell to do just what characters such as "A Real Ghost" and the woman of "Next Day" could not. At the end as at the beginning of the "Lost World" poems, Jarrell can see himself as part of a life course that connects him to the intimate affective relations and to the imaginative faculties of childhood. He can thereby manifest to others—to readers, to "you"—a life that can be articulated and shared.

Conclusion

"WHAT WE SEE AND FEEL AND ARE"

We have seen in the "Lost World" poems and throughout Jarrell's oeuvre how he took care to define and defend the self. We have seen how his lonely personae seek intersubjective confirmation and how his alienated characters resist the so-called social world. We have seen how Jarrell's divided, conflicted selves depend on psychoanalytic ideas—both those of a familiar Freudianism and those of later object-relations theories. We have seen how concepts of work and play, and related ideas about childhood, adolescence, and adulthood, both inform and confine the ways Jarrell's characters think about their lives. And we have seen how those people—among them the "Randall Jarrell" of the late autobiographical poetry—draw on Proust, Wordsworth, Rilke, Freud, and the poets and thinkers of Jarrell's era to create a self that exists in time, one whose capacity for imagination and recognition connects who we have been to who we are.

The selfhood, or memory, Jarrell ends up "holding" in "Thinking of the Lost World" is the goal of the poem, even of a life; and yet it is worth "nothing," can bring "no reward." Though we can try to manifest it to others—though it seems to be "nothing" without such manifestations—the self is always "nothing" in another sense: it carries no exchange value, cannot be traded for anything, and cannot bring its private character into any public world. Other people, other readers, and even nonreaders, have their own selfhoods too: the newspaper columns are, so to speak, full of them. The LOST AND FOUND columns of "Thinking of the Lost World" remember a smaller, now vanished Los Angeles (where newspapers ran such columns), but they also look back to the newspapers imagined in Jarrell's criticism, in one of his most often quoted passages. The relevant paragraph appeared in the *Nation* in 1946, where it introduced several brief, negative reviews.[1] He reprinted it, in *Poetry and the Age*, alone, under the heading "Bad Poets":

> Sometimes it is hard to criticize, one wants only to chronicle. The good and mediocre books come in from week to week, and I put them aside and read them and think of what to say; but the "worthless" books come in day after day, like the cries and truck sounds from the street, and there is nothing that anyone could think of that is good enough for them. In the bad type of the thin pamphlets, in hand-set lines on imported paper, people's hard lives and hopeless ambitions have expressed themselves more directly and heartbreakingly than they have ever been expressed in any work of art; it is as if the writers had sent you their ripped-out arms and legs, with "This is a poem" scrawled on them in lipstick. After a while one is embarrassed not so much for them as for poetry, which is for these poor poets one more of the openings against which everyone in the end beats his brains out; and one finds it unbearable that poetry should be so hard to write—a game of Pin the Tail on the Donkey in which there is for most of the players no tail, no donkey, not even a booby prize. If there were only some mechanism . . . for reasonably and systematically converting into poetry what we see and feel and are! When one reads the verse of people who cannot write poems—people who sometimes have more intelligence, sensibility, and moral discrimination than most of the poets—it is hard not to regard the Muse as a sort of fairy godmother who says to the poet, after her colleagues have showered on him the most disconcerting and ambiguous gifts, "Well, never mind. You're still the only one that can write poetry."
>
> (*Age* 176–177)

The bad poets' encapsulated lives cannot command respect as aesthetic objects—no more so than newspaper classifieds or severed limbs. They deserve respect, however, as parts of their authors' lives, as signs of that individual experience that amounts to "nothing" yet that makes persons count as ends. Where the robotized people of Jarrell's mass culture critique seemed distressingly empty of selfhood, the "bad poets" here (though perhaps more distressing) make clear that everyone has a self to lose.

What that famous passage about arms and legs acknowledges in "bad poets" and everyone else, as a good divorced from any formal good, is the *same* good that the formal intricacies of "Thinking of the Lost World" explore in Jarrell himself. It had once seemed to Jarrell a shame that an unimaginative girl's life would "add up to *yet!*" (*CP* 18). "Thinking" declares instead that all our lives add up to "yet": as private creations of individual, remembered experience, all lives are equally valuable or valueless. From the point of view of literature, bad poems and their authors' lives are "nothing at all." Yet from a less formal (or less professional) point of view those lives are the only sort of value that matters— not "use-value" or "exchange value" (as "The Night Before" articulated it) but "plain/Value." We recognize and value other lives, as others might value ours, not because anything in particular can always be learned or taken from them, but exactly because nothing can.

Jarrell thus faces the unavoidable and unanswerable contradiction between (on the one hand) a liberal ethics founded on the equal dignity of persons and (on the other) the inevitable, and seemingly "unfair," distinctions involved in aesthetic response. Jarrell quipped in *Pictures*, "Aesthetic discrimination seems no more just and rational to those discriminated against, than racial discrimination: the popular novelist would be satisfied with his income . . . if people would only admit that he is a better writer than Thomas Mann" (89). To be a secular leftist or a liberal, and an aesthetic critic, and a post-Wordsworthian poet—and Jarrell was all these things for all of his career—is to live aware of both human equality and human difference; it is to live with more than one mode of response to human endeavor and to be troubled by the dissonance between them. Arendt declared that "the public sphere is as consistently based on the law of equality as the private sphere is based on . . . difference and differentiation" (*Origins* 301). Though art can praise equality (just as private utterance can praise public action), the two modes of response can never be made one. In this sense (as in others), for Arendt, "the conflict between art and politics . . . cannot and must not be solved" (*Between* 218).

Depicting the inner life—but depicting it as "the nothing for which there's no reward"; portraying isolated people and their need for others; tying itself in knots (as the girl in "The Night Before" had) about others' bad taste and trying to reach out to them; and describing—while rejecting—public events and the public world, Jarrell's work seems (perhaps now more than in his lifetime) unmatched as a description of that dissonance, of that unsolvable problem. It is perhaps this strongly binocular vision—his dual insistence on human equality and on aesthetic judgment—that made him matter so much to Adrienne Rich, whose words about him, written after his death, emphasize the acts of speaking and listening so central to his poetics. Rich wrote in 1967 that for her as for many other poets, "if asked that old question: 'To what or whom do you address your poems?' the truthful answer would be 'To the mind of Randall Jarrell' " (*RJ* 183).

Trying to duplicate the messiness of real interaction between real people, and the different uncertainties of memory, Jarrell's style explores and reinforces his efforts to manifest a recognizable self. It is that effort that helps make some of Jarrell's poems so affecting and informs their peculiar integrity. This effort is linked to another project, a project that gives Jarrell's poems both their peculiar sort of ethics and their ontological slipperiness. Often the poems try *at once* to show how an inner life, a particular selfhood, is worth everything to its possessor and how, from another point of view, it is "nothing."² Jarrell had been exposed to such problems of value—of the uncertain status of all human value—since his days reading Wolfgang Köhler, who found that the contrast between "human experience" and "objective nature" made the resulting "problem of value . . . the eminent task of modern thought" (15, 36–37). Grounded both in Wordsworth's achievement and in such psychological perspectives, Jarrell began his career uniquely prepared to see how the inner, invisible self (a self we can trace to our childhoods) is the source of "plain / Value" and yet is in practical terms invisible, unverifiable, even insignificant. The poems play up and play out this existential contrast. And this is perhaps a final reason why they care so much about, and find so many formal equivalents for, the passage of time. Empson explained in *Seven Types of Ambiguity* (a book Jarrell studied intently):

> The human mind has two main scales on which to measure time. The large one takes the length of a human life as its unit, so that there is nothing to be done about life. . . . The small one takes as its unit the conscious moment, and it is from this that you consider . . . your personality. The scales are so far apart as almost to give the effect of defining two dimensions.
>
> (24)

Jarrell's effects involving interruption and multiple speakers govern his poems about loneliness and recognition. Effects involving pace and repetition govern poems (such as "The Lost Children," "Thinking," and "The Player Piano") that combine those intersubjective concerns with others about the life course and about mortality. These poems thus invoke Empson's "two dimensions." In them consciousness—consciousness of our past, of other people—can seem at once to be nothing and everything, "nothing" we can have and all we need.

This effect takes over Jarrell's most powerful war poems. Most of those poems cannot be called pacifist—but neither can it be said that they accept the war's "Losses" as necessary, or justified. Instead, their deliberately unstable tones incorporate both the perspective, the *longue durée*, from which the lost lives must, objectively, be sacrificed and the minute-by-minute perspective according to which each life is everything. Jarrell describes a soldier in his prose poem "1914": "He has been dead for months—that is to say for a minute, for a century; if because of his death his armies have conquered the world, and have brought to its peoples food, justice and art, it has been a good bargain for all of them but him" (CP 203). Either we see things from his point of view or we do not; either we credit his extinguished person with infinite value or we tally his corpse along with others—saying perhaps, as the (adult) authorities in "Losses" say, "the casualties were low" (CP 145). The most self-conscious characters in the war poems know just how these "two dimensions," personal and impersonal, have described them. They have in common their dual awareness that they are or have been objects, instruments, and that they are not, have never been, *mere* objects. The airman of "Siegfried" finds himself in "warfare, indispensable / In general, and in particular dispensable, / As a cartridge, a life" (CP 149). "[I]nside the infallible, invulnerable / Machines," he wants to come home, and to feel that he is himself again, even though such a self would "not matter": he finally prays "let nothing I do matter / To anybody, anybody. Let me be what I was" (CP 150).

In Jarrell's last published war poem, "The Survivor Among Graves," living and dead, "haunters and haunted," beg "each other" to "*say again / That life is—what it is not; / That, somewhere, there is—something, something*" (CP 207; italics in original). That "somewhere" is the place where inner lives, individual selves, endure and have meaning, where the equal dignity of persons is realized; it is like the "world entirely different from this," whose "unknown . . . precepts we bore in our hearts," that Proust imagined at the death of Elstir and that Jarrell invokes to end his essay "The Obscurity of the Poet" (Age 27). That other world is, at Jarrell's most optimistic, the realm of memory, of interpersonal speech, and of shared, accomplished imaginative creations. In Jarrell's less hopeful moods, the self has its real existence "somewhere" but only in the past or in dreams. Thus the mother in "The Lost Children," waking from dreams of her daughters, feels "comforted / That, somewhere, they still are" (CP 301). The same work that defends the self and its needs can worry that that self is indeed "nothing": "City, City" finds its insomniac narrator, "in yearning, // In loathing," reaching out "to the world," where "There is always something; and past that something / Something else: and all these somethings add to nothing" (CP 475). Jarrell's concentration on the ways in which our selves come into being, on how they exist in time and how they become manifest to one another, made him acutely and simultaneously conscious of the sense in which an individual life is the only value and of the sense (or perspective or time scale) in which it is "nothing," no sooner noticed than lost.

This sense gave him not only his unusual tones but his poems' peculiar, implicit ethics—interpersonal, specific, not lawlike but driven by sympathy. But theirs is also a version of sympathy compelled to recall how hard it is to know someone else, how hard it is to believe the self is more than "nothing," and that frequently finds itself (in consequence) unwillingly reduced from sympathy to pity. Such reductions take place in many war poems; they are captured elegantly in a 1964 lyric called "The Sign":

> Having eaten their mackerel, drunk their milk,
> They lie like two skeins of embroidery silk
> Asleep in the glider. The child repeats, "It's *such* a pity!"
> And paints on a piece of beaverboard, FREE KITTY.
>
> (CP 486)

The "sign" of the title is what the child paints, but it is also the whole tableau the poem yields. Child, phrase, painted sign, and kittens are presented as if they were a sufficient "sign" for the whole world. Like "The Night Before," the poem dares readers to find it sentimental. What could be softer, soppier, than rhyming couplets about a child giving away kittens? And yet the poem leaves us with the choice of feeling ("sentimental," extravagant, italicized) pity for these kittens or feeling that we do not feel enough—that we have become (like "The Snow Leopard" in Jarrell's earlier poem) "heartless" before the world's "brute and geometrical necessity" (CP 115). One might have to be a child, or else to feel childish, in order to feel intensely for the kittens. But their fate is ours as well: all of us are brought into the world, given some amount of care as we grow up, and finally left to make our own way in it. Not to care, as the child cares, for the free kitty would be to risk caring for nothing human.

In the same way, in "Terms," not to care, as Jarrell's "one-armed, one-legged, and one-headed" veteran cares, for the fall of one autumn leaf, might be not to care for a human life:

> "You're as good as dead,"
> Says the man, with a mocking smile, to the leaf [. . .]
> . . . .
> The leaf is alive, and it is going to be dead.
> It is like any other leaf.
>
> (CP 209–210)

In the veteran's dream, "The leaves fell one by one, like checks" (like his dis-ability checks) "Into the grave; / And I thought: I am my own grave." As an am-putee he may feel helpless, like the leaf; before death, we may all feel so help-less—may feel, too, inconsequential and all alike. On the other hand, to be "as good as dead," and to understand it and venture out to act among others any-way, is the human condition:

> As he opens the door
> He watches his hand opening the door
> And holds out his good hand—
> And stares at them both, and laughs;
> Then he says, softly, "I am a man."
>
> (CP 211)

There the poem ends: the self, the past, a child, "a man," are everything, worth everything, axiomatically, or else they are worth nothing.

The frequent helplessness and impracticality of Jarrell's characters—the maimed veteran, the powerless clerk, the distressed schoolgirl, the old house-wife—bring into sharp focus such dilemmas about the value of the self. The poems, when they carry ethical dimensions, ask us to seek (with difficulty) the perspectives in which such subjective goods do seem real and communicable. They recommend, with difficulty, the proximity their children maintain to their cats, rather than the inhuman heights of the snow leopard, "cold, fugitive, se-cure" on his peak. The perspective from which we feel for others may seem strained, sentimental, childish, embarrassing, inappropriate, hard to maintain—and yet (Jarrell's poems often insist) its alternative, indifference, would be worse.

"Washing" is rare and important among Jarrell's late poems because it chooses indifference:

> The washing flops on the line
> In absolute torment—
> And when the wind dies for a moment
> The washing has the collapsed abject
> Look of the sack of skin
> Michelangelo made himself in his *Last Judgment*.
>
> (CP 330)

The clothes on its clothesline are like the leaves in "Terms," wind-buffeted sym-bols for helplessness and mortality.[3] The laundry can do nothing to help itself, but neither, ultimately, could Michelangelo; from a perspective sufficiently far removed, neither Michelangelo's nor the laundry's pain seems more than trivial: "Its agonies / Are heartfelt as a sneeze." Blowing in the yard, the hanging laundry reminds Jarrell of "when Mama wrung a chicken's / Neck" (a scene already shown in *The Lost World*):

> The expression of its body was intense,
> Immense
> As this *Help! Help! Help!*
> The reeling washing shrieks to someone, Someone.

Like the helpless kittens, the washing represents any or all of us, and we have no basis except our sentiments on which to choose between extending pity to all of us and seeing ourselves as trivial objects in an indifferent world:

> The washing inhabits a universe
> Indifferent to the woes of washing,
> A world—as the washing puts it—
> A world that washing never made.

The poem's experiment with a cosmic perspective, in which human beings are no more than lost laundry, would be Frostian if it sounded more secure in its choices and its rhythms. Such a deliberately shaky approach to Frostian coldness and bareness may be what Jarrell had in mind: he found in one of Frost's late works "a cold certainty that nothing but mercy will do for *us*," though "what he really warms to is a rejection beyond either justice or mercy" (*Age* 35). As much as Jarrell admired, and learned from, Frost's way with spoken language, it is this awareness of rejection, of the perspective from which the self is nothing, that his essays on Frost tend to highlight: Frost sees "the universe that is incommensurable with us," whose "inhuman not-answer" is "a black-and-white one that is somehow not an answer at all" (*Age* 42, 50).

Frost knew, Jarrell wrote in another review, how "even [a life's] salvation, far back at the cold root of things, is make-believe, drunk from a child's broken and stolen goblet hidden among the ruins of the lost cultures" (*KA* 141).[4] That reading of "Directive" makes it one of the few poems, *outside* Jarrell and Rilke, to understand both the importance to adult selves, and the final insignificance, of the fictions children can believe and of the different fictions adults create about childhood—fictions that the "Lost World" poems placed in their family context and went on to defend. If Jarrell answers Frost's magnificently cold view in his own poetics, it is as the Bat-Poet answered the mockingbird. Jarrell's poems try hard, and find a style that tries hard, for sympathy, for the perspective not of the universe but of the tiny people who live in it, all of whom have to matter if any do.

Each of us was—as Rilke says in "The Grown-Up" (a poem Jarrell translated)— "a child once"; all of us are as leaves before death, as laundry in wind, if any of us are (CP 239). Examined and appreciated far less frequently than Jarrell's poems about children, his poems about cosmically helpless selves bring some of the same terms to bear on the same moral center. Many of them are poems about visual art; with them, this book can come to an end.[5] Comparing several centuries of European painters, Jarrell's "The Old and the New Masters" (as several readers have seen) functions as a sort of manifesto.[6] Where Auden's "Musée de Beaux Arts" declared, "About suffering they were never wrong, / The Old Masters," Jarrell explains that the masters "disagree" (237; CP 332). Describing real and imaginary nativities, Jarrell recommends an Old Master like van der Goes, for whom "everything / That was or will be in the world is fixed / On its small, helpless, human center." By contrast, the New Masters' undesirable cosmic perspectives treat the earth as one planet among many; they might even be indifferent to our demise (CP 333).[7]

More complex, more troubling ekphrastic poems share Jarrell's preference for a "human center" but explore doubts about its realization. Though (like anything else) it may be symbolized, the self, Jarrell's poems sometimes suggest, cannot be adequately, permanently, unquestionably depicted in visual media, since the self (unlike a painting or a sculpture) exists in time and has no final, unchanging form. Yet the same criteria suggest how hard it is for *verbal* art to represent the self: poems, too, however they may resist closure (or trope an ongoing conversation) are fixed sets of words with beginnings and ends of their own—the same words, no matter who reads them. Problems of how to get the ungraspable, intangible, self and its "value" into a work of art—of what techniques might do so, and of why we want so much to see it done—were problems Jarrell took up very early. He addressed them most fully, and most self-consciously, in the ekphrastic poetry of his final years.

By far his most famous poem about art is "The Bronze David of Donatello" (1958). Donatello's bronze *David* (1425–30?) depicts a slim and confident adolescent—nude, helmeted, and holding a sword—standing on Goliath's severed head. It is well known as the first freestanding, life-size sculptural nude since Roman times, and as an early example of Renaissance realism.[8] Jarrell's ambitious 1953 review of André Malraux's *The Voices of Silence* and his 1957 attack on Action Painting both recommend a return to such realism and to "the represented world" (*KA* 285–286). Given Jarrell's sophistication about art history, his anxiety about late-modernist autotelism, and his interest in defending the self, we might expect him to see in Donatello's *David* (as he saw in van der Goes's *Nativity*) an embodiment of the values he recommends. And yet Jarrell's notion of selfhood can never be David's: it is, the poem discovers, more like Goliath's, never self-sufficient, and more fully realized in defeat. Rather than admiring its sculptural realism, "The Bronze David of Donatello" turns David's triumphant self-presence into an anxious, anguished commentary about age and youth, about eros and gender, and about the distance that separates persons from their representations in art.[9]

"A sword in his right hand, a stone in his left hand," David stands "Shod and naked. Hatted and naked" (*CP* 273). His shamelessness, his elegance, and his youth combine to make him sexually appealing and to make that appeal disturbing:

> The boy David's
> Body shines in freshness, still unhandled,
> And thrusts its belly out a little in exact
> Shamelessness.

Exactly reversing Rilke's famous, headless "Archaic Torso of Apollo" (in which "there is no place that does not see you"), David's torso is all face and compels our attention without returning it

> The rib-case, navel, nipples are the features
> Of a face that holds us like the whore Medusa's—
> Of a face that, like the genitals, is sexless.

Most adults, now as in 1958, believe they are attracted to men or to women. If we find this shameless, powerful, sexless adolescent, this "boy who is like a girl," sexually compelling, as the poem seems surprised to find him, what does that say about him and about us?

Before it can answer such questions, the poem returns to David's anomalous status as an innocent victor, who "handles" swords, but is himself "unhandled." Untouched by the world and victorious within it, he is neither a vulnerable child nor a regretful, self-conscious adult—nor is he like the adolescent girl of "The Night Before" who was both vulnerable and self-conscious. David is instead almost her opposite, being everything about adolescence that *does not* represent the poet in Jarrell's poems. Donatello's *David* thus represents (even if Donatello the sculptor does not) a theory of art directly counter to Jarrell's aims. *David*'s

elegance draws subtly, supply,
Between the world and itself, a shining
Line of delimitation, demarcation.
The body mirrors itself.

(CP 273–274)

The "Night Before" girl and her relatives (of all genders) failed to see themselves either in their own bodies or in mirrors; David finds it hard to see anything else.

The poem has begun at David's head and moved down; it is about to reach Goliath's severed head. A simpler poem might see the giant as a defeated hero. Instead this Goliath is almost comic: "The head dreams what has destroyed it / And is untouched by its destruction."

The new light falls
As if in tenderness, upon the face —
Its masses shift for a moment, like an animal,
And settle, misshapen, into sleep: Goliath
Snores a little in satisfaction.

Goliath dreams almost as the child readers in Jarrell's library poems dream — he shows no compassion nor does he incarnate some more hopeful idea about art. Nevertheless, his defeated head invites sympathy. David, above Goliath and above the viewer, "looks down at the head and does not see it," just as he did not see us: "alone, now, in his triumph," he notices no one (neither men nor women). One of the things that makes him oddly, dangerously, sexually attractive is his apparent freedom from sexual needs: Jarrell's notes for the poem call David's "genitals sexless as a child's . . . since sex [is] that in which we lose ourselves / die" (UNC-Greensboro). The young David appears to exist prior to and above all the childish or grown-up desires that lead us to require satisfactions from one another rather than in ourselves:

Upon this head
As upon a spire, the boy David dances,
Dances, and is exalted.
          Blessed are those brought low,
Blessed is defeat, sleep blessed, blessed death.

(CP 275)

Like an abstract expressionist painter declaring independence from nature, David encapsulates all the victories art can win when it separates itself from an interpersonal matrix; its triumphant closures and completions make such a confident art false to our lives. In David, one draft has it, "No part / Breaks from its bounds, no part acknowledges / The unanswerable: the world of which it once was part[,] the useless and means-less end" (UNC-Greensboro). Having no concept of ends beyond himself, David leaves no room for the relations for which Jarrell's characters yearn—he is indeed a freestanding statue.

He is, even, a statue that seems to dance. "The dance," writes Suzanne Ferguson, "is a projection of David's inward triumph, his total indifference to his victim. He exists only in himself" (*Poetry* 184). The frightening David thus makes at once a bad moral example and a bad model for art, exactly because he is such a good model for artists' aspirations. This secularized, careless David becomes what Frank Kermode (discussing the dancers in modernist poems) has termed "a Herodiade emblem, representing at once the cruelty of the isolation [of modern art] and the beauty (distinct from life yet vital) of its product" (70). Modernist works in which art wants to be like a dance, however admirable, complete the work Donatello's *David* begins: they falsify the persons whom Jarrell seeks to draw out—persons visible through false starts, wrong moves, defeats, incompletions, awkward phraseology, all the aspects of life in a shared human world that are not and cannot be like dance and that resist certainty and closure.

Invented out of Wordsworthian Romanticism, Jarrell's poetics thus end by rejecting what Kermode names the Romantic image. What does Jarrell—what can art— offer in its stead? We saw in chapter 1 how the interruptions and awkwardly complex sentences of other poems mimed the incompleteness of real persons.[10] "The psychological correlate of [aesthetic] closure," Charles Altieri writes, "is the dream of a coherent and satisfying representation of the self, either as an individual or as someone in full possession of the terms by which he or she identifies with other people" (*Self* 148). Since, for Jarrell, selves are vulnerable, interdependent, and by definition alterable, such psychological closure can never be found. To the extent that works of art have closure—and no work can avoid it entirely—all works of art falsify the self. "The Bronze David" suggests that the human person cannot be accurately and compassionately represented in any *freestanding* sculpture, or in any sculpture of a *triumph*, except perhaps by figures of defeat.

The later poem "Man in Majesty" goes even further: it suggests that a human being cannot be fully represented in art *at all*, because what makes us human— our embeddedness in discourse, our ability to change, our intersubjective awareness—cannot be captured by any thing we can *make*. Jarrell's Pygmalionesque sculptor finds himself taken in by a work of art, almost as if he had been seduced by David. That sculptor "looks into the swan's-down of a statue," whose "alabaster, / Lit with his look's light, flames to him in pure / Seduction"

(CP 488). That statue makes its self-sufficiency a source of pride, and then of frustration, since it cannot be human:

> *I close about myself in bliss,*
> *But what is bliss? To be is to be beautiful,*
> The statue says, shut-mouthed, stone-nippled, silent.
> *What do I wish? To wake,* is sounded
> In the last notes under hearing, by the beating
> Of the alabaster's heart [. . .]

This statue seems to tell its maker, *"Touch me and I will wake"*; it aspires to full humanity. Yet its sculptor, for all his majestic talent, cannot satisfy those wishes—"the maker, man, in majesty / Touches the stone with his hand, to make it stone.//—The stone of another statue."

Learning that art works can never be fully human, Jarrell's failed Pygmalion learns instead to make art that is its own, abstract, unchanging end. This newer art, triumphantly autotelic (like *David*, like modernist poems for Kermode, or like modernist painting for Clement Greenberg), no longer asks of us more feeling than we can give, no longer yearns for what it cannot have, no longer entangles its spectators in dangerous, demanding emotions. On the other hand, it cannot be loved:

> Long ago the stone wished, and was flesh.
> The flesh wishes itself back, wishes the wish
> Unwished.
>
> *To look is to make; what I have made I see.*
> *What I have made I love; or love, almost, would love*
> *Except that—*
>
> He says each day, to each new statue, *Stay,*
> And his hand goes out to it: to make it a statue.
>
> (CP 488–489)

Viewers' *"hearts* go out to" the sculptures of "In Galleries"; this sculptor's "hand" goes out instead (CP 298; italics mine). Like the "New Masters" (and like Faust, to whom the last lines allude) this sculptor has made a disturbing bargain. Confronted with the ineluctable difference between representing a person in art and acknowledging persons outside art, he has given up even trying to represent people.

Instead he makes *things*. "*Homo faber*, the . . . producer of things," Arendt writes, "can find his proper relationship to other people only by exchanging his products with theirs, because these products themselves are always produced in isolation" (*Human* 161–162). No wonder this artist is lonely; but was he less so when he made human forms? Like Content in "The End of the Rainbow," this sculptor raises the possibility that a life spent on works of art is not well spent— is, even, a life unlived, precisely because we cannot have from works of art the recognition we seek from human beings. "Without my paintings," Content asks, "I would be— / Why, whatever would I be?" (*CP* 228) "Old enough to be invisible," Content has "spent her principal on dreams"; Jarrell's long poem about her asks, among other questions, whether the good of dreams, or of works of art, might be the only good we have: "How can a dream be bad / If it keeps one asleep?" (*CP* 228). Perhaps dreams, illusions, representations of other lives and other speakers are all we can find to alleviate our isolation—just as they were all that Goliath had left.

I have spent most of this book showing how Jarrell depicted interpersonal, interdependent, imagining selves, who speak and listen and play. Theories of such selves are now in demand, in some of the social sciences as well as in literary and cultural thought. Jarrell's poems manifest such selves; those manifestations show us what he accomplished. But poems such as "The Bronze David" and "The End of the Rainbow" also allow for a bleaker view: perhaps our senses of ourselves are not only interdependent but unsustainable. Perhaps, no matter how hard we look, we cannot find lasting recognition at all: we are so made as to seek what we cannot have, and art is our way of pretending to have it.

Can the self be manifest in art? To whom, and how? Is it something we understand only when we see it as hidden, or as under threat, or as "nothing," or as "lost"? Though any given work of art has an end, the project of manifesting the self *in* art is potentially endless. That project may be seen as a collaboration between an artist's past and her present, as well as a collaboration between past creators and present ones. The self might even be defined by, and *as*, our continuing, continually frustrated project of representing it to others. Such a project would proceed—over a career or over centuries—partly and paradoxically through a series of complaints that it is impossible. What may (on the basis of its forms and themes) be Jarrell's last poem about art makes just such a guardedly optimistic claim. Excluded from *The Complete Poems*, and rediscovered in 2000, the untitled poem appears here, for the first time:

> When, lit as in a painting of Latour's
> The first man—
> > but he is imaginary.

Our perspective vanishes into a point
Or trace that is subterranean, a grave
Upon whose ceiling, if one looks for stars
And has brought the light to see them by, one sees still
Animals seen by an animal.
A miner
Of natural graves, a painter of natural
Objects, he is unnatural. It is unarguable:
Whether he names in gardens, paints in caves
His animals, Adam is Adam.
Still awed
By what he kills, since he cannot always kill it,
He traces in ochre, umber, all the earths,
In the red or black of blood, all animals.
Man is the measure

Of all things; and, showing all the world
Except himself, is he not shown?
The deer whom the stagheaded dancer slew
And by the flame of whose fat he painted,
Lying here upon his back, as you below
The surface of the earth as Michelangelo
In the Sistine Chapel lay above it—
Who knows him or his slayer?
Who knoweth the spirit of man
That goeth upward, the spirit of the beast
That goeth downward?
Things last by being lost
Or broken: the shard is safest under the loess.
The Ark sails under the waters of the earth.

(Berg Collection)

Looking into the prehistory of art, the poem also looks back over Jarrell's career: the lost "shard" recalls the "broken" knife in "Thinking of the Lost World" (and the broken cup in Frost's "Directive"). And the biblical language, traced to its source (Ecclesiastes 3:21), becomes a question about the life course, survival, and mortality: the surrounding passage reads (in the Authorized Version)

All go unto one place: all are of the dust, and all turn to dust again. Who knoweth the spirit of man that goeth upward, and the spirit of the beast that goeth downward to the earth? Wherefore I perceive that there is nothing better, than that a man shall rejoice in his own works; for that is his portion: for who shall bring him to see what shall be after him?

(3:20–22)

The poem's core questions are originally religious, or metaphysical: do we have souls that survive our bodily deaths, or are we only "animals" despite our abilities? But (as in "Jerome" and "The Night Before") Jarrell gradually replaces these questions with psychological and aesthetic ones. The "souls" that matter, the psyches we develop (and that make us "unnatural") are displayed in art, because they are displayed in our impulse to make works of art. "Showing all the world," our representations of visible, audible, tangible things become the best evidence we have for that invisible, intangible thing, the self or psyche or soul, which (as Arendt had it) can "add constantly new things to the already existing world" only because it is not identical with that world (*Between* 217).

The self toward which Jarrell's rhetorical questions and broken-off sentences gesture becomes visible *as* the maker of utterances, the fabricator of things in the world, precisely because the self cannot be represented directly within them. The process by which art reveals the self is "unarguable" because it cannot be proven to take place. Our apprehension of other people's inner lives—in everyday life, just as in works of art—depends upon their own appeal to our interiority; explicit arguments (rather than demonstrations) that we have inner lives, or that art reveals them, are lost as soon as they need to be made. Moreover, all selves are "lost" in a different sense: we all die, and the works of art we make, though they may outlast us, can break, or corrode, or become unintelligible, or perish along with their civilizations. (An earlier poem, about the "Lost Colony" of Jamestown, declared, "All colonies are lost" [*CP* 286].) Arendt describes in *The Human Condition* the "reification and materialization without which no thought can become a tangible thing," but that impart to all art a material "deadness from which it can be rescued only when the dead letter comes again into contact with a life willing to resurrect it"; at the same time "this resurrection of the dead shares with all living things [the fact] that it, too, will die again" (169). That process, with its glory and its pathos, is what Jarrell's late poem about early paintings describes.

Arendt also believed that genuine art required at least the fiction of permanence: "only when we are confronted with things," she wrote, "whose quality remains always the same, do we speak of works of art" (*Between* 210). Jarrell's succession of key words argues otherwise. Repeating and repositioning "natural," "lost" (and its homonym "loess"), "show," "man" along with the negative prefixes *un-* and *not*, Jarrell's succession of interrupted sentences and rhetorical questions suggests that we apprehend art—and recognize one another—partly because it and we can never be permanent. The underground Ark with all its imagined animals, the artist in the cave with his cave paintings, the poet with his posthumous *Complete Poems*, exist in time and will finally be lost. At the same time they appeal for new life to those who encounter them. To see the painted animals (deer, or eland), to find the "shard" or hear the discovered poem, is like recognizing persons from the past—or like being recognized by them. The lonely makers of "lost" works have been waiting (in libraries, in caves) for us, just as we and the works of our age may await other listeners, viewers, readers: all the more reason for us to pay attention to them while we can.

NOTES

Introduction

1. For Taylor's skepticism about "contemporary neo-Nietzschean doctrines of over-coming the self or 'the subject,'" see 526–527; theories that "purport to reconnect us with some larger reality, social or natural" are in his view "less adequately described as negations of the self than they are as ways of understanding its embedding in interlocution" (527).

2. Relevant here are a broad range of more or less feminist, guardedly communitarian, and postpoststructuralist ways of reconstructing persons and agents, many of which appear in Levine; others can be found in Linda Marie Brooks's *Alternative Identities*. Brooks contrasts "the singular Western subject . . . whose existence rests on positing and . . . appropriating its objects" to several versions of what she and David Roberts name "the weak self"—a person or agent who exists, and has experiences, by means of relationships and within a historical frame (7, 12).

3. On Jarrell's relations with Bishop, see Longenbach 58–59, 62.

4. Another tradition of object-relations psychology is represented by Melanie Klein. On Jarrell's most Kleinian poems (such as "A Quilt-Pattern"), see Williamson, "Märchen"; see also chapter 3.

5. Hagenbuchle, who argues for the omnipresence of a Jungian "black goddess" in Jarrell's work, anticipates Williamson in some respects.

6. Charles Altieri also finds that our senses of self are bound up with our need for unique others and that we experience both in literary reading: "At the very core

of our being for itself we find impulses we realize are inseparable from the possibility of others playing their roles in this communal exchange of identifications and affirmations" (*Canons* 304–305).

7. See Williamson, "Märchen," passim. Eric Murphy Selinger has also used Jessica Benjamin to discuss poetry, though his book on American love poems does not mention Jarrell. For general remarks and cautions about object-relations psychology and literature, see Skura, esp. 173–174 and 185–190; see also her chapter 6.

8. Hammer argues that Jarrell's work and his life, with their emphases on the private, the feminine, and the domestic, react against and hence bear constant traces of (masculine) institutions; Longenbach agrees, but focuses on Jarrell's relations to older male poets and to Elizabeth Bishop. For more on both arguments, see my chapters 1 and 6.

9. For Jarrell's war poems as records of military life, see especially Fussell; on military *flying*, see Vardamis.

10. Tate recalled that Jarrell "was of Tennessee parentage, brought up, I believe, in California" (*RJ* 231). Ransom seems always to have believed that Jarrell was Jewish: he wrote to Tate in 1957, "I've always respected [Jarrell] for the way he will pitch into a question which puts the Jew at a disadvantage, even though he might pass for a Gentile if he kept quiet" (*Selected Letters* 395).

11. On the translations, see Cross and Seidler, both in *CE*.

Antechapter: Randall Jarrell's Life

1. The brothers were never close. Charles would move to France and marry a French woman, and he played almost no role in Randall's adult life. Mary recalls only one visit from Charles during her fourteen years of marriage to Randall, and the *Letters* record only one earlier stay.

2. For more on this letter and the Tennessee family, see Pritchard 13–15. Another commentator on the youthful Jarrell, Richard Flynn, tends to blame Jarrell's later troubles on his parents' divorce: see *Lost* 4–5.

3. Among other commentators on young Randall's troubles, Pritchard emphasizes Anna's uncertain mental state and Flynn the family's instability. Travisano and Williamson both find that the relations between the "narcissistic" Anna and the bookish young Randall follow patterns described in Alice Miller's *Drama of the Gifted Child*: see *Mid-Century* 100–105 and "Märchen" 289–290. Flynn, followed gingerly by Travisano, suspects physical or sexual abuse: see *Lost* 18 and *Mid-Century* 104–105.

4. For a good summary of Jarrell's high school writings, see Pritchard 21–22.

5. "I have a friend," Jarrell wrote Amy Breyer, "who is a good friend of Isherwood's, and who knows Auden; he says they think I am good, but that when he asked Auden how he liked my article on him Auden just looked sad" (Berg Collection, n.d.). For a long analysis of the supposedly oedipal quarrel with Auden, see Sansom.

6. "We have moved to Jamaica and see trees, birds and children outside our windows," Randall wrote to John Berryman in March (University of Minnesota, 28 March 1947).

7. Empson's *No Exit* review came too late to be used, because Empson had mailed it from China: it appeared, with my own introduction, in the *New York Review of Books* (21 June 2001).

8. Brooks' talk appeared in the program to the Yale memorial service for Jarrell; it is the only substantial talk there not reprinted in *RJ*.

9. According to Mary, Randall and Mackie had taken—and Randall therefore occupied alone—the house of Princeton professor Donald Stauffer, on leave for 1951–52; reports of Randall's untidiness during that year come mostly from his unwillingness to do dishes (Mary Jarrell, conversation).

10. Jarrell's former students at Greensboro—among them the writers Heather Ross Miller, Kelly Cherry, and Sylvia Wilkinson—wrote many reminiscences of his teaching; most appeared in Greensboro publications or remain in manuscript. The best discussion of these is Quinn, *Randall Jarrell*, 131–142.

11. The best account of debates about his death is probably Pritchard 290–298; others have ended up prurient or lurid.

12. Jarrell's local paper, the *Greensboro Record*, remarked in a 1975 tribute, "No ivory-tower poet-scholar, he was an avid and talented tennis player" (Beinecke, Randall Jarrell file). Jarrell perhaps played tennis in part so people would say this about him.

Chapter 1: *Jarrell's Interpersonal Style*

1. Sven Birkerts finds "Next Day" "as much as any poem can be, representative" ("Randall Jarrell" 86). Chris Wallace-Crabbe decides that " 'Solitary' is an excellent word for ["Next Day"] to end on, for that is what Jarrell's poetry . . . is all about" (58).

2. For more commentary on "Next Day," see Birkerts, "Randall Jarrell" 83–89, Pritchard 301–302, Shapiro, *RJ* 206–210, and Travisano, *Mid-Century* 275–276.

3. Even some of Jarrell's studious defenders have claimed that his poems never found a style of their own: Suzanne Ferguson's 1972 study found his achievement instead in "characters and themes" (5).

4. Suzanne Ferguson calls "90 North" "Jarrell's first fully characteristic poem, and one of his best," while Jarrell's biographer William Pritchard dubs "90 North" the "strongest early intimation of Jarrell's distinctiveness as a poet" (*Poetry* 19: 81).

5. See, for example, Beck *Worlds* 31 ("His speakers . . . never . . . benefit from human interaction"); for other such views, see Kinzie, Mazzaro, and Vendler, "Inconsolable."

6. Jarrell is sometimes credited with having coined the term *postmodernist*, in a 1947 review of Robert Lowell. John Crowe Ransom used the adjective to describe Jarrell's own poems in 1941—according to Thomas Travisano, the first use of *post-*

modernist with reference to literature; see Travisano's introduction to "Levels and Opposites" 695. For earlier uses of *postmodern*, see Longenbach 3.

7. For a later diagnosis of solitude as "part of the evolving self-image of modernism," see Bromwich, *Choice* 254–255.

8. The poem presents interesting problems for dating other poems, since on its verso are stanzas from "The Tower," which the *Complete Poems* dates to 1951 (the year it appeared in *Kenyon Review*); either Jarrell did not publish "The Tower" for several years after he wrote it, or he was interested in a tribute to Engels as late as 1950–51.

9. For Altieri's explanation of third-, second- and first-person commitments, see *Canons*: "When the 'I' turns to the singular 'you,' it seeks a relationships defined not by general rules but by specific conditions of adjustment and attunement. . . . The 'you' engages us concretely in what the 'he' or 'she' opens for us" (306).

10. None of the articles appeared; Charlotte Beck suggest that Jarrell never finished an essay on Wordsworth simply because no one had *commissioned* one (*Worlds* 11).

11. Longenbach claims plausibly that "when ['The End of the Line'] was published in the early forties, its argument was unheard of, except by devoted readers of Stevens" (10). David Perkins recalled in 1982 that as late at the 1950s "no powerful body of contemporary criticism . . . presented the romantics favorably" (561).

12. When Jarrell writes, in "A Front," of "bombers banging / Like lost trucks down the levels of the ice," he seems to be remembering the thunder in book 2 of *The Excursion*, "roaring sound, that ceases not to flow, / Like smoke, along the level of the blast" (*CP* 173; *Excursion* 2:699–703). When Jarrell writes, in "The Emancipators," "the apple shone / Like a seashell through your prism, voyager," he invokes Wordsworth's famous lines on a statue at Cambridge "Of Newton with his prism and silent face, / The marble index of a mind for ever / Voyaging through strange seas of Thought, alone" (*CP* 120; *Prelude* 1850 3:61–63). Helen Hagenbuchle finds links between Jarrell's early "The Skaters" and Wordsworth's ice-skating episode in the *Prelude* (104–106). For a detailed discussion of "The Emancipators" see Nemerov 193–197.

13. For more on Wordsworth, sympathy, and acknowledgement, see Bromwich, *Disowned*, esp. 23–25 and 88–91, and Cavell, "Knowing and Acknowledging."

14. Fussell explains that "try as [Jarrell] will to overcome the implications of [the war's] multitudinousness and . . . uniformity and consider this soldier as a unique person, he can't make it" (67). For more on wartime anonymity, see Fussell 59–63, 66–69, and chapter 6; see also my chapter 2.

15. For a longer, later excursus on this theme, along with its derivation from Freud, see "Stories" xii–xiii.

16. For Grossman on "hermeneutic friendship" and "care," see 284–287 and 368–371: "one [friend] seeks to keep the other in being" (370).

17. Spender noted the changes in meter from stanza to stanza in "The Island" in his review of *The Seven League Crutches* (182).

18. For more on "speech" and "The Christmas Roses," see Ferguson, *Poetry* 30, Longenbach 54–55, and Hammer "Who" 403–404.

19. See, for example, Longenbach 55 and Hammer 403.

20. Wallace-Crabbe, for example, diagnoses "Jarrell's indifference to *closure*, his unwillingness to assemble the well-made poem" (49).

21. On Jarrell's use of *War and Children*, see Flynn, *Lost* 46–47.

22. Dickey made "The Truth" a test case—one of his personae calls it "damned poor metrically," while the other exclaims, "if that doesn't move you, you ought to be boiled down for soap" (*RJ* 46).

23. Pritchard has noted the war poems' debt to Pyle: see 122–123. Wallace-Crabbe praises Jarrell's "other voices," Dickey his verisimilitude, both with specific reference to "Transient Barracks," whose "G.I. can of beets" gives Dickey part of his title (53; *Reader* 338–339). For other praise of "Transient Barracks," see Pritchard 124–127.

24. Bromwich comments on the same passage: see *Disowned* 22. For more on Arendt's often invoked distinction between solitude (a necessary condition for original thought) and loneliness (in which thought seems impossible), see *The Life of the Mind*, book 1, chapter 9, esp. 74–75. For more on Jarrell and Arendt, see chapter 2.

25. For other comments on mirrors in Jarrell, see Frances Ferguson, *CE* 170 and Quinn, *CE* 80; see also the discussion of "A Ghost, A Real Ghost" in chapter 4.

26. A considerable secondary literature concerns apostrophe and prosopopoeia (poetic address to an inanimate object), a device Jarrell rarely uses: see Kneale, esp. 141–146.

27. Alfred Kazin remembered that in person "Randall was as full of quotations as a Unitarian minister—they were his theology, too" (*RJ* 91). Keith Monroe has discussed "the submerged or unattributed quotation[s] and the altered cliché[s]" that animate Jarrell's criticism (*CE* 263–264).

28. Another sociolinguist, Jennifer Coates, records a widespread belief that "so" as an adverbial intensifies characterizes women's speech (20). Coates has also described the persistent, and sexist, belief "that women often produce half-finished sentences" (25).

29. Mary Kinzie explains that Jarrell "seemed to many [readers] to have split his imagination in two" (67). Vendler writes that Jarrell put "his passivity into his poetry, his ferocity into his criticism" ("Inconsolable" 36). See Longenbach, chapter 4 ("Randall Jarrell's Semi-Feminine Mind") for an extended, insightful discussion of this split.

30. For another discussion of this poem, "To Be Dead," see Longenbach 55.

31. For Mary's account of the genesis of "The Meteorite," see *Remembering* 9–11; for Randall's letter about the piece of obsidian that prompted it, see *Letters* 258; for the letter in which he enclosed the completed poem, see *Letters* 261–262.

32. Mary Jarrell identified the painting in a December 1977 letter to Sister Bernetta Quinn (cited in Quinn, *Randall Jarrell* 88). For more on "In Galleries," see Quinn, *Randall Jarrell* 86–89.

33. Russell Fowler argues that the woman of "Seele im Raum" is "childlike," therefore "exceptionally fortunate . . . She has not lost her 'soul,' like most of the 'adults' of Jarrell's poetry" (*CE* 183). Charlotte Beck, on the other hand, believes her "psychotic"; Pritchard considers the eland "a symbol for her sickness" (*Worlds* 19; 270). Suzanne Ferguson's nuanced reading explains the eland as a "projection" that

seems, after the woman is cured of her illness, to represent the incommunicability of experience: "the outer world inevitably falsifies the inner" (*Poetry* 151–154).

34. For Jarrell's own short note on the German sources, see *CP* 5.

35. On Complex Words and "Statements in Words," see Empson, *Complex*, chapter 2.

36. As early as 1952 Parker Tyler identified Jarrell's chief mode as "dramatic lyrism," though he did not define the term; William Meredith later pronounced Jarrell's "gift . . . essentially dramatic, like Browning's." Kinzie calls him "a great twentieth-century master of the dramatic monologue" (*CE* 140; *RJ* 120; 66).

37. Tucker finds this tendency false to the genre: for him, "dramatic monologue at its best asks us to do without . . . the figuration of inside and outside," of "soul" and "self," or of soul and society (234).

38. The rural people in "A Country Life," too, "are subdued to their own element" (*CP* 20). Jarrell's commentary confirms the allusion (*KA* 321). He spent the summer of 1939 on Shakespeare's sonnets, working alongside—and quarreling with—Ransom: see Robert Lowell's account (*RJ* 101–102). Auden published *The Dyer's Hand* in 1962, two years after *The Woman at the Washington Zoo*.

39. Michel Benamou devotes an entire essay to the repetitions in this poem: see *CE* 241–244. For a skeptical reading of "change" here and elsewhere in Jarrell, see Pritchard 274.

40. Benfey suggests that part of her wants to be raped; Suzanne Ferguson calls her "neurotically hysterical." (130; *Poetry* 188) Jarrell's own explication tells us that "her own life is so terrible to her that, to change, she is willing to accept" even "the obscene sexuality of the flesh-eating death-bird," whose sexual trappings are, "she hopes or pretends or desperately is sure . . . merely external" (*KA* 326).

41. Pritchard, for example, complains that its speaker is "not a real housewife" (300).

42. The Plato reader is actually one of Whyte's examples of well-functioning housewives, with "a rather keen consciousness of self—and the sophistication to realize that while individualistic tastes may raise eyebrows, exercising those tastes" won't necessarily get her ostracized (365). For more on Whyte, see chapter 2.

43. For one such reading, see Karl Shapiro, *CE* 206–207.

Chapter 2: Institutions, Professions, Criticism

1. Jarrell told Arendt, for example, "What you said about my 'Obscurity of the Poet' was a great pleasure to me because of the way you put it: that you were 'intoxicated with agreement "against a world of enemies" ' " (*Letters* 250).

2. David Laskin reports that among the New York intellectuals of the late forties, Jarrell and Arendt "were very much on the same wavelength"; "after *The Origins of Totalitarianism*," "Lowell, [Mary] McCarthy, Jarrell, [Alfred] Kazin, and [Elizabeth] Hardwick . . . all became zealous Arendt partisans" (158, 220). See also Laskin 158–160 and Pritchard 239.

3. Pitkin strives to disentangle "the social" from Arendt's other concepts—from Arendt's famous trio of labor, work, and action, and her account of public action

and freedom: see esp. 194–201. Another reading of Arendt's "social" is Lewis and Sandra Hinchman's: "On the one side the rise of the social has diminished the private sphere by absorbing its former functions; on the other, as politics is inundated by economic demands, it can no longer fulfill its role as an arena for self-disclosure, and that impulse is forced to take refuge in intimate relationships (à la Jaspers), the last stronghold of 'individuality' " (155).

4. For more on the *esprit sérieux*, see *Origins* 336.

5. Richard Flynn finds Riesman's critique of "other-direction" in Jarrell's later attacks on mass culture: see "Fairy" 8.

6. For a detailed summary of the many fifties critiques of conformity, see Pells, chapter 4. These critiques' focus on white, and white-collar, problems, their tendency toward overstatement, and their supposed neglect of class were pointed out at the time by Harold Rosenberg in "The Orgamerican Fantasy" and have been stressed by some more recent historians: see, for example, Lears. The important point, for the literature of the period is not whether white, and white-collar Americans *did* conform so completely but that they felt, and described, great pressure to do so.

7. For Riesman's comments on Stevenson and Eisenhower—made *before* Ike became President—see *Lonely* 214–215.

8. In certain ways Jarrell could not be—almost no poet or novelist has been—strictly Arendtian. George Kateb takes a plausible if extreme position when he writes that for Arendt, "in political action alone is a person revealed. . . . The political self, publicly presented, is thus the real self or what must pass for the real self" (8).

9. Riesman himself decided later that in a world of pressure toward togetherness, "the book . . . comes into its own as a guarantor of that occasional apartness which makes life viable" (*Abundance* 442).

10. A good example is "The Wide Prospect," which juxtaposes the Pacific war with the scientific and industrial revolutions: "Who could have figured, when the harnesses improved / And men pumped kobolds from the coal's young seams . . . The interest on that first raw capital?" (*CP* 185).

11. For more on this theme see Fussell, chapters 3 and 6; for more on "Losses" see Fussell 63.

12. For Jarrell's insistence that words in poems behaved like words outside poems, see his exchange of letters with Sister Bernetta Quinn (*Letters* 223–225).

13. For a brief, admiring overview of American "journalism-as-criticism," see Dickstein 63–67; on Jarrell's rivals and contemporaries, including Blackmur and Wilson, see Dickstein, chapters 5 and 6.

14. Monroe and Birkerts offer other useful lists of his rhetorical devices: see Monroe, *CE* 262–264 and Birkerts, "Randall Jarrell" 90–93.

15. Such as Richards' *Principles of Literary Criticism* (1925) and *Philosophy of Rhetoric* (1936), Burke's *Grammar of Motives* (1945) and *Rhetoric of Motives* (1950), and Frye's *Anatomy of Criticism* (1957).

16. Jarrell is paraphrasing Eliot's "The Perfect Critic" (1920): "the 'historical' and the 'philosophical' critics had better be called historians and philosophers quite sim-

ply. As for the rest, there are merely various degrees of intelligence" (58). On Eliot and professionalism, see also Menand, chapter 5. Eliot had also advocated "professionalism in art," in *The Egoist* 5 (1918), quoted in Menand 125.

17. Guillory's complex argument relates Eliot's concepts of form, tradition and orthodoxy to the same concepts in the work of Cleanth Brooks and F. R. Leavis, to the Marxian concept of ideology, and to the "mass culture debate"; see Guillory 141–155.

18. For separate arguments about "modernist" critics' "anti-professionalism," finding in it both "a ritual of professional legitimation" and a way of defending culture in general, see Robbins 74–75.

19. Tate even decried, in 1935, "The total loss of professionalism in letters . . . in our age" (*Essays* 519). Taking examples from Henry James, Nathanael West, and other fiction writers, Thomas Strychacz argues for "a profound identity between the structure of professional discourses and of modernist writing strategies"; for him, "the economic and social rewards accruing to professionals are comparable to the cultural rewards (the symbolic capital) accruing to modernist writers" (26). On literary *critics'* professionalism, see Strychacz 5–6, 22–44. On Tate's professionalism and modernist professionalism in general, see also Hammer, *Janus-Faced*, chapters 1 and 3.

20. Compare Geoffrey Hartman's uneasy 1982 remark (reviewing a book about deconstruction): "our very hope that criticism could save us from specialization . . . [has] identified it as *the* rehumanizing activity, so when it becomes technical or claims a field of its own—when criticism says, 'Let us be like other departments of knowledge'—it seems not only to mistake but even to betray its nature" (*Easy Pieces* 189).

21. For related arguments—available in Jarrell's youth—about the "nondiscursive" knowledge available in works of art, see Suzanne K. Langer, *Philosophy in a New Key* (New York: Mentor/NAL, 1948 [1941]).

22. Cavell writes, "Since we cannot know the world exists, its presentness to us cannot be a function of knowing. The world is to be *accepted*; as the presentness of other minds is not to be known, but acknowledged" (*Must* 324). Warner Berthoff makes a related, if less elaborate, argument about art and the apprehension of persons: "A work of literature . . . comes alive to imaginative consciousness . . . as . . . it makes us sensible of the reality of other persons, identified through an impressionability and power of response which we recognize and anticipate the return of in ourselves" (13).

23. A substantial body of sociological argument contrasts professions' "autonomy" with other workers' managed status ("heteronomy"). Eliot Friedson contrasts "administrative direction and the loss of autonomy" with "true professional autonomy"; he goes on to argue that disciplinary solidarity among professionals produces an imagined "institution" that professionals work together to defend. (71–73, 99–100). Such arguments do not contradict Jarrell's point: for him, literary criticism ought *not* aspire to autonomy *as a discipline*; it should instead be responsible to human life outside professional frameworks of reward and outside the limits of its special methods.

24. For Jarrell's initial, and equally negative, reaction to *The Age of Anxiety*, see *KA* 145–146.
25. Jarrell in 1941 called "Miss Emily and the Bibliographer" "the most brilliant attack on scholarship—*PMLA* variety—that I have ever seen" (*KA* 65).
26. Jarrell's commitment to private experience should thus be distinguished from others' commitment to "culture." From an Eliotic or an Arnoldian viewpoint, Robbins avers, "a professional discipline that takes culture as its objects must seem to have fallen from culture, to be untrue to culture, to be in a state of contradiction, from the very moment it *becomes* a discipline, that is, one discipline among others within a division of intellectual labor" (18). But a language directed always toward culture in general might prove just as inadequate for describing particular readers' experience as a language derived from "one discipline among others" would.
27. Birkerts similarly concludes that Jarrell's "criticism is . . . not criticism at all, but poetry carried on by other means" ("Randall Jarrell" 93).
28. Altieri's account of "first-person investments" also draws on Wordsworth: "In the case of disciplinary knowledge, our pleasure lies in coming to master specific practices, instruments leading to a deeper grasp of the world. But in [Wordsworth] our pleasure lies less in the contents of knowledge than in the state of the [human] subject. . . . The very terms of the pleasure become features of what we then reflect on as fundamental to humanity" (*Canons* 146).
29. Jarrell was certainly aware of the concept we now call "cultural capital" and aware that the humanities seemed to be retaining less and less of it: "We belong to a culture whose old hierarchy of values–which demanded that a girl read Pope just as it demanded that she go to church and play the pianoforte–has virtually disappeared" (*Age* 15–16).
30. It may be partly this aim that Marianne Moore lauded as "the abounding unsnobbishness of [Jarrell's] heart" (*RJ* 127).
31. "Back in the stacks, in libraries; in bookcases in people's living rooms; on brick-and-plank bookshelves beside studio couches, one sees big books in dark bindings, the *Collected Poems* of the great poets. Once, long ago, the poems were new: the book went by post—so many horses and a coach—to a man in a country house, and the letter along with it asked him to describe, evaluate and fix the place in English literature, in 12,000 words, by January 25, of the poems of William Wordsworth. And the man did. It is hard to remember that this is the way it was; harder to remember that this is the way it is" (*Third* 55).
32. It is, of course, also possible to read the project I have been discussing as essentially one of mystification, rendering technical insights as untechnical, expensively learned procedures as self-evident, in order to disguise the bad faith with which trained readers like Jarrell had in fact learned to make aesthetic judgments. If Jarrell's prose does not counter such charges, or at least render them implausible, it is very hard to imagine what critic and what style could.
33. For the binder, see *Letters* 279. Jarrell had promised to dedicate *Pictures* to Arendt; when his wife, Mary, objected, he dedicated the novel to them both (*Remembering* 1–2). Jarrell told Arendt that Gottfried and Irene were "very like you

in some of the big general things—in most of the medium sized things they're quite different" (*Letters* 392).

34. Philip Rahv seems to have turned down a chapter of *Pictures* for *Partisan Review* because he believed it portrayed McCarthy. Jarrell repeatedly minimized the resemblance, writing to Rahv that "readers who know Jean Stafford best think *she's* Gertrude" and complaining to Elizabeth Bishop that *Pictures* "to me is a serious book not about Mary McCarthy." Arranging with Ransom to have portions of *Pictures* appear in *Kenyon Review*, Jarrell distinguished President Robbins from Harold Taylor, then president of Sarah Lawrence, but offered to "change smaller things" to avoid "get[ing] me or *Kenyon* into trouble" (*Letters* 383, 413, 366).

35. McCarthy's novel places Jarrell in a list of poets considered for invitation to a conference: "Tate, Ransom, Miss Moore, Empson, Jarrell, Shapiro, Auden, Winters, Roethke, Lowell, Miss Bishop"(239). Jarrell noticed his name in McCarthy's novel: see *Letters* 324.

36. *Pictures*, Riesman wrote, "bursts with its tirade against a lady novelist who 'heartlessly' cases a college community (the book in turn cruelly cases the lady). But Jarrell, as befits the author of *The Age of Criticism*, is unusually self-conscious about reflexivity for a literary man; most novelists so far as I can make out . . . take exploitation of their 'material' for granted" (*Abundance* 509).

37. Flo's language reflects contemporary usage: Elizabeth Hardwick told David Laskin that at *Partisan Review* in the late 1930s "the Soviet Union, the Civil War in Spain, Hitler and Mussolini, were what you might call real life" (34).

38. For another view of Jarrell's deliberate plotlessness, see Suzanne Ferguson, *CE* 272, 280.

39. The same bit of Emerson (also quoted in T. S. Eliot's "Sweeney Erect") had turned up in one of Jarrell's fiction reviews: "As for the men whose shadows these institutions are—the men who make and break states, corporations, and academies—in Marquand's books they are a little gray, a little ghostly, except in so far as their organizations give them bone and hue" (*KA* 204).

40. Donald Davie, who cared very much for architecture but could not appreciate "classical" music, explicitly mapped the distinctions between public and private, social-ethical and purely aesthetic, onto the distinction between architecture and instrumental music: see *Companions* 8–9, 30–31. For Riesman's other-directed educators, "music as a way of escape in to one's individual creative life—a private refuge—would strike many . . . school authorities today as selfish" (*Lonely*, 166).

41. For a similar device at work in George Eliot's sentences, see Gallagher.

42. Pitkin explains that she called her book *Attack of the Blob* because the lurid fears in fifties disaster movies overlap with Arendt's fears of the social. Pitkin cites earlier essays by Susan Sontag, Naomi Goldenberg, and Michael Rogin relating fifties disaster films to topical concerns: "All three suggest that the real fear was psychological, reflecting people's sense of personal isolation, fragmentation, helplessness and dehumanization" (4).

43. Jarrell elsewhere calls himself "an old reader of science fiction"; he wrote to Mary, "Yesterday I was bored enough to buy not the good science fiction maga-

zine, which I buy every month, but one of the bad ones" (*KA* 324; *Letters* 323–324).

44. For more on the "mass culture critique," Dwight Macdonald, and the reception of the Frankfurt School in America, see Gorman, chapters 6 and 7, esp. 178–192. On "theories of mass culture as social decay," see Brantlinger, esp. p. 17ff.; another influential treatment is Huyssen, chapters 1–3. Debaters shared not just positions but key texts; readers of Bernard Rosenberg and David Manning White's 1957 anthology, *Mass Culture*, will find, for example, the Frankfurt School thinker Leo Löwenthal quoting the very same paragraph of Tocqueville Jarrell adduced in "The Intellectual in America" (*MC* 51; *SH* 8–9). Similar debates took place slightly earlier in Britain: a powerful response to these is Raymond Williams, esp. 300–319.

45. The only substantial analyses of these notebooks, as of *Sad Heart* in general, are Richard Flynn's: he argues that Jarrell's critique of "Eisenhower's America" contributes to the poems in *The Lost World*. See "Fairy" 5–6.

Chapter 3: *Psychology and Psychoanalysis*

1. Zaretsky adds that by World War II, American "analysis had become . . . a complex phenomenon, encompassing a profession, an evolving body of theory, and a vast process of cultural diffusion in which analytic ideas influenced both popular culture and lay intellectuals" ("Charisma" 331). Ellen Herman has shown how mid-century psychologists and analysts shaped public policy; see her chapters 3, 4, and 5.

2. The notes are undated; their presence at Greensboro (rather than the Berg Collection), and their handwriting, suggests the early or mid-fifties. Jarrell worked for years on an essay called "T. S. Eliot and Obsessional Neurosis." His extensive notes for that essay cite not only Freud and his peers but a bevy of articles from professional journals such as *Psychoanalytic Quarterly*. All that survives of the essay in his published work are a few sentences from "Fifty Years of American Poetry" (1962) in which Jarrell declares Eliot "from a psychoanalytical point of view . . . far and away the most interesting poet of [the twentieth] century" (*Third* 314).

3. Among the valuable psychoanalytic readings of Jarrell's life and character, Hammer, Lesser, Longenbach, and Williamson focus on gender, Travisano (*Mid-Century*, chapter 3) and Vendler ("The Inconsolable") on childhood. Vendler remarks that Freudian frameworks gave Jarrell the only "theory" he ever relied on—"a theory of life and not a theory of art" (*Part* 117–118).

4. For another view of the value Jarrell placed on "the unconscious," see Mazzaro, *CE* 83–85.

5. For Ian Sansom, "it was undoubtedly Auden who for various reasons felt the full force of Jarrell's subcontrary Oedipal urges" (280).

6. The same lecture incorporates Jarrell's published, very negative, 1947 review of *The Age of Anxiety*; see *KA* 145–146, and (for comments on it) Keith Monroe, *CE* 256, and Sansom generally.

7. For a long discussion of this theme in Jarrell's early poetry, see Flynn, *Lost* 17–21, and Hagenbuchle generally; see also my discussion of "The Death of the Ball Turret Gunner," below.

8. For more remarks on this long, disturbing, unwieldy, and sometimes beautiful poem, see Kinzie 70–72 and Flynn, *Lost* 30–31.

9. These poems and parts of poems, with their "womb-tomb asociation," drive Helen Hagenbuchle's 1975 monograph, *The Black Goddess*: for Hagenbuchle Jarrell's work imagines an all-engulfing Jungian "Great Mother" who gives the poet "the choice either to submit to her fatal will or to fight against her in ultimately futile rebellion" (5). Though Jarrell certainly read Jung, there is no reason to think he found Jung's theories especially congenial; Mary Jarrell remembers a Washington, D.C., psychoanalyst as "too Jungian for close friendship" with Randall, and Hagenbuchle bases her arguments not on Jarrell's conscious choice among psychoanalytic models but on what she takes to be the general truth of Jung's theories (*Remembering* 33).

10. Williamson finds this dynamic of preoedipal splitting at work also in Jarrell's personal life, in which he seems to have been, at times, quite aloof and at other times very needy ("Märchen" 290–291). Joseph Smith remarks appositely that "persons with the greatest difficulty" in moving past preoedipal splitting and idealization "have at least a chance for achieving the deepest understanding" (113).

11. Jarrell told Sister Bernetta Quinn, "when I have a *Selected Poems* with notes I believe I will quote a little sentence from a psychoanalyst like [Harry Stack] Sullivan about Good Me, Bad Me, and the Other" (the characters the child in the poem creates) (*Letters* 304). Jarrell's actual note in the 1955 *Selected* mentioned *good me* and *bad me* but quoted nobody (*CP* 6). Parker Tyler wrote in the *Kenyon Review* in 1952 that "A Quilt-Pattern" "verifies, to a spectacular degree, many insights of Freud, while emerging 'unbroken' in its own intuition and formal achievement" (*CE* 143).

12. Suzanne Ferguson gives the publication history: see *Poetry* 198.

13. For another appreciation of "A Hunt," see Bottoms 93–94.

14. For Köhler's version of object-relations, see 86–88; for models of mind-body or body-"self" dualism, see 181–194; on memory traces and the diachronic self, see 233–248 and 378–381.

15. Dream lyric is a recognized Renaissance subgenre, sometimes flagged, as in Milton's sonnet 23, by the opening "Methought": see Cook 235–247. During the 1920s, Claudia Morrison writes, "The central . . . concern to literary critics interested in the potential use of psychoanalytic theory was the nature of the relationship between art and the dream" (96).

16. For a very sophisticated discussion of analogies between literary works and dreams, see Skura, chapter 4, which focuses, however, almost entirely on short stories, novels, and plays. Frederick Hoffman's 1945 study also covers modernist uses of Freud.

17. Other critics have noticed Jarrell's attraction to boundary states, including the hypnopompic and hypnogogic: see Beck, *Worlds* 54, and Kinzie, Lesser, and Quinn, discussed below. Frances Ferguson identifies Jarrell's interest in dream

boundaries with a putative taking-apart of identity into a "choric voice": see *CE* 170–174. Travisano also links the dreams or dreamlike delusions in "Ball Turret Gunner," "Next Day," and "Seele in Raum" (*Mid-Century* 62).

18. A poem which uses (a) dream as (a) metaphor (especially as a metaphor for itself) incorporates dream as trope; a poem organized as dreams are (supposedly) organized uses dream as scheme. See Hollander, *Melodious* chapter 1, esp. 5–6.

19. Quinn wrote frequently on Jarrell and dreams; see especially *RJ* 139–154. For a long reading of another dream poem, "In the Ward: The Sacred Wood," see Suzanne Ferguson, *Poetry* 97–103.

20. The best recent take on the poem is probably Travisano's: see *Mid-Century* 62, 240–243. For other readings not cited in text, see Frances Ferguson, *CE* 169; Richard Fein, *CE* 155–158; and several brief essays in *Field* 35 (1986) (part of that journal's symposium on Jarrell).

21. Freud suggests in several places "that the act of birth is the source and prototype of the affect of anxiety" 16:397). Though he repudiated Otto Rank's "extreme inferences," Freud continued to believe in the thirties "that the experience of anxiety at birth is the model of all later situations of danger" (22:88).

22. For Williamson, the five-line poem "may have succeeded so well as an elegy on the indifference of war precisely because it is really an elegy for the primal separation" ("Märchen" 285).

23. For a relevant account of "strangeness," in dreams and in accounts of them, see Hejinian, esp. 33. See also Mary Jarrell, *Remembering* 112.

24. For more on time in this poem, see Frances Ferguson, *CE* 169 ("The poem so thoroughly manifests the lack of a middle . . . in the life and in the brevity of the poetry . . . that the time between birth and death is lost"); for more on time in dreams, see Hejinian 35.

25. The elaborate structure (four couplets, each beginning with four or five feet and ending with two) recalls the stanzaic mechanics of Wilfred Owen and especially the five-line units of "The Send-Off," which Jarrell had admired in his review of Owen (*KA* 169).

26. Suzanne Ferguson concludes that "The Black Swan" has no specific folk- or fairy-tale source (*Poetry* 125). Quinn links it to the ballet "Swan Lake" (*RJ* 146).

27. For more about "The Black Swan," Freud, and dreaming, see Beck, *Worlds* 53–54; Bottoms 92–93; Kinzie 82–84; and Quinn, *RJ* 146–147.

28. For more on "Field and Forest," see Ferguson, *Poetry* 201–202.

29. Decades earlier, Köhler had worried about specialization in similar terms; he wrote: "All the professors have their little farms which they are highly skilled in cultivating. . . . But every one of them has been careful to erect a fence against that vast, uncharted country beyond his farm in which we others try to find our way and cannot" (4).

30. The original (translated) Freud can be found in "A Metapsychological Supplement to the Theory of Dreams" (14:222).

31. This is also Travisano's position; see *Mid-Century* 108–109. His readings, more biographical than mine, rely primarily on Alice Miller's *The Drama of the Gifted*

Child. Travisano does mention Winnicott with reference to Jarrell's array of "sacred objects," photographs, and reproductions of paintings, which he installed in each of his houses and offices: these " 'transitional objects,' as D. W. Winnicott terms them, allowed Jarrell to recreate his identity, surrounded by his 'chosen family,' no matter where he happened to be" (*Mid-Century* 109).

32. One of several possible sources in Freud is "Recommendations to Physicians Practicing Psychoanalysis": there psychoanalytic technique "consists simply in not directing one's notice to anything in particular and in maintaining the same 'evenly-suspended attention' (as I have called it) in the face of all that one hears" (12:111–112).

33. Explaining how many thinkers in the twenties compared literary work to dreaming, Morrison adds that the comparison between literature and the process of analysis was much less common: Floyd Dell, who wrote preeminently about novelists (and who brought in Marx as well as Freud) seems almost alone in arguing that "the artist . . . is the psychoanalyst of human society" (quoted in Morrison 137).

34. For more on "A Game at Salzburg" see Longenbach 59–60 (stressing its postwar feel) and Suzanne Ferguson, *Poetry* 132.

35. Jarrell's note to "A Game" tells us: "It seemed to me that if there could be a conversation between the world and God, this would be it" (*CP* 6). Readers of Freud will associate it with the *fort-da* game, too.

36. Freud claimed in *Three Essays on the Theory of Sexuality* that "the riddle of where babies come from . . . in a distorted form which can easily be rectified, is the same riddle that was propounded by the Theban Sphinx" (7:195).

37. For an appreciation of "Jerome" that draws on deconstruction and on psychoanalysis, see Frances Ferguson, *CE* 170ff. For one built around Saint Jerome in visual art, see Quinn, *Randall Jarrell* 76–79. Another brief, attentive reading is Bryant 147–151.

38. Sansom traces the toads to Chamfort, via Zola and Auden's "New Year Letter" (283).

39. Suzanne Ferguson notes that "in some fairly developed drafts of the poem, Jarrell included . . . an allusion to the psychiatrist's own analysis many years before, the traditional analysis all classical Freudian analysts undergo to prepare themselves for practice" (*Poetry* 171).

40. For more angels in Jarrell, see Quinn, "Randall Jarrell and Angels."

41. Jarrell invoked Saint Jerome's lion in a 1953 review: there the "quieter personal and domestic values," "what St. Jerome felt for his lion instead of what he felt for his church—hardly exist for [André] Malraux; his mind is large and public" (*KA* 184). Richard Flynn's reading of "Jerome" is precisely the reverse of mine: for him it is a condemnation of secular modernity, where "the possibility of adoration has vanished under the light of reason," which leads society to "self-destruction" (*Lost* 92).

42. Mary Jarrell relates one of many stories about Randall's investment in Kitten: "Once at a cocktail party on a campus we were visiting, a professor began drawing Randall out on Kitten. Delighted to escape from General Conversation, Randall was animated and voluble and a circle soon formed. At this point, to be

funny perhaps, the professor interjected a story he'd heard about Randall giving his meat-ration coupons to the cat during the war. 'Why of course!' Randall flashed sparks. 'What would you *expect*? He's only a poor cat, and has to eat what he can. People can eat anything. What an absurd remark' " (*Remembering* 139). For more on Kitten, see *Letters* passim. Kitten died in the spring of 1956, "hit at the side of the road by a car" (*Letters* 414; *Remembering* 139).

43. Rogers also argues that twentieth-century writers have been more likely than their predecessors both to present "cat-human relationships . . . as friendships between equals" and to make them represent "enviable liberation" (129, 141). For Czeslaw Milosz, human affection for cats even refutes all "arguments that there is no human nature" (161).

44. Eve Sedgwick, perhaps recalling Jarrell, imagines telling her therapist "I need you *to change me*"; "The space of [her therapist] is both myself and not. / The place where talking / to someone else is also / talking to myself" (*Dialogue* 51, 115). For Sedgwick on Jarrell, see *Fat Art, Thin Art* 21.

45. Jarrell wrote later that the poem was divided up into "color and colorlessness" (*KA* 323).

46. In Bollas's theories, "transformational object-seeking" is always a more specific quest to "recurrently enact a pre-verbal ego memory" of maternal care (16).

47. *The Woman at the Washington Zoo* came out in 1960, but most of the poems in it had been written years earlier; *The Seven-League Crutches* (1951) coincided with Lowell's *The Mills of the Kavanaughs.* (Travisano argues that some of Jarrell's dream poems from that volume react to Lowell's.) For Jarrell's private approval of *Life Studies*, see *Letters* 443, 457–459; for his only public comments on Lowell's fifties work, see *Third* 332–334.

48. Charles Altieri now dislikes *Life Studies* for more or less this reason: see *Postmodernisms* 94.

49. For another discussion of these lines and their relations to Lowell, see Longenbach 57–58.

50. Vendler has suggested that Berryman's *Dream Songs* owe something as a sequence, to "the successivity . . . of therapeutic interviews"; but, as Vendler also shows, Berryman's protagonist, "the shamefully-acting self of his mad or alcoholic moments," has very deliberately not integrated itself with any other kind of identity nor fully acknowledged its dependence on others (*Given* 32).

51. Trilling found Freud's emphasis on the drives a welcome defense against "the social," since such inherited motivations (however irrational or amoral) are aspects of humanity no cultural engineering can erase: "somewhere in this child, somewhere in the adult, there is a hard, irreducible, stubborn core of biological urgency, and biological necessity, and biological *reason*, which culture cannot reach, and which reserves the right, which sooner or later it will exercise, to judge the culture and resist and revise it" (54).

52. Such a reading makes up one strand of Vereen Bell's *Robert Lowell: Nihilist as Hero.*

53. One such disappointed reader is Vendler, who noted in 1969 the love poems' lack of sex and described in 1990 the poems' "passivity" as against the essays' "feroc-

ity." Michael Hofmann and Michael Wood, among more recent reviewers, also wish the poems were more aggressive.

54. These are not—if it needs saying—new ideas: see Freud's own "Observations on Transference Love" (1915).

55. The poem also responds to Adrienne Rich's "The Roof-walker"; see *Letters* 469.

Chapter 4: Time and Memory

1. For more on "The Elementary Scene," see Pritchard 37–38 and Quinn, *CE* 203–204.

2. For more references to Proust, see the numerous invocations in *Letters*, as well as the poem "A Man Meets a Woman in the Street," where "Proust, dying, is swallowing his iced beer / And changing in proof the death of Bergotte / According to his own experience" (*CP* 352).

3. The poem carries an epigraph from *Der Rosenkavalier*: "*Die alte Frau, die alte Marschallin!*" Hofmannsthal's Marschallin anticipates looking in a mirror someday and seeing that she has grown old; the poem's speaker might be an older Marschallin or might be anyone who knows the opera. Beck ties "The Face" specifically to the Rilke translation "Faded," which Jarrell probably completed in 1952 (*CE* 197–198; *CP* 480).

4. For Ransom, the poem encapsulated "the tragedy of Everywoman": what would he have said had he known that earlier drafts made the speaker "not handsome?" (*RJ* 173). On these and other issues of gender in "The Face," see Longenbach 55. Benfey finds in "The Face" both male narcissism and a defense of male privilege, since the poem depicts a woman who wants other people to look at her (125–126). For a response to Benfey, see chapter 1. The best general discussion of "The Face" is Lesser 12; another is Suzanne Ferguson, *Poetry* 116–117.

5. Published in the *Kenyon Review* in 1946, the poem was omitted from subsequent volume of verse until Jarrell placed it, with very minor changes, in his 1960 *The Woman at the Washington Zoo*. Some brief readings of "A Ghost, A Real Ghost" are Bryant 145–146 and Kinzie 84; Suzanne Ferguson dismisses its "monotonous flatness" (*Poetry* 185). Flynn notes the resemblance between the speaker of "A Ghost," the man in "Windows," and the disembodied adult in "The Elementary Scene" (*Lost* 82).

6. Proust writes also: "For to 'recognize' someone and, *a fortiori*, to learn someone's identity after having failed to recognize him, is to predicate two contradictory things of a single subject, it is to admit that what was here, the person whom one remembers no longer exists, and also that what is now here is a person whom one did not know to exist; and to do this we have to apprehend a mystery almost as disturbing as that of death, of which it is, indeed, as it were the preface and harbinger" (3:982).

7. On military songs during World War II in general, see Fussell 262–267: "Bitterness is the general tone of these songs, together with disdain for civilian ignorance and pomposity" (264).

8. For more on "our sense of a past and our impressions of the rate of time's passage," see Friedman (2).
9. The Berg Collection holds an Audenesque early sestina beginning "Now night braids with her fingers"; Jarrell seems to have found a model for both in Auden's sestina "We have brought you, they said, a map of the country," included in *The Orators*. For "A Story" as "autobiography," see *Letters* 66; for other comments on the poem, see Ferguson, *Poetry* 12–13; Flynn, *Lost* 26–27; and Mazzaro, *CE* 91.
10. Few critics give the poem more than a couple of sentences; exceptions are Chappell, "Moving," and Flynn, *Lost* 39–40.
11. See Winnicott 1–6. Another paper of Winnicott's relevant to "Moving" is "The Place Where We Live" (104–110).

Chapter 5: *Childhood and Youth*

1. For more reactions to his apparent childlikeness, see Travisano, *Mid-Century* chapter 3.
2. Most notoriously, Joseph Bennett attacked Jarrell's "doddering infantilism." For discussions of that 1965 review and Jarrell's reaction, see Pritchard 299 and Longenbach 63.
3. Jarrell's other versions of Rilke's poems about childhood include "The Grown-Up," "The Child," and "Requiem for the Death of a Boy," all in *The Woman at the Washington Zoo*. On Jarrell's translations and Rilke's originals, see Seidler and Cross, *CE* 300–301 and 315–317.
4. Gertrude, unsurprisingly, feels very differently about Derek: she "couldn't understand why [children] didn't act more like grown-ups—a little more like, anyway; it seemed to her almost affectation on their part" (193).
5. The minor character Camille Batterson enters Jarrell's novel to chasten our admiration of "potential": "One can hardly help being primitively attracted to the Romantic belief that potentiality is always better than actuality, that nothing is always better than Anything; yet, looking at Miss Batterson, one could not help doubting it" (92).
6. On Sara Starr as the model for Constance, see Flynn, "Jarrell's Wicked Fairy" 7–8.
7. Gottfried Rosenbaum had also wished for "some people to come from another planet and make me their pet" (*Pictures* 152).
8. For other comments on "A Sick Child," see Pritchard 247 and Flynn, *Lost* 50–51.
9. For Sandra Beckett, "Crosswriting is a characteristic feature of the children's classics that constitute the core of the children's literature canon": it therefore *differentiates* them from the age-graded books Jarrell dislikes, which denies that grown-ups and children have something (inner) in common (xii). On Jarrell's children's books, cross-writing, and mid-century literary theory, see also Travisano, "Dialectic" 26–28.
10. For more such readings, see Finney, *CE* 289, Griswold 53–61, and Pritchard 280–282.

11. For a willfully optimistic reading of the book as a parable of family—analogous to the later *The Animal Family*—see Flynn, *Lost* 105–107. For other readings of *The Bat-Poet*, see Bryant 122–124 and Quinn, *Randall Jarrell* 94–100.

12. After one face-to-face meeting with Frost, Jarrell told Lowell that Frost "felt faintly, comfortably, mocking about everything in me that hadn't written those articles [on Frost's poetry]: after all, nothing I did was the way *he'd* have done it" (*Letters* 483). For the mockingbird as Frost, see Pritchard 282, Griswold 56 ("The resemblance . . . is unmistakable"), and Mary Jarrell, *Remembering* 105 (seeing also a resemblance to Robert Lowell). Quinn thinks the mockingbird represents Ezra Pound; see her *Randall Jarrell* 100.

13. So traditional, in fact, as to have prompted the title of A. D. Nuttall's *Why Does Tragedy Give Pleasure?* (New York: Oxford University Press, 1996).

14. Most accounts trace the rise of American interest in adolescence to the psychologist G. Stanley Hall; see Spacks, chapter 9.

15. Many commentators have noticed how young Jarrell's soldiers seem: Alex Vardamis's work on his airmen, typically, describes their "ingenuousness," "innocence," and "childlike faith" (66). Vendler praises the "adolescent soldiers" of "Losses, "with their pitiful reality of high school—high school!—as the only notching stick of experience" (*Part* 112).

16. The full quotation from Plautus (*Asinaria* 495) reads *Lupus est homo homini, non homo, quom qualis sit non novit*: "Man is a wolf to man, when he hasn't discovered what he's like"; the familiar truncated "Man is a wolf to man" appears in Robert Burton's *Anatomy of Melancholy* (1.1.1).

17. For more on "Eighth Air Force," see Brooks and Flynn (discussed in text) and also Ferguson, *Poetry* 85–88; Fein, *CF* 158–162; Quinn, *Randall Jarrell* 45–47; Bryant 51; and Vardamis 76–81.

18. Every critic who addresses the passage glosses the New Testament allusions differently (though most stress the soldiers' innocence). For Richard Fein, "This is a poem of forgiveness for man as murderer, and forgiveness remakes the image of man"; for Sister Bernetta Quinn, "it is an elegy for, and at the same time an exoneration of, all the American combatants" (161; *Randall Jarrell* 46). But for Flynn, "the pilot who speaks the poem does not absolve himself of guilt; if he cannot find fault in the 'other murderers,' it is primarily because he recognizes that he, too, is not without sin" (*Lost* 35).

19. The comment occurs in Jarrell's 1945 discussion of Auden's *For the Time Being: A Christmas Oratorio*. The whole passage has some bearing on Jarrell's poem: "Why on Earth should Auden choose to represent *Herod* as the typical Liberal? It would have been far more natural and far more plausible to pick Pontius Pilate (at that time the only regular subscriber to *The Nation* in all Palestine); but Auden could not risk the sympathy for Pilate which, increasingly injected into the Gospels as they developed—as anti-Semitic propaganda, incidentally—has been inherited by all of us" (*Third* 161).

20. Suzanne Ferguson also finds Pyle relevant to "Eighth Air Force": see *Poetry* 86.

21. Quinn's formally attentive reading also connects Jarrell's poem to Lowell's conscientious objection: see her *Randall Jarrell* 46–47. For Lowell's letter, objecting to "an almost apocalyptic series of all-out air raids" on German cities, see Hamilton 87–88. On his jail time, see Hamilton 92–100.

22. Pritchard considers "Aging" a good test of Jarrell's achievement, filled as it is with "provocations to the charge of sentimentality" (255).

23. For Travisano's comments on all three memorial sonnets, see *Mid-Century* 279–281.

24. For the 1957 Phillipe Halsman photo of Jarrell behind the wheel, see the last of the photos inserted in *RJ* and the book jacket for *No Other Book*; for a 1954 photo of the Jarrell family driving, see the photo insert in Pritchard. One of Jarrell's most enthusiastic occasional essays is a paean to auto racing (*KA* 197–200).

25. The entire paragraph from Yeats's "Reveries Over Childhood and Youth" is relevant: Yeats wrote, "For some months now I have lived with my own youth and childhood, not always writing indeed but thinking of it almost every day, and I am sorrowful and disturbed. It is not that I have accomplished too few of my plans, for I am not ambitious; but when I think of all the books I have read, and of the wise words I have heard spoken, and of the anxiety I have given to parents and grandparents, and of the hopes that I have had, all life weighed in the scales of my own life seems to me a preparation for something that never happens" (70). Jarrell quoted the autobiographies in "The Development of Yeats' Sense of Reality" (1942) (*KA* 89).

26. Stressing continuities between children's and grownups' reading, Jarrell differs sharply from almost all other fifties writers who attack mass culture. Dwight Macdonald, for example, complained in 1953 of "adultized children and infantile adults" and of a "merging of the child and grown-up audience" (*MC* 66). Leo Löwenthal sought "to know whether the consummation of popular culture really presupposes a human being with preadult traits or whether modern man has a split personality: half multilated child and half standardized adult" (*MC* 57). Such generalizations provided rhetorical ammunition for highbrow proponents of popular culture: Leslie Fiedler called himself, in 1955, one of the few intellectuals "who can boast that he has read more comic books than attacks on comic books" (*MC* 537).

27. Riesman's explanation is worth consulting: art "objects are hardly given meaning in private and personal values when they are so heavily used as counters in a preferential method of relating oneself to [one's] peers" (*Lonely* 77).

28. In his introduction to *The Vanishing Adolescent*, Riesman wrote of the "morally and culturally impoverished young whose basic passivity makes heroic demands on those who must daily cope with them in or out of school" (9). Jarrell seems to have felt the same way about some of his pupils at the Woman's College, where he began teaching in 1947; he wrote to Hannah Arendt that though some of his students were bright, "the only thing to do with the freshmen here is to write a ballet with a Chorus of Peasant Girls for them" (*Letters* 180).

29. It represents Jarrell in the *Norton Anthology of Poetry*, third ed. (1983), where the only other Jarrell poems are "Ball Turret Gunner" and "Well Water." (More recent Norton anthologies make different choices.) Quinn, too, compares the poem to "The Rape of the Lock:": see *Randall Jarrell* 66. More recently Pritchard has praised the poem at length (193–198).

30. Sandra Brown encountered the poem as a student at Greensboro during the 1950s; her surprising essay offers just that critique: "[When] I took copies of 'A Girl in a Library' to my class . . . I wanted to know . . . if they identified with being peasants the way I once did" (153).

31. For more on "A Girl in a Library," see Ferguson *Poetry* 136–140, Quinn, *Randall Jarrell* 63–67, Lesser 11 (finding in the poem's mixed feelings a "self-lacerating despair"), and Chappell, "Indivisible" 12–13.

32. I quote Walter Arndt's translation, published by Dutton in 1963, eleven years after Jarrell's poem. Arndt taught in Greensboro—at the Women's College and at Guilford College—during the early fifties, leaving only in 1956. Quinn suggests that Arndt's presence in Greensboro drew Jarrell's attention to Pushkin (*Randall Jarrell* 65).

33. Jarrell glossed these lines for Quinn: "many people have, like dolphins, leaped up for a moment, from the world of what Leibnitz [sic] calls 'brute and geometrical necessity,' up into the purer world of—oh, art, mysticism, philosophy, love; but the poor girl sleeps placidly in the trap, and has never even felt the need to escape" (*Letters* 239).

34. A 1941 essay compares homosexuality in the early Auden to "Greek homosexuality in Naomi Mitchison"; the king of Sparta and his lover are important characters in *The Corn King* (*Third* 127).

35. Flynn notes that its situation reflects Jarrell's own youth with the sexes reversed: "rather than a little boy living with his mother and without his father, the fourteen-year-old girl in the poem lives with her father, and her mother is dead" (*Lost* 57). Beck sees the poet both in the girl who speaks and in the sick boy who occasionally responds: "The sick boy and the unlovely, unloved woman are, after all, Jarrell's favorite self-projections; and in 'The Night Before the Night Before Christmas' he uses both" (*Worlds* 85). For more on "The Night Before," see Flynn, Kinzie, Longenbach, and Travisano (discussed in text and in notes 37–39 below), and also Quinn, *CE* 68–71 (on dreams), Ferguson, *Poetry* 143–148, and Bryant 25–27.

36. Slogans play a similar role in "The Times Worsen," which ends: "Life is that 'wine like Mother used to make—/ So rich you can almost cut it with a knife' " (*Age* 20).

37. Longenbach writes that "the girl's mind wanders between the 'real' world [her] books describe and a dream-world populated by her mother and pet squirrel, both of whom have recently died" (61). This "dream world" is itself helped into being by her books; her psyche is divided not so much *between* the real and the fantastic, or between the dead and the living (which her dream merges), but *among* the modes of representation she knows.

38. Some critics find this poem closer to Christian doctrine than I do. Travisano focuses on its angels: "the child feels a transitory yet powerful impulse to perceive at work the hand of a God whose existence she believes, intellectually, that she must deny" (*Mid-Century* 143–144). For more on Jarrell's angels, see Quinn, "Angels."

39. Kinzie has aptly described "the long emotional crescendo of the last five pages of the poem," which lead readers "not just to a sympathy with the essential being of the girl—her knowledge that her brother is dying, that she and he are suspended in an ambiguous universe together, and that she cannot help any of it—but to a manifestation of Jarrell's victory over his own limitations" (82).

40. Richard Eberhart remembered that James Laughlin of New Directions sent him the *Pisan Cantos* manuscript for review in fall 1946. At the time, Jarrell was living in New York City and editing the book review pages at *The Nation*; he would probably have seen the manuscript as soon as Laughlin circulated it (Homberger 375).

41. I count Jarrell's very long, very early "Orestes at Tauris" as apprentice work; so did he (*CP* 3, 406).

42. Jarrell wrote: "probably the best poem by a living poet, *Four Quartets*, has only one real character, the poet, and a recurrent state of that character which we are assured is God; even the ghostly mentor encountered after the air-raid is half Eliot himself, a sort of Dostoievsky double" (*Age* 241).

Chapter 6: Men, Women, Children, Families

1. Among recent discussions of Jarrell and gender, Hammer and Longenbach have considered his literary-historical motives for writing in the voices of women and girls, while Benfey and (more convincingly) Williamson offer psychoanalytic readings; Benfey, Lesser, and others decide that Jarrell's women sound too much like men or too much like him. For more on these arguments, see especially Hammer, "Who" 392, 401–405.

2. Thus the speakers in "Seele im Raum" and "Next Day" are not just *women* but also *aging housewives*. The girl of "The Night Before. " is an *American adolescent girl*, a *young reader*, and a thirties reader to boot.

3. Jarrell has taken his Freudian quotation from the Standard Edition's English version of Freud's "Some Psychic Consequences of the Anatomical Distinction Between the Sexes" (19:257) For Chodorow's comments on the same passage, see *Mothering*, chapters 9 and 10, esp. 166ff: "feminine development . . . may lead to a superego more open to persuasion and the judgments of others, that is, not so independent of its emotional origins" (169).

4. For Jarrell's role in the writing of *A Wilderness of Ladies*, see Eleanor Ross Taylor's own account ("Altogether we had three sessions going over my poems") and also Mary's (*RJ* 239, *Remembering* 71).

5. Experts, Benjamin has written, "have only just begun to think about the mother as a subject in her own right, principally because . . . contemporary feminism . . . made us aware of the disastrous results for women of being reduced to the mere

extension of a two-month-old" (*Bonds* 23). She describes one "mother who, when asked what care and support *mothers* need, could not understand the question and finally replied, 'Someone taking care of *me?* . . . *I'm* the mother, *I'm* the one, I take care of *him!*' " (*Bonds* 214; italics hers).

6. For more of Mary's comments on "The Lost Children," see *Remembering* 122–128. The poem may also, as Suzanne Ferguson suggests, owe something to Kipling's story " 'They' ": see *Poetry* 210–212. For more on "The Lost Children," see Bryant 163–165, Lesser 11, and Pritchard 303–304.

7. For more on "Windows," see Bryant 136–137, Flynn, *Lost* 81–84, Hagenbuchle 77–78, and Pritchard 259–262. For the probable original of the snowstorm in "Windows," see *Letters* 338.

8. Drafts of the poem sharpen the sense of reunion with the mother: they have its speaker "look up, nodding, into a kind of love, / A speechess face, and there for me forever" (UNC-Greensboro).

9. See, for example, Brantlinger, Huyssen (esp. chapters 1 and 3), Pitkin, Rogin, and Zaretsky, "Charisma"; see also the last section of my chapter 2.

10. On *Fly-by-Night* considered as a whole book, with emphases on its Freudian overtones, see Griswold 74–94 and Flynn, *Lost* 105–107; for another appreciative reading, see Getz.

11. In Flynn's summary, the husband "replicates his own unstable childhood in his marriage. . . . In his feeling that he has, perhaps, married his mother, he feels that he has become his father by incorporating his father's worst characteristics" (*Lost* 120–121). Ferguson is the only other critic to discuss "Hope" in more than biographical terms: see *Poetry* 205–210.

12. For antimaternal sentiments in forties and fifties popular culture, see Rogin, chapter 8; a flagrant example is Philip Wylie's *Generation of Vipers*, whose dangerous "Momism," Rogin comments, "is the demonic version of domestic ideology" (241).

13. For the psychoanalyst Joseph Smith, "the more persons protest that they are completely different from the mother the more they reveal a lack of separateness—a secret holding-on that betrays the fear of individuation" (116).

14. On the writing of *The Animal Family*, and on some of its sources, see *Remembering* 107–113.

15. The best and longest discussions of *The Animal Family* are Griswold's and Flynn's; see, respectively, Griswold 119–128 and *Lost* 109–115. For other comments, see Finney, *CE* 289–291; Quinn, *Randall Jarrell* 101–105; Pritchard, 313–315; and Williamson, "Märchen" 296–298.

16. Pritchard describes the plot, quite plausibly, as the successive fulfillment of the hunter's wishes (314). Flynn writes, "it is apparent from the beginning that the hunter lacks more than an audience: what he misses, what makes his loneliness profound, is a family—not just a mother, as has been suggested, but a complete family, consisting of father and mother and child" (*Lost* 111).

17. Both Mary Jarrell and Griswold point out that the mermaid is perhaps the only mother figure in Jarrell's oeuvre who has no hint of being a bad, archetypal

Mother: see *Remembering* 109 and Griswold 120–122. Williamson ties this family's happiness to "the fact that none of [them] have actually emerged from each other's bodies" ("Märchen" 297).

18. *The Lost World*, the triptych, links up in many respects with the later poem "Thinking of the Lost World," which ends the book also entitled *The Lost World*.

19. The poem does not, however, quote from the letters, which can be read at the Berg Collection; for discussions of the letters themselves, see Pritchard 16–17 and 288, and also Williamson 289–290.

20. Several critics have already examined the poem, or parts of it, at some length. Ferguson focuses on its nostalgic elements and on its debts to Proust (*Poetry* 212–221). Flynn's book finds in the poem a happy child threatened by the approach of adolescent sexuality and also reads into it Jarrell's hostility to fifties mass culture (*Lost* 121–134). For him, the triptych portrays a "childhood paradise . . . on the brink of its disapperance" in "awakening adolescence" (*Lost* 122). Flynn's recent, more nuanced "Jarrell's Wicked Fairy" finds thematic and verbal continuities between the prose of *Sad Heart* and the "Lost World" poems; see also his "Infant Sight" 114–115. Quinn and Travisano treat the poems as autobiographical record: see *Randall Jarrell* 24–25; *Mid-Century* 102–105. Pritchard offers a remarkable defense of the poems' style: see 305–310. Bryant provides an admiring description: see 166–171. For remarks on the poem by Jarrell's contemporaries, see Bishop, *One Art* 432–435 and *RJ* 55, 60–62, 266–271.

21. The title "Children's Arms," with its faint Virgilian echo, nods to Dante's guide, Virgil; in general, though, Dantean allusions serve the poem as grace notes or sidebars—one cannot read the whole poem well through them.

22. Are these lines a source for Elizabeth Bishop's "Crusoe in England"? After reading *The Lost World*, Bishop told Jarrell, in a letter he may never have read, "some of the Lost World hasn't quite been lost here yet, I feel, on the days I still like living in this backward place." For Bishop's extensive comments on *The Lost World* (and on *The Bat-Poet*), see *One Art* 432–435. For the beginnings of "Crusoe" and their dates, see Millier 446–447.

23. The link between "habit" and "happiness" is one among several of Jarrell's allusions to an epigram Pushkin borrowed from Chateaubriand and that Jarrell probably found in Pushkin: "Heaven gives us habits to take the place of happiness" (*Onegin* 2:31). For more "habit" and "happiness" in Jarrell's late poetry, see "Aging," "Well Water," and "A Man Meets a Woman" (*CP* 234, 300, 351).

24. On this and other Proustian references in Jarrell, see Ferguson, *Poetry* 212–213.

25. Flynn writes: "The game of dominoes with the great-grandmother underscores the confusion of the child-speaker in his new role as adolescent. He sense that the roles of parent and child are curiously reversed, and, in a sense, feels guilty for wishing to remain a child, when he feels that what is expected of him is to become responsible like an adult" (*Lost* 127).

26. Compare Jarrell's futile apology to Dandeen with Proust's futile apology to his grandmother: "never should I be able to eradicate from my memory that contraction of her face, that anguish of her heart, or rather of mine; for as the dead exist

only in us, it is ourselves that we strike without respite when we persist in recall-
ing the blows that we have dealt them. I clung to this pain, cruel as it was, with
all my strength, for I realised that it was the effect of the memory I had of my
grandmother, the proof that this memory was indeed present within me" (2:786).

27. Poets of other generations also decided that to acquire selfhood was to imagine
one's death. James Merrill imagined that in the next world our spirits "appear to
others" at "THE AGE / AT WHICH IT FIRST SEEMS CREDIBLE TO DIE"
(16; capitals in original).

28. The only *Life Studies* poem to merge adult and child selves is "Grandparents,"
whose climactic passage sounds as if Lowell had been learning from Jarrell:
"Grandpa! Have me, hold me, cherish me! / Tears smut my fingers . . . " A few
lines later Lowell decides that he is "disloyal still" (*LS/FUD* 69).

29. For much more on Mignonette's song, see Steedman, *Strange*, chapter 1.

30. This is the effect Jarrell's last poems seem to have had on Bishop, who read them
as reminiscences not of childhood but of a historical period: she wrote Jarrell,
apropos of "The Player Piano," "Heavens, I remember the false armistice—but
for some reason, not the real one" (*One Art* 433). Flynn notes that this blurring of
Gay Nineties and Gay Twenties occurs to Jarrell first in the *Sad Heart* notebooks,
where he complains that the younger generation seems to lack a historical sense
("Fairy" 12).

31. For Jarrell's "nothing" as a version of Stevens's "Snow Man" "nothing," see Denis
Donoghue, *RJ* 61, and also Longenbach 64; another reading is John Crowe Ran-
som's (*RJ* 181).

Conclusion: "What We See and Feel and Are"

1. The poets reviewed were Arnold Stein (later a well-known Milton scholar), Oscar
Williams, Stanton Coblentz, and Ruth Pitter. For the reviews, see *KA* 137–139.

2. Such ambiguities may be one reason Grossman finds in Jarrell only "the trace of
a great enterprise . . . a set of brilliant and, on the whole, evasive fragments" (33).

3. Jarrell is probably remembering Elizabeth Bishop's "Songs for a Colored Singer":
"A washing hangs upon the line / But it's not mine / None of the things that I can
see / Belong to me" (*Poems* 47).

4. For much more about Frost's influence on Jarrell, see the remarks throughout
Pritchard, esp. 214–215.

5. Other relevant poems on visual art include the early "Dummies;" "The Knight,
Death and the Devil"; parts of "The End of the Rainbow," a poem I have only
been able to touch on here; and "The Augsburg Adoration" (*CP* 21, 385, 219,
346). On "The Knight," a good commentary is Hollander, *Gazer's* 255–258; "Jar-
rell's knight is in some ways more like a successful analysand than a soldier of the
faith" (257).

6. For other discussions of "The Old and the New Masters," see Sansom 285–287,
Ferguson, *Poetry* 195–198, and Quinn, *Randall Jarrell* 79–86. The poem interacts

with, and to some extent duplicates, Jarrell's prose attack on abstract expressionism: see *KA* 285–289.

7. The poem's consideration of "objectivity" recalls Köhler's, twenty-five years earlier; he too brought in the analogy of painting while rebuking his fellow scientists for emphasizing the insignificance of "man": "We do not evaluate paintings in terms of square inches, although we *can* measure them on this scale, and shall then find them practically non-entities in comparison with the Sahara. Thus man *can* be seen in a merely astronomical scheme of things; and, if he appears in this scheme as almost non-existent, a corresponding statement will be 'correct.' And yet, always in that same sense, such a statement will be altogether untrue" (20; italics in original).

8. Jarrell would have seen the sculpture during the summer of 1958, which he and Mary spent with the Taylors in Italy.

9. For other readings of "The Bronze David" see Bryant 151–153; Ferguson, *Poetry* 181–184; Flynn, *Lost* 95–97; Quinn, *Randall Jarrell* 68–71, and Williamson, *Almost a Girl* 24–26.

10. Compare Donald Davie's description of Poundian style: "If he is sure that there is more to his subject (more perhaps to any subject) than he got out of it," Davie writes, "then, like Michelangelo leaving some portion of stone unworked in his sculptures, the poet will deliberately seek an effect of improvisation . . . . For only in this way can he be true to his sense of the inexhaustibility of the human and non-human nature he is working with, a sense which makes him feel not noble but humble" (*Ezra Pound* 86–87).

BIBLIOGRAPHY

Certain titles are cited in the text by abbreviations:

CE	Ferguson, ed., *Critical Essays on Randall Jarrell*
CP	Jarrell, *The Complete Poems*
IA	Stein, Vidich, and Manning White, eds. *Identity and Anxiety*
KA	Jarrell, *Kipling, Auden and Co.*
LS/FUD	Lowell, *Life Studies/For the Union Dead*
MC	Rosenberg and Manning White, eds., *Mass Culture*
RJ	Lowell, Taylor, and Penn Warren, eds., *Randall Jarrell 1914–1965*
SH	Jarrell, *A Sad Heart at the Supermarket*

Where other citations require titles, they are given as key words. For example, Jessica Benjamin's *The Bonds of Love* appears as *Bonds*.

Adorno, Theodor. *Prisms*. Trans. Samuel and Sherry Weber. Cambridge: MIT Press, 1997 (1981).
Altieri, Charles. *Canons and Consequences: Reflections on the Ethical Force of Imaginative Ideals*. Evanston, Ill.: Northwestern University Press, 1990.
——— . *Postmodernisms Now: Essays on Contemporaneity in the Arts*. University Park, Pa.: Pennsylvania State University Press, 1998.
——— . *Self and Sensibility in Contemporary American Poetry*. Cambridge: Cambridge University Press, 1984.

Arendt, Hannah. *Between Past and Future.* New York: Penguin, 1968.

———. *Essays in Understanding, 1930–1954.* Ed. Jerome Kohn. New York: Harcourt, Brace. 1994.

———. "French Existentialism." *The Nation,* February 23, 1946. Repr. in *The Nation, 1865–1990,* ed. Katrina Vanden Heuvel, New York: Thunder's Mouth, 1990. 171–175.

———. *The Life of the Mind.* Ed. Mary McCarthy. New York: Harcourt, Brace, 1978.

———. *The Origins of Totalitarianism.* 2d expanded ed. Cleveland: Meridian/World, 1958 (1951).

———. "Randall Jarrell." *RJ* 3–9.

Arendt, Hannah, and Mary McCarthy. *Between Friends: The Correspondence of Hannah Arendt and Mary McCarthy, 1949–1975.* Ed. and introd. Carol Brightman. New York: Harcourt, Brace, 1995.

Atlas, James. "Randall Jarrell." *American Poetry Review* 41 (Jan.-Feb. 1975): 26–28.

Auden, W. H. *The English Auden.* Ed. Edward Mendelson. London: Faber and Faber, 1977.

Bakhtin, M. M. *The Dialogic Imagination.* Trans. Caryl Emerson and Michael Holquist; ed. Michael Holquist. Austin: University of Texas Press, 1981.

Baldwin, James. *The Price of the Ticket: Collected Nonfiction, 1948–1985.* New York: St. Martin's, 1985.

Bauerlein, Mark. *Literary Criticism: An Autopsy.* Philadelphia: University of Pennsylvania Press, 1997.

Beck, Charlotte. "Randall Jarrell's Modernism: The Sweet Uses of Personae." *South Atlantic Review* 50, no. 2 (May 1985): 67–73.

———. "Unicorn to Eland: The Rilkean Spirit in the Poetry of Randall Jarrell." *Southern Literary Journal* 12 (1979): 3–17. Repr. *CE* 191–202.

———. *Worlds and Lives: The Poetry of Randall Jarrell.* Port Washington, N.Y.: Associated University Presses, 1983.

Sandra L. Beckett, ed. *Transcending Boundaries: Writing for a Dual Audience of Children and Adults.* New York: Garland, 1999.

Bedient, Calvin. "Randall Jarrell and Poetry and the Age." *Southern Review* 93, no. 1 (winter 1985): 128–135.

Bell, Vereen. *Robert Lowell: Nihilist as Hero.* Cambridge: Harvard University Press, 1983.

Benamou, Michel. "The Woman at the Zoo's Fearful Symmetry." *Analects* 1, no. 2 (1961): 2–4. Repr. *CE* 241–245.

Benfey, Christopher. "The Woman in the Mirror: Randall Jarrell and John Berryman." In *Men Writing the Feminine,* edited by Thaïs E. Morgan. Albany: State University of New York Press, 1994. 123–138.

Benjamin, Jessica. *The Bonds of Love.* New York: Pantheon, 1988.

———. *Like Subjects, Love Objects: Essays on Recognition and Sexual Difference.* New Haven: Yale University Press, 1995.

———. *The Shadow of the Other.* New York: Routledge, 1998.

Berryman, John. "Randall Jarrell" and "Op. post. no. 13." *RJ* 14–19.

———. "Roethke's Yule." *Gettysburg Review* 4, no. 4 (autumn 1991): 559.

Berthoff, Warner. *Literature and the Continuances of Virtue.* Princeton: Princeton University Press, 1986.

Birkerts, Sven. "Randall Jarrell." *Parnassus* 16, no. 2 (1991): 78–93.

———. *Readings.* St. Paul, Minn.: Graywolf, 1999.

Bishop, Elizabeth. *The Complete Poems: 1927–1979.* New York: Farrar, Straus and Giroux, 1983.

———. *One Art: Letters.* Ed. Robert Giroux. New York: Farrar Straus and Giroux, 1994.

Blackmur, R. P. *The Lion and the Honeycomb.* New York: Harcourt, Brace, 1955.

Bogart, Leo. "The Growth of Television." In *Mass Communications,* ed. Wilbur Schramm. 2d ed. Urbana: University of Illinois Press, 1969 (1960). 95–111.

Bollas, Christopher. *The Shadow of the Object: Psychoanalysis of the Unthought Known.* New York: Columbia University Press, 1987.

Booth, Philip. *Relations.* New York: Viking, 1986.

Bottoms, David. "The Messy Humanity of Randall Jarrell." *South Carolina Review* 17, no. 1 (fall 1984): 82–95.

Brantlinger, Patrick. *Bread and Circuses: Theories of Mass Culture as Social Decay.* Ithaca, N.Y.: Cornell University Press, 1983.

Brenkman, John. *Straight Male Modern: A Cultural Critique of Psychoanalysis.* New York: Routledge, 1993.

Breslin, Paul. *The Psycho-Political Muse.* Chicago: University of Chicago Press, 1987.

Bromwich, David. *A Choice of Inheritance: Self and Community from Edmund Burke to Robert Frost.* Cambridge: Harvard University Press, 1989.

———. *Disowned by Memory: Wordsworth's Poetry of the 1790s.* Chicago: University of Chicago Press, 1999.

Brooks, Cleanth, and Robert Penn Warren. *Understanding Poetry.* 3d ed. New York: Holt, Rinehart and Winston, 1960.

Brooks, Linda Marie, ed. *Alternative Identities: The Self In Literature, History, Theory.* New York: Garland, 1995.

Brooks, Peter, and Alex Woloch, eds. *Whose Freud?: The Place of Psychoanalysis in Contemporary Culture.* New Haven: Yale University Press, 2000.

Brown, Sandra M. "Poetry and the Age: 'A Girl in a Library' to Randall Jarrell." In *The Intimate Critique: Autobiographical Literary Criticism,* edited by Diane P. Freeman, Olivia Frey, and Frances Zuhar. Durham: Duke University Press, 1993. 151–162.

Bryant, J. A., Jr. *Understanding Randall Jarrell.* Columbia: University of South Carolina Press, 1986.

Burt, John. *Robert Penn Warren and American Idealism.* New Haven: Yale University Press, 1988.

Butsch, Richard. *The Making of American Audiences: From Stage to Television, 1750–1990.* Cambridge: Cambridge University Press, 2000.

Cavell, Stanley. *Must We Mean What We Say?* Cambridge: Cambridge University Pres, 1981 (1969).

———. *Pursuits of Happiness: The Hollywood Comedy of Remarriage.* Cambridge: Harvard University Press, 1981.

Chappell, Fred. "The Indivisible Presence of Randall Jarrell." *North Carolina Literary Review* 1, no. 1 (summer 1992): 8–13.

——— . "Moving." *Field* 35 (fall 1986): 23–29.

Chodorow, Nancy. *The Power of Feelings: Personal Meaning in Psychoanalysis, Gender, and Culture.* New Haven: Yale University Press, 1999.

——— . *The Reproduction of Mothering: Psychoanalysis and the Sociology of Gender.* Berkeley: University of California Press, 1978.

Coates, Jennifer. *Women, Men, and Language.* 2d ed. Harlow: Longman, 1993.

Coleridge, Samuel Taylor. *Complete Poetical Works in Two Volumes.* Ed. Ernest Hartley Coleridge. Oxford: Clarendon, 1967 (1912).

——— . *Works.* Vol. 4, *The Friend.* Ed. Barbara E. Rooke. Princeton, N.J.: Princeton University Press, 1969.

Cook, Eleanor. *Against Coercion: Games Poets Play.* Stanford: Stanford University Press, 1998.

Coveney, Peter. *Poor Monkey: The Child in Literature.* London: Rockliff, 1957.

Cross, Richard. "Jarrell's Translations: The Poet as Elective Middle European." *CE* 310–320.

Cummins, James. "Calliope Music: Notes on the Sestina." *Antioch Review* 55, no. 2 (spring 1997): 148–159.

Davie, Donald. *Ezra Pound: Poet as Sculptor.* New York: Oxford University Press, 1964.

——— . *These the Companions.* Cambridge: Cambridge University Press, 1982.

Demos, John. *Past, Present, and Personal: The Family and Its Life Course in American History.* New York: Oxford University Press, 1986.

Denney, Reuel. "American Youth Today: A Bigger Cast, a Wider Screen." In Erikson, *Youth* 155–179.

Dickey, James. *The James Dickey Reader.* Ed. Henry Hart. New York: Simon and Schuster, 1999.

——— . "Randall Jarrell." *RJ* 33–48.

Dickstein, Morris. *Double Agent: The Critic and Society.* New York: Oxford University Press, 1992.

Dinnerstein, Dorothy. *The Mermaid and the Minotaur.* New York: Harper Colophon, 1976.

Donoghue, Denis. "The Lost World." *RJ* 49–62.

Elias, Norbert. *Time: An Essay.* Trans. Edmund Jephcott. Oxford: Blackwell, 1992.

Eliot, T. S. *Selected Prose of T. S. Eliot.* Ed. Frank Kermode. London: Faber and Faber, 1975.

Empson, William. *Seven Types of Ambiguity.* Rev. ed. New York: New Directions, 1967 (1947, 1930).

——— . *The Structure of Complex Words.* Cambridge: Harvard University Press, 1989. (1951)

Erikson, Erik. *Childhood and Society.* New York: Norton, 1950.

——— , ed. *The Challenge of Youth.* New York: Anchor, 1965 (1963).

Fein, Richard. "Randall Jarrell's World of War." *Analects* 1, no. 2 (1961): 14–23. Repr. *CE* 149–162.

Ferguson, Frances C. "Randall Jarrell and the Flotations of Voice." *Georgia Review* 28 (fall 1974): 423–439. Repr. CE 163–174.

Ferguson, Suzanne. *The Poetry of Randall Jarrell.* Baton Rouge: Louisiana State University Press, 1971.

——— . "To Benton with Love and Judgment: Jarrell's *Pictures from an Institution*." CE 272–283.

——— , ed. *Critical Essays on Randall Jarrell.* Boston: G. K. Hall, 1983.

Fiedler, Leslie. "The Middle Against Both Ends." MC 537–547.

Finney, Kathe Davis. "The Poet, Truth, and Other Fictions: Randall Jarrell as Storyteller." CE 284–297.

Fish, Stanley. *Is There a Text in This Class?* Cambridge; Harvard University Press, 1980.

——— . *Professional Correctness: Literary Studies and Political Change.* Oxford: Clarendon, 1995.

Fishman, Pamela. "Conversational Insecurity." In *The Feminist Critique of Language: A Reader,* edited by Deborah Cameron. 2d ed. New York: Routledge, 1998. 253–258.

Flax, Jane. *Thinking Fragments: Psychoanalysis, Feminism, and Postmodernism in the Contemporary West.* Berkeley: University of California Press, 1990.

Flint, R. W. "Jarrell as Critic." *Partisan Review* 20, no. 6 (1953): 702–708.

Flynn, Richard. " 'Infant Sight': Romanticism, Childhood, and Postmodern Poetry." In *Literature and the Child,* edited by James McGavran. Iowa City: University of Iowa Press, 1999. 105–129.

——— . "Jarrell's Wicked Fairy: Cultural Criticism, Childhood, and the 1950s." Paper delivered at "Jarrell, Bishop, Lowell and Co." Conference, Case Western Reserve University, April 2000.

——— . *Randall Jarrell and the Lost World of Childhood.* Athens, Ga.: University of Georgia Press, 1990.

Frank, Joseph. *The Idea of Spatial Form.* New Brunswick, N.J.: Rutgers University Press, 1991.

Fowler, Russell. "Randall Jarrell's 'Eland': A Key to Motive and Technique in His Poetry." *Iowa Review* 5, no. 2 (1974): 113–126. Repr. CE 176–190.

Freud, Sigmund. *The Standard Edition of the Complete Psychological Works of Sigmund Freud.* Translated under the general editorship of James Strachey, with Anna Freud, Alix Strachey, and Alan Tyson. 23 vols. London: The Hogarth Press and the Institute of Psychoanalysis, 1953–58.

Friedenberg, Edgar Z. *The Vanishing Adolescent.* New York: Dell, 1959.

Friedman, William. *About Time: Inventing the Fourth Dimension.* Cambridge: MIT Press, 1990.

Friedson, Eliot. *Professionalism Reborn.* Cambridge: Polity, 1994.

Frost, Robert. *The Poetry of Robert Frost.* Ed. Edward Connery Lathem. New York: Henry Holt, 1969.

Frye, Northrop. *Anatomy of Criticism.* Princeton, N.J.: Princeton University Press, 1971 (1957).

Fussell, Paul. *Wartime: Understanding and Behavior in the Second World War.* New York: Oxford University Press, 1989.

Gallagher, Catherine. "George Eliot, Immanent Victorian." *Proceedings of the British Academy,* 94. London: The British Academy, 1997. 157–172.

Getz, Thomas. "Memory and Desire in *Fly-by-Night.*" *Children's Literature* 11 (1983). 125–134.

Gilligan, Carol. *In a Different Voice: Psychological Theory and Women's Development.* Cambridge: Harvard University Press, 1993 (1982).

Gopnik, Adam. "Celestial Navigator." *The New Yorker,* July 19, 1999. 92–97.

Gorman, Paul R. *Left Intellectuals and Popular Culture in Twentieth-Century America.* Chapel Hill: University of North Carolina Press, 1996.

Graff, Gerald. *Professing Literature: An Institutional History.* Chicago: University of Chicago Press, 1987.

Griswold, Jerome. *The Children's Books of Randall Jarrell.* Athens, Ga.: University of Georgia Press, 1988.

Grossman, Allen, and Mark Halliday. *The Sighted Singer: Two Works on Poetry for Readers and Writers.* Baltimore: Johns Hopkins University Press, 1992.

Guillory, John. *Cultural Capital.* Chicago: University of Chicago Press, 1993.

Hagenbuchle, Helen. *The Black Goddess: A Study of the Archetypal Feminine in the Poetry of Randall Jarrell.* Zurich: Francke Verlag, 1975.

Halberstam, Judith. *Female Masculinity.* Durham, N.C.: Duke University Press, 1998.

Halliday, Mark. *Stevens and the Interpersonal.* Princeton, N.J.: Princeton University Press, 1991.

Hamilton, Ian. *Robert Lowell: A Biography.* New York: Vintage, 1983.

Hammer, Langdon. *Janus-Faced Modernism: Hart Crane and Allen Tate.* Princeton, N.J.: Princeton University Press, 1993.

——. "Who Was Randall Jarrell?" *Yale Review* 79, no. 3 (spring 1990): 389–405.

Haney, David P. "Aesthetics and Ethics in Gadamer, Levinas, and Romanticism: Problems of Phronesis and Techne." *PMLA* 114, no. 1 (January 1999): 32–45.

Hartman, Geoffrey. *A Critic's Journey: Literary Reflections, 1958–1998.* New Haven: Yale University Press, 1999.

——. *Easy Pieces.* New York: Columbia University Press, 1985.

——. *The Fateful Question of Culture.* New York: Columbia University Press, 1997.

——. *Wordsworth's Poetry, 1787–1814.* New Haven: Yale University Press, 1971 (1964).

Hecht, Anthony. "Le Byron de Nous Jours." *Grand Street* 2, no. 3 (spring 1983): 32–48.

Hejinian, Lyn. "Strangeness." *Poetics Journal* 8 (1989): 32–45.

Herbert, Christopher. *Culture and Anomie: Ethnographic Imagination in the Nineteenth Century.* Chicago: University of Chicago Press, 1991.

Herman, Ellen. *The Romance of American Psychology.* Berkeley: University of California Press, 1995.

Hernnstein Smith, Barbara. *Poetic Closure: A Study of How Poems End.* Chicago: University of Chicago Press, 1968.

Hinchman, Lewis P., and Sandra K. Hinchman, eds. *Hannah Arendt: Critical Essays.* Albany: State University of New York Press, 1994.

Hoffman, Frederick. *Freudianism and the Literary Mind.* Baton Rouge: Louisiana State University Press, 1945.

Hofmann, Michael. "Child Randall." *Times Literary Supplement*, September 4, 1991. 20.

Hollander, John. *The Gazer's Spirit*. Chicago: University of Chicago Press, 1999.

——. *Melodious Guile*. New Haven: Yale University Press, 1988.

——. *The Work of Poetry*. New York: Columbia University Press, 1997.

Homberger, Eric, ed. *Ezra Pound: The Critical Heritage*. London: Routledge, 1972.

Horn, Bernard. "The Tongue of Gods and Children: Blakean Innocence in Randall Jarrell's Poetry." *Children's Literature* 2 (1973): 148–151.

Horney, Karen. *The Neurotic Personality of Our Time*. New York: Norton, n.d. (1937).

Howard, Richard. *Fellow Feelings*. New York: Atheneum, 1976.

Howe, Irving. "The Self in Literature." In Levine, *Constructions* 249–268.

Huyssen, Andreas. *After the Great Divide: Modernism and Mass Culture*. London: Macmillan, 1988.

Jarman, Mark. "John and Randall, Randall and John." *Gettysburg Review* 4, no. 4 (autumn 1991): 565–579.

Jarrell, Mary von S. "Introduction." In Randall Jarrell, *Jerome: The Autobiography of a Poem*. New York: Grossman, 1971.

——. *Remembering Randall*. New York: HarperCollins, 1999.

Jarrell, Randall. "About Popular Culture." National Book Awards address, March 11, 1958. MS. in Library of Congress, Poetry Consultant archive.

——. *The Animal Family*. Decorations by Maurice Sendak. New York: HarperCollins, 1993 (1965).

——. *The Bat-Poet*. Pictures by Maurice Sendak. New York: HarperCollins, 1964.

——. *Complete Poems*. New York: Farrar Straus and Giroux, 1969.

——. *Fly by Night*. Pictures by Maurice Sendak. New York: Farrar, Straus and Giroux, 1976.

——. *The Gingerbread Rabbit*. Pictures by Garth Williams. New York: Macmillan, 1964.

——. "Interview." *Analects* 1 (spring 1961): 5–10.

——. *Kipling, Auden, and Co.* New York: Farrar, Straus and Giroux, 1980.

——. *The Letters of Randall Jarrell*. Ed. Mary von S. Jarrell. Boston: Houghton Mifflin, 1985.

——. "Levels and Opposites." Ed. and introd. Thomas Travisano. *Georgia Review* 50, no. 4 (winter 1996): 697–713.

——. *No Other Book*. Ed. Brad Leithauser. New York: HarperCollins, 1999.

——. *Pictures from an Institution*. Chicago: University of Chicago Press, 1980 (1954).

——. *Poetry and the Age*. Gainesville: University Press of Florida, 2001 (1953).

——. "Previously unpublished poems." *AGNI* 53 (2001): 188–96.

——. *A Sad Heart at the Supermarket: Essays and Fables*. New York: Atheneum, 1962.

——. " 'Sayings of the Bloksberg Post' and 'The Pound Affair.' " Ed. and introd. Stephen Burt. *Thumbscrew* 14 (1999): 2–20.

——. *The Third Book of Criticism*. New York: Farrar Straus and Giroux, 1969.

——. "Two Poems." *Southern Review* 1, no. 1 (July 1935): 84–86.

——. "Woman." *Botteghe Oscure* 11 (1953): 382–389.

——. Manuscripts and papers at the Berg Collection, New York Public Library.

——— . Manuscripts and papers at the University of North Carolina-Greensboro.

——— . Manuscripts and papers in the Poetry Consultant archive of the Library of Congress, Washington, D.C.

Jenks, Chris. *Childhood.* London: Routledge, 1996.

Kalstone, David. "A Critic Apart." *The New Republic,* June 3, 1985. 32–36.

Kateb, George. *Hannah Arendt: Politics, Conscience, Evil.* Totowa, N.J.: Rowan and Allanheld, 1983.

Kazin, Alfred. "Randall: His Kingdom." *RJ* 86–96.

Keenan, Thomas. "Windows: Of Vulnerability." In Robbins, *Phantom* 121–141.

Kermode, Frank. *Romantic Image.* New York: Chilimark, 1957.

Kinzie, Mary. *The Cure of Poetry in an Age of Prose.* Chicago: University of Chicago Press, 1993.

Kirsch, Adam. "The Insects of a Day." *Times Literary Supplement,* August 6, 1999. 24.

Klein, Melanie. *Envy and Gratitude and Other Works.* New York: Macmillan/Free Press, 1975.

Kneale, J. Douglas. "Romantic Aversions: Apostrophe Reconsidered." *ELH* 58, no. 1 (spring 1991): 141–166.

Knoepflmacher, U. C., and Mitzi Myers. "From the Editors: Cross-Writing and the Reconceptualizing of Children's Literary Studies." *Children's Literature* 25 (1997): vii–xvii.

Koffka, Kurt. *Principles of Gestalt Psychology.* London: Routledge and Kegan Paul, 1935.

Köhler, Wolfgang. *The Place of Value in a World of Facts.* New York: Liveright, 1938.

Kramer, Lawrence. "Freud and the Skunks: Genre and Language in *Life Studies.*" In *Robert Lowell: Essays on the Poetry,* edited by Steven Gould Axelrod and Helen Deese. Cambridge: Cambridge University Press, 1986. 80–98.

Kristeva, Julia. "Psychoanalysis and the Imaginary." In Levine, *Constructions* 285–298.

Lakoff, Robin Tolmach. *Talking Power.* New York: Basic Books, 1990.

Langbaum, Robert. *The Poetry of Experience,* New York: Norton, 1957.

Laskin, David. *Partisans: Marriage, Politics, and Betrayal Among the New York Intellectuals.* New York: Simon and Schuster, 1999.

Lears, Jackson. "A Matter of Taste: Corporate Cultural Hegemony in a Mass-Consumption Society." In *Recasting America: Culture and Politics in the Age of Cold War,* edited by Lary May. Chicago: University of Chicago Press, 1989. 38–57.

Lechlitner, Ruth. "Music of Despair: *Blood for a Stranger,* by Randall Jarrell." *New York Herald Tribune Review of Books,* November 29, 1942. 22. Repr. *CE* 17–18.

Lesser, Wendy. "Through the Looking Glass." *Threepenny Review* (spring 1990): 10–12.

Levine, George, ed. *Constructions of the Self.* New Brunswick, N.J.: Rutgers University Press, 1992.

Longenbach, James. *Modern Poetry After Modernism.* New York: Oxford University Press, 1998.

Lowell, Robert. *Life Studies* and *For the Union Dead.* New York: Farrar, Straus and Giroux, 1964 (1959, 1964).

——— . *Notebook.* New York: Farrar, Straus and Giroux, 1970.

———. "Randall Jarrell." *RJ* 101–112.

Lowell, Robert, Peter Taylor, and Robert Penn Warren, eds. *Randall Jarrell 1914–1965*. New York: Farrar Straus and Giroux, 1967.

Löwenthal, Leo. "Historical Perspectives of Popular Culture." *American Journal of Sociology* 55 (1950): 323–332. Repr. in *MC* 46–57.

———. *Literature and Mass Culture: Communication in Society*. Vol. 1. New Brunswick, N.J.: Transaction, 1984.

Macdonald, Dwight. "A Theory of Mass Culture." *Diogenes* 3 (summer 1953): 1–17. Repr. in *MC* 59–73.

May, Elaine Tyler. "The Commodity Gap: Consumerism and the Modern Home." In *Consumer Society in American History: A Reader*, edited by Lawrence Glickman. Ithaca, N.Y.: Cornell University Press, 1999. 298–315.

Mazzaro, Jerome. "Between Two Worlds: The Post-Modernism of Randall Jarrell." *Salmagundi* 17 (fall 1971): 93–113. Repr. *CE* 82–100.

McAlexander, Hubert. *Peter Taylor: A Writer's Life*. Baton Rouge: Louisiana State University Press, 2001.

McCarthy, Mary. *The Groves of Academe*. New York: Plume, 1971 (1952).

Melson, Gail F. *Why the Wild Things Are: Animals in the Lives of Children*. Cambridge: Harvard University Press, 2001.

Meredith, William. "The Lasting Voice." *RJ* 118–124.

Merrill, James. *The Changing Light at Sandover*. New York: Atheneum, 1992.

Millier, Brett. *Elizabeth Bishop: Life and the Memory of It*. Berkeley: University of California Press, 1993.

Milosz, Czeslaw. *Road-Side Dog*. New York: Farrar, Straus and Giroux, 1998.

Mitchison, Naomi. *The Corn King and the Spring Queen*. Woodstock, N.Y.: Overlook, 1990 (1930).

Monroe, Keith. "Principle and Practice in the Criticism of Randall Jarrell." *CE* 256–265.

Moore, Marianne. "Randall Jarrell." *RJ* 125–132.

Moran, Ronald. "Randall Jarrell as Critic of Criticism." *South Carolina Review* 17, no. 1 (fall 1984): 60–65.

Morrison, Claudia. *Freud and the Critic: The Early Use of Depth Psychology in Literary Criticism*. Chapel Hill: University of North Carolina Press, 1968.

Naegele, Kaspar. "Youth and Society: Some Observations." In Erikson, *Youth* 51–75.

Nemerov, Howard, *Figures of Thought*. Boston: David R. Godine, 1978.

Nodelman, Perry. "The Craft or Sullen Art of a Mouse and a Bat." *Language Arts* 55, no. 4 (April 1978): 467–472.

Parfit, Derek. *Reasons and Persons*. New York: Oxford University Press, 1986.

Peltason, Timothy. "The Way We Read and Write Now: The Rhetoric of Experience in Victorian Literature and Contemporary Criticism." *ELH* 66, no. 4 (1999): 985–1014.

Pells, Richard. *The Liberal Mind in a Conservative Age: American Intellectuals in the 1940s and 1950s*. New York: Harper and Row, 1985.

Perkins, David. "How It Was." *Studies in Romanticism* 21, no. 4 (winter 1982): 560–562.

Person, Ethel Spector. *The Sexual Century.* New Haven: Yale University Press, 1999.

Piotrkowski, Chaya S. *Work and the Family System.* New York: Free Press, 1978.

Pitkin, Hanna Fenichel. *Attack of the Blob: Hannah Arendt's Concept of the Social.* Chicago: University of Chicago Press, 1998.

Pritchard, William. *Randall Jarrell: A Literary Life.* New York: Farrar, Straus and Giroux, 1990.

Proust, Marcel. *Remembrance of Things Past (A la recherche de temps perdu).* Trans. C. J. Scott-Moncrieff and Terence Kilmartin. New York: Penguin: 1989 (1981).

Pushkin, Alexander. *Eugene Onegin.* Trans. Walter Arndt. Rev. ed. New York: E. P. Dutton, 1983 (1963).

Quinn, Sister Bernetta. "Landscapes of Life and *Life*." *Shenandoah* 20, no. 2 (1969): 49–78. Repr. *CE* 203–227.

———. "Metamorphoses in Randall Jarrell." *RJ* 139–154.

———. *Randall Jarrell.* Boston: Twayne, 1981.

———. "Randall Jarrell and Angels." *South Carolina Review* 17, no. 1 (fall 1984): 65–71.

Quinney, Laura. *The Poetics of Disappointment.* Charlottesville: University of Virginia Press, 1999.

Ransom, John Crowe. "The Making of a Modernist: The Poetry of George Marion O'Donnell." *Southern Review* 1, no. 4 (spring 1936): 864–874.

———. *The New Criticism.* Norfolk, Conn.: New Directions, 1941.

———. "The Rugged Way of Genius." *RJ* 155–181.

———. *Selected Letters of John Crowe Ransom,* ed. Thomas Daniel Young and George Core. Baton Rouge: Louisiana State University Press, 1985.

———. *The World's Body.* New York: Scribner, 1938.

———, ed. *The Kenyon Critics: Studies in Modern Literature from the Kenyon Review.* Cleveland: World, 1951.

Rich, Adrienne. "For Randall Jarrelll." *RJ* 182–183.

———. *Of Woman Born: Motherhood as Experience and Institution.* 2d ed. New York: Norton, 1995 (1986, 1976).

Ricoeur, Paul. *Oneself as Another.* Trans. Kathleen Blamey. Chicago: University of Chicago Press, 1992.

Riesman, David. *Abundance for What?* New Brunswick, N.J.: Transaction, 1993.

Riesman, David, with Reuel Denney and Nathan Glazer. *The Lonely Crowd: A Study of the Changing American Character.* New Haven: Yale University Press, 1950.

Rilke, Rainer Maria. *Selected Poetry o f Rainer Maria Rilke.* Ed. and trans. Stephen Mitchell; introd. Robert Hass. Bilingual ed. New York: Vintage, 1984.

Robbins, Bruce. *Secular Vocations: Intellectuals, Professionalism, Culture.* New York: Verso, 1993.

———, ed. *The Phantom Public Sphere.* Minneapolis: University of Minnesota Press, 1993.

Rogers, Katharine M. *The Cat and the Human Imagination.* Ann Arbor: University of Michigan Press, 1998.

Rogin, Michael. *Ronald Reagan, the Movie.* Berkeley: University of California Press, 1987.

Rollin, Lucy. *Twentieth-Century Teen Culture by the Decades: A Reference Guide.* Westport, Conn.: Greenwood Press, 1999.

Rosenberg, Bernard, and David Manning White, eds. *Mass Culture: The Popular Arts in America.* Glencoe, Ill.: Free Press/Falcon's Wing, 1957.

Rosenberg, Harold. "The Orgamerican Fantasy." In *The Tradition of the New.* New York: Horizon, 1959. 269–285. Repr. *IA* 319–328.

Rudnytsky, Peter L., ed. *Transitional Objects and Potential Spaces: The Literary Uses of D. W. Winnicott.* New York: Columbia University Press, 1993.

Sachs, Hanns. *The Creative Unconscious.* Cambridge, Mass.: Sci-Art Publishers, 1942.

Sansom, Ian. " 'Flouting Papa': Randall Jarrell and W. H. Auden." In *"In Solitude, For Company": W. H. Auden After 1940,* edited by Katherine Bucknell and Nicholas Jenkins. Oxford: Clarendon Press, 1995. 273–288.

Sass, Louis. "The Self and Its Viccisitudes in the Psychoanalytic Avant-Garde." In Levine, *Constructions* 17–58.

Schafer, Roy. *The Analytic Attitude.* New York: Basic Books, 1983.

Schapiro, Barbara. *Literature and the Relational Self.* New York: New York University Press, 1994.

Schechtman, Marya. *The Constitution of Selves.* Ithaca, N.Y.: Cornell University Press, 1996.

Schwartz, Delmore. "The Dream From Which No One Wakes." *The Nation.* December 1, 1945. 590. Repr. *CE* 19–21.

Sedgwick, Eve Kosofsky. *A Dialogue on Love.* Boston: Beacon, 1999.

——. *Fat Art, Thin Art.* Durham, N.C.: Duke University Press, 1994.

Selinger, Eric Murphy. *What Is It Then Between Us?: Traditions of Love in American Poetry.* Ithaca, N.Y.: Cornell University Press, 1998.

Sendak, Maurice, interviewed by James Marcus. "Unlimited Partnership: Maurice Sendak on Randall Jarrell." http://www.amazon.com/exec/obidos/ts/feature/6306 /107–5416464–4064516, viewed April 22, 2002.

Shapiro, Karl. *The Bourgeois Poet.* New York: Random House, 1964.

——. "The Death of Randall Jarrell." *RJ* 195–229.

Siedler, Ingo. Excerpt from "Jarrell and the Art of Translation." *Analects* 1, no. 2 (1961): 40–48. Repr. *CE* 298–309.

Simpson, David. *The Academic Postmodern and the Rule of Literature: A Report on Half-Knowledge.* Chicago: University of Chicago Press, 1995.

Simpson, Eileen. *Poets in Their Youth: A Memoir.* New York: Farrar, Straus and Giroux, 1982.

Skura, Meredith. *The Literary Use of the Psychoanalytic Process.* New Haven: Yale University Press, 1981.

Smith, Joseph H. "Equality and Difference." In *Psychoanalysis, Feminism and the Future of Gender,* edited by Joseph H. Smith and Afaf M. Mahfouz. Baltimore: Johns Hopkins University Press, 1994. 109–120.

Spacks, Patricia Meyer. *The Adolescent Idea.* New York: Basic Books, 1981.

Spender, Stephen. "Form and Feeling." *The Nation,* February 23, 1952. 182–183.

Stallworthy, Jon, ed. *The Norton Anthology of Poetry*. 3d ed. (shorter). New York: Norton, 1987.

Steedman, Carolyn. *Landscape for a Good Woman: A Story of Two Lives*. New Brunswick, N.J.: Rutgers University Press, 1987.

——. *Strange Dislocations: Children and the Idea of Human Interiority, 1780–1930*. London: Virago, 1995.

Stein, Maurice, Arthur Vidich, and David Manning White, eds. *Identity and Anxiety: Survival of the Person in Mass Society*. New York: Free Press, 1960.

Steiner, George. *After Babel*. New York: Oxford University Press, 1969.

Stevens, Wallace. *Collected Poetry and Prose*. Ed. Frank Kermode and Joan Richardson. New York: Library of America, 1998.

Strychacz, Thomas. *Modernism, Mass Culture, and Professionalism*. Cambridge: Cambridge University Press, 1993.

Tate, Allen. *Essays of Four Decades*. Chicago: Swallow Press, 1968.

——. "Young Randall." *RJ* 230–232.

Taylor, Charles. *Sources of the Self*. Cambridge: Harvard University Press, 1989.

Taylor, Eleanor Ross. "Greensboro Days." *RJ* 233–240.

Taylor, Peter. *Conversations with Peter Taylor*. Ed. Hubert H. McAlexander. Jackson: University of Mississippi Press, 1987.

——. "That Cloistered Jazz." In *The Writer's Craft: Hopwood Lectures 1965–1981*, edited by Robert A. Martin. Ann Arbor: University of Michigan Press, 1982. 20–36.

Thurston, Michael. "Robert Lowell's Monumental Vision: History, Form, and the Cultural Work of Postwar American Lyric." *American Literary History* 12, nos. 1–12 (2000): 79–112.

Travisano, Thomas. *Mid-Century Quartet: Bishop, Jarrell, Lowell, Berryman. and the Making of a Postmodern Poetics*. Charlottesville: University of Virginia Press, 1999.

——. "Of Dialectic and Divided Consciousness: Intersections Between Children's Literature and Childhood Studies." *Children's Literature* 28 (2000): 22–29.

Trilling, Lionel. *Freud and the Crisis of Our Culture*. Boston: Beacon, 1955.

Tucker, Herbert F. "Dramatic Monologue and the Overhearing of Lyric." In *Lyric Poetry: Beyond New Criticism*, edited by Chaviva Hošek and Patrica Parker. Ithaca, N.Y.: Cornell University Press, 1985. 226–246.

Tyler, Parker. "Randall Jarrell's Dramatic Lyrism." *Poetry* 79 (1952): 335–346. Repr. *CE* 140–149.

Van den Haag, Ernest, and Ralph Ross. *The Fabric of Society: An Introduction to the Social Sciences*. New York: Harcourt, Brace, 1957.

Vardamis, Alex. "Randall Jarrell's Poetry of Aerial Warfare." *War, Literature and the Arts* 2, no. 1 (spring 1990): 63–82.

Vendler, Helen. *The Given and the Made*. Cambridge: Harvard University Press, 1995.

——. "The Inconsolable." *The New Republic*, July 23, 1990. 32–36.

——. *The Music of What Happens*. Cambridge: Harvard University Press, 1988.

——. *Part of Nature, Part of Us: Modern American Poets*. Cambridge: Harvard University Press, 1980.

Vidich, Arthur J., and Maurice Stein. "The Dissolved Identity in Military Life." *IA* 493–506.

Voigt, Ellen Bryant. "Frost, Jarrell, and the 'Tones That Haven't Been Brought to Book.' " Paper delivered at "Jarrell, Bishop, Lowell and Co." Conference, Case Western Reserve University, April 2000.

Walker, David. "The Shape on the Bed." *Field* 35 (fall 1986): 64–67.

Wallace-Crabbe, Chris. *Toil and Spin: Two Directions in Modern Poetry.* Melbourne: Hutchinson, 1980.

Warren, Robert Penn. "Twelve Poets." *American Review* 3, no. 2 (May 1934): 212–228.

Whyte, William H., Jr. *The Organization Man.* New York: Simon and Schuster, 1956.

Williams, Raymond. *Culture and Society, 1780–1950.* New York: Harper and Row, 1958.

Williams, William Carlos. *Paterson.* New York: New Directions, 1958.

Williamson, Alan. *Almost a Girl: Male Writers and Female Identification.* Charlottesville: University Press of Virginia, 2001.

——. *Introspection and Contemporary Poetry.* Cambridge: Harvard University Press, 1984.

——. "Jarrell, the Mother, the Märchen." *Twentieth Century Literature* 40, no. 3 (fall 1994): 283–299.

Winnicott, D. W. *Playing and Reality.* New York: Basic Books, 1971.

Wilson, Edmund. *Axel's Castle.* London: Fontana Library, 1961 (1931).

Wolheim, Richard. "On Persons and Their Lives." In *Explaining Emotions,* edited by Amélie Oksenberg Rorty. Berkeley: University of California Press, 1980. 299–322.

Wood, Linda. "Loneliness." In *The Social Construction of Emotions,* edited by Rom Harré. Oxford: Basil Blackwell, 1986. 184–208.

Wood, Michael. "Keeping the Reader Alive." *New York Review of Books,* December 2, 1999. 43–48.

Woolf, Virginia. *The Captain's Death Bed and Other Essays.* New York: Harcourt Brace Jovanovich, 1978 (1950).

Wordsworth, William. *Poetical Works.* Ed. Thomas Hutchinson and E. de Selincourt. New York: Oxford University Press, 1936.

——. *The Prelude: The Four Texts.* Ed. Jonathan Wordsworth. London: Penguin, 1995.

Wordsworth, William, and Samuel Taylor Coleridge. *Lyrical Ballads.* Ed. R. L. Brett and A. R. Jones. London: Routledge, 1991.

Wright, Stuart. *Randall Jarrell: A Descriptive Bibliography.* Charlottesville: University of Virginia Press, 1986.

Wrong, Dennis. *The Modern Condition: Essays at Century's End.* Stanford, Calif.: Stanford University Press, 1998.

Yeats, William Butler. *The Autobiographies of William Butler Yeats.* Garden City, N.Y.: Doubleday, 1958.

Zaretsky, Eli. *Capitalism, the Family, and Personal Life.* New York: Harper Colophon, 1976.

——. "Charisma or Rationalization? Domesticity and Psychoanalysis in the United States in the 1950s." *Critical Inquiry* 26, no. 2 (winter 2000): 328–353.

INDEX